PSALMS, BOOKS 4–5

WISDOM COMMENTARY

Volume 22

Psalms Books 4–5

Nancy L. deClaissé-Walford

Linda M. Maloney
Volume Editor

Barbara E. Reid, OP
General Editor

A Michael Glazier Book

LITURGICAL PRESS
Collegeville, Minnesota

www.litpress.org

A Michael Glazier Book published by Liturgical Press

Cover design by Ann Blattner. *Chapter Letter 'W', Acts of the Apostles, Chapter 4,* Donald Jackson, Copyright 2002, *The Saint John's Bible,* Saint John's University, Collegeville, Minnesota USA. Used by permission. All rights reserved.

1	2	3	4	5	6	7	8	9

Library of Congress Cataloging-in-Publication Data

Names: DeClaissé-Walford, Nancy L., 1954– author.
Title: Psalms : books 4-5 / Nancy L. DeClaissé-Walford ; Linda M. Maloney, volume editor ; Barbara E. Reid, OP, general editor.
Description: Collegeville, Minnesota : Liturgical Press, 2020. | Series: Wisdom commentary; volume 22 | "A Michael Glazier book." | Includes bibliographical references and index. | Summary: "This commentary on Psalms, Books 4-5 provides a feminist interpretation of Scripture in serious, scholarly engagement with the whole text, not only those texts that explicitly mention women. It addresses not only issues of gender but also those of power, authority, ethnicity, racism, and classism"— Provided by publisher.
Identifiers: LCCN 2020013681 (print) | LCCN 2020013682 (ebook) | ISBN 9780814681213 (hardcover) | ISBN 9780814681466 (epub) | ISBN 9780814681466 (mobi) | ISBN 9780814681466 (pdf)
Subjects: LCSH: Bible. Psalms, XC-CL—Feminist criticism. | Catholic Church—Doctrines.
Classification: LCC BS1430.52 .D435 2020 (print) | LCC BS1430.52 (ebook) | DDC 223/.2077—dc23
LC record available at https://lccn.loc.gov/2020013681
LC ebook record available at https://lccn.loc.gov/2020013682

Contents

Abbreviations

ANET	*Ancient Near Eastern Texts Relating to the Old Testament.* Edited by James B. Pritchard. 3rd ed. Princeton: Princeton University Press, 1969.
AOTC	Abingdon Old Testament Commentaries
BAR	*Biblical Archaeology Review*
BBR	*Bulletin for Biblical Research*
BCOT	Baker Commentaries on the Old Testament
BHS	*Biblia Hebraica Stuttgartensia*
BibInt	*Biblical Interpretation*
BibInt	Biblical Interpretation Series
BJSUCSD	Biblical and Judaic Studies from the University of California, San Diego
BL	*Bibel und Liturgie*
BRev	*Bible Review*
BSac	*Bibliotheca Sacra*
BZAW	Beihefte zur Zeitschrift für die alttestamentliche Wissenschaft
CEB	Common English Bible
CBQ	*Catholic Biblical Quarterly*
CC	Continental Commentary
ECC	Eerdman's Critical Commentary

ESV	English Standard Version
FAT	Forschungen zum Alten Testament
FCB	Feminist Companion to the Bible
FOTL	Forms of Old Testament Literature
GBS	Guides to Biblical Scholarship
HALOT	*The Hebrew and Aramaic Lexicon of the Old Testament.* Ludwig Koehler, Walter Baumgartner, and Johann J. Stamm. Translated and edited under the supervision of Mervyn E. J. Richardson. 4 vols. Leiden: Brill, 1994–1999.
HAT	Handbuch zum Alten Testament
HBT	*Horizons in Biblical Theology*
IBC	Interpretation: A Biblical Commentary for Teaching and Preaching
IFT	Introductions in Feminist Theology
Int	*Interpretation*
JFSR	*Journal of Feminist Studies in Religion*
JSOT	*Journal for the Study of the Old Testament*
JSOTSup	Journal for the Study of the Old Testament Supplement series
KJV	King James Version
LCBI	Literary Currents in Biblical Interpretation
LXX	Septuagint
MLBS	Mercer Library of Biblical Studies
MT	Masoretic Text
NASB	New American Standard Bible
NCBC	New Cambridge Bible Commentary
NIB	*New Interpreter's Bible* in Twelve Volumes
NICOT	New International Commentary on the Old Testament
NIV	New International Version
NRSV	New Revised Standard Version
OBT	Overtures to Biblical Theology
RevExp	*Review & Expositor*

SBLDS	Society of Biblical Literature Dissertation Series
StBibLit	Studies in Biblical Literature
SymS	Symposium Series
TDOT	*Theological Dictionary of the Old Testament.* Edited by G. Johannes Botterweck and Helmer Ringgren. Translated by John T. Willis et al. 15 vols. Grand Rapids: Eerdmans, 1974–2006.
VT	*Vetus Testamentum*
VTSup	Supplements to *Vetus Testamentum*
WBC	Word Biblical Commentary
WBiC	Westminster Bible Companion
WCS	Wisdom Commentary Series

Acknowledgments

When I was approached by Liturgical Press to write a "broadly feminist" commentary on books 4 and 5 of the Psalter, I was flattered, flabbergasted, and fearful. I had spent the previous twenty-five years of my academic career focusing on the shape and shaping of the book of Psalms: first its metanarrative and then the narrative shaping of smaller groups of psalms. This commentary for Liturgical Press would prove to be a whole new undertaking for me, expanding my reading and understanding of this well-loved book.

The studies of the Psalter I subsequently undertook revealed to me myriad topics addressed in the words of the Psalter that had somehow not surfaced in my previous studies of the book. First, the Psalter contains many feminine images of God and feminine understandings of God, both of which I was aware but never incorporated into my research and commentary on the book. And, equally important, the book addresses societal and human rights issues that continue to be concerns in our twenty-first-century world: economic disparities, power inequalities, social inequalities, ecological issues, and basic issues of human rights, among others.

This author's assignment by Liturgical Press was to write 75 percent of the commentary and then, for the other 25 percent, incorporate other voices, voices rarely, if ever, included in a scholarly commentary on a biblical book. I have, over the years, cultivated strong ties to a number of universities in South Africa and have witnessed firsthand on many occasions the deep-seated feelings of oppression by Africans living in South Africa, particularly females. Twenty-five years after the end of apartheid, issues of racial, economic, ecological, and social inequality remain a major issue for both blacks and whites in South Africa as they struggle to live together in a postapartheid world.

Thus I determined to incorporate South African voices as the contributing voices in this commentary on books 4 and 5 of the Psalter. A generous Sabbatical Research Grant from the Louisville Institute in Louisville, Kentucky, and a sabbatical leave from Mercer University allowed me to travel to South Africa for six weeks in the spring of 2018 and interview and recruit a group of mostly first-generation African theology students who contributed eighteen moving reflections to the commentary.

I am most grateful to the McAfee School of Theology at Mercer University for giving me, over the years, the opportunities to pursue the research and writing agendas that I so love, and to the Louisville Institute for its support.

And, as always, my heartfelt love to my husband, Steve, for his patient indulging of my academic pursuits and all the time I spend in my study researching and writing. None of this would be possible without him.

Nancy L. deClaissé-Walford
Advent 2019

Contributors

Agnes Besigye (Nkuna) is an administrative assistant in the Department of Classics at the University of Pretoria. She is the only black person in her department at the university but does not feel in any way marginalized. She was born before the end of apartheid and has memories of it herself as well as what her parents and grandparents have shared with her.

Siphokazi Dlwati is a master's degree student in the Department of Theology at the University of the Free State in Bloemfontein. She also works in the department as a student academic adviser. She comes from a rural village in the Eastern Cape where tradition is very strong. Ancestor worship and belief in Jesus go hand in hand in her village, with much ritual surrounding appeasing the ancestors, often involving a costly purchase of a cow, a sheep, etc. Siphokazi is disturbed by the high cost of such rituals and has trouble reconciling them with faith in Jesus. She expresses concern about how the "academics" of theology can be translated to the church. She is an active member of a church called Divine Restoration Ministries.

William Chisa is from Malawi in central Africa and is a master's degree student at the University of Kwa Zulu Natal in Pietermaritzburg. William's master's thesis will be an examination of Malawi's stance on termination of pregnancies. In 2016 the government of Malawi began a reexamination of the current law that allows termination only if the life of the mother is at stake, with an eye to expanding it to cases of rape, incest, and other circumstances. The Malawi Council of Churches has gotten involved in the debate. William would like to examine the debate using the story of the woman in Mark 5:25-34 as an example of someone who was considered unclean because of her condition but dared to approach Jesus and was healed.

Belinda Crawford is the program coordinator for Body Theology in the Ujamaa Centre at the University of Kwa Zulu Natal's Pietermaritzburg Campus. The word "ujamaa" is Swahili for "familyhood" or "extended family." The centre in Pietermaritzburg describes itself this way: "The Ujamaa Centre is an interface between socially engaged biblical and theological scholars, organic intellectuals, and local communities of the poor, working-class, and marginalized. Together we use biblical and theological resources for individual and social transformation."

Belinda is of mixed race and so her African mother could not keep her; she was raised in a reformatory school, a repository for children of mixed race during South Africa's apartheid era. That move probably saved her life, but Belinda did not know of her mixed parentage until her mother told her when she was twenty-two years old. Belinda states that she feels somewhat robbed socially and culturally because she does not belong in either the "white world" or the "black world" of South Africa. She has experienced a variety of religious contexts, including Conservative Pentecostal and Seventh-Day Adventist. She identifies as Seventh-Day Adventist. Before coming to the University of Kwa Zulu Natal she attended Heldeberg Bible College in Cape Town and, after graduation, ran a shelter for women and children there.

Nikki Carroll Hardeman is director of outreach and alumni relations at the McAfee School of Theology at Mercer University. She completed her master of divinity degree at the McAfee School of Theology in 2005 and served in local churches and the Cooperative Baptist Fellowship Offices in Georgia before returning to McAfee in 2015.

Thanyani Mahanya is assistant to the deputy dean and head of the Department of Old Testament at the University of Pretoria. She was raised by her mother and grandmother after her grandmother took her mother away from a polygamist marriage. She states that women in South Africa are taught that family matters are private matters, so they should not be talked about. "We are not to air our dirty laundry." So women dress in their best finery for church and sit and talk as if they have no problems, but many are very broken and damaged, often because of "the myth of marriage and motherhood." She believes women need a safe place to talk and air their feelings, their hurts, their despairs.

Nellie Zania Mahlangu is a domestic worker in three households. While she completed high school and began training in computer science, she had to discontinue her studies and find work because of her family situation. She is the "head of house" at the moment, living with and caring for her unemployed mother, brother, sister, and nephew and raising a young son alone. She travels two hours each day to get to her work and then back home again, rising at four o'clock in the morning. She is very involved in the Zion Christian Church and would like to continue her education at some point in the future.

Christine Nel is the theology librarian at the University of Pretoria. She is Afrikaans and grew up on a farm in Kwa Zulu Natal. Her father and mother had African workers, but she states that they treated them like members of the family and many of the workers stayed on the farm for decades. She expressed a great love for African culture and for the African students with whom she works, saying that in so many instances her African friends were so much more open, willing to share, and embrace than her Afrikaans friends.

Gweneth Ntamo is a master's degree student in the Department of Theology at the University of the Free State in Bloemfontein. She is a first-generation college student who started out in the sociology department (to please her parents) but knew all along that she wanted to do theology. She comes from the Isixhosa tribe of the Northern Cape but knows Afrikaans and English better than her own tribal language. She states that since she is light skinned she is regularly considered "colored," that is, of mixed race; thus she often finds herself treated as an outsider because of her skin color and because she is in college. In her church, Empowerment Ministries International, she is ordained and runs home cells, is on the worship team, and teaches children's Sunday School.

Yenziwe Shabalala graduated from the University of Kwa Zulu Natal in 2017 and now is a volunteer at the Ujamaa Centre at the university. She lives in a large extended household of ten persons and her mother is the only source of income for the family. She feels a great deal of pressure to contribute to the family income and has dreams of a food services business on the campus of the University of Kwa Zulu Natal, since virtually none exists. Yenzi and her partners have made two proposals to the university but so far have not been successful in gaining a contract.

Yenzi is a member of the Seventh-Day Adventist Church. She states that black women find it difficult to voice their opinions in the church and in society, and she is concerned to empower women, particularly from rural areas, to be able to do so. She states that she is "Afro-centric" but recognizes much gender inequality in the culture.

Lodewyk Sutton is Afrikaans and is professor of Old Testament in the Department of Theology at the University of the Free State in Bloemfontein. He came to theology after earning degrees in business and law and thus is also an advocate in criminal law in South Africa. He began his theological studies emphasizing the New Testament, but when he took Hebrew he "converted" to the Old Testament and took a special interest in warfare imagery in the book of Psalms.

Lesego Temane is an administrator, master's degree student, and part-time lecturer in the Department of Theology at the University of Pretoria. She has a master's degree in philosophy and is completing a master's degree in theology. In addition, she is a minister in her church congregation, working in pastoral counseling and youth ministry.

Lesego described her father as an abusive man, and therefore she now views God as the father she never had. Thus she calls God "he" as a father figure, but she encounters many women who find it difficult to see God as "he" when they have been so hurt by men. And for many women, God is silent.

Foreword

"Tell It on the Mountain"—or, "And You Shall Tell Your Daughter [as Well]"

Athalya Brenner-Idan

Universiteit van Amsterdam/Tel Aviv University

W hat can Wisdom Commentary do to help, and for whom?
The commentary genre has always been privileged in biblical studies.
Traditionally acclaimed commentary series, such as the International
Critical Commentary, Old Testament and New Testament Library, Hermeneia, Anchor Bible, Eerdmans, and Word—to name but several—
enjoy nearly automatic prestige, and the number of women authors who
participate in those is relatively small by comparison to their growing
number in the scholarly guild. There certainly are some volumes written
by women in them, especially in recent decades. At this time, however,
this does not reflect the situation on the ground. Further, size matters. In
that sense, the sheer size of the Wisdom Commentary is essential. This
also represents a considerable investment and the possibility of reaching
a wider audience than those already "converted."

Expecting women scholars to deal especially or only with what are considered strictly "female" matters seems unwarranted. According to Audre Lorde, "The master's tools will never dismantle the master's house."[1] But this maxim is not relevant to our case. The point of this commentary is not to destroy but to attain greater participation in the interpretive dialogue about biblical texts. Women scholars may bring additional questions to the readerly agenda as well as fresh angles to existing issues. To assume that their questions are designed only to topple a certain male hegemony is not convincing.

At first I did ask myself: is this commentary series an addition to calm raw nerves, an embellishment to make upholding the old hierarchy palatable? Or is it indeed about becoming the Master? On second and third thoughts, however, I understood that becoming the Master is not what this is about. Knowledge is power. Since Foucault at the very least, this cannot be in dispute. Writing commentaries for biblical texts by feminist women and men for women and for men, of confessional as well as non-confessional convictions, will sabotage (hopefully) the established hierarchy but will not topple it. This is about an attempt to integrate more fully, to introduce another viewpoint, to become. What excites me about the Wisdom Commentary is that it is not offered as just an alternative supplanting or substituting for the dominant discourse.

These commentaries on biblical books will retain nonauthoritative, pluralistic viewpoints. And yes, once again, the weight of a dedicated series, to distinguish from collections of stand-alone volumes, will prove weightier.

That such an approach is especially important in the case of the Hebrew Bible/Old Testament is beyond doubt. Women of Judaism, Christianity, and also Islam have struggled to make it their own for centuries, even more than they have fought for the New Testament and the Qur'an. Every Hebrew Bible/Old Testament volume in this project is evidence that the day has arrived: it is now possible to read *all* the Jewish canonical books as a collection, for a collection they are, with guidance conceived of with the needs of women readers (not only men) as an integral inspiration and part thereof.

In my Jewish tradition, the main motivation for reciting the Haggadah, the ritual text recited yearly on Passover, the festival of liberation from

---

1. Audre Lorde, "The Master's Tools Will Never Dismantle the Master's House," in *Sister Outsider: Essays and Speeches* (Berkeley, CA: Crossing Press, 1984, 2007), 110–14. First delivered in the Second Sex Conference in New York, 1979.

bondage, is given as "And you shall tell your son" (from Exod 13:8). The knowledge and experience of past generations is thus transferred to the next, for constructing the present and the future. The ancient maxim is, literally, limited to a male audience. This series remolds the maxim into a new inclusive shape, which is of the utmost consequence: "And you shall tell your son" is extended to "And you shall tell your daughter [as well as your son]." Or, if you want, "Tell it on the mountain," for all to hear.

This is what it's all about.

Editor's Introduction to Wisdom Commentary

"She Is a Breath of the Power of God" (Wis 7:25)

Barbara E. Reid, OP

General Editor

Wisdom Commentary is the first series to offer detailed feminist interpretation of every book of the Bible. The fruit of collaborative work by an ecumenical and interreligious team of scholars, the volumes provide serious, scholarly engagement with the whole biblical text, not only those texts that explicitly mention women. The series is intended for clergy, teachers, ministers, and all serious students of the Bible. Designed to be both accessible and informed by the various approaches of biblical scholarship, it pays particular attention to the world in front of the text, that is, how the text is heard and appropriated. At the same time, this series aims to be faithful to the ancient text and its earliest audiences; thus the volumes also explicate the worlds behind the text and within it. While issues of gender are primary in this project, the volumes also address the intersecting issues of power, authority, ethnicity, race, class, and religious belief and practice. The fifty-eight volumes include the books regarded as canonical by Jews (i.e., the Tanakh); Protestants (the "Hebrew Bible" and the New Testament); and Roman Catholic, Anglican, and Eastern Orthodox Communions (i.e., Tobit, Judith, 1 and

2 Maccabees, Wisdom of Solomon, Sirach/Ecclesiasticus, Baruch, including the Letter of Jeremiah, the additions to Esther, and Susanna and Bel and the Dragon in Daniel).

A Symphony of Diverse Voices

Included in the Wisdom Commentary series are voices from scholars of many different religious traditions, of diverse ages, differing sexual identities, and varying cultural, racial, ethnic, and social contexts. Some have been pioneers in feminist biblical interpretation; others are newer contributors from a younger generation. A further distinctive feature of this series is that each volume incorporates voices other than that of the lead author(s). These voices appear alongside the commentary of the lead author(s), in the grayscale inserts. At times, a contributor may offer an alternative interpretation or a critique of the position taken by the lead author(s). At other times, she or he may offer a complementary interpretation from a different cultural context or subject position. Occasionally, portions of previously published material bring in other views. The diverse voices are not intended to be contestants in a debate or a cacophony of discordant notes. The multiple voices reflect that there is no single definitive feminist interpretation of a text. In addition, they show the importance of subject position in the process of interpretation. In this regard, the Wisdom Commentary series takes inspiration from the Talmud and from *The Torah: A Women's Commentary* (ed. Tamara Cohn Eskenazi and Andrea L. Weiss; New York: Women of Reform Judaism, Federation of Temple Sisterhood, 2008), in which many voices, even conflicting ones, are included and not harmonized.

Contributors include biblical scholars, theologians, and readers of Scripture from outside the scholarly and religious guilds. At times, their comments pertain to a particular text. In some instances they address a theme or topic that arises from the text.

Another feature that highlights the collaborative nature of feminist biblical interpretation is that a number of the volumes have two lead authors who have worked in tandem from the inception of the project and whose voices interweave throughout the commentary.

Woman Wisdom

The title, Wisdom Commentary, reflects both the importance to feminists of the figure of Woman Wisdom in the Scriptures and the distinct wisdom that feminist women and men bring to the interpretive process. In the Scriptures, Woman Wisdom appears as "a breath of the power of God, and a pure emanation of the glory of the Almighty" (Wis 7:25), who was present and active in fashioning all that exists (Prov 8:22-31; Wis 8:6). She is a spirit who pervades and penetrates all things (Wis 7:22-23), and she provides guidance and nourishment at her all-inclusive table (Prov 9:1-5). In both postexilic biblical and nonbiblical Jewish sources, Woman Wisdom is often equated with Torah, e.g., Sirach 24:23-34; Baruch 3:9–4:4; 38:2; 46:4-5; 2 Baruch 48:33, 36; 4 Ezra 5:9-10; 13:55; 14:40; 1 Enoch 42.

The New Testament frequently portrays Jesus as Wisdom incarnate. He invites his followers, "take my yoke upon you and learn from me" (Matt 11:29), just as Ben Sira advises, "put your neck under her [Wisdom's] yoke and let your souls receive instruction" (Sir 51:26). Just as Wisdom experiences rejection (Prov 1:23-25; Sir 15:7-8; Wis 10:3; Bar 3:12), so too does Jesus (Mark 8:31; John 1:10-11). Only some accept his invitation to his all-inclusive banquet (Matt 22:1-14; Luke 14:15-24; compare Prov 1:20-21; 9:3-5). Yet, "wisdom is vindicated by her deeds" (Matt 11:19, speaking of Jesus and John the Baptist; in the Lukan parallel at 7:35 they are called "wisdom's children"). There are numerous parallels between what is said of Wisdom and of the *Logos* in the Prologue of the Fourth Gospel (John 1:1-18). These are only a few of many examples. This female embodiment of divine presence and power is an apt image to guide the work of this series.

Feminism

There are many different understandings of the term "feminism." The various meanings, aims, and methods have developed exponentially in recent decades. Feminism is a perspective and a movement that springs from a recognition of inequities toward women, and it advocates for changes in whatever structures prevent full flourishing of human beings and all creation. Three waves of feminism in the United States are commonly recognized. The first, arising in the mid-nineteenth century and lasting into the early twentieth, was sparked by women's efforts to be involved in the public sphere and to win the right to vote. In the 1960s and 1970s, the second wave focused on civil rights and equality for women. With the third wave, from the 1980s forward, came global feminism and the emphasis on the contextual nature of interpretation. Now a fourth wave may be emerging, with a stronger emphasis on the intersectionality of women's concerns with those of other marginalized groups and the increased use of the internet as a platform for discussion and activism.[1] As feminism has matured, it has recognized that inequities based on gender are interwoven with power imbalances based on race, class, ethnicity, religion, sexual identity, physical ability, and a host of other social markers.

Feminist Women and Men

Men who choose to identify with and partner with feminist women in the work of deconstructing systems of domination and building structures of equality are rightly regarded as feminists. Some men readily identify with experiences of women who are discriminated against on the basis of sex/gender, having themselves had comparable experiences; others who may not have faced direct discrimination or stereotyping recognize that inequity and problematic characterization still occur, and they seek correction. This series is pleased to include feminist men both as lead authors and as contributing voices.

Feminist Biblical Interpretation

Women interpreting the Bible from the lenses of their own experience is nothing new. Throughout the ages women have recounted the biblical stories, teaching them to their children and others, all the while interpreting them afresh for their time and circumstances.[2] Following is a very brief sketch of select foremothers who laid the groundwork for contemporary feminist biblical interpretation.

One of the earliest known Christian women who challenged patriarchal interpretations of Scripture was a consecrated virgin named Helie, who lived in the second century CE. When she refused to marry, her

---

1. See Martha Rampton, "Four Waves of Feminism" (October 25, 2015), at http://www.pacificu.edu/about-us/news-events/four-waves-feminism; and Ealasaid Munro, "Feminism: A Fourth Wave?," https://www.psa.ac.uk/insight-plus/feminism-fourth-wave.

2. For fuller treatments of this history, see chap. 7, "One Thousand Years of Feminist Bible Criticism," in Gerda Lerner, *Creation of Feminist Consciousness: From the Middle Ages to Eighteen-Seventy* (New York: Oxford University Press, 1993), 138–66; Susanne Scholz, "From the 'Woman's Bible' to the 'Women's Bible,' The History of Feminist Approaches to the Hebrew Bible," in *Introducing the Women's Hebrew Bible*, IFT 13 (New York: T&T Clark, 2007), 12–32; Marion Ann Taylor and Agnes Choi, eds., *Handbook of Women Biblical Interpreters: A Historical and Biographical Guide* (Grand Rapids: Baker Academic, 2012).

parents brought her before a judge, who quoted to her Paul's admonition, "It is better to marry than to be aflame with passion" (1 Cor 7:9). In response, Helie first acknowledges that this is what Scripture says, but then she retorts, "but not for everyone, that is, not for holy virgins."[3] She is one of the first to question the notion that a text has one meaning that is applicable in all situations.

A Jewish woman who also lived in the second century CE, Beruriah, is said to have had "profound knowledge of biblical exegesis and outstanding intelligence."[4] One story preserved in the Talmud (b. Berakot 10a) tells of how she challenged her husband, Rabbi Meir, when he prayed for the destruction of a sinner. Proffering an alternate interpretation, she argued that Psalm 104:35 advocated praying for the destruction of sin, not the sinner.

In medieval times the first written commentaries on Scripture from a critical feminist point of view emerge. While others may have been produced and passed on orally, they are for the most part lost to us now. Among the earliest preserved feminist writings are those of Hildegard of Bingen (1098–1179), German writer, mystic, and abbess of a Benedictine monastery. She reinterpreted the Genesis narratives in a way that presented women and men as complementary and interdependent. She frequently wrote about the Divine as feminine.[5] Along with other women mystics of the time, such as Julian of Norwich (1342–ca. 1416), she spoke authoritatively from her personal experiences of God's revelation in prayer.

In this era, women were also among the scribes who copied biblical manuscripts. Notable among them is Paula Dei Mansi of Verona, from a distinguished family of Jewish scribes. In 1288, she translated from Hebrew into Italian a collection of Bible commentaries written by her father and added her own explanations.[6]

Another pioneer, Christine de Pizan (1365–ca. 1430), was a French court writer and prolific poet. She used allegory and common sense

3. Madrid, Escorial MS, a II 9, f. 90 v., as cited in Lerner, *Feminist Consciousness*, 140.

4. See Judith R. Baskin, "Women and Post-Biblical Commentary," in *The Torah: A Women's Commentary*, ed. Tamara Cohn Eskenazi and Andrea L. Weiss (New York: Women of Reform Judaism, Federation of Temple Sisterhood, 2008), xlix–lv, at lii.

5. Hildegard of Bingen, *De Operatione Dei*, 1.4.100; PL 197:885bc, as cited in Lerner, *Feminist Consciousness*, 142–43. See also Barbara Newman, *Sister of Wisdom: St. Hildegard's Theology of the Feminine* (Berkeley: University of California Press, 1987).

6. Emily Taitz, Sondra Henry, Cheryl Tallan, eds., *JPS Guide to Jewish Women 600 B.C.E.–1900 C.E.* (Philadelphia: Jewish Publication Society of America, 2003), 110–11.

to subvert misogynist readings of Scripture and celebrated the accomplishments of female biblical figures to argue for women's active roles in building society.[7]

By the seventeenth century, there were women who asserted that the biblical text needs to be understood and interpreted in its historical context. For example, Rachel Speght (1597–ca. 1630), a Calvinist English poet, elaborates on the historical situation in first-century Corinth that prompted Paul to say, "It is well for a man not to touch a woman" (1 Cor 7:1). Her aim was to show that the biblical texts should not be applied in a literal fashion to all times and circumstances. Similarly, Margaret Fell (1614–1702), one of the founders of the Religious Society of Friends (Quakers) in Britain, addressed the Pauline prohibitions against women speaking in church by insisting that they do not have universal validity. Rather, they need to be understood in their historical context, as addressed to a local church in particular time-bound circumstances.[8]

Along with analyzing the historical context of the biblical writings, women in the eighteenth and nineteenth centuries began to attend to misogynistic interpretations based on faulty translations. One of the first to do so was British feminist Mary Astell (1666–1731).[9] In the United States, the Grimké sisters, Sarah (1792–1873) and Angelina (1805–1879), Quaker women from a slaveholding family in South Carolina, learned biblical Greek and Hebrew so that they could interpret the Bible for themselves. They were prompted to do so after men sought to silence them from speaking out against slavery and for women's rights by claiming that the Bible (e.g., 1 Cor 14:34) prevented women from speaking in public.[10] Another prominent abolitionist, Isabella Baumfree, who adopted the name Sojourner Truth (ca. 1797–1883), a former slave, quoted the Bible liberally in her speeches[11] and in so doing challenged cultural assumptions and biblical interpretations that undergird gender inequities.

---

7. See further Taylor and Choi, *Handbook of Women Biblical Interpreters*, 127–32.

8. Her major work, *Women's Speaking Justified, Proved and Allowed by the Scriptures*, published in London in 1667, gave a systematic feminist reading of all biblical texts pertaining to women.

9. Mary Astell, *Some Reflections upon Marriage* (New York: Source Book Press, 1970, reprint of the 1730 edition; earliest edition of this work is 1700), 103–4.

10. See further Sarah Grimké, *Letters on the Equality of the Sexes and the Condition of Woman* (Boston: Isaac Knapp, 1838).

11. See, for example, her most famous speech, "Ain't I a Woman?," delivered in 1851 at the Ohio Women's Rights Convention in Akron, OH; http://www.fordham.edu/halsall/mod/sojtruth-woman.asp.

Another monumental work that emerged in nineteenth-century England was that of Jewish theologian Grace Aguilar (1816–1847), *The Women of Israel*,[12] published in 1845. Aguilar's approach was to make connections between the biblical women and contemporary Jewish women's concerns. She aimed to counter the widespread notion that women were degraded in Jewish law and that only in Christianity were women's dignity and value upheld. Her intent was to help Jewish women find strength and encouragement by seeing the evidence of God's compassionate love in the history of every woman in the Bible. While not a full commentary on the Bible, Aguilar's work stands out for its comprehensive treatment of every female biblical character, including even the most obscure references.[13]

The first person to produce a full-blown feminist commentary on the Bible was Elizabeth Cady Stanton (1815–1902). A leading proponent in the United States for women's right to vote, she found that whenever women tried to make inroads into politics, education, or the work world, the Bible was quoted against them. Along with a team of like-minded women, she produced her own commentary on every text of the Bible that concerned women. Her pioneering two-volume project, *The Woman's Bible*, published in 1895 and 1898, urges women to recognize that texts that degrade women come from the men who wrote the texts, not from God, and to use their common sense to rethink what has been presented to them as sacred.

Nearly a century later, *The Women's Bible Commentary*, edited by Carol A. Newsom and Sharon H. Ringe (Louisville: Westminster John Knox, 1992), appeared. This one-volume commentary features North American feminist scholarship on each book of the Protestant canon. Like Cady Stanton's commentary, it does not contain comments on every section of the biblical text but only on those passages deemed relevant to women. It was revised and expanded in 1998 to include the Apocrypha/Deuterocanonical books, and the contributors to this new volume reflect the global face of contemporary feminist scholarship. The revisions made in the third edition, which appeared in 2012, represent the profound advances in feminist biblical scholarship and include newer voices. In both the second and third editions, *The* has been dropped from the title.

---

12. The full title is *The Women of Israel or Characters and Sketches from the Holy Scriptures and Jewish History Illustrative of the Past History, Present Duty, and Future Destiny of the Hebrew Females, as Based on the Word of God.*

13. See further Eskenazi and Weiss, *The Torah: A Women's Commentary,* xxxviii; Taylor and Choi, *Handbook of Women Biblical Interpreters,* 31–37.

Also appearing at the centennial of Cady Stanton's *The Woman's Bible* were two volumes edited by Elisabeth Schüssler Fiorenza with the assistance of Shelly Matthews. The first, *Searching the Scriptures: A Feminist Introduction* (New York: Crossroad, 1993), charts a comprehensive approach to feminist interpretation from ecumenical, interreligious, and multicultural perspectives. The second volume, published in 1994, provides critical feminist commentary on each book of the New Testament as well as on three books of Jewish Pseudepigrapha and eleven other early Christian writings.

In Europe, similar endeavors have been undertaken, such as the one-volume *Kompendium Feministische Bibelauslegung*, edited by Luise Schottroff and Marie-Theres Wacker (Gütersloh: Gütersloher Verlagshaus, 2007), featuring German feminist biblical interpretation of each book of the Bible, along with apocryphal books, and several extrabiblical writings. This work, now in its third edition, has recently been translated into English.[14] A multivolume project, *The Bible and Women: An Encylopaedia of Exegesis and Cultural History*, edited by Irmtraud Fischer, Adriana Valerio, Mercedes Navarro Puerto, Christiana de Groot, and Mary Ann Beavis, is currently in production. This project presents a history of the reception of the Bible as embedded in Western cultural history and focuses particularly on gender-relevant biblical themes, biblical female characters, and women recipients of the Bible. The volumes are published in English, Spanish, Italian, and German.[15]

Another groundbreaking work is the collection The Feminist Companion to the Bible Series, edited by Athalya Brenner (Sheffield: Sheffield Academic, 1993–2015), which comprises twenty volumes of commen-

---

14. *Feminist Biblical Interpretation: A Compendium of Critical Commentary on the Books of the Bible and Related Literature*, trans. Lisa E. Dahill, Everett R. Kalin, Nancy Lukens, Linda M. Maloney, Barbara Rumscheidt, Martin Rumscheidt, and Tina Steiner (Grand Rapids: Eerdmans, 2012). Another notable collection is the three volumes edited by Susanne Scholz, *Feminist Interpretation of the Hebrew Bible in Retrospect*, Recent Research in Biblical Studies 7, 8, 9 (Sheffield: Sheffield Phoenix, 2013, 2014, 2016).

15. The first volume, on the Torah, appeared in Spanish in 2009, in German and Italian in 2010, and in English in 2011 (Atlanta: Society of Biblical Literature). Five more volumes are now available: *Feminist Biblical Studies in the Twentieth Century*, ed. Elisabeth Schüssler Fiorenza (2014); *The Writings and Later Wisdom Books*, ed. Christl M. Maier and Nuria Calduch-Benages (2014); *Gospels: Narrative and History*, ed. Mercedes Navarro Puerto and Marinella Perroni; English translation ed. Amy-Jill Levine (2015); *The High Middle Ages*, ed. Kari Elisabeth Børresen and Adriana Valerio (2015); and *Early Jewish Writings*, ed. Eileen Schuller and Marie-Theres Wacker (2017). For further information, see http://www.bibleandwomen.org.

taries on the Old Testament. The parallel series, Feminist Companion to the New Testament and Early Christian Writings, edited by Amy-Jill Levine with Marianne Blickenstaff and Maria Mayo Robbins (Sheffield: Sheffield Academic, 2001–2009), contains thirteen volumes with one more planned. These two series are not full commentaries on the biblical books but comprise collected essays on discrete biblical texts.

Works by individual feminist biblical scholars in all parts of the world abound, and they are now too numerous to list in this introduction. Feminist biblical interpretation has reached a level of maturity that now makes possible a commentary series on every book of the Bible. In recent decades, women have had greater access to formal theological education, have been able to learn critical analytical tools, have put their own interpretations into writing, and have developed new methods of biblical interpretation. Until recent decades the work of feminist biblical interpreters was largely unknown, both to other women and to their brothers in the synagogue, church, and academy. Feminists now have taken their place in the professional world of biblical scholars, where they build on the work of their foremothers and connect with one another across the globe in ways not previously possible. In a few short decades, feminist biblical criticism has become an integral part of the academy.

Methodologies

Feminist biblical scholars use a variety of methods and often employ a number of them together.[16] In the Wisdom Commentary series, the authors will explain their understanding of feminism and the feminist reading strategies used in their commentary. Each volume treats the biblical text in blocks of material, not an analysis verse by verse. The entire text is considered, not only those passages that feature female characters or that speak specifically about women. When women are not apparent in the narrative, feminist lenses are used to analyze the dynamics in the text between male characters, the models of power, binary ways of thinking, and the dynamics of imperialism. Attention is given to how the whole text functions and how it was and is heard, both in its original context and today. Issues of particular concern to women—e.g., poverty, food, health, the environment, water—come to the fore.

---

16. See the seventeen essays in *Her Master's Tools? Feminist and Postcolonial Engagements of Historical-Critical Discourse,* ed. Caroline Vander Stichele and Todd Penner (Atlanta: Society of Biblical Literature, 2005), which show the complementarity of various approaches.

One of the approaches used by early feminists and still popular today is to lift up the overlooked and forgotten stories of women in the Bible. Studies of women in each of the Testaments have been done, and there are also studies on women in particular biblical books.[17] Feminists recognize that the examples of biblical characters can be both empowering and problematic. The point of the feminist enterprise is not to serve as an apologetic for women; it is rather, in part, to recover women's history and literary roles in all their complexity and to learn from that recovery.

Retrieving the submerged history of biblical women is a crucial step for constructing the story of the past so as to lead to liberative possibilities for the present and future. There are, however, some pitfalls to this approach. Sometimes depictions of biblical women have been naïve and romantic. Some commentators exalt the virtues of both biblical and contemporary women and paint women as superior to men. Such reverse discrimination inhibits movement toward equality for all. In addition, some feminists challenge the idea that one can "pluck positive images out of an admittedly androcentric text, separating literary characterizations from the androcentric interests they were created to serve."[18] Still other feminists find these images to have enormous value.

One other danger with seeking the submerged history of women is the tendency for Christian feminists to paint Jesus and even Paul as liberators of women in a way that demonizes Judaism.[19] Wisdom Commentary aims to enhance understanding of Jesus as well as Paul as Jews of their day and to forge solidarity among Jewish and Christian feminists.

---

17. See, e.g., Alice Bach, ed., *Women in the Hebrew Bible: A Reader* (New York: Routledge, 1998); Tikva Frymer-Kensky, *Reading the Women of the Bible* (New York: Schocken Books, 2002); Carol Meyers, Toni Craven, and Ross S. Kraemer, *Women in Scripture* (Grand Rapids: Eerdmans, 2000); Irene Nowell, *Women in the Old Testament* (Collegeville, MN: Liturgical Press, 1997); Katharine Doob Sakenfeld, *Just Wives? Stories of Power and Survival in the Old Testament and Today* (Louisville: Westminster John Knox, 2003); Mary Ann Getty-Sullivan, *Women in the New Testament* (Collegeville, MN: Liturgical Press, 2001); Bonnie Thurston, *Women in the New Testament: Questions and Commentary*, Companions to the New Testament (New York: Crossroad, 1998).

18. Cheryl Exum, "Second Thoughts about Secondary Characters: Women in Exodus 1.8–2.10," in *A Feminist Companion to Exodus to Deuteronomy*, FCB 6, ed. Athalya Brenner (Sheffield: Sheffield Academic, 1994), 75–97, at 76.

19. See Judith Plaskow, "Anti-Judaism in Feminist Christian Interpretation," in *Searching the Scriptures: A Feminist Introduction*, ed. Elisabeth Schüssler Fiorenza (New York: Crossroad, 1993), 1:117–29; Amy-Jill Levine, "The New Testament and Anti-Judaism," in *The Misunderstood Jew: The Church and the Scandal of the Jewish Jesus* (San Francisco: HarperSanFrancisco, 2006), 87–117.

Feminist scholars who use historical-critical methods analyze the world behind the text; they seek to understand the historical context from which the text emerged and the circumstances of the communities to whom it was addressed. In bringing feminist lenses to this approach, the aim is not to impose modern expectations on ancient cultures but to unmask the ways that ideologically problematic mind-sets that produced the ancient texts are still promulgated through the text. Feminist biblical scholars aim not only to deconstruct but also to reclaim and reconstruct biblical history as women's history, in which women were central and active agents in creating religious heritage.[20] A further step is to construct meaning for contemporary women and men in a liberative movement toward transformation of social, political, economic, and religious structures.[21] In recent years, some feminists have embraced new historicism, which accents the creative role of the interpreter in any construction of history and exposes the power struggles to which the text witnesses.[22]

Literary critics analyze the world of the text: its form, language patterns, and rhetorical function.[23] They do not attempt to separate layers of tradition and redaction but focus on the text holistically, as it is in its present form. They examine how meaning is created in the interaction

---

20. See, for example, Phyllis A. Bird, *Missing Persons and Mistaken Identities: Women and Gender in Ancient Israel* (Minneapolis: Fortress, 1997); Elisabeth Schüssler Fiorenza, *In Memory of Her: A Feminist Theological Reconstruction of Christian Origins* (New York: Crossroad, 1983); Ross Shepard Kraemer and Mary Rose D'Angelo, eds., *Women and Christian Origins* (New York: Oxford University Press, 1999).

21. See, e.g., Sandra M. Schneiders, *The Revelatory Text: Interpreting the New Testament as Sacred Scripture*, rev. ed. (Collegeville, MN: Liturgical Press, 1999), whose aim is to engage in biblical interpretation not only for intellectual enlightenment but, even more important, for personal and communal transformation. Elisabeth Schüssler Fiorenza (*Wisdom Ways: Introducing Feminist Biblical Interpretation* [Maryknoll, NY: Orbis Books, 2001]) envisions the work of feminist biblical interpretation as a dance of Wisdom that consists of seven steps that interweave in spiral movements toward liberation, the final one being transformative action for change.

22. See Gina Hens-Piazza, *The New Historicism*, GBS, Old Testament Series (Minneapolis: Fortress, 2002).

23. Phyllis Trible was among the first to employ this method with texts from Genesis and Ruth in her groundbreaking book *God and the Rhetoric of Sexuality*, OBT (Philadelphia: Fortress, 1978). Another pioneer in feminist literary criticism is Mieke Bal (*Lethal Love: Feminist Literary Readings of Biblical Love Stories* [Bloomington: Indiana University Press, 1987]). For surveys of recent developments in literary methods, see Terry Eagleton, *Literary Theory: An Introduction*, 3rd ed. (Minneapolis: University of Minnesota Press, 2008); Janice Capel Anderson and Stephen D. Moore, eds., *Mark and Method: New Approaches in Biblical Studies*, 2nd ed. (Minneapolis: Fortress, 2008).

between the text and its reader in multiple contexts. Within the arena of literary approaches are reader-oriented approaches, narrative, rhetorical, structuralist, post-structuralist, deconstructive, ideological, autobiographical, and performance criticism.[24] Narrative critics study the interrelation among author, text, and audience through investigation of settings, both spatial and temporal; characters; plot; and narrative techniques (e.g., irony, parody, intertextual allusions). Reader-response critics attend to the impact that the text has on the reader or hearer. They recognize that when a text is detrimental toward women there is the choice either to affirm the text or to read against the grain toward a liberative end. Rhetorical criticism analyzes the style of argumentation and attends to how the author is attempting to shape the thinking or actions of the hearer. Structuralist critics analyze the complex patterns of binary oppositions in the text to derive its meaning.[25] Post-structuralist approaches challenge the notion that there are fixed meanings to any biblical text or that there is one universal truth. They engage in close readings of the text and often engage in intertextual analysis.[26] Within this approach is deconstructionist criticism, which views the text as a site of conflict, with competing narratives. The interpreter aims to expose the fault lines and overturn and reconfigure binaries by elevating the underling of a pair and foregrounding it.[27] Feminists also use other postmodern approaches, such as ideological and autobiographical criticism. The former analyzes the system of ideas that underlies the power and

24. See, e.g., J. Cheryl Exum and David J. A. Clines, eds., *The New Literary Criticism and the Hebrew Bible* (Valley Forge, PA: Trinity Press International, 1993); Edgar V. McKnight and Elizabeth Struthers Malbon, eds., *The New Literary Criticism and the New Testament* (Valley Forge, PA: Trinity Press International, 1994).

25. See, e.g., David Jobling, *The Sense of Biblical Narrative: Three Structural Analyses in the Old Testament*, JSOTSup 7 (Sheffield: University of Sheffield, 1978).

26. See, e.g., Stephen D. Moore, *Poststructuralism and the New Testament: Derrida and Foucault at the Foot of the Cross* (Minneapolis: Fortress, 1994); *The Bible in Theory: Critical and Postcritical Essays* (Atlanta: Society of Biblical Literature, 2010); Yvonne Sherwood, *A Biblical Text and Its Afterlives: The Survival of Jonah in Western Culture* (Cambridge: Cambridge University Press, 2000).

27. David Penchansky, "Deconstruction," in *The Oxford Encyclopedia of Biblical Interpretation*, ed. Steven McKenzie (New York: Oxford University Press, 2013), 196–205. See, for example, Danna Nolan Fewell and David M. Gunn, *Gender, Power, and Promise: The Subject of the Bible's First Story* (Nashville: Abingdon, 1993); David Rutledge, *Reading Marginally: Feminism, Deconstruction and the Bible*, BibInt 21 (Leiden: Brill, 1996).

values concealed in the text as well as that of the interpreter.[28] The latter involves deliberate self-disclosure while reading the text as a critical exegete.[29] Performance criticism attends to how the text was passed on orally, usually in communal settings, and to the verbal and nonverbal interactions between the performer and the audience.[30]

From the beginning, feminists have understood that interpreting the Bible is an act of power. In recent decades, feminist biblical scholars have developed hermeneutical theories of the ethics and politics of biblical interpretation to challenge the claims to value neutrality of most academic biblical scholarship. Feminist biblical scholars have also turned their attention to how some biblical writings were shaped by the power of empire and how this still shapes readers' self-understandings today. They have developed hermeneutical approaches that reveal, critique, and evaluate the interactions depicted in the text against the context of empire, and they consider implications for contemporary contexts.[31] Feminists also analyze the dynamics of colonization and the mentalities of colonized peoples in the exercise of biblical interpretation. As Kwok Pui-lan explains, "A postcolonial feminist interpretation of the Bible needs to investigate the deployment of gender in the narration of identity, the negotiation of power differentials between the colonizers and the colonized, and the reinforcement of patriarchal control over spheres where these elites could exercise control."[32] Methods and models from sociology and cultural anthropology are used by feminists to investigate

---

28. See Tina Pippin, ed., *Ideological Criticism of Biblical Texts: Semeia* 59 (1992); Terry Eagleton, *Ideology: An Introduction* (London: Verso, 2007).

29. See, e.g., Ingrid Rosa Kitzberger, ed., *Autobiographical Biblical Interpretation: Between Text and Self* (Leiden: Deo, 2002); P. J. W. Schutte, "When *They, We*, and the Passive Become *I*—Introducing Autobiographical Biblical Criticism," *HTS Teologiese Studies / Theological Studies* 61 (2005): 401–16.

30. See, e.g., Holly Hearon and Philip Ruge-Jones, eds., *The Bible in Ancient and Modern Media: Story and Performance* (Eugene, OR: Cascade, 2009).

31. E.g., Gale Yee, ed., *Judges and Method: New Approaches in Biblical Studies* (Minneapolis: Fortress, 1995); Warren Carter, *The Gospel of Matthew in Its Roman Imperial Context* (London: T&T Clark, 2005); *The Roman Empire and the New Testament: An Essential Guide* (Nashville: Abingdon, 2006); Elisabeth Schüssler Fiorenza, *The Power of the Word: Scripture and the Rhetoric of Empire* (Minneapolis: Fortress, 2007); Judith E. McKinlay, *Reframing Her: Biblical Women in Postcolonial Focus* (Sheffield: Sheffield Phoenix, 2004).

32. Kwok Pui-lan, *Postcolonial Imagination and Feminist Theology* (Louisville: Westminster John Knox, 2005), 9. See also, Musa W. Dube, ed., *Postcolonial Feminist Interpretation of the Bible* (St. Louis: Chalice, 2000); Cristl M. Maier and Carolyn J. Sharp,

women's everyday lives, their experiences of marriage, childrearing, labor, money, illness, etc.[33]

As feminists have examined the construction of gender from varying cultural perspectives, they have become ever more cognizant that the way gender roles are defined within differing cultures varies radically. As Mary Ann Tolbert observes, "Attempts to isolate some universal role that cross-culturally defines 'woman' have run into contradictory evidence at every turn."[34] Some women have coined new terms to highlight the particularities of their socio-cultural context. Many African American feminists, for example, call themselves *womanists* to draw attention to the double oppression of racism and sexism they experience.[35] Similarly, many US Hispanic feminists speak of themselves as *mujeristas* (*mujer* is Spanish for "woman").[36] Others prefer to be called "Latina feminists."[37] Both groups emphasize that the context for their theologizing is *mestizaje* and *mulatez* (racial and cultural mixture), done *en conjunto* (in community), with *lo cotidiano* (everyday lived experience) of Hispanic women as starting points for theological reflection and the encounter with the divine. Intercultural analysis has become an indispensable tool for working toward justice for women at the global level.[38]

Prophecy and Power: Jeremiah in Feminist and Postcolonial Perspective (London: Bloomsbury, 2013).

33. See, for example, Carol Meyers, *Discovering Eve: Ancient Israelite Women in Context* (New York: Oxford University Press, 1991); Luise Schottroff, *Lydia's Impatient Sisters: A Feminist Social History of Early Christianity*, trans. Barbara and Martin Rumscheidt (Louisville: Westminster John Knox, 1995); Susan Niditch, *"My Brother Esau Is a Hairy Man": Hair and Identity in Ancient Israel* (Oxford: Oxford University Press, 2008).

34. Mary Ann Tolbert, "Social, Sociological, and Anthropological Methods," in *Searching the Scriptures*, 1:255–71, at 265.

35. Alice Walker coined the term (*In Search of Our Mothers' Gardens: Womanist Prose* [New York: Harcourt Brace Jovanovich, 1967, 1983]). See also Katie G. Cannon, "The Emergence of Black Feminist Consciousness," in *Feminist Interpretation of the Bible*, ed. Letty M. Russell (Philadelphia: Westminster, 1985), 30–40; Renita Weems, *Just a Sister Away: A Womanist Vision of Women's Relationships in the Bible* (San Diego: Lura Media, 1988); Nyasha Junior, *An Introduction to Womanist Biblical Interpretation* (Louisville: Westminster John Knox, 2015).

36. Ada María Isasi-Díaz (*Mujerista Theology: A Theology for the Twenty-First Century* [Maryknoll, NY: Orbis Books, 1996]) is credited with coining the term.

37. E.g., María Pilar Aquino, Daisy L. Machado, and Jeanette Rodríguez, eds., *A Reader in Latina Feminist Theology* (Austin: University of Texas Press, 2002).

38. See, e.g., María Pilar Aquino and María José Rosado-Nunes, eds., *Feminist Intercultural Theology: Latina Explorations for a Just World*, Studies in Latino/a Catholicism (Maryknoll, NY: Orbis Books, 2007).

Some feminists are among those who have developed lesbian, gay, bisexual, and transgender (LGBT) interpretation. This approach focuses on issues of sexual identity and uses various reading strategies. Some point out the ways in which categories that emerged in recent centuries are applied anachronistically to biblical texts to make modern-day judgments. Others show how the Bible is silent on contemporary issues about sexual identity. Still others examine same-sex relationships in the Bible by figures such as Ruth and Naomi or David and Jonathan. In recent years, queer theory has emerged; it emphasizes the blurriness of boundaries not just of sexual identity but also of gender roles. Queer critics often focus on texts in which figures transgress what is traditionally considered proper gender behavior.[39]

Feminists also recognize that the struggle for women's equality and dignity is intimately connected with the struggle for respect for Earth and for the whole of the cosmos. Ecofeminists interpret Scripture in ways that highlight the link between human domination of nature and male subjugation of women. They show how anthropocentric ways of interpreting the Bible have overlooked or dismissed Earth and Earth community. They invite readers to identify not only with human characters in the biblical narrative but also with other Earth creatures and domains of nature, especially those that are the object of injustice. Some use creative imagination to retrieve the interests of Earth implicit in the narrative and enable Earth to speak.[40]

Biblical Authority

By the late nineteenth century, some feminists, such as Elizabeth Cady Stanton, began to question openly whether the Bible could continue to be regarded as authoritative for women. They viewed the Bible itself as

39. See, e.g., Bernadette J. Brooten, *Love between Women: Early Christian Responses to Female Homoeroticism* (Chicago and London: University of Chicago Press, 1996); Mary Rose D'Angelo, "Women Partners in the New Testament," *JFSR* 6 (1990): 65–86; Deirdre J. Good, "Reading Strategies for Biblical Passages on Same-Sex Relations," *Theology and Sexuality* 7 (1997): 70–82; Deryn Guest, *When Deborah Met Jael: Lesbian Feminist Hermeneutics* (London: SCM, 2011); Teresa Hornsby and Ken Stone, eds., *Bible Trouble: Queer Readings at the Boundaries of Biblical Scholarship* (Atlanta: Society of Biblical Literature, 2011).

40. E.g., Norman C. Habel and Peter Trudinger, *Exploring Ecological Hermeneutics*, SymS 46 (Atlanta: Society of Biblical Literature, 2008); Mary Judith Ress, *Ecofeminism in Latin America*, Women from the Margins (Maryknoll, NY: Orbis Books, 2006).

the source of women's oppression, and some rejected its sacred origin and saving claims. Some decided that the Bible and the religious traditions that enshrine it are too thoroughly saturated with androcentrism and patriarchy to be redeemable.[41]

In the Wisdom Commentary series, questions such as these may be raised, but the aim of this series is not to lead readers to reject the authority of the biblical text. Rather, the aim is to promote better understanding of the contexts from which the text arose and of the rhetorical effects it has on women and men in contemporary contexts. Such understanding can lead to a deepening of faith, with the Bible serving as an aid to bring flourishing of life.

Language for God

Because of the ways in which the term "God" has been used to symbolize the divine in predominantly male, patriarchal, and monarchical modes, feminists have designed new ways of speaking of the divine. Some have called attention to the inadequacy of the term *God* by trying to visually destabilize our ways of thinking and speaking of the divine. Rosemary Radford Ruether proposed *God/ess*, as an unpronounceable term pointing to the unnameable understanding of the divine that transcends patriarchal limitations.[42] Some have followed traditional Jewish practice, writing *G-d*. Elisabeth Schüssler Fiorenza has adopted *G*d*.[43] Others draw on the biblical tradition to mine female and non-gender-specific metaphors and symbols.[44] In Wisdom Commentary, there is not one standard way of expressing the divine; each author will use her or his preferred ways. The one exception is that when the tetragrammaton, YHWH, the name revealed to Moses in Exodus 3:14, is used, it will be without vowels, respecting the Jewish custom of avoiding pronouncing the divine name out of reverence.

---

41. E.g., Mary Daly, *Beyond God the Father: A Philosophy of Women's Liberation* (Boston: Beacon, 1973).

42. Rosemary Radford Ruether, *Sexism and God-Talk: Toward a Feminist Theology* (Boston: Beacon, 1983).

43. Elisabeth Schüssler Fiorenza, *Jesus: Miriam's Child, Sophia's Prophet; Critical Issues in Feminist Christology* (New York: Continuum, 1994), 191 n. 3.

44. E.g., Sallie McFague, *Models of God: Theology for an Ecological, Nuclear Age* (Philadelphia: Fortress, 1987); Catherine LaCugna, *God for Us: The Trinity and Christian Life* (San Francisco: Harper Collins, 1991); Elizabeth A. Johnson, *She Who Is: The Mystery of God in Feminist Theological Discourse* (New York: Crossroad, 1992). See further Elizabeth A. Johnson, "God," in *Dictionary of Feminist Theologies*, 128–30.

Nomenclature for the Two Testaments

In recent decades, some biblical scholars have begun to call the two Testaments of the Bible by names other than the traditional nomenclature: Old and New Testament. Some regard "Old" as derogatory, implying that it is no longer relevant or that it has been superseded. Consequently, terms like Hebrew Bible, First Testament, and Jewish Scriptures and, correspondingly, Christian Scriptures or Second Testament have come into use. There are a number of difficulties with these designations. The term "Hebrew Bible" does not take into account that parts of the Old Testament are written not in Hebrew but in Aramaic.[45] Moreover, for Roman Catholics and Eastern Orthodox believers, the Old Testament includes books written in Greek—the Deuterocanonical books, considered Apocrypha by Protestants.[46] The term "Jewish Scriptures" is inadequate because these books are also sacred to Christians. Conversely, "Christian Scriptures" is not an accurate designation for the New Testament, since the Old Testament is also part of the Christian Scriptures. Using "First and Second Testament" also has difficulties, in that it can imply a hierarchy and a value judgment.[47] Jews generally use the term Tanakh, an acronym for Torah (Pentateuch), Nevi'im (Prophets), and Ketuvim (Writings).

In Wisdom Commentary, if authors choose to use a designation other than Tanakh, Old Testament, and New Testament, they will explain how they mean the term.

Translation

Modern feminist scholars recognize the complexities connected with biblical translation, as they have delved into questions about philosophy of language, how meanings are produced, and how they are culturally situated. Today it is evident that simply translating into gender-neutral formulations cannot address all the challenges presented by androcentric texts. Efforts at feminist translation must also deal with issues around authority and canonicity.[48]

---

45. Gen 31:47; Jer 10:11; Ezra 4:7–6:18; 7:12-26; Dan 2:4–7:28.

46. Representing the *via media* between Catholic and reformed, Anglicans generally consider the Apocrypha to be profitable, if not canonical, and utilize select Wisdom texts liturgically.

47. See Levine, *The Misunderstood Jew*, 193–99.

48. Elizabeth Castelli, "*Les Belles Infidèles*/Fidelity or Feminism? The Meanings of Feminist Biblical Translation," in *Searching the Scriptures*, 1:189–204, here 190.

Because of these complexities, the editors of the Wisdom Commentary series have chosen to use an existing translation, the New Revised Standard Version (NRSV), which is provided for easy reference at the top of each page of commentary. The NRSV was produced by a team of ecumenical and interreligious scholars, is a fairly literal translation, and uses inclusive language for human beings. Brief discussions about problematic translations appear in the inserts labeled "Translation Matters." When more detailed discussions are available, these will be indicated in footnotes. In the commentary, wherever Hebrew or Greek words are used, English translation is provided. In cases where a wordplay is involved, transliteration is provided to enable understanding.

Art and Poetry

Artistic expression in poetry, music, sculpture, painting, and various other modes is very important to feminist interpretation. Where possible, art and poetry are included in the print volumes of the series. In a number of instances, these are original works created for this project. Regrettably, copyright and production costs prohibit the inclusion of color photographs and other artistic work. It is our hope that the web version will allow a greater collection of such resources.

Glossary

Because there are a number of excellent readily available resources that provide definitions and concise explanations of terms used in feminist theological and biblical studies, this series will not include a glossary. We refer you to works such as *Dictionary of Feminist Theologies*, edited by Letty M. Russell with J. Shannon Clarkson (Louisville: Westminster John Knox, 1996), and volume 1 of *Searching the Scriptures*, edited by Elisabeth Schüssler Fiorenza with the assistance of Shelly Matthews (New York: Crossroad, 1992). Individual authors in the Wisdom Commentary series will define the way they are using terms that may be unfamiliar.

A Concluding Word

In just a few short decades, feminist biblical studies has grown exponentially, both in the methods that have been developed and in the number of scholars who have embraced it. We realize that this series is limited and will soon need to be revised and updated. It is our hope that

Wisdom Commentary, by making the best of current feminist biblical scholarship available in an accessible format to ministers, preachers, teachers, scholars, and students, will aid all readers in their advancement toward God's vision of dignity, equality, and justice for all.

———◦◦◦———

Acknowledgments

There are a great many people who have made this series possible: first, Peter Dwyer, director of Liturgical Press, and Hans Christoffersen, publisher of the academic market at Liturgical Press, who have believed in this project and have shepherded it since it was conceived in 2008. Editorial consultants Athalya Brenner-Idan and Elisabeth Schüssler Fiorenza have not only been an inspiration with their pioneering work but have encouraged us all along the way with their personal involvement. Volume editors Mary Ann Beavis, Carol J. Dempsey, Gina Hens-Piazza, Amy-Jill Levine, Linda M. Maloney, Song-Mi Susie Park, Ahida Pilarski, Sarah Tanzer, and Lauress Wilkins Lawrence have lent their extraordinary wisdom to the shaping of the series, have used their extensive networks of relationships to secure authors and contributors, and have worked tirelessly to guide their work to completion. Four others who have contributed greatly to the shaping of the project are Linda M. Day, Mignon Jacobs, Seung Ai Yang, and Barbara E. Bowe of blessed memory (d. 2010). Editorial and research assistant Susan M. Hickman has provided invaluable support with administrative details and arrangements. I am grateful to Brian Eisenschenk and Christine Henderson who have assisted Susan Hickman with the Wiki. I am especially thankful to Lauren L. Murphy and Justin Howell for their work in copyediting; and to the staff at Liturgical Press, especially Colleen Stiller, production manager; Stephanie Lancour, production editor; Angie Steffens, production assistant; and Tara Durheim, associate publisher.

Author's Introduction

Wrestling with the Book of Psalms

How does one go about writing a feminist commentary on the book of Psalms in general and books 4 and 5 of the Psalter in particular? The Psalter mentions only one woman by name (Bathsheba). She appears in the superscription of Psalm 51 but does not figure in the poetry of the psalm itself. The remainder of the book refers to women sporadically, but only in very general terms: Psalms 22:9-10 (my mother); 27:10 (my mother); 35:14 (a mother); 45:9-15 (daughters of kings, a queen [consort], a princess, virgins); 48:6 (a woman in labor); 68:5, 25 (widows, girls [young women]); 71:6 (my mother); 78:63, 64 (girls [virgins], widows); 94:6 (the widow); 106:37-38 (their daughters); 109:9, 14 (wife, widow, his mother); 113:9 (barren woman, mother); 123:2 (a maid [female servant], her mistress [lady, queen]); 128:3 (your wife); 131:2 (mother); 139:13 (mother); 144:12 (our daughters); 146:9 (the widow); 148:12 (young women [virgins]).[1]

But a few observations are in order. First, the reader may be interested to see that the book of Psalms offers no negative words about women as do some other biblical books, such as Proverbs, Ecclesiastes, and Ben

---

1. All Scripture references are to the New Revised Standard Version unless otherwise indicated.

Sirach. In Proverbs, for instance, the "students" are warned to beware of "the lips and the speech of the loose/strange [זרה] woman" (Prov 5:3) whose "feet go down to death" (Prov 5:5), who "with much seductive speech . . . persuades . . . (and) with smooth talk . . . compels" (Prov 7:21). In the book of Ecclesiastes the teacher muses: "I found more bitter than death the woman who is a trap, whose heart is snares and nets, whose hands are fetters; one who pleases God escapes her, but the sinner is taken by her" (Qoh 7:26). Ben Sirach writes: "Any iniquity is small compared to a woman's iniquity; may a sinner's lot befall her! . . . From a woman sin had its beginning, and because of her we all die. . . . Keep strict watch over a headstrong daughter, or else, when she finds liberty, she will make use of it" (Sir 25:19, 24; 26:10).

Second, the book of Psalms abounds in references to humanity in a generic, general, all-inclusive sense. The word אנוש, meaning human beings in general and variously translated in the NRSV as "mortals," "human," "human beings," and "others," occurs thirteen times.[2] אדם and the related term בני־אדם, translated variously in the NRSV as "one/ones," "everyone," "those," "people," "man/men," "everyone," "all people," "mortal/mortals," "humankind," "human beings," and "human/humans," occur no fewer than fifty times.[3]

Third, an observation closely tied to the second: the human voices and players within individual psalms are rarely named specifically; they remain as generic manifestations of all walks of humanity. The singer of Psalm 106 says, "Remember me, O LORD . . . that I may glory in your heritage" (106:4-5); Psalm 73 laments the arrogant and the prosperity of the wicked (73:3); Psalm 37 offers assurance that "the righteous shall be kept safe forever, but the children of the wicked shall be cut off" (37:28); in Psalm 7 the psalmist pleads with God to "save me from all my pursuers, and deliver me" (7:1); in Psalm 122 the people cry, "Our feet are standing within your gates, O Jerusalem" (122:2). The voices and the players—"me," "the arrogant," "the wicked," "the righteous," "the children of the wicked," "pursuers," "our feet"—are not assigned gender but rather are portrayed as human beings in relation to God and to others. The words of the psalms are the words of all people in all places and times. The exigencies of life that women dealt with in the time of the formation of the biblical text, however, were intrinsically different from

2. See Pss 8:4; 9:19, 20; 10:18; 55:13; 56:1; 66:12; 73:5; 90:3; 103:15; 104:15 (2x); 144:3.
3. See, for example, Pss 8:4; 17:4; 21:10; 22:7; 36:6; 56:11; 66:5; 64:9; 76:10; 80:17; 89:47; 90:3; 107:8, 15, 21, 31.

those dealt with by men, for the most part, and that reality continues in many ways today.

Appropriating the Psalmic Words

A number of barriers present themselves when one attempts to read the Psalter from a feminist perspective. First, a "voice" is assigned to many psalms in their superscriptions, most often the voice of David (Pss 3–41, etc.), but also the sons of Korah (Pss 42–49, 84–85, 87–88), Asaph (Pss 50, 73–83), Heman (Ps 88), Ethan (Ps 89), Solomon (Pss 72 and 127), and Moses (Ps 90).[4] This can make it difficult to "hear" the voice of all humanity in the psalms, since all those named are men and David and Solomon are royalty.

Second, commentators speculate that many of the psalms were recited at the temple in Jerusalem by priests and worshipers (often the king), thus effectively removing them from the realm of common humanity; this is especially true for women, who could enter the temple only as far as the women's court, and for men living in outlying towns and villages who could travel to the temple only for the occasional holy day. Hans-Joachim Kraus states, for instance, that the *Sitz im Leben* of Psalm 4 may be easily assumed to be "an experience in the temple" in which "an innocent person who has been persecuted and accused" has had his rights restored through a divine verdict in the temple.[5] He further contends that "the '*Sitz im Leben*' of Psalm 24" is "a cultic antiphonal song, a liturgical ceremonial address, which doubtless is connected with an entrance of the holy ark to the temple in Jerusalem."[6] In books 4 and 5 the enthronement Psalms, 93–100, seem almost universally to be associated with temple worship,[7] and Kraus writes that Psalm 113 "is unquestionably a cultic hymn that has been intoned by a group."[8]

---

4. The Korahites, the Asaphites, Heman, and Ethan were cultic singers during the reigns of David and Solomon. See 1 Chr 6:31-48; 9:19-34; 15:16-22; 2 Chr 5:11-13.

5. Hans-Joachim Kraus, *Psalms 1–59: A Commentary* , trans. Hilton C. Oswald, CC (Minneapolis: Augsburg, 1988), 146.

6. Ibid., 312.

7. See Marvin E. Tate, *Psalms 51–100*, WBC 20 (Nashville: Thomas Nelson, 2000), 474–75, for a full bibliography. See also Sigmund Mowinckel, *The Psalms in Israel's Worship*, 2 vols., trans. D. R. Ap-Thomas (Nashville: Abingdon, 1962).

8. Hans-Joachim Kraus, *Psalms 60–150: A Commentary*, trans. Hilton C. Oswald, CC (Minneapolis: Augsburg, 1993), 367. See also Leslie C. Allen, *Psalms 101–150*, WBC 21 (Nashville: Thomas Nelson, 2002), 134.

Third, God as king and God as judge—both overtly masculine images—are arguably the dominant words describing God in the Psalter.[9]
God as king first appears in Psalm 5: "Listen to the sound of my cry, my
King and my God" (v. 2), and it occurs no fewer than twenty-five times
in the book.[10] Psalm 7:8 states: "The LORD judges [ידין] the peoples," and
we find this metaphor no fewer than twenty-five times as well.[11]

These two are not the only metaphors for God in the book of Psalms,
however. One powerful image has its roots in Exodus 34:6-7, where God
pronounces God's self-identity to Moses on Mount Sinai. One of God's
self-descriptive words is רחום, translated most often as "merciful" or
"compassionate." The word derives from the noun רחם, which literally
means "womb." References to God's רחום and רחמים, God's "womb love,"
perhaps, occur no fewer than twenty times in the book of Psalms.[12] In
Psalm 119:156 we read: "Great is your mercy [רחמיך], O LORD; give me
life according to your justice." In an interesting juxtaposition of metaphors, Psalm 103:13 affirms: "As a father has compassion [כרחם אב] for
his children, so the LORD has compassion [יהוה רחם] for those who fear
him." And in Psalm 77:9 the psalm singer cries out, "Has God forgotten
to be gracious? Has he in anger shut up his compassion [רחמיו]?" bringing to mind the words of 1 Samuel 1:6, a notice that YHWH had "closed"
Hannah's womb (רחם), and the words of Isaiah 66:9 in which God asks
"shall I, the one who delivers, shut the womb [מוליד]?"[13]

Psalm 22 takes the metaphor a step further and connects God's self-
identification with "womb-love" to the physical referent for the metaphor. In verse 10 the psalmist cries to God: "Upon you I was cast from
my birth" (literally "the womb," רחם). Here God is intimately tied to the
life-giving womb and is further pictured as midwife.[14] Phyllis Trible describes the image in Psalm 22 as a "semantic movement from a physical

9. "Judge," however, in contemporary times is becoming more and more an oc-
cupation of both women and men.

10. See Pss 5:2; 10:16; 24:7, 8, 9, 10; 29:10; 44:4; 47:2; 47:6, 7, 8; 48:2; 68:24; 74:12; 84:3;
89:18; 93:1; 95:3; 96:10; 97:1; 98:6; 99:1; 145:1; 149:2.

11. See Pss 1:5; 7:6, 8, 11; 9:4, 7, 16; 50:4, 6; 51:4; 67:4; 75:2, 7; 76:8, 9; 82:2, 8; 94:2;
96:10, 13; 98:9; 110:6; 119:84; 143:2; 149:9.

12. See, for example, Pss 25:6; 40:11; 69:16; 77:9; 79:8; 103:13.

13. The word "womb," רחם, does not occur in Isa 66:9, but the context strongly
suggests such an understanding. Hence the NRSV translation.

14. See L. Juliana M. Claasens, "Rupturing God-Language: The Metaphor of God
as Midwife in Psalm 22," in *Engaging the Bible in a Gendered World*, ed. Katherine Doob
Sakenfeld, et al. (Louisville: Westminster John Knox, 2006), 166–75.

organ of the female body to a psychic mode of being."[15] We find similar imagery in Psalm 71:6. There the psalm singer cries out to God: "Upon you I have leaned from my birth [מֵעֶה]; it was you who took me from my mother's womb [literally "belly, inward part," מְעֵי אִמִּי].

Another prominent metaphor for God in the Psalter is "refuge," often imaged as shelter under the wings (כְּנָפִים) of God. We read in Psalm 17:8, "Guard me as the apple of the eye; hide me in the shadow of your wings [כְּנָפֶיךָ]"; in Psalm 36:7, "All people may take refuge in the shadow of your wings [כְּנָפֶיךָ]"; and in Psalm 61:4, "Let me abide in your tent forever; find refuge under the shelter of your wings [כְּנָפֶיךָ]."[16] Protective wings bring to mind the image of a mother bird caring for her young, keeping them warm, providing shelter, and warning off predators (as we see in Matt 23:37).[17]

Finally, wisdom is a prominent feature in the Psalter. The characterization of wisdom in the biblical text is multifaceted and ever-evolving. Wisdom is depicted variously as something of a consort or feminine counterpart to God in the books of Job, Proverbs, Ben Sirach, the Wisdom of Solomon, and Baruch. She is hidden from and inaccessible to humanity according to Job 28; she is present in the midst of humanity, crying out in the streets and at the entrance to the city gates in Proverbs 1, and she was there at creation, working beside God and delighting in the human race in Proverbs 8. In the Wisdom of Solomon she is sought after as the desired spouse of Solomon, having the "knowledge" of "things of old" and giving "good counsel"; she teaches "self-control and prudence, justice and courage" (Wis 7:22–8:9). In Ben Sirach, Wisdom states that she "came forth from the mouth of the most high" (Sir 24:3) at creation and was destined to dwell in Israel. The sexually evocative language of Ben Sirach equates the pleasures of knowing Woman Wisdom with the pleasures of knowing the Torah (Sir 24:19-22). Ben Sirach 24:23 states, in fact, "All this is the book of the covenant of the Most High God, the law [νόμον] that Moses commanded us," and Baruch 4:1 says, "She is the book of the commandments of God, the law [νόμος] that endures forever."

---

15. Phyllis Trible, *God and the Rhetoric of Sexuality*, OBT (Philadelphia: Fortress, 1978), 33.

16. See also Pss 57:1; 63:7; 91:4.

17. For a full treatment of this metaphor see the commentary on Psalm 91, along with Carolyn Blevins, "Under My Wings: Jesus' Motherly Love; Matthew 23:37-39," *RevExp* 104 (2007): 365–74. Joel LeMon offers an alternate view of the "winged image" of YHWH in the Psalter: see his *Yahweh's Winged Form in the Psalms: Exploring Congruent Iconography and Texts* (Fribourg: Academic Press, 2010).

The book of Psalms equates wisdom with Torah, specifically in Psalms 1 and 119, thereby inviting the reader to hear in the wisdom psalms and the wisdom elements of the psalms the voice of Woman Wisdom, the feminine iteration of Yʜᴡʜ, calling humankind to search out the path to a right relationship with Yʜᴡʜ through obedience to the Torah. Athalya Brenner reminds us that in the book of Proverbs Torah (תורה) is attributed to the mother figure, never to the father (1:8; 6:20; 31:26; the NRSV translates each instance of Torah [תורה] in these verses as "teaching" rather than "law").[18] Claudia Camp maintains that in the Psalter Wisdom actually replaces the earthly king as the mediator between God and humanity.[19]

The Metaphors of the Psalms

Feminist interpretation of the book of Psalms cannot confine itself solely to finding biological sex-specific "female attributes and affinities" of God, such as womb-love (רחם, compassion) and a mother's protective wings (כנפים). Melody Knowles writes: "Naming and associating behaviors as feminine runs the danger of composing an essentialized femininity that conforms to socially prescribed behaviors and attributes—reifying 'feminine' into a construction that constricts women instead of understanding it as cultural performance."[20] The biblical text is essentially a patriarchal document that presents an androcentric view of the world. The presentation of women is, by and large, a "constricted" one that reflects the traditional male-dominated role of women in ancient Israelite society—mother, daughter, widow, queen, seductress, etc.[21] Thus feminist interpretations often involve reading "against the text" or "from the underside of the text," asking "What is the text not telling us?" and "What is the text trying to tell us, but cannot?"

---

18. Athalya Brenner and Fokkelien Van Dijk-Hemmes, *On Gendering Texts: Female and Male Voices in the Hebrew Bible* (Leiden: Brill, 1993), 119.

19. Claudia V. Camp, *Wisdom and the Feminine in the Book of Proverbs* (Sheffield: Almond Press, 1985), 272–80; see also Silvia Schroer, *Wisdom Has Built Her House: Studies on the Figure of Sophia in the Bible*, trans. Linda M. Maloney and William McDonough (Collegeville, MN: Liturgical Press, 2000), 26–68; and Gerlinde Baumann, *Die Weisheitsgestalt in Proverbien 1–9: Traditionsgeschichtliche und theologische Studien*, FAT 16 (Tübingen: Mohr [Siebeck], 1996), 300–303.

20. Melody D. Knowles, "Feminist Interpretation of the Psalms," in *The Oxford Handbook of the Psalms*, ed. William P. Brown (Oxford: Oxford University Press, 2014), 424–36, at 426.

21. There are exceptions, of course: see, for example, Tamar (Gen 38); Deborah (Judg 4–5); Abigail (2 Sam 25); and Huldah (2 Kgs 22).

Therefore when we as readers encounter and contemplate metaphors in a quest to understand the God of the Hebrew Bible, we must keep in mind a number of things. First, a metaphor is nothing more than, nothing less than, a linguistic symbol. It attempts to tie a hard-to-describe, perhaps indescribable object or concept to one that is familiar and understandable to readers and hearers. Scholars use a number of terms to describe the relationship between the two entities, including "tenor" (the object or concept) and "vehicle" (the metaphor), "target domain" (the object or concept) and "source domain" (the metaphor), "primary subject" (the object or concept) and "secondary subject" (the metaphor), "occasion" (the object or concept) and "image" (the metaphor).[22] Whatever the language used to describe the relationship between the metaphor and what it is attempting to describe, it is in the end simply the juxtaposition of language symbols.

Second, metaphors are "contextually conditioned," that is, semantic and cultural contexts impact how a writer constructs a metaphor, how that metaphor is received by the reader or hearer, and how it is interpreted. David Rensberger writes: "Metaphor, simile, and their kin are inherently both accurate and inaccurate. They point toward some truth about an entity, but they do not claim to express entire truth or pure truth; not *everything* about the thing compared is meant to apply to the entity under discussion."[23] The metaphors the psalm singers use to describe and attempt to understand God are human constructs, employing images and ideas that other human readers or hearers are able to appropriate from their own life experiences. The biblical text is the product of a male-dominated undertaking; therefore we as readers and interpreters of the Psalter must be sensitive to its use of language about God and about humanity.

Third, William P. Brown, in *Seeing the Psalms*, reminds us:

> When metaphors . . . become literalized to the point that they exclude other metaphors for the same subject or target domain, particularly in the case of God, they function as idols. . . . Put theologically, if any metaphor, no matter how profound, becomes absolutized, as though it were itself considered ultimate, idolatry becomes the norm.[24]

22. William P. Brown, *Seeing the Psalms: A Theology of Metaphor* (Louisville: Westminster John Knox, 2002), 5.

23. David Rensberger, "Ecological Use of the Psalms," in Brown, *The Oxford Handbook of the Psalms*, 613.

24. Brown, *Seeing the Psalms*, 10.

The beauty of metaphoric imagery for God in the Psalter is that it allows for a multiplicity of conceptualizations or, as Luis Alonso Schökel suggests, "a vast collection of interwoven images."[25] Therefore we should not, ought not, be constrained to a single metaphoric conceptualization of God in the book of Psalms.

Words for All People

The Psalter is a rich and varied collection of poetry from the life of ancient Israel that expresses a wide range of emotions and feelings, including joy, sorrow, fear, oppression, hurt, amazement, and yearning, and it addresses a wide variety of topics, such as interpersonal relationships, enemies, illnesses, national crises, the splendor of creation, the goodness of God, Israel's history, and personal sins, nearly all of which are not tied or restricted to any specific historical or easily identified personal event.[26] What this means is that the words of the psalmists are genderless and timeless; they are the words of every person in every time and place and testify to the multifaceted dimensions of humanity's relationship with God and one another in all times and places. The experiences of each person affects how they appropriate the words of the book of Psalms into their own lives. Women, for the most part, will hear its word differently than will men, and women of privilege will read the Psalter's word differently from women living in poverty and

25. Luis Alonso Schökel, *A Manual of Hebrew Poetics*, trans. Adrian Graffy (Rome: Editrice Pontificio Istituto Biblico, 1998), 10.

26. Psalm 71's words, "Rescue me, O my God, from the hand of the wicked, from the grasp of the unjust and cruel" (v. 4), or Ps 101's "I will study the way that is blameless. When shall I attain it? I will walk with integrity of heart within my house; I will not set before my eyes anything that is base" (vv. 3-4) lack a specific referent and are open to myriad appropriations.

In addition we must view the superscriptions, such as Psalm 51's "A Psalm of David, when the prophet Nathan came to him, after he had gone in to Bathsheba," as initial "hooks" on which to "hang" the psalms, that is, as initial "story worlds" for their words. But we must not leave the psalms "anchored" in the past. The sentiments expressed in them are not time-, class-, or gender-exclusive; they are the words of every human. Thus we read the heartfelt words of Psalm 13, "How long, O LORD? Will you forget me forever? How long will you hide your face from me?" (v. 1); Psalm 81's glorious "Sing aloud to God our strength; shout for joy to the God of Jacob. Raise a song, sound the tambourine, the sweet lyre with the harp" (vv. 1-2); and the wonder of Psalm 139: "For it was you who formed my inward parts; you knit me together in my mother's womb" (v. 13).

oppression. The Psalter's words meet every person in their own place and time and circumstance.

Another dimension to "finding the feminine" in the Psalter is attention to cultural and social location. Feminist interpretations of the biblical text ask, "How would a feminine-gendered person read and appropriate a text?" Feminine images of God, women, and/or the voice of Wisdom need not be present in the text in order for us to "find the feminine." In examining the psalms in books 4 and 5 of the Psalter this author will attend to issues in reading the psalms that, while not exclusively the concern of "feminine-gendered persons," are or may be of special concern to them: marginalized voices; economics; power inequities; the environment; access to education; food distribution; violence against women, men, and children; and so forth. The commentary will examine the texts of each psalm in its entirety, attempting to understand how a particular psalm functioned in its "original" setting and suggesting how it might be heard and appropriated in the twenty-first century.

Two insightful examples of "finding the feminine" in psalms outside the scope of this commentary volume may be found in Ulrike Bail's 1998 essay " 'Oh God, Hear My Prayer': Psalm 55 and Violence against Women" and Maria Häusl's 2002 essay "Ps 17—Bittgebet einer kinderlosen Frau?" Bail suggests that the words of Psalm 55 could be the prayer of a woman who has suffered rape at the hands of a close acquaintance. She stresses that neither the original historical setting of the psalm nor its original author can be known and therefore we are permitted to appropriate the text to various acts of violence, including rape.[27] Häusl, in like manner, reads Psalm 17 as the prayer of a childless woman asking for protection from tormentors (and, in an interesting aside, in v. 8 we encounter the image of "the shadow of God's wings").[28]

Many Perspectives

Melody Knowles reminds us that "because feminist criticism self-consciously foregrounds the experience of the interpreter, it is never a

27. Ulrike Bail, " 'O God Hear My Prayer': Psalm 55 and Violence against Women," in *Wisdom and Psalms,* FCB, 2nd ser., ed. Athalya Brenner and Carole Fontaine (Sheffield: Sheffield Academic, 1998), 242–63.

28. Maria Häusl, "Ps 17—Bittgebet einer kinderlosen Frau?," in *"Wer darf hinaufsteigen zum Berg YHWH's": Beiträge zu Prophetie und Poesie des alten Testaments,* ed. Hubert Irsigler (St. Ottilien: EOS Verlag, 2002), 205–22.

purely consistent reading strategy." Feminist criticism allows for a multiplicity of approaches to the text, so that one interpreter may claim "multiple identities."[29] That is certainly the case with this commentator. I have spent most of my academic career studying the shape and shaping of the book of Psalms. But along the way I discovered that I have employed a number of other critical approaches in my interpretations. One such approach was rhetorical criticism: that is, what is the text attempting to persuade the reader to conclude, to believe? In a 2008 article on Psalm 44 I mused:

> As a canonical critic, I have spent my career looking, for the most part, at the big picture—the shaping of a book of the Bible (the Psalter) to convince the postexilic Israelite people that they could survive as a separate and identifiable entity in a world in which they were simply one of many vassal nations. Thus, the book of Psalms is a shaping of words to convince. In the process of pondering this statement, a question came to mind. Had I perhaps been delving into rhetorical criticism without realizing it? Is canonical criticism a "cousin" of rhetorical criticism?[30]

Canonical criticism and rhetorical criticism both examine a text's attempt to persuade readers and hearers to adopt a certain mind-set, to accept a certain set of givens, and to adhere to a certain set of societal norms.

In the current undertaking this canonical/rhetorical biblical interpreter is attempting to look at the text through a new lens, one that reads against the dominant mind-set, refuses to accept the givens, and seeks to uncover a hidden/alternate/parallel set of societal norms. How to begin?

The Shape and Shaping of the Psalter

I am unashamedly persuaded by the "story of the shaping of the Psalter" as formulated by scholars over the past thirty years. That will be my beginning point as I examine the psalms in books 4 and 5 and attempt to bring feminist lenses to the interpretation of the text.

The Psalter begins in book 1 with the story of the reign of King David. Book 2 continues the story of David's reign and ends with the succession of Solomon as king. Book 3 narrates the Divided Kingdoms and their eventual destructions by the Assyrians and the Babylonians; book 4,

---

29. Knowles, "Feminist Interpretation of the Psalms," 424–25.

30. Nancy L. deClaissé-Walford, "Psalm 44: O God, Why Do You Hide Your Face?," in *My Words Are Lovely*, ed. Robert L. Foster and David M. Howard (New York: T&T Clark, 2008), 121–31, at 123.

set in exile in Babylon, relates the struggle of the exiles to find identity and meaning in a world of changed circumstances; book 5 celebrates the return to Jerusalem and the reestablishment of temple worship, but without an earthly king. Now God is sovereign.

Book 1: The Reign of David

Book 1 opens with words encouraging fidelity to the Torah (Ps 1:2). It continues with words of warning to the nations and their rulers to recognize the God of Israel as king over all (Ps 2:10-11). Readers thus enter the Psalter with two admonitions: diligently study and delight in the Torah and acknowledge God as sovereign.

Thirty-nine psalms "of David" make up book 1 of the Psalter. The overwhelming majority of them (59 percent) are laments and provide insight into every facet of David's life: as king, as human being, as warrior, as parent, as servant of the Lord. David's life was fraught with conflict and oppression from without and within the nation-state he founded: with the Philistines, Saul, David's own family (see 1 Sam 19:11; 29:1; 31:1; 2 Sam 3:1; 5:22; 15:6, 10; 20:1; 1 Kgs 1:24-25).

Book 2: The Succession of Solomon[31]

Book 2, like book 1, contains many laments, but not all of them are attributed to David. The Korahites, who according to the book of Chronicles were temple singers during the reigns of David and Solomon,[32] mingle their voices with David's in singing the laments of book 2 (Pss 42–49). But, interestingly, fifteen psalms of David (Pss 51–65) appear in the middle of book 2; fourteen of them are laments, and eight of the fourteen are connected, in their superscriptions, to particular events in the life of David. These psalms remind readers once again that David's life was one of turmoil and strife, but they also depict a person who loved the Lord and strove to serve the Lord with fervor.

Psalm 72, the closing psalm of book 2, is one of only two psalms in the Psalter ascribed to Solomon.[33] H.-J. Kraus describes Psalm 72 as a collection of wishes and prayers for the well-being of the king, probably

31. See Denise Dombkowski Hopkins, *Psalms Books 2–3*, WCS 21 (Collegeville, MN: Liturgical Press, 2016).

32. See 1 Chr 6:31-37; 9:19.

33. The other is one of the Songs of Ascents, Ps 127.

used at an enthronement ceremony for a king in Jerusalem.[34] Brevard Childs suggests that the canonical placement of Psalm 72 indicates that the psalm "is 'for' Solomon, offered by David."[35] Book 2 ends with the words "The prayers of David son of Jesse are ended" (72:20).

Book 3: The Divided Kingdoms

Book 3 opens with "A Psalm of Asaph" (Ps 73). Like the sons of Korah, Asaph, according to Chronicles, was a temple singer during the reigns of David and Solomon.[36] Fifteen of the seventeen psalms in book 3 are attributed to Asaph and the sons of Korah. Only one, Psalm 86, is attributed to David. With the close of book 2, David moves into the background. The focus is now on David's descendants, who will determine the future of ancient Israel.

In Psalm 73 the psalm singer looks at the world and sees the wicked prospering while the righteous suffer and questions whether conventional theology and mores still hold true in life.[37] There seems to be no reasoned connection between righteousness and reward, wickedness and punishment. In despair, the psalm singer enters the sanctuary of the Lord and there finds order in the seeming chaos of life (Ps 73:17).

Psalm 73 begins a new chapter in the Psalter's story; it signals a turning point. David's reign has come to an end, and Solomon's reign will conclude with the nation divided into two rival kingdoms that will be in constant conflict with one another and with the nations around them. Community laments and community hymns dominate book 3. The voice of David, the individual, gives way to the voices of the communities of

---

34. Kraus, *Psalms 60–150*, 76–77.

35. Brevard S. Childs, *Introduction to the Old Testament as Scripture* (Philadelphia: Fortress, 1979), 516.

36. 1 Chr 6:39; 25:1, 2; 2 Chr 5:12 state that Asaph was a descendant of Levi, part of one of the great families or guilds of musicians and singers in preexilic Israel. See Harry P. Nasuti, *Tradition History and Psalms of Asaph*, SBLDS 88 (Atlanta: Scholars Press, 1988).

37. Humankind in the ancient Near East believed in a basic moral governance of the world. Act and consequence were connected: thus, the good prospered and the wicked perished. Sages and wisdom teachers taught that there was a fundamental order in the world that could be discerned by experience, that the gods had established the order, and that all humanity was bound by the rules governing that order. For a detailed treatment, see John G. Gammie and Leo G. Perdue, eds., *The Sage in Israel and the Ancient Near East* (Winona Lake, IN: Eisenbrauns, 1990).

faith, which are attempting to make sense of all the turmoil, internal and external, political and religious, that is taking place.

Psalm 88, placed at the end of book 3, is a lament, but a lament like no other in the Psalter. Psalms of lament in the Hebrew Psalter typically consist of five elements: (1) an invocation, in which the psalmist calls on the name of God; (2) a complaint, in which the psalmist tells God what is wrong; (3) a petition, in which the psalmist tells God what the psalmist wants God to do; (4) words of trust, in which the psalmist outlines the reasons for trusting that God can and will answer the psalmist's petition; and (5) words of praise, in which the psalmist celebrates the goodness and sovereignty of God.[38] Psalm 88 is almost wholly composed of the element of complaint. Invocation and petition are brief lines within the psalm, and words of trust and words of praise are missing completely.

Psalm 89 follows. It begins, in verses 1-37, with praise to God for the good provisions to David, the king of God's choosing. But the psalm takes a sudden turn in verse 38, asking God why God has "spurned and rejected," "renounced the covenant," "removed the scepter from his hands" (vv. 38, 39, 44).

In 722 BCE the Assyrians destroyed the city of Samaria and scattered the population of Israel. In 587 BCE the Babylonians destroyed Jerusalem and took a major portion of its population into captivity in Babylon. The nations of Israel and Judah were no more; Davidic kingship was ended; the people were exiled from their homeland. Book 3 of the Psalter ends with the community of faith lamenting and asking questions of its God: "Who are we? Who will lead us? Who will help us to survive in this new world?"

Book 4: In Exile in Babylon

Book 4 opens with "A Prayer of Moses, the Man of God." It is the only psalm in the Hebrew Psalter so designated. Not just Psalm 90 but the whole of book 4 of the Psalter is dominated by the person of Moses. Otherwise Moses is mentioned only once in the Psalter (Ps 77:21); in book 4 he is mentioned seven times (Pss 90:1; 99:6; 103:7; 105:26; 106:16, 23, 32).[39]

The community of faith in exile in Babylon cannot effect a return to the days of King David. They can only move forward. Moses intervenes with God on behalf of the people just as he did in the time of the

---

38. Nancy L. deClaissé-Walford, *Introduction to the Psalms: A Song from Ancient Israel* (St. Louis: Chalice, 2004), 23–25.

39. Marvin Tate describes book 4 as a "Moses Book." See his *Psalms 51–100*, xxvi.

wilderness wandering (Ps 90:13; see Exod 32:12), and he points the way forward.[40] Enthronement psalms, celebrating God as sovereign over the people rather than a king of the Davidic line, lie at the center of book 4 (Pss 93–100).

At the end of book 4 two psalms recount the history of God's dealings with the community of faith throughout its long history. Psalm 105, a hymn of praise, recalls how God provided for, protected, and sustained them throughout their history. Psalm 106 also recounts the history of God and the people of Israel, but it is a community lament that reminds the people of their repeated unfaithfulness to God despite God's good provision for them.

Book 4 ends very differently from book 5. While Psalm 89 at the end of book 3 hurls questions at God about why Israel is suffering in its present situation, the end of book 4 offers a simple petition to the Lord to "save us and gather us" (v. 47). In 539 BCE the Persian army under the leadership of Cyrus II captured Babylon, the capital city of the Babylonian Empire. In the following year Cyrus issued a decree allowing captive peoples to return to their homelands, to rebuild, and to resume their religious practices. The repatriated peoples would remain part of the vast Persian Empire, subject to Persian law. Cyrus's decree meant that the Israelites could rebuild their temple and continue their religious practices, but they could not restore their nation-state under the leadership of a king of the line of David.

Book 5: Return from Exile

Book 5 opens with Psalm 107, a hymn that celebrates God's graciousness in delivering the community of faith from perilous circumstances. Verses 33-41 outline the beneficence the sovereign God is able to bestow on the community of faith, and the psalm closes with an admonition to "the wise" to heed God's good provisions. Beginning with Psalm 108, David, who has been virtually absent from the Psalter since his final words in book 2 (Ps 72:20), returns.[41] Psalms 108–110; 122; 124; 131;

---

40. See David Noel Freedman, "Other than Moses . . . Who Asks (or Tells) God to Repent?," *BRev* 1 (1985): 56–59.

41. Recall that in book 3 only one psalm is "of David" (Ps 86), and in book 4 only two psalms are "of David" (Pss 101 and 103).

138–145 are "of David" and in them David leads the Israelites in praise of God as sovereign. In the middle of the book, with psalms of David forming an *inclusio* around them, are psalms used in various celebrations and commemorations in Jewish life:

- Psalms 113–118, the Egyptian Hallel, recited during Passover
- Psalm 119, a wisdom acrostic about Torah piety, recited during the feast of Pentecost
- Psalms 120–134, the Songs of Ascents, recited during the feast of Booths (Tabernacles or Sukkoth)

David leads and the people join in to praise and give thanks to the God who sustained, protected, and guided them throughout their history. The last psalm of David in book 5, Psalm 145, is a masterful alphabetic acrostic that celebrates the sovereignty of God over the community of faith and over all creation.

Thus the five books of the Psalter narrate the history of ancient Israel, the very history recorded in the books of Samuel, Kings, Chronicles, Ezra, Nehemiah, and a number of the prophets. The story of the shaping of the Psalter is the story of the shaping of survival. The Psalter, together with the other texts that make up the Hebrew Scriptures, was a constitutive document of identity for postexilic Israel. Within that collection of texts the community of faith found a new structure for existence and identity that transcended traditional concepts of nationhood. The story of the Psalter gave the postexilic community a new rationale for existence, a new statement of national identity. With Yhwh as sovereign the people could survive as a separate and identifiable entity within the vast empires—Persian, Greek, and Roman—of which they were a part.

Conclusion

The task of bringing the feminist lens to the whole of the text of the Psalter is not an easy one. Few have undertaken the task. As pointed out in the general introduction to the Wisdom Commentary series, numerous women throughout the millennia have challenged traditional patriarchal interpretations of the biblical text, but feminist interpretations of and commentaries on the Psalter are rare. The probable reason for this is that, as stated above, images of women occur only sporadically in the text of the Psalter—none is named except Bathsheba—and the roles assigned to them are the traditional ones within a male-dominated culture.

Elizabeth Cady Stanton's 1898 *The Woman's Bible* describes its goal as "to revise only those texts and chapters directly referring to women, and those also in which women are made prominent by exclusion."[42] Only two psalms are briefly mentioned: Psalms 45 and 51. The commentator writes: "There is a passing mention of the existence of women as imaginary beings in the Psalms, the Proverbs, and The Song of Solomon, but not illustrated by any grand personalities or individual characters."[43]

Nonetheless, the book of Psalms has been a powerful source of prayer and meditation for women and men for millennia. Women who lived cloistered lives under the Rule of St. Benedict in tenth-century Europe developed a set of eight daily readings of the Psalms called "The Little Office of the Blessed Virgin Mary." This work was eventually incorporated into "The Book of Hours," a popular book of personal devotion in western Europe in the late Middle Ages and Renaissance.[44] The Book of Hours includes scores of Psalms and some were bound together with complete Psalters (the most popular books, both hand-copied and printed, in this time period). Ownership inscriptions, patron portraits, and feminine grammatical forms in the prayers indicate that women both within and outside cloister walls owned and used the Book of Hours.[45]

In a powerful and thought-provoking essay titled "Take Back the Bible!" the Hebrew Bible scholar Phyllis Trible discusses her personal struggles with the male-dominated and -oriented biblical text. She writes: "To know that one is a feminist and to know that one loves the Bible is, in the thinking of many, be they feminists or opponents, an oxymoron. It will not work." She ponders that, if this be true, "then I was of all women most wretched—or whatever adjective seems fitting: schizophrenic, misguided, conservative, or just plain wrong."[46]

And then Trible came across a familiar story in the Bible—that of Jacob wrestling at the Jabbok in Genesis 32. In comparing her wrestling with

---

42. Elizabeth Cady Stanton, *The Woman's Bible* (New York: Prometheus Books, 1999), 5.

43. Ibid., 96–97.

44. See Edmund Bishop, *Liturgica Historica: Papers on the Liturgy and Religious Life of the Western Church* (Oxford: Clarendon, 1918), 211–37.

45. Eamon Duffy, *Marking the Hours: English People and Their Prayers 1240–1750* (New Haven: Yale University Press, 2006), 1–64.

46. Phyllis Trible, "Take Back the Bible," *RevExp* 97 (2000): 425–31, at 428.

that of Jacob and the outcome of his struggle, she concludes: "Do not abandon the Bible to the bashers and the thumpers. Take back the text. Do not let go until it blesses you. Indeed, make it work for blessing, not for curse, so that you and your descendants, indeed so that all the families of the earth, may live."[47]

This volume of the Wisdom Commentary will "wrestle with the text." It will not abandon the text to traditional, entrenched interpretations. It will ask hard questions; it will demand from the text its inmost meanings; it will not give up until the text reveals itself in profound ways. "So that you and your descendants, indeed so that all the families of the earth, may live" is the assurance that our creator God cares for each of us, regardless of race, creed, nationality, or gender, and that our creator God cares for this world that God so painstakingly created and that is so fragile.

Traditional recent commentaries on the book of Psalms are numerous. I commend to readers J. Clinton McCann Jr.'s work in *The New Interpreter's Bible*; the work of Rolf A. Jacobson, Beth LaNeel Tanner, and myself in Eerdmans's New International Commentary on the Old Testament series; John Goldingay's contribution to the Baker Commentary on the Old Testament series; Walter Brueggemann and William H. Bellinger Jr.'s work in the New Cambridge Bible Commentary series; and Frank Lothar Hossfeld and Erich Zenger's *Psalms 2* and *Psalms 3* in the Hermeneia series.[48] This commentary will employ somewhat different methods than do most commentaries. The canonical storyline of the Psalter will be the guiding principle of interpretation. Matters of original dating and provenance of psalms and/or redactional issues will rarely be addressed. While the psalms are, individually, magnificent poetic compositions, each is part of the larger 150-psalm collection we know as the Psalter or the book of Psalms, and each plays an integral role in the story of the Psalter. Many psalms are "standalone" entities, but it seems that the "shapers" of the Psalter grouped some together intentionally. When, in the eyes of the

---

47. Ibid., 431.

48. J. Clinton McCann Jr., "The Book of Psalms," *NIB*, vol. 4 (Nashville: Abingdon, 1996), 639–1280; Nancy L. deClaissé-Walford, Rolf A. Jacobson, and Beth LaNeel Tanner, *The Book of Psalms*, NICOT (Grand Rapids: Eerdmans, 2014); John Goldingay, *Psalms*, vol. 3: *Psalms 90–150*, BCOT (Grand Rapids: Baker Academic, 2008); Walter Brueggemann and William H. Bellinger Jr., *Psalms*, NCBC (Cambridge: Cambridge University Press, 2014); and Frank-Lothar Hossfeld and Erich Zenger, *Psalm 2*, trans. Linda M. Maloney, Hermeneia (Minneapolis: Fortress, 2005) and *Psalms 3*, trans. Linda M. Maloney, Hermeneia (Minneapolis: Fortress, 2011).

commentator, this seems to be the case we will examine groups of psalms rather than individual psalms.

In addition, this commentary, generally speaking, will not provide strict verse-by-verse expositions. Rather, it will examine themes and messages that relate to the position of the psalm groupings in the overall "storyline" of the Psalter and then move to the appropriation of those texts for our own lives in the twenty-first century.

Other Voices

In the spring of 2018 I had the privilege of traveling to South Africa for six weeks, funded by a generous grant from the Louisville Institute. There I met with and interviewed some thirty individuals in anticipation that they would contribute reflections for this commentary volume. Of the thirty individuals interviewed, eleven submitted eighteen reflections, and one other American voice has contributed. I introduce them above in the list of contributors.

Book 4 of the Psalter
(Pss 90–106)

Psalms 90–92

So That We May Gain a "Heart of Wisdom"

Psalms 90–92 open book 4 of the Psalter. Scholars have long recognized a connectedness among the three psalms, one that includes wisdom motifs, concern with the human condition, and finding security in Yhwh.[1] With Erich Zenger, I consider Psalms 90–92 to be *"eine Komposition"* (a single composition) that is linked by keyword motifs, by questions in one psalm that are answered in a following psalm, and with a Mosaic *inclusio*.[2] We can see movement in the three psalms from lament in Psalm 90 to promise in Psalm 91 to thanksgiving in Psalm 92.[3]

---

1. See David Howard, "A Contextual Reading of Psalms 90–94," in *The Shape and Shaping of the Psalter*, ed. J. Clinton McCann Jr., JSOTSup 159 (Sheffield: JSOT Press, 1993); Robert E. Wallace, *The Narrative Effect of Book Four of the Hebrew Psalter* (New York: Peter Lang, 2007), 18–31; Jerome Creach, *Yahweh as Refuge and the Editing of the Hebrew Psalter* (Sheffield: Sheffield Academic, 1996), 93–96.

2. Erich Zenger, "The God of Israel's Reign over the World," in *The God of Israel and the Nations: Studies in Isaiah and the Psalms*, ed. Norbert Lohfink and Erich Zenger, trans. Everett R. Kalin (Collegeville, MN: Liturgical Press, 2000), 167–68.

3. Frank-Lothar Hossfeld and Erich Zenger, *Psalms 2*, trans. Linda M. Maloney, Hermeneia (Minneapolis: Fortress, 2005), 442.

Psalm 90

The "storyline" of the Psalter (see the introduction, pp. l–lv) places Psalm 90 in the period of the Babylonian exile of the Israelites, but it calls to mind the exodus from Egypt and the wilderness wanderings—another time in the people's history when they were outside the land of promise and longing to return. I read the psalm as a "lament,"[4] a plea to God that continues the despairing questions posed at the end of Psalm 89—"How long, O Lord? Will you hide yourself forever? How long will your wrath burn like fire?" (Ps 89:46).

It is the only psalm in the Psalter attributed to Moses and echoes many of the words uttered by Moses in the books of Exodus and Deuteronomy. In Exodus 32:12, in the aftermath of the Golden Calf incident, Moses pleads with God to "turn" (שוב) and "change your mind" (נחם), the same Hebrew words used in verse 13 of Psalm 90, though נחם is translated as "have compassion" in Psalm 90. The words of Psalm 90:1, "you have been our dwelling place in all generations," echo Moses's words in Deuteronomy 32:7, while the words of Deuteronomy 32:14 are reiterated in Psalm 90:2, "Before the mountains were brought forth, or ever you had formed the earth and the world," and the unusual morphological forms "days" (ימות) and "years" (שנות) in Psalm 90:15 occur also in Deuteronomy 32:7. Marvin Tate writes: "The similarities of language between Ps 90 and the song of Moses in Deut 31:30–32:47 was probably the starting point for either the composition of Ps 90 and/or its assignment to Moses."[5] David Noel Freedman suggests that "the composer of the psalm based it on the episode in Exodus 32 and imagined in poetic form how Moses may have spoken in the circumstances of Exodus 32."[6] Many commentators label book 4 the "Moses Book." Outside of book 4, Moses is mentioned only one time in the Psalter (77:21). In book 4, however, he is referred to seven times (90:1; 99:6; 103:7; 105:26; 106:16, 23, 32).

On the surface, then, Psalm 90 seems very nationalistic and male (Moses)-oriented, recalling the events that led to the formation of Israel as a national identity during the wilderness wanderings and the hope of national survival during the Babylonian exile. But we must not forget that women, as well as men, endured the hardships of the exodus

---

4. Hossfeld and Zenger, *Psalms 2*, 442.

5. Marvin M. Tate, *Psalms 51–100*, WBC 20 (Nashville: Thomas Nelson, 2000), 438.

6. David Noel Freedman, "Other than Moses . . . Who Asks (or Tells) God to Repent?," *BRev* 1 (1985): 59.

Psalm 90:1-17

A Prayer of Moses, the man of God.

¹Lord, you have been our dwelling
    place
  in all generations.
²Before the mountains were brought
    forth,
  or ever you had formed the earth
    and the world,
  from everlasting to everlasting you
    are God.
³You turn us back to dust,
  and say, "Turn back, you mortals."
⁴For a thousand years in your sight
  are like yesterday when it is past,
  or like a watch in the night.
⁵You sweep them away; they are like
  a dream,

like grass that is renewed in the
    morning;
⁶in the morning it flourishes and is
    renewed;
  in the evening it fades and
    withers.
⁷For we are consumed by your anger;
  by your wrath we are
    overwhelmed.
⁸You have set our iniquities before
    you,
  our secret sins in the light of your
    countenance.
⁹For all our days pass away under
    your wrath;
  our years come to an end like a
    sigh.

---

from Egypt and the exile in Babylon and carried the memories of them. After the Israelites crossed the Reed Sea in Exodus 15, Miriam led the women in song and dance according to the words of verses 20-21.[7] Thus, Miriam—though mentioned only sporadically in the biblical text[8]—was, I suggest, an ever-present reality, especially among the women and children, during the wilderness wanderings, as were other strong women. What were their roles among the travelers? Women heavy with pregnancy, enduring childbirth, nursing infants, tending to crying toddlers,

---

7. Some scholars suggest that the whole song in Exod 15:1-21 was sung by Miriam and the women of the Exodus. Judg 11:34; 1 Sam 18:7; and Jer 31:4 indicate that women were the leaders of the victory songs and dances at the conclusion of battles. George J. Brooke, "A Long-Lost Song of Miriam," *BAR* 20 (1994): 62–65, proposes that a separate Song of Miriam, partially suppressed in the book of Exodus, has survived in the Dead Sea Scrolls text 4Q365. See also Rita J. Burns, *Has the Lord Indeed Spoken Only Through Moses? A Study of the Biblical Portrait of Miriam*, SBLDS 84 (Atlanta: Scholars Press, 1987); Phyllis Trible, "Bringing Miriam Out of the Shadows," *BRev* 5 (1989): 14–25; J. Gerald Janzen, "Song of Moses, Song of Miriam: Who Is Seconding Whom?," *CBQ* 54 (1992): 211–20; and Wilda C. Gafney, *Daughters of Miriam: Women Prophets in Ancient Israel* (Minneapolis: Fortress, 2008).

8. Exod 2 and Num 12 and 20.

Psalm 90:1-17 (cont.)

¹⁰The days of our life are seventy
   years,
   or perhaps eighty, if we are
     strong;
even then their span is only toil and
   trouble;
   they are soon gone, and we fly
     away.
¹¹Who considers the power of your
   anger?
   Your wrath is as great as the fear
     that is due you.
¹²So teach us to count our days
   that we may gain a wise heart.
¹³Turn, O LORD! How long?
   Have compassion on your
     servants!

¹⁴Satisfy us in the morning with your
   steadfast love,
   so that we may rejoice and be
     glad all our days.
¹⁵Make us glad as many days as you
   have afflicted us,
   and as many years as we have
     seen evil.
¹⁶Let your work be manifest to your
   servants,
   and your glorious power to their
     children.
¹⁷Let the favor of the Lord our God be
   upon us,
   and prosper for us the work of our
     hands—
   O prosper the work of our hands!

and worrying about the source of the next meal surely turned to them for encouragement and advice. And thus I maintain that we are able to read women's voices within the text of Psalm 90.

The words of verse 2 are particularly evocative. A literal translation of the Masoretic Text (MT)[9] is, "Before the mountains were born, you, God, writhing in labor [the verbal root is חיל in the *polel* verbal stem] birthed the earth [ארץ] and the habitable world [תבל]."[10] "Earth" is the same word used in conjunction with "heavens [שמים]" in the creation story in Genesis 1:1 to describe the universal creation. "Habitable world," on the other hand, tends to connote the inhabited places on the earth—places of solidity and permanence.[11]

The history of translation of the verb חיל in Psalm 90 is an interesting study. The Septuagint (LXX), along with Aquila, Symmachus, the Vul-

9. The Masoretic Text (MT) is the basis of most Hebrew Bibles today and is the standard text for critical study of the Hebrew text of the Old Testament. It is the text of the Leningrad Codex, the oldest complete manuscript of the Hebrew Bible, dating to 1008 CE and housed in the National Library of Russia in St. Petersburg.

10. Deut 32:18 contains similar language—"you have forgotten the God who writhed in labor with you."

11. Heinz-Josef Fabry and N. van Meeteren, "חיל," *TDOT*, 4:344–55. See also Prov 8:31.

gate, and the Targums, alters the *polel* form to a *polal* translation, making "the earth and the inhabited world" the subject of a passive *polal* verb rather than the object of an active *polel* verb—thus it (the earth and the inhabited world) "was formed, or came to birth."[12] Were the LXX translators and those who followed wrong in their reinterpretation of the text? Eugene Boring posits that language suggestive of YHWH as what he terms "earth mother" may have "sounded too much like Canaanite or Greek fertility goddesses to the LXX translators."[13]

The concerns of the LXX translators, however, were not the concerns of later translators. While they maintained the Masoretic Text's active verbal aspect, they failed to convey fully the rich meaning of חיל in Psalm 90. English translations, beginning with the Geneva Bible of 1560 and continuing with the Common English Bible of 2011, render the verb variously as "you formed," "you brought forth," and "you birthed." The *qal*, *polel*, *polal*, and *hifil* stem forms of חיל, in almost every instance of their occurrences in the Hebrew Bible, are used in reference to the birthing process,[14] and where they are not, they connote twirling, writhing, or great distress.[15] Verse 2 of Psalm 90 thus depicts the creator God writhing in childbirth, bringing forth the world.[16]

12. Interestingly, this passive translation was retained in the Douay-Rheims translation of 1610 and the New Jerusalem Bible produced in 1985.

13. M. Eugene Boring, "Psalm 90—Reinterpreting Tradition," *Mid-Stream* 40 (January–April 2001): 119–28, at 123. He quotes Andre Lacocque, who maintained that to consider the development of Scripture as complete with the establishment of its final redaction is "almost as though one were to give the funeral eulogy of someone yet alive." André Lacocque and Paul Ricoeur, *Thinking Biblically: Exegetical and Hermeneutical Studies*, trans. David Pellauer (Chicago: University of Chicago Press, 1998), xii. He refers also to the words of Northrop Frye, who maintains that every text is a "picnic to which the author brings the words and the reader the meaning." See Northrop Frye, *Fearful Symmetry: A Study of William Blake* (Princeton, NJ: Princeton University Press, 1969), 427.

14. See Deut 32:18; Isa 13:8; 23:4; 26:17, 18; 45:10; 51:2; 54:1; 66:7, 8; Jer 4:31; Job 15:7; 39:1; Ps 51:5 (7); Prov 8:24, 25; 25:23.

15. See Deut 2:25; Isa 23:5; Jer 4:19; 5:3, 22; 51:29; Joel 2:6.

16. Tate, *Psalms 51–100*, 431, translates the phrase as "you travailed with." Various Christian communities' patriarchal conceptions of God seem to be so strong that they have missed or downplayed a powerful feminine image of the God of the Israelites. L. Juliana M. Claassens, in *Mourner, Mother, Midwife* (Louisville: Westminster John Knox, 2012), asserts that female images, e.g., birthing, take on greater prominence in exilic/postexilic experience of traumatized Israel. See especially chapter 3: "God as Mother."

The feminine imagery continues as the singer of Psalm 90 reminds God of the fragility of human life. The terms "humankind" (אנוש)[17] and "mortals" (בני־אדם) in verse 3 are reminiscent of Psalm 8's and Psalm 144's wonder at humanity's place in the created order.[18] In 90:16 the psalm singers request that God reveal God's works (פעלים) and majesty (הדר) to the people and their children (בניהם). While all members of the Israelite community were concerned with the survival of the people, a feminist reading of these verses highlights the vulnerability of the un-born, newborn, and young children and their mothers during difficult times like the wilderness wanderings and the Babylonian exile. Infant and mother mortality rates were high in the ancient Near East, and thus I suggest that when a woman in exile in Babylon heard the words of Psalm 90 her mind conjured up images of the great vulnerability of women, newborns, and young children, each of whom were important keys to the survival of ongoing generations.

The central focus of Psalm 90, in my opinion and that of many others, is verses 11–12.[19] The psalmist acknowledges the power (עז) of God's anger and requests of God, according to the NRSV, "teach us to count our days that we may gain a wise heart [לבב חכמה]." This commentator suggests a translation of "teach us to number our days so that we may approach what we do with a heart of wisdom." The phrase "a heart of wisdom" is unique to Psalm 90 but, interestingly, the phrase "wise of heart [חכם לב]" is used four times in the Exodus narratives to describe the craftspersons who constructed the tabernacle and fashioned its furnishings.[20] Do the words of Psalm 90:12—"and we will approach what we do with a heart of wisdom"—suggest that the people were being admonished to be content with whatever tasks and endeavors confronted them daily? Erich Zenger writes: "If 'wisdom' means the art of living, then the ability here asked of God to say yes to life and to live that yes (in the midst of the many things that deserve a no) is Wisdom's art of living par excellence."[21] The closing words of Psalm 90 appear to validate such an understanding of "a heart of wisdom." In verse 14 the people ask God to "satisfy us" (שבע)

---

17. The text of the NRSV has "us," while the MT has "humankind" (אנוש).

18. See Ps 8:4 and Ps 144:3.

19. See, for instance, Hossfeld and Zenger, *Psalms 2*, 422.

20. See Exod 28:3; 31:6; 36:1, 2. In addition, Woman Wisdom is depicted in Prov 8:30 as אמון, "master worker" (NRSV) or "master of crafts" (CEB).

21. Hossfeld and Zenger, *Psalms 2*, 423.

"with your steadfast love [חסד[22]], so that we may rejoice [רנן] and be glad [שמח]," and in verse 17 they request that God "prosper for us the work of our hands—O prosper the work of our hands!" The word translated "prosper" is כון, which means "to establish, set up, fix in place." The singers of Psalm 90 were asking God not for prosperity but rather for a sense of satisfaction and accomplishment for the works of their hands, whatever those works might be.

Thus with Moses's words in Psalm 90 the women and men in the time of the wilderness wanderings and the Babylonian exile cry out to God, who birthed the world (v. 2), to remember that they are mere mortals (v. 3) and to turn and change God's mind (v. 13) about their present situation. In the meantime they ask that God give them "a heart of wisdom" (v. 12) so that they might find meaning and importance in the work of their hands (v. 17).

"Sister, Your Silence Is Not a Show of Strength"

"Lord, you have been our dwelling place in all generations. . . . Satisfy us in the morning with your steadfast love, so that we may rejoice and be glad all our days." (Ps 90:1, 14)

Women in my culture are taught as they are brought up that home affairs are private. Thus they often do not share their problems with others but rather feel they must be strong and deal with them on their own. This is the case even in many Christian communities, and thus we women dress up in our finest clothes and sit together in silence, pretending that everything in life is fine because to do otherwise would show a lack of faith. The sad reality is that many women are abused in their homes: wives in polygamous marriages, subject to incest and rape, left to raise children on their own, poorly educated, and forced to work long hours to provide food and shelter for their families. These women sitting together silently in church honestly look good. But do not be fooled, every imaginable secret is found in the house of God. My sister is an abused wife, my sister is in a polygamous marriage, my sister has been raped, my sister is a substance addict, my sister is filled with insecurities and depression, my sister is hungry, my sister's husband has abandoned her.

Sister, your silence is not a show of strength. Sister, sharing

22. For a discussion of חסד, see the commentaries for Pss 92:2 and 103:8.

your pain is not a lack of faith. So many women live with their situation of pain for so long that they come to believe that that is how life was meant to be for them and that they have no other choice. God's people have problems, and what we all need to do is face them. They come with the turf of a world that has been turned upside down by sin. It is not a matter of lack of faith or not being saved. It is a fact of life in a fallen world. The church is filled with private problems, with practical, real-life issues. In chapter 11 of the book of Hebrews great "heroes of the faith" are celebrated: Noah, Abraham, Moses, Rahab, Gideon, David, Samuel, the prophets, and great women of faith. Each of them faced difficulties, but they did not sit in silence. They spoke up and they acted and God blessed them.

The singers of Psalm 90 recall that God has been their "dwelling place" for all generations, recall their fragile human state, and cry out to God to "satisfy" so that they can "rejoice." Stand up, sister, and don't be afraid to speak! Express your anger, your fear, your doubt, your pain. Demand that God satisfy you so that you may rejoice!

Thanyani Mahanya

Psalm 91

Psalm 91 seems to offer an answer to the people's plea to God in Psalm 90:13 and 14 to "turn [שוב] . . . have compassion [נחם]. . . and satisfy [שבע] us in the morning," thus affirming Erich Zenger's characterization of Psalm 91 as "promise."[23] In words of confident praise the singer of the psalm celebrates the many ways that God cares for and ultimately "satisfies" (שבע) (v. 16) those who trust.

Psalm 91 opens in verses 1-2 with vivid imagery of a God who shelters, delivers, and provides refuge. The verses also present an awkward verbal construction: masculine singular participle ("you who live," ישׁב), followed by a third-person masculine singular imperfect ("who abide," יתלונן), and then a first-person singular imperfect ("[I] will say," אמר). Hermann Gunkel suggests that the awkward verbal construction of verses 1-2 could be resolved by adding אשׁרי to the beginning of verse 1 and altering the Masoretic Text's first-person common singular imperfect form of אמר in verse 2 to a masculine singular participle—thereby not

23. Hossfeld and Zenger, *Psalms 2*, 442.

Psalm 91:1-16

¹You who live in the shelter of the
  Most High,
  who abide in the shadow of the
    Almighty,
²will say to the LORD, "My refuge and
    my fortress;
  my God, in whom I trust."
³For he will deliver you from the
    snare of the fowler
  and from the deadly pestilence;
⁴he will cover you with his pinions,
  and under his wings you will find
    refuge;
  his faithfulness is a shield and
    buckler.
⁵You will not fear the terror of the
    night,
  or the arrow that flies by day,
⁶or the pestilence that stalks in
    darkness,
  or the destruction that wastes at
    noonday.
⁷A thousand may fall at your side,
  ten thousand at your right hand,
  but it will not come near you.
⁸You will only look with your eyes

and see the punishment of the
    wicked.
⁹Because you have made the LORD
    your refuge,
  the Most High your dwelling place,
¹⁰no evil shall befall you,
  no scourge come near your tent.
¹¹For he will command his angels
    concerning you
  to guard you in all your ways.
¹²On their hands they will bear you up,
  so that you will not dash your foot
    against a stone.
¹³You will tread on the lion and the
    adder,
  the young lion and the serpent
    you will trample under foot.
¹⁴Those who love me, I will deliver;
  I will protect those who know my
    name.
¹⁵When they call to me, I will answer
    them;
  I will be with them in trouble,
  I will rescue them and honor them.
¹⁶With long life I will satisfy them,
  and show them my salvation.

requiring an emendation of the consonantal text.[24] This would render a translation of "Content is the one who lives in the shelter of the Most High; that one will abide in the shadow of the Almighty, saying to the LORD, 'My refuge and my fortress.'" Whether אשרי was omitted or is simply to be understood (Gunkel does not make this clear), such a conjecture's wisdom ties[25] bolster the argument that Psalm 91 is an answer to Psalm 90:12's request for "a heart of wisdom." If Psalm 91 begins with

24. Hermann Gunkel, *An Introduction to the Psalms: The Genres of the Religious Lyric of Israel*, trans. James D. Nogalski, MLBS (Macon, GA: Mercer University Press, 1998), 222–35.

25. See Pss 1, 112, and 119, for example.

אשרי (overt or implied), then we are able to read its words as the path to that "heart of wisdom" requested of God by the singers of Psalm 90:12.

Verse 1 of Psalm 91 states that the one who lives in the shelter of the Most High (עליון) will lodge in the shadow of the Almighty (שדי).[26] Some suggest that the basic meaning of the word "Almighty—Shaddai" is "breast" (שד),[27] while others maintain that "mountain" is the referent[28] and thus understand "Shaddai" as "God of the mountains." But let us move backward to Psalm 90:2 and then forward to Psalm 91:4 as we attempt to find a meaning for verse 1's use of "Shaddai." Psalm 90:2 depicts God birthing (חיל) the earth and the inhabitable world, and in verses 3, 12, and 14 the psalmists request that God give "humankind [אנוש]" and "mortals [בני־אדם]" a "heart of wisdom [לבב חכמה]" and that God "satisfy [שבע] humanity."

The epithet "Shaddai" in Psalm 91:1 may be understood as a reference to the nurturing, nourishing God who gave birth to the earth (Ps 90:2) and now suckles it—satisfies it—as it learns to have a "heart of wisdom" (Ps 90:12). References that tie nurturing breasts to God and God's goodness are numerous in the Hebrew Bible. Genesis 49:25 connects the blessing of Shaddai with the breasts (שדים) and the womb (רחם). In Isaiah 66:11, Zion is a "consoling breast" (שד). Naomi laments in Ruth 1:20-21, "Shaddai [שדי] has dealt bitterly with me [and] . . . brought calamity upon me," a reflection perhaps of her now "barren" state, and in Psalm 22:9-10 the psalmist says to God: "you kept me safe on my mother's breasts [שדי אמי]. On you I was cast from my birth [רחם]."[29] Job 20:21 suggests that the children of the wicked will "drink the wrath" of "Shaddai" (שדי).[30]

Verses 3 and 4 of Psalm 91 employ avian imagery to depict the dangers that especially threaten young birds—the fowler's snare and the threat of predators—to provide assurance that God will shelter the psalmist with protective wings (כנפים) and pinions and will ensure safety and

---

26. Only here and in Ps 68:15 is God called "Shaddai" in the Psalter.

27. See especially Harriet Lutzky, "Shadday as a Goddess Epithet," *VT* 48 (1998): 15–36; and Phyllis Trible, *God and the Rhetoric of Sexuality* (Philadelphia: Fortress, 1978), 60–62.

28. See, e.g., Hans-Joachim Kraus, *Psalms 60–150: A Commentary*, trans. Hilton C. Oswald, CC (Minneapolis: Fortress, 1993), 52–53.

29. The Midrash on Ps 22 attributes the psalm to Esther. Esth. Rab. 6:5; y. B. Meg. 13a.

30. References to God as "Shaddai" are most numerous in the books of Genesis (6x) and Job (23x). Interestingly, the only reference to God as Shaddai outside the biblical text is found in the Deir Allah inscriptions.

nurturing.[31] While there are varying understandings of winged-god images in the ancient Near East,[32] in the context of Psalms 90 and 91 YHWH's winged protection in 91:4 is best understood as the protection a mother gives to the child she has born, suckled, and taught to live with wisdom in a world where adversity presents itself on every side. Thus the psalmist will not fear, in the words of verses 5 and 6, the terror and pestilence of the night or the arrow and destruction of the day.

The words of verses 7-13 continue the theme of protection by the birthing, nurturing God: the wicked will be punished (v. 8), no evil will come near your tent (v. 10), you will not dash your foot against a stone (v. 12), and you will tread on the lion and the adder (v. 13). J. Clinton McCann writes: "The psalmist affirms that no place, no time, no circumstance that befalls us is beyond God's ability to protect us."[33] God's repeated promise to care for and protect the psalm singers leads to the declaration in verse 16 that God will finally "satisfy [שבע]"—the very request made by the psalmists in 90:14. These words of promise, of course, are heard in dissonance by those whom God has not satisfied in the midst of so many trials and setbacks in life. But they perhaps offer a hope of the eventuality of satisfaction to those who seek to live with a "heart of wisdom."

Psalm 92

Psalm 92, a thanksgiving psalm, culminates the three-psalm grouping of Psalms 90–92 that begins with lament (Ps 90) and continues with promise (Ps 91).[34] In Psalm 92 all that is asked for in Psalm 90 and promised in Psalm 91 comes to fruition.

The superscription provides a description of the psalm, "A psalm," and further indicates its function, "A song for the Sabbath Day." The psalm opens with calls to praise (vv. 1-5) and continues with descriptive

---

31. Hossfeld and Zenger, *Psalms 2*, 430. The image of God's sheltering wings occurs six times in the Psalter, in Pss 17:8; 36:7; 57:1; 61:4; 63:7; and 91:4. In addition, Jesus employs sheltering wings imagery in his lament over Jerusalem in Matt 23:37 and Luke 13:34.

32. See Joel LeMon, *Yahweh's Winged Form in the Psalms: Exploring Congruent Iconography and Texts* (Fribourg: Academic Press, 2010), for a full treatment of the varying viewpoints.

33. J. Clinton McCann Jr., "The Book of Psalms," in *NIB*, vol. 4 (Nashville: Abingdon, 1996), 1047. See McCann further, p. 1048, for commentary on the use of vv. 11-12 in Luke 4:9-12. See also Matt 4:6.

34. Hossfeld and Zenger, *Psalms 2*, 442.

Psalm 92:1-15

A Psalm.
A Song for the Sabbath Day.

¹It is good to give thanks to the LORD,
to sing praises to your name, O
Most High;
²to declare your steadfast love in the
morning,
and your faithfulness by night,
³to the music of the lute and the harp,
to the melody of the lyre.
⁴For you, O LORD, have made me
glad by your work;

at the works of your hands I sing
for joy.
⁵How great are your works, O LORD!
Your thoughts are very deep!
⁶The dullard cannot know,
the stupid cannot understand this:
⁷though the wicked sprout like grass
and all evildoers flourish,
they are doomed to destruction
forever,
⁸but you, O LORD, are on high
forever.

words about YHWH's good works on behalf of the psalm singer and the righteous ones (vv. 6-15).

The words of verse 1 are rich with references back to Psalms 90 and 91 that precede it and glimpses forward into the enthronement psalms (Pss 93–100) that follow. The epithet "Most High" (עליון) recalls the opening words of Psalm 91 (v. 1), while "name" (שם) echoes the psalm's closing words (v. 14). In the middle of Psalm 92:1 the verb translated "sing praises" (זמר) prepares readers for the songs of praise they will encounter in the enthronement psalms (see Pss 95:2 and 98:4, 5). The retrospect and prospect continue throughout Psalm 92. In verse 2 the psalm singer celebrates YHWH's steadfast love (חסד) in the morning (בקר) and YAHWEH's faithfulness by night (לילה), confirming Psalm 91:5's promise of protection from the terror of the night (לילה) and the arrow by day (יומם). A key word in this verse is "steadfast love" (חסד). It has to do with relationship—one based on the covenant made between God and the Israelites at Sinai. The word describes both who God is and what God does as well as who the people of God are to be and what they are expected to do; thus it encompasses both the internal character and the external actions that are required to maintain a life-sustaining relationship between God and people.

Psalm 92:3-4 invoke the lute, the harp, and the lyre in praise of God's good care, just like the lyre, the trumpets, and the horn in Psalm 98:5, 6. The verses' "glad[ness]" (שמח) and "sing[ing] for joy" (רנן), along with the cause of that gladness and joyful singing, God's "work" (פעל, v. 4), recall the "rejoicing" (רנן) and "gladness" (שמח) of Psalm 90:14 and the

⁹For your enemies, O Lᴏʀᴅ,
    for your enemies shall perish;
    all evildoers shall be scattered.
¹⁰But you have exalted my horn like
    that of the wild ox;
    you have poured over me fresh oil.
¹¹My eyes have seen the downfall of
    my enemies;
    my ears have heard the doom of
        my evil assailants.
¹²The righteous flourish like the palm
    tree,

and grow like a cedar in
    Lebanon.
¹³They are planted in the house of the
    Lᴏʀᴅ;
    they flourish in the courts of our
        God.
¹⁴In old age they still produce fruit;
    they are always green and full of
        sap,
¹⁵showing that the Lᴏʀᴅ is upright;
    he is my rock, and there is no
        unrighteousness in him.

praise of God's "work" (פעל) in Psalm 90:16. Additionally, the psalmist's anticipation of gladness and joyful singing in Psalm 92:4 is realized in the gladness expressed in Psalms 96:11 and 97:1, 11, 12, and the joyful singing in Psalms 95:1; 96:12; 98:4, 8.

An interesting occurrence of joyful singing (רנן) as we find in Psalm 92:4 is in Proverbs 1:20. There we read that (Woman) Wisdom "cries out" (רנן) in the street, proclaiming her words of admonition to those who will listen. Further, references to the "dullard" (בער), the "stupid" (כסיל), and the "wicked" (רשעים) in Psalm 92:6, 7 are found frequently in the book of Proverbs[35] and perhaps are used purposefully by the singer of Psalm 92 to tie the words of verse 4 not only to the pleas of the psalmist in Psalm 90 and the joyful words of the enthronement psalms but also to the admonitions of (Woman) Wisdom in Proverbs. Psalm 90:12 requests of God "a heart of wisdom"; Wisdom provides that path but the dullard, the fool, and the wicked cannot know it. Verse 7 of Psalm 92 continues by stating that the wicked sprout like "grass" (עשב), and "evildoers" (פעלי און) "flourish" (צוץ), recalling the words of Psalm 90:5, 6 that the years of the psalmist are like "grass" (עשב) that "flourishes" (צוץ) in the morning but fades and withers in the evening. Following the path of Wisdom and achieving a "heart of wisdom" results in a very different fate.

35. "Dullard" occurs in Prov 12:1 and 30:2; "fool" is found some fifty times in the book (see, e.g., 1:22; 9:13; 12:23; 17:21; 26:1; 29:11), and the very common "wicked" occurs over seventy times (see, e.g., 3:33; 10:6; 12:5; 15:6; 21:4; 29:7).

The words of verses 12-14 of Psalm 92 are particularly intriguing from a gender standpoint. Here the "righteous" (צַדִּיק), in contrast to the "dullard," the "stupid," the "wicked," and "evildoers" (92:6-7), are likened to the palm tree and the cedar of Lebanon. The two are common images of strength and longevity in the ancient Near East, set alongside one another in poetic parallelism. The palm tree (תמר, *tamar*) here is most likely the date palm,[36] a long-lived tree that provided many staple items of the ancient Near Eastern diet for both humans and animals as well as wood for various household projects. It is also a symbol of life-giving water in the biblical text. Recall that just after crossing the Reed Sea the wandering Israelites came to Elim, where there were twelve springs of water and seventy palm trees.[37] Tamar (תמר) is, additionally, the name of three female biblical characters: the daughter-in-law of Judah in Genesis 38, the daughter of David in 2 Samuel 13, and the daughter of Absalom in 2 Samuel 14.[38] The word is used in Song of Songs 7:7-8 as a metaphor for a desirable woman, where we read: "You are stately as a palm tree, and your breasts are like its clusters." Judges 4:5 states that Deborah sat under a palm tree as she judged Israel.[39] Thus the palm tree was often associated with the feminine and fertility.[40]

The cedars (ארז) of Lebanon convey a more masculine imagery. They were connected with longevity, majesty, and strength and were symbols of royal power. King Hiram of Tyre sent wood from the cedars of Lebanon to build David's palace (2 Sam 5:11; 7:2, 7) and to Solomon for the construction of the temple in Jerusalem (1 Kgs 5:6-10). The singer of Psalm 29 cries, "The voice of the LORD breaks the cedars; the LORD breaks the cedars of Lebanon" (v. 5), and in Song of Songs the protagonist describes her lover's appearance as "like Lebanon, choice as the cedars" (5:15).[41] Thus the palm tree and the cedar of Lebanon were two powerful images of the strength and resilience of the people of God—one feminine, the other masculine.

---

36. Richard D. Patterson, "Psalm 92:12-15: The Flourishing of the Righteous," *BSac* 166 (2009): 271–88, at 275.

37. See Exod 15:27 and Num 33:9. See also Deut 34:3 (Jericho) and Judg 1:16; 3:13.

38. See Gen 38:6; 2 Sam 13:1; 2 Sam 14:27.

39. See also Isa 9:14 and Joel 1:12 as examples of judgments on the people of Israel.

40. See also Peter Shäfer, *Mirrors of His Beauty: Feminine Images of God from the Bible to the Early Kabbalah* (Princeton, NJ: Princeton University Press, 2002).

41. See also Judg 9:15; 2 Kgs 19:23; Job 40:17; Pss 104:16; 148:9; Isa 2:13; 14:8; 37:24.

The tree imagery of Psalm 92 recalls the metaphoric imagery of the wisdom psalm that opens the Psalter in which the righteous person, the one called "happy" (אשרי, Ps 1:1), is likened to "a tree planted by streams of water" (1:3). In addition, the righteous person in Psalm 1 "meditates" (הגה, v. 2) on the Torah, the same verbal root that occurs in Psalm 90:9, "our years come to an end like a sigh [הגה]," and in Psalm 92:3 "to the melody [*higgiyon*, from the root הגה] of the lyre," perhaps suggesting an additional tie between the Psalter's opening words of wisdom and the wisdom elements of Psalms 90 and 92 (see the introduction, pp. xlv–xlvi).[42]

Psalm 92 continues in verse 13 with an assurance that the righteous will be planted in the "house" of YHWH and will thrive in its courtyards. Verse 14 promises that "in old age they [will] still produce fruit" and will be "always green and full of sap." The promised fertility of the righteous in Psalm 92 renders null and void Psalm 90's lament that "You sweep [our years] away; they are like a dream, like grass that is renewed in the morning; in the morning it flourishes and is renewed; in the evening it fades and withers" (vv. 5-6).[43]

Those especially concerned with the vulnerability of the young, the newborn, and those yet to be born in the exilic community in Babylon, and those concerned with the vulnerable in today's world, hear in the words of Psalm 90 the admonition that the next generation will indeed survive *if* the people embrace the "wise heart—heart of wisdom" for which the singer of Psalm 90:12 asks and will be "satisfied" (Ps 90:14) with the "work of our hands" (90:17); accept Psalm 91's promise of being "satisfied" with long life (Ps 91:16); and embrace the assurance of Psalm 92 that "the righteous [will] flourish" (92:12). Having heard the words of assurance that God will satisfy their needs, the people now offer praise to the source of their hopeful expectation for the future in the words of book 4's enthronement psalms (Pss 93–100).

42. The root הגה occurs only twenty-five times in the Psalter.
43. See also Ps 92:8.

Psalms 93–100

God Is Sovereign:
Let the Earth Give a Ringing Cry

Psalms 93 and 95–99, along with Psalm 47, are categorized as enthronement psalms. They depict Yhwh as sovereign over creation (Pss 47:2; 93:1; 94:2; 95:4-5; 96:10), more majestic than all other gods (Pss 95:3; 96:4-5; 97:9), able to conquer the chaos of raging waters (Pss 93:3-4; 95:5; 98:7-8), and an arbiter in matters pertaining to human welfare (Pss 94:2, 10; 96:13; 99:4). The enthronement psalms have five basic characteristics:

1. Concern with all the earth, all peoples, or all nations
2. References to other gods
3. Songs of exaltation and kingship
4. Characteristic acts of Yhwh: making, establishing, sitting, judging, etc.
5. Expressions of the attitude of praise before the heavenly king[1]

---

1. Marvin E. Tate, *Psalms 51–100*, WBC 20 (Nashville: Thomas Nelson, 2000), 474.

This commentary will include Psalms 94 and 100 in its examination of the enthronement psalms, offering rationales for reading the somewhat disturbing Psalm 94 within the context of praise of the enthronement psalms and understanding Psalm 100 as a closing doxological psalm for the group.

According to the storyline of the Psalter (see the introduction, pp. l–lv), book 4 is set in the period of the Babylonian exile and its psalms call to mind the time of the wilderness wanderings, the two times in the history of the ancient Israelites when they were outside the land promised to them by God, anticipating a return. Three psalms in book 4 precede the enthronement psalms. Psalm 90 calls on the God who, according to verse 2, "formed" ("birthed," חיל) the "earth" (ארץ) and the (habitable) "world" (תבל) to remember that the psalm singers are mere humans (אנוש) and mortals (בני־אדם) (v. 3). The psalmists ask God in verse 12 to give them a "wise heart" ("heart of wisdom," לבב חכמה) and plead with God to "turn" (שוב) and "have compassion" (נחם) (v. 13) and to "satisfy" them (שבע) (v. 14).

Psalm 91's words of promise follow; the God who birthed the earth now suckles it (שדי, v. 1), protects it under motherly wings (כנפים, vv. 3-4), and finally "satisfies" (שבע, v. 16). Psalm 92, a psalm of thanksgiving, provides rich connections to Psalms 90 and 91 and glimpses of what the reader will encounter in the enthronement psalms. The words "Most High" (עליון) and "name" (שם) in Psalm 92:1 echo the beginning and ending of Psalm 91 (vv. 1 and 14), while the "gladness" (שמח) and "joyful singing" (רנן) at God's "work" (פעל) in Psalm 92:4 recall the words of Psalm 90:14-16 and anticipate the words of Psalms 96:11; 97:8; 100:2 (שמח) and 95:1; 96:12; 98:8; 100:2 (רנן). Psalm 92 continues with the promise that, in contrast to the "wicked," who will sprout like the "grass" (עשב, v. 7) that, according to Psalm 90:5-6, "fades and withers," the righteous, female and male, will be planted in the "house of the LORD" (v. 13) and even in old age will "flourish" and be "green and full of sap" (v. 14).

Psalms 90–92 thus may be read as words of assurance to the exilic community that God creates, nourishes, protects, and teaches to have a "heart of wisdom" and then ultimately "satisfies," regardless of life's exigencies. Having heard the words of assurance that God will satisfy their needs in Psalms 90–92, the people now offer praise to the source of their hopeful expectation for the future as they celebrate God's sovereignty over them and all the earth in the words of book 4's enthronement psalms.

Psalm 93

Verse 1 begins with the words, "The Lᴏʀᴅ is king [יהוה מלך]." The word translated "is king" is actually a verbal form (as it is in Pss 96:10; 97:1; 99:1)[2] and is better translated as "reigns," as we find in the CEB, the NIV, the NASB, and the KJV.

TRANSLATION MATTERS

The difference between "is king" and "reigns" at first glance may seem minor, but "is king" immediately brings to mind male images of God. Since the phrase יהוה מלך is a metaphor using words to attempt to describe God's relationship to the world and its inhabitants, a translation of מלך that evinces a broader metaphorical conception, such as "reigns," allows for both feminine and masculine metaphorical imagery of God. The metaphors the psalm singers use to describe and attempt to understand God are human constructs, employing images and ideas that other human readers or hearers are able to appropriate from their own life experiences. The biblical text is the product of a male-dominated undertaking; therefore we as readers and interpreters of the Psalter must be sensitive to its use of language about God. For more on metaphors for God, see the introduction, pp. xlvi–xlviii.

Verse 1 ends, "He has established [כון] the world [תבל]; it shall never be moved [מוט]." A translation that encompasses the rich meaning of the Hebrew words is "As well, the habitable world [תבל] stands firm [כון]; it will not be shaken [מוט]." תבל, which refers to the earth's habitable spaces, places of solidity and permanence for God's creation,[3] occurs fifteen times in the Psalter, with six occurrences in the six enthronement psalms.[4] The only occurrence of the word in book 4 outside of the enthronement psalms is in Psalm 90:2, where we read that God birthed (חיל) the earth (ארץ) and the habitable world (תבל). Psalm 93:1 states confidently that this habitable world, birthed by God,[5] is firmly established; it cannot be moved.[6]

---

2. The noun form of מלך occurs in Pss 95:3; 98:6; 99:4.

3. Heinz Josef Fabry and N. van Meeteren, "תבל," *TDOT*, 15:557–64.

4. Pss 93:1; 96:10, 13; 97:4; 98:7, 9.

5. See the commentary for Ps 90:2.

6. See Ps 96:10, where these words are repeated as a further affirmation of God's sovereignty over the world.

Psalm 93:1-5

¹The LORD is king, he is robed in majesty;
the LORD is robed, he is girded with strength.
He has established the world; it shall never be moved;
²your throne is established from of old;
you are from everlasting.
³The floods have lifted up, O LORD,
the floods have lifted up their voice;
the floods lift up their roaring.
⁴More majestic than the thunders of mighty waters,
more majestic than the waves of the sea,
majestic on high is the LORD!
⁵Your decrees are very sure;
holiness befits your house,
O LORD, forevermore.

Verses 3-4 abound with references to water. Verse 3's "The floods have lifted up, O LORD, the floods have lifted up their voice; the floods lift up their roaring" conjures up images of overwhelming inundation and potential death.⁷ Water was a common metaphor for chaos in ancient Near Eastern stories—chaos that needed to be overcome in order to create the world.⁸ But according to verse 4, "more majestic than the thunders of mighty waters, more majestic than the waves of the sea, majestic on high is the LORD." In the context of Psalm 93 and in the overall context of book 4, the words of verses 3 and 4 assure the reader and hearer that in the process of birthing the habitable world God overcame the primordial chaos, and the waters that threatened are less majestic than the majesty of God. An added note of assurance to the readers and hearers of the psalm is the fivefold repetition of YHWH ("the LORD" in the NRSV), God's personal name revealed to Moses at the burning bush (Exod 3:14) in verses 1, 3, 4, and 5.

Psalm 94

Most commentaries do not include Psalm 94 in the grouping of enthronement psalms in book 4. The psalm is classified as a community lament and further as an imprecatory or vengeance psalm, based on

---

7. See also Pss 42:7; 46:2-3; 69:1-2; 88:7.
8. See, for example, the Babylonian creation story Enuma Elish, the Ugaritic Baal Cycle, and the Egyptian stories of Ra and Apep. In Gen 1:2-3 we read "and darkness was over the face of the deep [תהום] and the spirit of God hovered over the face of the waters. And God said, 'Let there be light.'" See also Job 38:8-11; Ps 77:16; 104:5-9; Prov 8:27-29; Jer 5:22.

Psalm 94:1-23

¹O LORD, you God of vengeance,
you God of vengeance, shine forth!
²Rise up, O judge of the earth;
give to the proud what they
deserve!
³O LORD, how long shall the wicked,
how long shall the wicked exult?
⁴They pour out their arrogant words;
all the evildoers boast.
⁵They crush your people, O LORD,
and afflict your heritage.
⁶They kill the widow and the stranger,
they murder the orphan,

⁷and they say, "The LORD does not see;
the God of Jacob does not
perceive."
⁸Understand, O dullest of the people;
fools, when will you be wise?
⁹He who planted the ear, does he not
hear?
He who formed the eye, does he
not see?
¹⁰He who disciplines the nations,
he who teaches knowledge to
humankind,
does he not chastise?

the twofold use of the word "vengeance" (נקם) in verse 1.⁹ Are words of vengeance appropriate in a celebration of the sovereignty of God? In addition, Psalm 94 makes no mention of God as sovereign (מלך) as do the other psalms classified as "enthronement." A number of characteristics of Psalm 94, though, confirm its integral function within the group.

First, while Psalm 93 celebrates God's sovereignty and majesty and affirms the stability of the (habitable) world, Psalm 94 calls on God to act on Israel's behalf against the proud (v. 2), the wicked (vv. 3, 16, 20), those who "pour out their arrogant words" and "boast" (v. 4), those who "crush" and "afflict" (v. 5), those who "kill the widow and the stranger" and "murder the orphan" (v. 6), the "dullest of the people" and "fools" (v. 8), and the evildoers and "those who contrive mischief" (v. 20).¹⁰ The word translated "proud" (גאה) in 94:2 is from the same verbal root as the word translated "majesty" in 93:1, while "crush" (דכא) in reference to what the wicked do to the people of God in 94:5 is the same word used in 93:3 to describe the roaring of the floods. Thus the two psalms contrast the proud and wicked who assert their own "pride" and "crush" the people with the "majestic" God who calms the "roaring" chaos of threatening waters.

9. For a full discussion of "imprecatory," see the commentary for Ps 109.

10. God as a God of vengeance is a common theme in the Old Testament. See, for example, Deut 32:35; Pss 8:3; 18:48; 99:8; 149:7; Isa 1:24; 34:8; 35:4; 61:2; Jer 5:29; 11:20; Ezek 25:17; Nah 1:2.

Psalm 94:1-23 (cont.)

¹¹The LORD knows our thoughts,
   that they are but an empty breath.
¹²Happy are those whom you
      discipline, O LORD,
   and whom you teach out of your
      law,
¹³giving them respite from days of
      trouble,
   until a pit is dug for the wicked.
¹⁴For the LORD will not forsake his
      people;
   he will not abandon his heritage;

¹⁵for justice will return to the
      righteous,
   and all the upright in heart will
      follow it.
¹⁶Who rises up for me against the
      wicked?
   Who stands up for me against
      evildoers?
¹⁷If the LORD had not been my help,
   my soul would soon have lived in
      the land of silence.
¹⁸When I thought, "My foot is slipping,"

In the ancient Near East a people's stability, livelihood, and protection were ensured by allegiance to the ruler of the city or district, the (habitable) land of their inheritance. Being subject to the ruler guaranteed a secure way of life.[11] If people moved beyond their own city or district they were likely to come under a different ruler, one who might or might not look favorably on them.

When the Israelites left Egypt and settled in the Promised Land one of the first issues they faced was how to have a ruler who would guarantee their safety and a good way of life (1 Sam 8–16). The prophet Samuel anointed Saul and then David as king over the Israelites, but when the Babylonians destroyed Jerusalem and took the people captive such a protected and guaranteed life disappeared. Israel no longer had its own king—its own protector. Its people were subjects of a foreign king. Imagine the fear, the questions, the searching. Who would protect them, guarantee their livelihood and survival as individuals and as a people, and mete out justice? Embracing God as sovereign was a way for the Israelites in captivity in Babylon to maintain a sense of identity as royal subjects, not of the Babylonian king, but of their own divine ruler.

Specifically named in the complaint against the wicked in Psalm 94 is their oppression of the widow (אלמנה), the stranger (גר), and orphans (יתום) (v. 6). Repeatedly in the biblical text these three are named as the most vulnerable in society, those who require special consideration and

---

11. See Pss 72; 107:33-43; 145 for models of an ideal sovereign in ancient Israel.

your steadfast love, O LORD, held
me up.
¹⁹When the cares of my heart are
many,
your consolations cheer my soul.
²⁰Can wicked rulers be allied with you,
those who contrive mischief by
statute?
²¹They band together against the life
of the righteous,

and condemn the innocent to
death.
²²But the LORD has become my
stronghold,
and my God the rock of my refuge.
²³He will repay them for their iniquity
and wipe them out for their
wickedness;
the LORD our God will wipe them
out.

care.[12] Such care was especially important to the women in the community, and we thus may hear the voices of women as well as those of men calling on God as sovereign to "right this wrong."

Second, Psalm 94 employs language that connects it to the Song of Moses in Deuteronomy 32 and 33, reinforcing book 4's ties to Moses.[13] The singer of Psalm 94 calls on the God of "vengeance" (נקם) in verse 1 to act on behalf of the people and states in verse 18 that God kept her "foot" (רגל) from "slipping" (מוט). In Deuteronomy 32:35, Moses speaks these words of God to the people, "Vengeance [נקם] is mine, and recompense, for the time when their foot [רגל] shall slip [מוט]." Psalm 94's use of the words "vengeance" in verse 1 and "foot" and "slip" in verse 18 is framed by "foot" in Psalm 91:12, "moved [מוט, slip]" in Psalm 93:1, and "vengeance" ("avenger" in the NRSV) in Psalm 99:8, forming something of an *inclusio* with a center in the words of Psalm 94.[14] Additionally, the psalmist's request of YHWH in 94:1 to "shine forth" (יפע) parallels Moses's description of YHWH's appearance from Mount Sinai (Deut 33:2).

Third, Psalm 94 uses wisdom language echoing that found in the opening psalms of book 4, particularly Psalm 92. The dullard (בער) and the stupid/fool (כסיל) who cannot know or understand in 92:6 are called on to do so in 94:8.[15] The wicked (רשעים) and evildoers (פעלי און) who sprout

12. See, for instance, Lev 19:10, 34; Exod 22:21; Deut 24:17; Isa 1:23; Mal 3:5.

13. See the commentary for Ps 90.

14. Robert E. Wallace, *The Narrative Effect of Book IV of the Hebrew Psalter*, StBibLit 112 (New York: Peter Lang, 2007), 40.

15. While "dullard" (בער) occurs only twice in the book of Proverbs (12:1; 30:2), "stupid/fool" (כסיל) occurs some fifty times.

like grass and flourish in 92:7 and exult and pour out arrogant words in 94:3-4 find their end with YHWH's justice in 94:16. Both psalms contrast the fate of the wicked (רשעים; Pss 92:7; 94:16) with the fate of the righteous (צדיק/צדק; Pss 92:12; 94:15).[16]

Verse 12 of Psalm 94 is a wisdom saying introduced by "happy" (אשרי) and declaring that the "law" (תורה) is the path to a life well-lived, paralleling the wisdom sayings in Psalms 1 and 119. The Psalter equates wisdom and Torah and invites the reader or hearer to recall the words of Woman Wisdom, who, according to Proverbs 8, was there at creation, God's "delight" (שעשעים, v. 30) who in turn "delights" (שעשע, v. 31) in the "human race" (בני־אדם, v. 31). Kathleen O'Connor writes of Woman Wisdom that in all the texts in which she appears "the most important aspect of her existence is her relationships. . . . She is closely joined to the created world. . . . She exists in it as if it were a tapestry of connected threads, patterned into an intricate whole of which she is the center."[17]

The word "delight" (שעשע) occurs five times in Psalm 119,[18] always in reference to the Torah (the law), further confirming the connection between Wisdom and Torah. At creation God delighted in Wisdom, who in turn delighted in humanity. That delight continues with adherence to the Torah. Claudia Camp suggests that, in the Psalter, Wisdom (identified with Torah), actually replaces the earthly king as the mediator between God and humanity.[19] Thus in the context of book 4's enthronement psalms, Psalm 94 affirms God's sovereignty and status as judge and arbiter (vv. 1-2) but also provides a tangible connection to God in the form of Wisdom as embodied in Torah (vv. 12-15).

Psalm 95

Psalm 95 begins with a call to "sing [רנן]" and "make a joyful noise [רוע]" with "songs of praise [זמר]" (vv. 1-2). The verb רנן in 95:1 recalls the words of Psalm 90:14, in which the people implore God: "Satisfy us in the morning . . . so that we may rejoice [רנן] and be glad all our days." רנן, better

---

16. "Wicked" (רשעים) and "righteous" (צדיק/צדק) each occur well over one hundred times in the books of Job, Proverbs, and Qoheleth.

17. Kathleen M. O'Connor, *The Wisdom Literature* (Collegeville, MN: Liturgical Press, 1988), 59.

18. Verses 24, 77, 92, 143, and 174. Outside of Ps 119 and Prov 8, the term occurs only in Isa 5:7 and Jer 31:20.

19. Claudia V. Camp, *Wisdom and the Feminine in the Book of Proverbs* (Sheffield: Almond, 1985), 272–80.

Psalm 95:1-11

¹O come, let us sing to the LORD;
  let us make a joyful noise to the
    rock of our salvation!
²Let us come into his presence with
    thanksgiving;
  let us make a joyful noise to him
    with songs of praise!
³For the LORD is a great God,
  and a great King above all gods.
⁴In his hand are the depths of the
    earth;
  the heights of the mountains are
    his also.
⁵The sea is his, for he made it,
  and the dry land, which his hands
    have formed.
⁶O come, let us worship and bow
    down,
  let us kneel before the LORD, our
    Maker!

⁷For he is our God,
  and we are the people of his
    pasture,
  and the sheep of his hand.
O that today you would listen to his
    voice!
⁸Do not harden your hearts, as at
    Meribah,
  as on the day at Massah in the
    wilderness,
⁹when your ancestors tested me,
  and put me to the proof, though
    they had seen my work.
¹⁰For forty years I loathed that
    generation
  and said, "They are a people
    whose hearts go astray,
  and they do not regard my ways."
¹¹Therefore in my anger I swore,
  "They shall not enter my rest."

translated as "give a ringing cry," is almost always used in a positive sense in the Hebrew Bible and is connected with joyous outbursts—never with cries of oppression, warfare, etc.[20] An interesting occurrence of רנן is in Proverbs 1:20. There we read that Wisdom "cries out [רנן] in the streets," proclaiming her words of admonition to those who would listen. The occurrence of רנן in Psalm 95:1 and Proverbs 1:20 signals for the reader or hearer ties between Wisdom's "ringing cry" in Proverbs, Psalm 94's wisdom call to heed the "law" (תורה, vv. 12-15), and the "ringing cry" (רנן) celebrating God's sovereignty over creation in Psalm 95.

Psalm 95:3 states, like Psalm 93:1, that the God of Israel is sovereign (מלך)[21] but adds that God is sovereign over all gods (כל־אלהים). Verses 4 and 5 echo the creation language of Psalm 93, but with words that speak less about chaotic waters and more about God's creative work—"the depths of the earth; the heights of the mountains," "the sea . . . and the dry land, which his hands have formed." The only direct mention of

20. Jutta Hausmann, "רנן" (*rānan*), *TDOT*, 13:515–22.
21. For a discussion of God as "sovereign," see the excursus for Ps 93.

water occurs in verse 5, where the psalmist says, "the sea is his, for he made it." Even so, the final verses of Psalm 95 (vv. 8-11) recall one of the Israelite people's times of grumbling during the wilderness wandering. The story of Meribah and Massah, related in Exodus 17, is about provision of water. It occurs not long after God delivered the people from the Egyptian army at the Reed Sea (Exod 14–15). The people camped at Rephidim but there was no water to drink. They complained against Moses, saying, "Why did you bring us out of Egypt, to kill us and our children and livestock with thirst?" (Exod 17:3). God instructs Moses to strike the rock at Horeb with his staff, and water comes gushing out (Exod 17:6).[22] The God who tamed the chaotic waters at creation (Gen 1:2) and provided water to the thirsty Israelites in the wilderness continues to provide the essential elements of life to God's people. The words of Psalm 95:8-11 would have been powerful to the Israelites in exile in Babylon and to members of the postexilic community; they remain powerful words today to women and men living in various "wildernesses" and "exiles."

Psalm 96

Psalm 96:1 calls the people to sing to the Lord a "new song" (שיר חדש).[23] The new song comes as a response to the history lesson in Psalm 95:8-11, which reassures the reader or hearer that the creator God who is sovereign over all can and will tame the chaotic waters and turn them into sustaining waters, and, as Marvin Tate suggests, "The 'new song' is to express a new realization and acknowledgment that the future belongs to Yahweh."[24]

The words of verses 1-4 affirm the universal nature of God's rule. "All the earth" is called to sing the new song; thus the reader or hearer is urged to "declare his glory among the nations [גוים]" and "his marvelous works among all the peoples [עמים]" because YHWH is "above all gods" (כל־אלהים; see Pss 95:3 and 97:9).[25] In 96:9 the psalmist calls on "all the earth" to "tremble" before the Lord. The word translated "tremble" is derived from חיל, the same verbal root used in Psalm 90:2 in reference to the beginnings of the world, where God birthed (חיל, "formed" in the

22. Other references to Meribah and Massah occur in Num 20:2-13, 24; Deut 6:16; 9:22; 32:15; 33:8; and Pss 81:7; 106:32.

23. The same phrase opens Ps 98.

24. Tate, *Psalms 51–100*, 514.

25. Judg 11:34; Sam 18:7; and Jer 31:4 indicate that women were the leaders of the victory songs and dances at the conclusion of battles.

Psalm 96:1-13

¹O sing to the LORD a new song;
   sing to the LORD, all the earth.
²Sing to the LORD, bless his name;
   tell of his salvation from day to day.
³Declare his glory among the nations,
   his marvelous works among all
      the peoples.
⁴For great is the LORD, and greatly to
      be praised;
   he is to be revered above all gods.
⁵For all the gods of the peoples are
      idols,
   but the LORD made the heavens.

⁶Honor and majesty are before him;
   strength and beauty are in his
      sanctuary.
⁷Ascribe to the LORD, O families of the
      peoples,
   ascribe to the LORD glory and
      strength.
⁸Ascribe to the LORD the glory due his
      name;
   bring an offering, and come into
      his courts.
⁹Worship the LORD in holy splendor;
   tremble before him, all the earth.

NRSV) the earth (אֶרֶץ) and the (habitable) world (תֵבֵל).[26] Now, in Psalm 96:9, the earth is called on to participate with God in the ongoing creative "birthing" process.

The verb חִיל is an interesting lexical study. It is closely related to and often combined lexically with חוּל, "to twirl in dance," allowing for a variety of ways to understand its meaning in various contexts. Arthur Walker-Jones, in *The Green Psalter*, translates Psalm 96:9 as "Worship the LORD in sacred glory; Dance before him all the Earth."[27] Walker-Jones's translation provides yet another means of tying Psalm 96:9 to Psalm 90:2. Is God, in Psalm 96, calling the earth that God "birthed" in Psalm 90 to joyously "dance" in God's presence? Or is the earth to "tremble—writhe along with God" at God's wondrous "birthing" of the earth? Whatever meaning we choose for חִיל, the singer of Psalm 96 calls on the earth to participate in one way or another in the "new song" (שִׁיר חָדָשׁ) in answer to the work of God in creation.[28]

---

26. The basic meaning of חִיל is "twirl, twist, or writhe," and nearly every occurrence of the word in the Hebrew Bible is in direct reference to the birthing process; where it is not it most often connotes writhing, anguish, and great distress. See the commentary on Ps 90 and Deut 32:18; Isa 13:8; 23:4; 26:17, 18; 45:10; 51:2; 54:1; 66:7, 8; Jer 4:31; Job 15:7; 39:1; Ps 51:5 (7); Prov 8:24, 25; 25:23.

27. Arthur Walker-Jones, *The Green Psalter* (Louisville: Westminster John Knox, 2009), 136.

28. In Peter's speech at Pentecost in Acts 2:24, he describes Jesus' release from death after the crucifixion as λύσος τὰς ὠδῖνας τοῦ θανάτου. The word ὠδῖνας is the Septuagint translation of the Hebrew root חִיל. The Authorized Version (KJV) translates the phrase as "having loosed the pains (ὠδῖνας) of death."

Psalm 96:1-13 (cont.)

¹⁰Say among the nations, "The LORD is king!
The world is firmly established; it shall never be moved.
He will judge the peoples with equity."
¹¹Let the heavens be glad, and let the earth rejoice;
let the sea roar, and all that fills it;
¹²let the field exult, and everything in it.
Then shall all the trees of the forest sing for joy
¹³before the LORD; for he is coming, for he is coming to judge the earth.
He will judge the world with righteousness,
and the peoples with his truth.

Psalm 96:10 admonishes the hearer or reader to declare, "The LORD is king,"[29] and states that the (habitable) world that God birthed (Ps 90:2) is "firmly established [כון]" and "shall never be moved [מוט]," echoing the words of Psalm 93:1 in which the psalm singer assures her listeners that the habitable world (תבל) will not be moved (מוט) (v. 1) despite the threat of inundating waters in the form of crashing river waves and the thundering breakers of the great waters and the sea (v. 4). Psalm 95 reverses the threatened inundation and affirms that the sea belongs to him and "he made it," and Psalm 96 frames Psalm 93's assurance that the (habitable) world stands firm.

Verses 11-12 of Psalm 96 depict the earth's response to verse 9's call to participate in singing the "new song" to God: "Let the heavens be glad [שמח], and let the earth rejoice [גיל]; let the sea roar . . . the field exult . . . all the trees of the forest sing for joy [רנן]."[30] Framing the depiction of the earth's participation in the "new song" are verses 10 and 13, stating that God who reigns[31] will judge the peoples (עמים) and the (habitable) world in uprightness, righteousness, and truth. Such an affirmation of God's sovereignty over all provided the women and men living in exile in Babylon and those who returned to the land to live under Persian rule the needed motivation and encouragement to go on, to nurture new lives, to cherish old lives, and to trust that God would provide.[32]

---

29. For a discussion of God as "king/sovereign," see the excursus for Ps 93.
30. See the commentary on Ps 95:1.
31. See the commentary on Ps 93:1.
32. For a similar admonishment, see Jer 29:4-7.

Cosmic Humility:
An Ecological Virtue

Verses 11-12 of Psalm 96 call on the heavens to "be glad," the earth to "rejoice," the fields to "exult," and the trees of the forest to "sing for joy [רנן]." While such displays of exuberance are most often associated in the Hebrew Bible with humanity, nonhuman members of creation are also called to "be glad" (the heavens in 1 Chr 16:31 and the coastlands in Ps 97:1), to "rejoice" (the earth in 1 Chr 16:31; Ps 97:1; Isa 49:13), and, most frequently, "sing for joy [רנן]." In 1 Chronicles 16:33 and Psalm 96:12 the trees of the forest "sing for joy," and the wings of the ostrich do so in Job 39:13, as do Mount Tabor and Mount Hermon in Psalm 89:12, the mountains in Psalm 98:8, and the heavens and the earth in Jeremiah 51:48, suggesting that not just humanity but all of creation actively participates in God's ongoing creative acts. Thus, we might well ask, "What is humanity's place in creation?"

We begin at the beginning. In Genesis 1:28, God says to the newly formed human creatures: "Be fruitful and multiply, and fill the earth and subdue it; and have dominion over [רדה] . . . every living thing," conveying a sense of power and authority. Then, in Genesis 2:19, "So out of the ground the LORD God formed every animal of the field and every bird of the air, and brought them to the man [אדם, human] to see what the

man [אדם, human] would call them; and whatever the man [אדם, human] called every living creature, that was its name." Subdue, have dominion, name: it seems that humanity has something of a privileged, superior position in the created order. The theme continues in the Psalter. In Psalm 8:3-6 the psalmist marvels:

> When I look at your heavens,
>   the work of your fingers,
>   the moon and the stars that
>   you have established;
> what are human beings that you
>   are mindful of them,
>   mortals that you care for
>   them?
> Yet you have made them a
>   little lower than God [or "the
>   gods"]. . . .
> You have given them dominion
>   over the works of your
>   hands.

In Psalm 8, however, the word translated "dominion" is not רדה but משל, which means "to rule over" and, interestingly, "to be wise about." The use of משל in Psalm 8 provides a needed corrective insight into the language of Genesis 1. It suggests that humanity is not given *carte blanche* to "have dominion" over the earth but rather to rule over it wisely, choosing to preserve the earth's natural resources and animal habitats rather than destroying them to build and sustain habitats for ourselves, honoring the earth rather than using it for our devices.

In *The Bible and Ecology* Richard Bauckham, a professor at the University of St. Andrews in Scotland, writes:

> The image of a community of creation, in which we humans are fellow-members with God's other creatures, is a helpful way of synthesizing important aspects of the relevant biblical material. It also provides a broader context within which to situate the special and distinctive roles of humans in creation, recognizing these without lifting humans out of creation as though we were demi-gods set over it. All God's creatures are first and foremost creatures, ourselves included. All earthly creatures share the same Earth, and all participate in an interrelated and interdependent community.[33]

The enthronement psalms convey Bauckham's sentiments well. Psalm 93, which, incidentally, never mentions humanity, celebrates the firm stability of the world (v. 2) that God birthed (Ps 90:2)—it shall never be shaken. In verses 3 and 4, though the floods lift up their voices with roaring, God is more majestic than the thunders of mighty waters.

Psalm 95 invites humanity to join in the joyful noise, adding its voice to the voice of the pounding waves because "In [God's] hand are the depths of the earth; the heights of the mountains are [God's] also. The sea is [God's], for [God] made it, and the dry land, which [God's] hands have formed." In Psalm 96 the psalmist calls on the whole earth to sing to the Lord a new song and tremble (or dance, חיל) before God. The voice and actions of humanity mix with the voice and actions of all creation in a celebration of God's rule over the world. And in Psalm 97, Psalm 96's call to sing and tremble (or dance) is realized.

Over and over again in the enthronement psalms in book 4 not just humanity but all of creation celebrates God's sovereignty over the created world. Nowhere in their words is there any reference to a superior position of humanity within creation. We humans and this world around us, all of us, are God's good creation, placed on this earth for a purpose, a part of the larger divine directive. In this view what is the meaning of the words "subdue" and "have dominion," of being "co-creators"?

How do we proceed? Should humanity intervene in threatened extinctions of various species of plants and animals? Should humanity assume the role of "God" in maintaining the cosmic order? Or should humanity accept that there is a natural ebb and flow to the

---

33. Richard Bauckham, *The Bible and Ecology* (Waco, TX: Baylor University Press, 2010), 64.

cosmos? And ought we to accept that while we can control many things there are many things we cannot? Richard Bauckham writes again:

> Cosmic humility is a much needed ecological virtue. We need the humility to recognize that our place in the world is a limited one. We need the humility to "walk more lightly upon the Earth, with more regard for the life around us." We need the humility to recognize the unforeseeable risks of technology before we ruin the world in pursuit of technological fixes to all our problems. We need the humility to know ourselves as creatures within creation, not gods over creation, the humility of knowing that only God is God.[34]

Nancy L. deClaissé-Walford

Psalm 97

Psalm 97 opens with the familiar words, "The LORD is king [reigns]"[35] and calls on the earth and the coastlands to rejoice and be glad. It continues in verses 2-5 with theophany language, describing God's ongoing presence in the created world: clouds and thick darkness, fire, lightnings, and mountains melting like wax. One of the most significant theophanic appearances of God in the Hebrew Bible is at Sinai in Exodus 19,[36] and thus the opening words of Psalm 97 are another call to the reader or hearer to remember the time of the wilderness wanderings (see the introduction, pp.liii–liv).

Verse 4 states that the earth ("habitable world," תבל) "trembles" in response to the presence of God, using the same verbal root (חיל) this commentator translated "birthed" in Psalm 90:2 (NRSV: "formed") and suggested could be translated in Psalm 96:9 as either "birth" or "twirl in dance." חיל occurs in the imperative in 96:9 but here in Psalm 97:4 in the imperfect with *vav*-consecutive. Thus the call to "birth" or "dance" in Psalm 96 is answered by a realization of that call in Psalm 97. The image of the habitable world "dancing" before God in Psalms 96 and 97 conjures up the image of Exodus 15:20-21, where the prophet Miriam leads the women in dance (a noun derived from חיל/חול) to celebrate the defeat of the Egyptians whom God "has thrown into the sea." The

---

34. Ibid., 46.
35. For a discussion of God as "king," see the excursus for Ps 93.
36. Other examples include 1 Kgs 19; Ezek 1; and Ps 18.

Psalm 97:1-12

¹The LORD is king! Let the earth rejoice;
  let the many coastlands be glad!
²Clouds and thick darkness are all
    around him;
  righteousness and justice are the
    foundation of his throne.
³Fire goes before him,
  and consumes his adversaries on
    every side.
⁴His lightnings light up the world;
  the earth sees and trembles.
⁵The mountains melt like wax before
    the LORD,
  before the Lord of all the earth.
⁶The heavens proclaim his
    righteousness;
  and all the peoples behold his
    glory.
⁷All worshipers of images are put to
    shame,

those who make their boast in
    worthless idols;
  all gods bow down before him.
⁸Zion hears and is glad,
  and the towns of Judah rejoice,
  because of your judgments, O
    God.
⁹For you, O LORD, are most high over
    all the earth;
  you are exalted far above all
    gods.
¹⁰The LORD loves those who hate evil;
  he guards the lives of his faithful;
  he rescues them from the hand of
    the wicked.
¹¹Light dawns for the righteous,
  and joy for the upright in heart.
¹²Rejoice in the LORD, O you
    righteous,
  and give thanks to his holy name!

creator God, who overcame the watery chaos at creation (Gen 1:2) and "birthed" the earth and the habitable world (Ps 90:2), controls the waters[37] and delivers the people from Egypt. And the women, very much a part of the habitable world, lead out in dance.

A connection with the Exodus narrative is strengthened by the repeated mention in Psalms 96 and 97 of "other gods." Psalm 96:5 states: "All the gods of the peoples are idols [אלילים, literally 'worthless things']," and Psalm 97:7, "All worshipers of images are put to shame, those who make their boast in worthless idols [אלילים]." In Exodus 7 Moses demonstrated to Pharaoh and his magicians that YHWH is, in the words of Psalm 97:9, "most high over all the earth; . . . exalted far above all gods."[38]

The women of the exodus, who danced with timbrels, gave hope to the women and men living in Babylon that the same God who delivered

---

37. See also Ps 95:8-11, where the psalmist reminds her readers and hearers of God's provision of water during the wilderness wandering.

38. See Exod 7:1-13 and Pss 95:3 and 96:4.

them at the Reed Sea could and would deliver them from their exile on the shores of the Euphrates River. Psalm 97:8 says: "Zion hears and is glad [שָׂמַח], and the towns [בְּנוֹת, daughters] of Judah rejoice." שׂמח occurs four times in Psalm 97, in verses 1, 11, and 12 (see also Pss 96:11 and 100:2). In Psalm 90:14-15 the psalm singers ask for God's steadfast love so that "we may . . . be glad [שָׂמַח] all our days" and additionally that God "make us glad [רנן]." The gladness requested of God by the singers of Psalm 90 is realized in the praise of Psalm 97, celebrating God's reign over Zion (Jerusalem), the towns of Judah, and all gods.

Psalm 98

The singer of Psalm 98, as does the singer of Psalm 96, calls the people to sing to YHWH "a new song" (שִׁיר חָדָשׁ) and, like Psalm 95, attributes the song to YHWH's "victory" (ישׁע). ישׁע occurs nearly fifty times in the Psalter and is variously translated as "salvation," "deliverance," "help," "protection," "victory." It appears three times in Psalm 98. In verse 1 the psalm singer proclaims that YHWH's right hand and holy arm have achieved "victory,"[39] in verse 2 that the Lord has made known his "victory," and in verse 3 that all the ends of the earth have seen the "victory" of God. Thus we observe a movement in Psalm 98 of the promise of "victory" (ישׁע)—from being told of it to knowing it to actually experiencing it.

In verses 4-8, Psalm 98 calls on the people and all of creation to "make a joyful noise" (רוע in vv. 4 and 6), "sing" (רנן in vv. 4 and 8), and "sing praises" (זמר in vv. 4 and 5), echoing the words of Psalm 95:1-2.[40] The words of praise in Psalm 98, though, move beyond the praise of Psalm 95, incorporating the lyre, trumpets, and the horn (shofar) (vv. 5 and 6).

Psalm 98 concludes with echoes of Psalms 95 and 96—the sea and the floods that thunder and clap their hands and the hills that sing (vv. 7 and 8; see Pss 95:4-5 and 96:11-12), followed by the assurance that God has come to judge the (habitable) world (תבל) in righteousness and the peoples with equity (v. 9; see Ps 96:10, 13). The assurance of YHWH's victory (vv. 2-3) and the promise that YHWH will judge the entire world and all the peoples provided the women and men in exile in Babylon and those who returned to the land after the exile and lived under Persian

---

39. See similar language in Isa 52:10.
40. For a full treatment of these words, see the comment on Pss 95:1-2 and 103:8.

Psalm 98:1-9

A Psalm

[1]O sing to the LORD a new song,
  for he has done marvelous things.
His right hand and his holy arm
  have gotten him victory.
[2]The LORD has made known his victory;
  he has revealed his vindication in
    the sight of the nations.
[3]He has remembered his steadfast
    love and faithfulness
  to the house of Israel.
All the ends of the earth have seen
  the victory of our God.
[4]Make a joyful noise to the LORD, all
    the earth;
  break forth into joyous song and
    sing praises.

[5]Sing praises to the LORD with the lyre,
  with the lyre and the sound of
    melody.
[6]With trumpets and the sound of the
    horn
  make a joyful noise before the
    King, the LORD.
[7]Let the sea roar, and all that fills it;
  the world and those who live in it.
[8]Let the floods clap their hands;
  let the hills sing together for joy
[9]at the presence of the LORD, for he is
    coming
  to judge the earth.
He will judge the world with
    righteousness,
  and the peoples with equity.

rule with confidence of a secure future despite the exigencies of life. Thus the "new song" celebrates YHWH's goodness to the people in the past and offers a firm promise for the future.

Psalm 99

Psalm 99 begins with the familiar words "The LORD is king [sovereign],"[41] but it introduces a number of new concepts to that theme. Perhaps the most prominent feature of the psalm is its seemingly exclusive concern with the welfare of the Israelite people and Zion (vv. 2, 4-6, 9) as opposed to a concern for all peoples (see Pss 96:7, 10 and 98:9). In addition, it does not mention the habitable world (תבל, see Pss 93:1; 96:10, 13; 97:4; 98:7, 9), creation's celebration of YHWH (see Pss 93:3-4; 95:4-5; 96:11-12; 97:1-6; 98:4, 7-8), or water, a recurring motif in the enthronement psalms (see Pss 93:3-4; 95:5, 8-9; 96:11; 98:7-8).

Verse 1 of Psalm 99 contains seemingly familiar words: "let the peoples tremble." While the NRSV translation of "tremble" appears to echo the words of Psalms 96:9 and 97:4, the word translated "tremble" in 99:1 is

41. For a discussion of God as "king/sovereign," see the excursus for Ps 93.

Psalm 99:1-9

[1]The Lord is king; let the peoples
tremble!
He sits enthroned upon the
cherubim; let the earth
quake!
[2]The Lord is great in Zion;
he is exalted over all the
peoples.
[3]Let them praise your great and
awesome name.
Holy is he!
[4]Mighty King, lover of justice,
you have established equity;
you have executed justice
and righteousness in Jacob.
[5]Extol the Lord our God;
worship at his footstool.
Holy is he!

[6]Moses and Aaron were among his
priests,
Samuel also was among those
who called on his name.
They cried to the Lord, and he
answered them.
[7]He spoke to them in the pillar of
cloud;
they kept his decrees,
and the statutes that he gave
them.
[8]O Lord our God, you answered them;
you were a forgiving God to them,
but an avenger of their
wrongdoings.
[9]Extol the Lord our God,
and worship at his holy mountain;
for the Lord our God is holy.

a different Hebrew word than the "tremble" we encounter in 96:9 and
97:4.[42] Here the word is רגז, which means "tremble, quake, be afraid."
The admonition is issued not to "the people" but to "the peoples" (עמים),
thus not to the people of Israel but to all peoples.[43] The words preface
the declaration that the Lord is the God of Zion, who establishes justice,
equity, and righteousness in Jacob (v. 4), resuming the promises issued
in Psalms 96:10, 13; 97:2; 98:9, but adding the note that while YHWH is
God over all peoples (v. 2), Israel has become God's special possession
(vv. 6-8).

Verses 6-9 recall the time of the wilderness wandering and the initial
settlement in the land of promise, thereby bringing many of the themes
in book 4 in general and the enthronement psalms in particular full circle.
Moses is a prominent figure and voice in book 4, with Psalm 90's ascrip-
tion to Moses setting the stage for reading the book in the context of the
wilderness wanderings. Psalm 93's fivefold repetition of "YHWH," the

42. See the commentaries on Pss 90:2; 96:9; 97:4.
43. See also Ps 97:7, 10.

personal name of God given at the burning bush (in vv. 1, 3, 4, and 5), reinforces the Moses connection, as do Psalm 94's echoes of Moses's last words to the people in Deuteronomy 32–33 and the story of the waters of Meribah and Massah in Psalm 95. In Psalm 96:9 the reader or hearer is invited into the celebration of Exodus 15, when the women led out in dance and song after crossing the Reed Sea, while the theophany language in Psalm 97 recalls the Israelites' encounter with Yhwh at Mount Sinai, "his holy mountain" (Ps 99:7, 9). Psalm 98's threefold declaration of the victory of Yhwh provides the assurance of continued care in the exilic and postexilic lives of the people, and Psalm 99 reaffirms the special position of God's chosen possession.

Psalm 100

While Psalm 100 is classified as a Hymn of Praise rather than as an enthronement psalm, it is a fitting conclusion to this grouping of psalms in book 4, with numerous parallels to the psalms that precede it.[44] The superscription's opening word, "a psalm," is from the Hebrew root זמר, which occurs in Psalms 95:2 and 98:4, 5 (translated in the NRSV as "sing praises"). Verse 1's "make a joyful noise [רוע]" parallels the invitation given to the readers or hearers in Psalms 95:1 and 98:4, 6. שׂמח, translated as "gladness" in Psalm 100:2, occurs also in Psalms 96:11 and 97:1, 8 as "glad," in 97:11 as "joy," and in 97:12 as "rejoice." The call to sing (רנן) echoes the repeated call to sing ("give a ringing cry") in Psalms 90:14; 92:5; 95:1; 96:12; 98:4, 8.

Verse 3 of Psalm 100 admonishes readers or hearers to "know" that God made us and we belong to God, and then invites us into the "gates" (שׁער) and the "courts" (חצר), the very courts in which Psalm 92:13-14 promised that the righteous, like the palm tree and the cedar of Lebanon, would be planted and would flourish, "always green and full of sap." The closing words of the psalm are words of confident praise that Yhwh is good, with steadfast love (חסד)[45] and faithfulness to all generations—those living in exile in Babylon, those who returned from the exile and dwelt as vassals of the Persian Empire, and those enduring various "exilic" life situations today.

---

44. See Tate, *Psalms 51–100*, 535; and Wallace, *The Narrative Effect of Book Four*, 47–48.
45. For a discussion of חסד, see the commentaries for Pss 92:2 and 103:8.

Psalm 100:1-5

A Psalm of thanksgiving.

¹Make a joyful noise to the LORD, all
the earth.
²Worship the LORD with gladness;
come into his presence with
singing.
³Know that the LORD is God.
It is he that made us, and we are
his;
we are his people, and the sheep
of his pasture.
⁴Enter his gates with thanksgiving,
and his courts with praise.
Give thanks to him, bless his name.
⁵For the LORD is good;
his steadfast love endures forever,
and his faithfulness to all
generations.

Inclusive Praise Silences Oppression

Psalm 100 is a call to all the earth, to everything and everyone in it to make a joyful noise to the Lord. The call is inclusive and holistic, since praise is at its most complete when made by all creation. In contrast, in Psalm 137:4, we find people protesting against singing praise to the Lord when they find themselves in a position of oppression, weakness, and repression. They ask: "How can we sing the Lord's song when our position of belonging is compromised?" Oppression silences the call to joyfully praise the Lord. When we are complete we respond fully to the call of Psalm 100. We should do so not only by coming to God with joyful praise but also by not hindering others from coming to God with the same exultation we enjoy.

I grew up in the most divided society in the world. Until the end of apartheid in 1994, segregation that divided people on the basis of their race was the law in South Africa. Each was not allowed to be a part of the other (part of the whole). This segregation and resultant idea of the superiority of one race over another was theologically justified by most white churches. Though the unjust laws of apartheid fell upon all, they were most felt by women and children. Somehow my father managed to shield his family from the negative outlook toward people of color that prevailed in our country. On his farm my father treated his employees with respect, living by the philosophy that "you must work for your workers." My father's attitude toward the black farmworkers transformed us. Though I was as aware then as I am now of my privilege as a white female in South Africa, I did not view being white as justification for undermining or oppressing others; instead, it was to be a tool to uplift and advocate for social cohesion.

Apartheid is no longer the law in South Africa, but it seems that the South African people still find it difficult to respond to a call made in verse 1 of Psalm 100. The Bible teaches us about a God who not only gives life but also enables human beings to be most fully themselves. To be able to fully appreciate this assertion we need an understanding of the Bible that is particularly sensitive to the complexities of race, class, gender, and issues of inclusivity in our world. If the entire creation is called to "make a joyful noise" to the Lord, then the voices of the marginalized as well as the privileged must be heard and recognized.

In verse 3, Psalm 100 gives a fourfold rationale for the call to make a "joyful noise": the Lord is God, the Lord made us, we belong to the Lord, and we are the sheep of the Lord's pasture. The psalmist confronts the reader or hearer with the reality of God's sovereignty. The affirmation that we were made by and therefore belong to something greater than ourselves challenges any form of authority that might try to impose restrictions or rules concerning how, where, or when someone can praise the Lord based on gender, race, age, or social status. We are not self-made; we are created by God and we belong to God alone.

Verse 4 of Psalm 100 issues a collective call to all worshipers to enter into the Lord's gates and courts, reminding the reader or hearer that praise is a communal act. We are not autonomous individuals; instead we are called to live, work, play, and worship in community. In response to the call to worship we must continually ask ourselves whom we are leaving behind, whom we are excluding, whom we are ignoring when we enter the gates and the courts. What unwritten rules do we have; what hidden prejudices do we carry; what are the unspoken structures of society that foster exclusion, that undermine people coming together as a whole to praise the creator and sustainer God? As long as racism, sexism, classism, and all forms of marginalization persist, no part of creation can be truly free to "make a joyful noise" to the Lord.

My father's openness to and respect for others has informed how I understand God and how I relate to the people around me, whether on the street where I live, in the shopping malls of Pretoria, or in the university library helping students find resources for course work. If we truly desire to respond to the call to praise the God who made all things (Gen 1), we must be prepared to embrace all of God's good creation. "The earth is the LORD's, and all that is in it, the world, and those who live in it" (Ps 24:1). The joyful praise unto God must come from the acknowledgment that God is the Lord and that we are the sheep of God's pasture; we belong to God. Together, as all of God's good creation, we must praise God with a joyful noise.

Christine Nel

Psalms 93–100: Concluding Words

The enthronement psalms reflect the language and culture of the societies within which they were composed and handed on generation after
generation. For interpreters in the twenty-first century, that must be the
starting point for reading and appropriating the texts. But the process
does not stop there. We can "read against" the text, asking questions
about what the text does *not* say and posing questions that perhaps the
text was never intended to answer. Then we can "read through" the text,
seeking out new understandings of traditional language and allowing the
metaphoric language to speak to us in our own contexts. So where do we
begin? Can we discover a deeper, more robust understanding of the God
of the Psalter through the words of the enthronement psalms of book 4?

The enthronement psalms are the heart of book 4, which, according
to the storyline of the Psalter, is set in the exilic period of the life of ancient Israel but calls on the people to recall the exodus and wilderness
wanderings of their ancestors. The Babylonian exile and the wilderness
wanderings were "bookends," both times when the people of YHWH were
outside the land of promise, waiting to return to that land. These were
undoubtedly times of great insecurity and questioning for the people.
If we listen closely to the words of the enthronement psalms, though,
some profoundly "settling" and "secure" ideas confront us.

First, these psalms emphasize the sovereignty of God over and over
with the words "The LORD is king" (מלך, "reigns") in Psalms 93:1; 96:10;
97:1; 99:1, and this sovereignty extends not only to the people of Israel
but to all peoples (עמים in Pss 96:7, 10; 98:9; 99:2) and all creation (תבל,
"the habitable world," in Pss 93:1; 96:10, 13; 97:4; 98:7, 9). Second, if we
embrace the full meaning of the verb חיל, first encountered in Psalm 90:2
and again in Psalms 96:9 and 97:4, and picture God "birthing" the (habitable) world and all creation, then the call to humanity and all creation
in Psalm 96:9 to "dance" or "birth" that is realized in Psalm 97:4 reflects
creation's shared responsibility to care for and celebrate the created world
over which God is sovereign.[46] Third, the singers of the enthronement
psalms repeatedly call on humanity and all creation to "sing, give a ringing
cry" (רנן) to the Lord: "us" in Psalm 95:1; "the trees of the forest" in 96:12;
"all the earth" in 98:4; "the hills" in 98:8. The call to "sing, give a ringing
cry" is for all—all humanity and all creation, even what we consider to
be inanimate objects. And recall that in the book of Proverbs, Wisdom

---

46. See commentary on Ps 96:9.

"sings, gives a ringing cry" (Prov 1:20) and, according to Proverbs 8, participates with God in the creation of the inhabited world (תבל) and delights (שעשעי) in humanity.

What can we learn from the enthronement psalms? The opening words of Psalm 90 ponder humanity's place within creation. Over and over in book 4 we encounter language that addresses the question: what is the relationship between humanity and the rest of creation? The Israelites living in exile in Babylon and those who wandered for forty years in the wilderness certainly questioned their place within the created order. The words of the enthronement psalms reminded the people of their groundedness, the very essence of their being.

Psalms 101–104

In the Midst of My Anguish, Let Me Walk with Integrity

Psalms 101–104 are an interesting mix of psalm types and themes that can be somewhat puzzling when attempting to read the psalms in book 4 as a purposeful collection (see the introduction, pp. liii–liv). How do these psalms contribute to the "storyline" of book 4? Further, what is their message?

The four psalms can be read in pairs, Psalm 101 paired with Psalm 102 and Psalm 103 with Psalm 104.[1] This four-psalm grouping should not, however, be read in isolation from the psalms surrounding them. Psalm 101, for example, is an apt sequel to Psalm 100, the concluding psalm of the enthronement grouping, offering words of confident trust in Yhwh's "loyalty" (חסד). The opening words of Psalm 102 (vv. 1-11) offer a stark contrast to the sentiment of Psalm 101, but the psalm singer returns in verse 12 to words affirming the enduring reign of Yhwh as sovereign. Psalm 103, a celebration of God's care for humanity, "heightens the theme sounded in Psalm 102 of Yhwh's mercy as the fundamental power of

---

1. Erich Zenger, "The God of Israel's Reign over the World (Psalms 90–106)," in *The God of Israel and the Nations: Studies in Isaiah and the Psalms*, ed. Norbert Lohfink and Erich Zenger, trans. Everett R. Kalin (Collegeville, MN: Liturgical Press, 2000), 161–90, at 183–85.

YHWH's reign."[2] Psalm 104 continues the theme of God's mercy and sovereignty, but in the spirit of the enthronement psalms (Pss 93–100) expands God's mercy and sovereignty to all creation. Psalms 105 and 106, treated in the next chapter, return to the theme of God's mercy to humanity, but with historical reminders of humanity's past encounters with God's mercy and sovereignty.

Psalm 101

Psalm 101's superscription, "Of David. A Psalm [לדוד מזמור]," connects it with Psalm 103, the only other psalm in book 4 attributed to David, and with Psalm 100's superscription, "A Psalm of thanksgiving." Psalm 101 answers Psalm 100's call to all the earth to "make a joyful noise" (רוע, 100:1) and to come into the presence of YHWH "with singing" (רנן, 100:2), with the psalm singer's declaration that she will "sing [שיר and זמר]" to YHWH. Although the verbal roots for the expression of praise to YHWH are not the same in Psalms 100 and 101, each word occurs numerous times in Psalms 90–99. The reader or hearer encounters רוע in Psalms 95:1, 2 and 98:4, 6; רנן in 90:14; 92:5; 95:1; 96:12; 98:4, 8; שיר in 92:1; 96:1, 2; 98:1; and זמר in 92:2; 95:2; 98:4, 5.

In addition, Psalm 100:5's proclamation that YHWH's steadfast love (חסד) endures forever is echoed in Psalm 101:1's declaration, "I will sing of loyalty [חסד]." The decision of the NRSV to translate חסד in different ways in the two psalms masks the connection between the two psalms.

The singer of Psalm 101 states in verse 2 that her intent is to "study the way that is blameless [תמים]" and "walk with integrity [תם]." The result of that study is, first, that she will not condone the acts described in verses 3-5 and 7; second, that she will be well-disposed to anyone who "walks in the way that is blameless" (תמים, v. 6); and third, that she will destroy all of the wicked and cut off all the evildoers from the city (v. 8).

Many scholars maintain that the words of Psalm 101 were originally composed and used at the inauguration of a king of Israel or at a celebration of kingship.[3] In the context of book 4, J. Clinton McCann further

---

2. Ibid., 185.

3. See, for example, John Goldingay, *Psalms*, vol. 3: *Psalms 90–150*, BCOT (Grand Rapids: Baker Academic, 2008), 139; James L. Mays, *Psalms*, IBC (Louisville: Westminster John Knox, 1994), 321; J. Clinton McCann Jr., "The Book of Psalms," in *NIB*, vol. 4 (Nashville: Abingdon, 1996), 1081; Robert E. Wallace, *The Narrative Effect of Book Four of the Hebrew Psalter*, StBibLit 112 (New York: Peter Lang, 2007), 53.

Psalm 101:1-8

Of David. A Psalm.

¹I will sing of loyalty and of justice;
　to you, O Lord, I will sing.
²I will study the way that is blameless.
　When shall I attain it?
I will walk with integrity of heart
　within my house;
³I will not set before my eyes
　anything that is base.
I hate the work of those who fall
　away;
　it shall not cling to me.
⁴Perverseness of heart shall be far
　from me;
　I will know nothing of evil.
⁵One who secretly slanders a
　neighbor

I will destroy.
A haughty look and an arrogant heart
　I will not tolerate.
⁶I will look with favor on the faithful in
　the land,
　so that they may live with me;
whoever walks in the way that is
　blameless
　shall minister to me.
⁷No one who practices deceit
　shall remain in my house;
no one who utters lies
　shall continue in my presence.
⁸Morning by morning I will destroy
　all the wicked in the land,
cutting off all evildoers
　from the city of the Lord.

suggests that its words are the "voice of an imagined future king" who says, "in effect, 'I shall do everything right,' implying that the monarchy should be restored."⁴ Erhard Gerstenberger offers another suggestion for the provenance of the psalm, maintaining that its language and imagery "point to the early Jewish community, not to monarchic society, as the original setting," and thus it is "a portrait of the ideal believer in Yahweh."⁵

Interpretations of Psalm 101 abound, but a common thread is the suggestion that the psalm singer is someone, real or imagined, who has authority over and responsibility for house (בַּיִת, vv. 2, 7), land (אֶרֶץ, v. 6), and city (עִיר, v. 8). While the so-called original setting for the psalm may have been the royal court, in its position in book 4 Psalm 101 conveys a broader message. The psalms that precede it remind humanity that we are part of a larger, intertwined, and complex world (Pss 93–100), one that God birthed (Ps 90:2), nurtures, and cares for (Ps 91), and with the promise that the righteous will be planted in the house (בַּיִת) of the Lord (Ps 92:13). The words of Psalm 101, then, may be heard as those of the

---

4. McCann, "The Book of Psalms," 1081.

5. Erhard S. Gerstenberger, *Psalms, Part 2, and Lamentations*, FOTL 15 (Grand Rapids: Eerdmans, 2001), 209.

righteous person seeking to share in the nurturing and care of God's world and thereby sounding a clarion cry to all who have authority or responsibility—no matter how great or small—to heed its words.[6]

We have only to open our web browsers, turn on the news, or pick up the morning newspaper to read or hear about those with responsibility and authority who, in their own best interest rather than in the interest of those for whom they are responsible, demonstrate perverseness of heart (v. 4), slander a neighbor (v. 5), have a haughty look and an arrogant heart (v. 5), or practice deceit and utter lies (v. 7). The list is endless: human traffickers, domestic abusers, self-centered political entities, the careless rich, corporate machines, drug cartels, animal poachers, racial cleansers.

Psalm 101 calls humanity "back from the brink" of self-aggrandizement toward the nurture and care for all of God's created world. The psalm can "be understood as an articulation of the values that God wills to be concretely embodied among humans."[7] Those values are summed up in the word translated "loyalty" in verse 2, the Hebrew word חסד—the covenant agreement made between God and the Israelites at Sinai. In Exodus 19:5 God says to the people: "If you obey my voice and keep my covenant, you shall be my treasured possession."[8] Further, Psalm 101 provides a "way," a "path" to that end—via wisdom. Wisdom themes in Psalm 101 include "study" (שכל, v. 2), "way" (דרך, vv. 2, 6), "blamelessness" (תמים, vv. 2, 6), "integrity" (תמים, תם, v. 2), "deceit" (רמיה, v. 7), "lies" (שקרים, v. 7), and "wicked" (רשעים, v. 8).[9]

The wisdom language of Psalm 101 points the reader or hearer to the words of Woman Wisdom in the book of Proverbs who was there at creation, "rejoicing in [God's] inhabited world and delighting in the human race" (Prov 8:31). In the book of Psalms, Wisdom is equated with Torah, which is depicted as the "way" or "path" of the righteous in Psalm 119.[10] William P. Brown writes: "The metaphor of the pathway 'maps' both

6. See Nancy L. deClaissé-Walford, Rolf A. Jacobson, and Beth LaNeel Tanner, *The Book of Psalms*, NICOT (Grand Rapids: Eerdmans, 2014), 747; Goldingay, *Psalms 90–150*, 145; Mays, *Psalms*, 322.

7. McCann, "The Book of Psalms," 1083.

8. For a full discussion of חסד see the commentary for Pss 92 and 103.

9. For occurrences of שכל—translated in the *hiphil* stem in v. 2—in the wisdom literature of the Hebrew Bible, often translated "be wise" or "be prudent," see Prov 1:3; 12:8; 15:24. For "way [דרך]," see Ps 1:1; 119:30; Prov 6; 23; 14:2. For "blameless [תמים, תם]," often translated "integrity" or "perfect," see Job 37:16; Ps 19:8; Prov 11:5; 28:18.

10. See the commentary for Ps 119, particularly vv. 1, 27, 29, 30, 32, and 33.

God's *tôrâ* and the speaker's response to *tôrâ*, imbuing them with a sense of dynamic, mutual engagement."[11] Thus those who seek to embody and enact the words of Psalm 101 have a dialogic "pathway" to that end.

Psalm 102

The words of Psalm 102 are a stark contrast to the words of Psalm 101. Its superscription introduces us to the singer of the psalm who, in a rather lengthy composition, voices anguish intermingled with words of hope. How may we understand the juxtaposition of Psalms 101 and 102? Commentators who place the origins of Psalm 101 at the inauguration of a king of Israel maintain that Psalm 101 presents an idealized future Davidic ruler who vows to have nothing to do with those who are perverse of heart (v. 4), slanderers (v. 5), and deceivers and liars (v. 7); in fact the singer of the psalm states that they will be destroyed and cut off from the city of YHWH (v. 8).

The singer of Psalm 102 laments that her days pass away like smoke (v. 3); her bones cling to her skin (v. 5) and burn like a furnace (v. 3); she is like an owl in the wilderness (v. 6) and a lonely bird on the housetop (v. 7); her enemies taunt her and curse her name (v. 8); she eats ashes for bread and mingles tears with her drink (v. 9); she withers away like grass (v. 11). Where is the fulfillment of the promise to destroy and cut off the wicked and the evildoers (Ps 101:8) so that the faithful may live in the land (Ps 101:6)?

The one to whom the psalm singer cries out in the midst of her suffering, though, is not an imagined future human ruler but YHWH.[12] Her accusations are harsh: YHWH in indignation and anger has lifted her up and thrown her aside (v. 10); YHWH has broken her strength in midcourse (v. 23). In its place in book 4, Psalm 102 may be read as the communal words of the people of Israel—though voiced by an individual—reflecting on their exilic situation.[13] They no longer have a king to hold accountable for what is happening. The preceding enthronement psalms (Pss 93–100)

11. William P. Brown, *Seeing the Psalms: A Theology of Metaphor* (Louisville: Westminster John Knox, 2002), 33.

12. Wallace, *The Narrative Effect of Book Four*, 60.

13. See McCann, "The Book of Psalms," 1086; Wallace, *The Narrative Effect of Book Four*, 59; Leslie C. Allen, *Psalms 101–150*, WBC 21 (Nashville: Thomas Nelson, 2002), 16. Allen writes: "A bewildering multiplicity of interpretations have been offered for this complex psalm."

Psalm 102:1-28

A prayer of one afflicted, when faint and
pleading before the Lord.

¹Hear my prayer, O LORD;
   let my cry come to you.
²Do not hide your face from me
   in the day of my distress.
Incline your ear to me;
   answer me speedily in the day
      when I call.
³For my days pass away like smoke,
   and my bones burn like a furnace.
⁴My heart is stricken and withered
      like grass;
   I am too wasted to eat my bread.
⁵Because of my loud groaning
   my bones cling to my skin.

⁶I am like an owl of the wilderness,
   like a little owl of the waste places.
⁷I lie awake;
   I am like a lonely bird on the
      housetop.
⁸All day long my enemies taunt me;
   those who deride me use my
      name for a curse.
⁹For I eat ashes like bread,
   and mingle tears with my drink,
¹⁰because of your indignation and
      anger;
   for you have lifted me up and
      thrown me aside.
¹¹My days are like an evening shadow;
   I wither away like grass.

celebrate God as sovereign rather than an earthly ruler; thus the people turn to YHWH. They call on YHWH to hear their prayer and their cry, not to hide YHWH's face from them, to incline the ear and answer (vv. 1-2).

The psalm singer contrasts the transience of her life with the enduring years of YHWH (v. 24) through numerous allusions to Psalms 90–92. Twice in Psalm 102 the psalmist says she withers like the grass in the evening (עשׂב, vv. 4, 11), recalling the words of Psalm 90:5 and 6 and Psalm 92:7. In Psalm 102:23-24 the singer accuses God of "shortening" her days and beseeches God not to take her away "at the midpoint of my life" (v. 24), recalling the assertion in Psalm 90 that the duration of human life is seventy or eighty years, and "even then their span is only toil and trouble" (v. 10). Psalm 91:15-16, though, promises that those who love, know the name of, and call on YHWH will be satisfied with long life, and Psalm 92 states that the righteous will be planted in the house of YHWH and will always be green and full of sap (vv. 12-14).

The first eleven verses of Psalm 102 do not evince any of the hope expressed in Psalms 90–92, but, in the spirit of the lament psalms,[14] the

14. Psalms of lament can consist of five elements: (1) an invocation, in which the psalmist calls on the name of God; (2) a complaint, in which the psalmist tells God what is wrong; (3) a petition, in which the psalmist tells God what the psalmist wants

¹²But you, O Lᴏʀᴅ, are enthroned
forever;
your name endures to all
generations.
¹³You will rise up and have
compassion on Zion,
for it is time to favor it;
the appointed time has come.
¹⁴For your servants hold its stones
dear,
and have pity on its dust.
¹⁵The nations will fear the name of
the Lᴏʀᴅ,
and all the kings of the earth your
glory.
¹⁶For the Lᴏʀᴅ will build up Zion;
he will appear in his glory.

¹⁷He will regard the prayer of the
destitute,
and will not despise their prayer.
¹⁸Let this be recorded for a
generation to come,
so that a people yet unborn may
praise the Lᴏʀᴅ:
¹⁹that he looked down from his holy
height,
from heaven the Lᴏʀᴅ looked at
the earth,
²⁰to hear the groans of the prisoners,
to set free those who were
doomed to die;
²¹so that the name of the Lᴏʀᴅ may
be declared in Zion,
and his praise in Jerusalem,

address turns in verse 12 from words of lament to words of trust in
Yʜᴡʜ (vv. 12-14, 25-27) and a celebration of Yʜᴡʜ's promised goodness
(vv. 15-22, 28). Verse 12's assertion that Yʜᴡʜ is "enthroned forever"
(עולם ישב), verse 24's that Yʜᴡʜ's "years endure throughout all generations" (בדור דורים), and verse 27's that Yʜᴡʜ is "the same and [Yʜᴡʜ's]
years have no end" echo Psalm 90's words, "from everlasting to everlasting [מעולם עד־עולם] you are God" (v. 2), and Psalm 92's "You O Lᴏʀᴅ, are
on high forever" (מרום עולם, v. 8).

Verses 13-22 voice words of assurance that Yʜᴡʜ is enthroned as
sovereign over Zion and Jerusalem. The psalm singer states with confidence in verse 15 that "the nations" and "all the kings of the earth" will
fear the "name" and the "glory" of Yʜᴡʜ.

The words of verse 17 are particularly interesting in their context
within the psalm. The word translated "regard" (פנה) is a verb derived

---

God to do; (4) words of trust, in which the psalmist outlines the reasons for trusting that God can and will answer the psalmist's petition; and (5) words of praise,
in which the psalmist celebrates the goodness and sovereignty of God. See Nancy
L. deClaissé-Walford, *Introduction to the Psalms: A Song from Ancient Israel* (St. Louis:
Chalice Press, 2004), 23–25.

Psalm 102:1-28 (cont.)

²²when peoples gather together,
and kingdoms, to worship the Lᴏʀᴅ.
²³He has broken my strength in midcourse;
he has shortened my days.
²⁴"O my God," I say, "do not take me away
at the midpoint of my life,
you whose years endure throughout all generations."
²⁵Long ago you laid the foundation of the earth,
and the heavens are the work of your hands.
²⁶They will perish, but you endure;
they will all wear out like a garment.
You change them like clothing, and they pass away;
²⁷but you are the same, and your years have no end.
²⁸The children of your servants shall live secure;
their offspring shall be established in your presence.

from the Hebrew word "face," conveying the idea of Yʜᴡʜ "turning to face" the sound of the prayer of the psalm singer, referencing the plea to Yʜᴡʜ in verse 2, "do not hide your face [פָּנֶה]." The twofold occurrence of the word translated "prayer" (תְּפִלָּה) in verse 17 echoes the twofold occurrence of the word in the psalm's superscription and first verse. The word translated "despise" (בָּזָה) in verse 17 means literally "to raise the head loftily and disdainfully." That Yʜᴡʜ will not do so is a further confirmation that Yʜᴡʜ will "regard" (פָּנָה) the prayer of the destitute one and affirms the statement in verse 19 that Yʜᴡʜ "looked down from his holy height."

The words of Psalm 102 can thus be understood as the cries of the exilic Israelites to their God, questioning their present situation, but in the context of the twenty-first century they may be appropriated as the words of an individual or a community crying out to God for restoration of dignity and well-being in the face of abuse, despair, and deprivation, while those with responsibility and authority (see Ps 101) turn a blind eye. We hear in the words of Psalm 102 the voices of abused children and spouses, victims of human trafficking, families driven from their homes by acts of terrorism, hardworking people who cannot escape the cycle of poverty, activists constantly thwarted in their quest to preserve and maintain, and parents watching their children being absorbed into a life of drug abuse.

In the midst of the abuse, despair, and deprivation, though, the psalm singer finds hope. She still sees the worth of bringing her petitions before God (vv. 1-2), and she envisions a restoration of order and goodness—in

Psalm 102 couched in words of restoration, deliverance, and creation (vv. 18-22, 25-27). She sings, "Long ago you laid the foundations of the earth . . . your years have no end" (vv. 25 and 27) and reminds us that there is hope for "the children of your servants" and for "their offspring" (v. 28), affirming that God is "from everlasting to everlasting" (see Ps 90:2) and "on high forever" (see Ps 92:8).

When God Is Silent

"Hear my prayer, O Lord. . . . Do not hide your face from me in the day of my distress; . . . answer me speedily when I call."

Have you ever faced a life situation in which you could not find a way to describe to others what has happened or to express how you feel? Someone asks you what is going on and you cannot find words to describe your anguish. Silently, you call on God. But what if God seems silent; what if God's voice does not come to you? And what if time and time again you suffer in silence, and the voice of God seems silent? In my culture in South Africa, if something bad happens to you it must be because of some sin that you committed. So silence is easier than sharing your anguish with those who are likely to tell you that God is punishing you for something you have done—and in your own silence God can seem silent as well.

Psalm 102 is a cry by someone who is afflicted and overwhelmed, who pours out her anguish to God, demanding that God hear her lamenting words. Something tragic has happened, but the reader of the psalm is not given the details of the psalmist's anguish. When we are overwhelmed by utter anguish and oppression, giving a detailed description of the source of that anguish is so very often difficult. Thus, rather than outlining the details of the trauma surrounding her the psalm singer graphically describes how she feels in the midst of the anguish: her bones are burning and they cling to her flesh; her heart is withered; she is an owl in the wilderness, a lonely bird on a housetop.

From those whose experiences are too painful to express in their own words:

- women who have suffered endless abuse at the hands of the men in their lives—fathers, uncles, husbands
- children and teens who have been sexually abused by fathers, stepfathers, and uncles
- a young woman who is gang-raped at a party because "her skirt was too short"
- women and children who are sexually abused by trusted clergy
- women who bravely determine to leave

abusive relationships and are ostracized by their communities

So many times I have heard these words:

- "God was silent. He never replied to my prayer."
- "I asked him to stop them from raping me, but he did not."
- "For years I asked God to make this man stop, but God never listened; he left me suffering in this man's hands for years."
- "I thought God loves me. How can he allow this to happen to me?"

Psalm 102 gives words to those who long to cry out to a seemingly silent God, those who have no words of their own. Its words say: "Yes, we can cry out." "Yes, we can talk about how we feel, even if the details of what has happened to us are too painful to talk about." "Yes, we can demand that God listen and respond." God does not condone silence on our part in times of anguish any more than in times of praise. God invites persistent demands on our part that God hear, even when it seems to us that God is silent. So, with the singer of Psalm 102, keep crying out: "My strength is broken; my days are shortened; I eat ashes; I wither like grass."

Why? Because God does hear. Isaiah 59:1 assures us: "See, the LORD's hand is not too short to save, nor his ear too dull to hear." In Acts 10:31 Cornelius is assured that God has heard his prayers: "Cornelius, your prayer has been heard and your alms have been remembered before God." Daniel is also assured that God has heard his prayers: "Do not fear, Daniel, for from the first day that you set your mind to gain understanding and to humble yourself before your God, your words have been heard, and I have come because of your words" (Dan 10:12). Does God ever seem to be silent? Job laments the silence of God: "I cry to you and you do not answer me; I stand, and you merely look at me" (Job 30:20). The singer of Psalm 22:1 cries: "My God, my God, why have you forsaken me? Why are you so far from helping me, from the words of my groaning?"

When God seems to be silent it does not mean that God is not hearing our prayers. We have to allow ourselves to see God at work in our situation through the eyes of our faith. Maybe then we can start opening our ears in faith to hear God's voice through the silence.

The singer of Psalm 102, in the midst of her anguish, first acknowledges God's sovereignty over all: "But you, O LORD, are enthroned forever; your name endures to all generations" (v. 12), and then states confidently in verse 17, "He will regard the prayer of the destitute, and will not despise their prayer." In the midst of the traumatic situations for which there seem to be no words, find in the words of Psalm 102 a voice to express what seems inexpressible.

Lesego Temane

Psalm 103

The superscription of Psalm 103, like Psalm 101, attributes it to David, and thus Psalms 101 and 103 form something of a "framing" around Psalm 102. Erich Zenger's suggestion that Psalm 103 be read in conjunction with Psalm 104 further ties all four of the psalms together.[15] Psalm 101's cry for justice followed by Psalm 102's words of despair (vv. 1-11, 23-26) and then hope (vv. 12-22, 27-28) is met in Psalm 103 with words of the promise of wholeness. Zenger states, "Psalm 103 heightens the theme sounded in Psalm 102 of YHWH's mercy as the fundamental power of YHWH's reign."[16]

TRANSLATION MATTERS

The words "Bless the LORD" (ברך יהוה) open and close Psalm 103, in verses 1-2 and 20-22. In verses 1 and 2 the psalmist calls on the "soul" (נפש) to bless YHWH.

The most common English translation of נפש is "soul" (AV, NASB, NIV, NRSV, ESV). The concrete, basic meaning of the word is "throat," the organ that allows one to breathe, eat, and speak. It thus conveys much more than the Western idea of a disembodied "soul"; rather, this "soul" is one's very life force. In Genesis 2:7, when God creates the first human, God breathes into the human's nostrils the breath of life and the human becomes a נפש חיה, "a living being." Thus the נפש may be understood as the "all of who one is" and should perhaps be better translated as "inmost being" or "whole being."

Verses 20-22 expand the call to bless to YHWH's "angels" (מלאכים), "mighty ones" (גבור), "hosts" (צבאות), "ministers" (משרתים), and "all of YHWH's works" (מעשים).

The word "all" (כל) occurs seven times in the psalm (vv. 1, 2, 3, 6, 19, 20, and 21), particularly at its beginning and end, suggesting that the psalm singer intends for the psalm to be a comprehensive summary of all that YHWH has done and will continue to do as sovereign over the world (v. 19). J. Clinton McCann points out as well that while the psalm is not an acrostic, "its twenty-two lines—the number of letters in the Hebrew alphabet—also suggest the psalmist's intent is to say it all."[17] The acrostic

---

15. See the Introduction to Psalms 101–104 and Zenger, "The God of Israel's Reign," 185.

16. Ibid., 185.

17. McCann, "The Book of Psalms," 1090.

Psalm 103:1-22

Of David.

¹Bless the LORD, O my soul,
and all that is within me,
bless his holy name.
²Bless the LORD, O my soul,
and do not forget all his benefits—
³who forgives all your iniquity,
who heals all your diseases,
⁴who redeems your life from the Pit,
who crowns you with steadfast
love and mercy,
⁵who satisfies you with good as long
as you live
so that your youth is renewed like
the eagle's.
⁶The LORD works vindication
and justice for all who are
oppressed.

⁷He made known his ways to Moses,
his acts to the people of Israel.
⁸The LORD is merciful and gracious,
slow to anger and abounding in
steadfast love.
⁹He will not always accuse,
nor will he keep his anger forever.
¹⁰He does not deal with us according
to our sins,
nor repay us according to our
iniquities.
¹¹For as the heavens are high above
the earth,
so great is his steadfast love
toward those who fear him;
¹²as far as the east is from the west,
so far he removes our
transgressions from us.

poem (see, for example, Pss 111, 112, and 119, Prov 31, and the book of Lamentations) is a wisdom literary device that suggests the author has covered the subject from א to ת—from A to Z. Nothing more can be or need be said about it. In addition, by employing the acrostic form the poet has used all the letters of the Hebrew alphabet and so, while not actually using all the words in the Hebrew language, the poet has offered all of the possible words in the language to discuss the subject at hand.[18]

Following the initial call to the "soul" (נפש) to bless the Lord in verses 1 and 2, the psalmist continues in verses 3-7 with a series of active participles—indicating ongoing activity—outlining YHWH's generous care for humanity by "forgiving iniquity" and "healing diseases" (v. 3), "redeeming life" and "crowning with steadfast love and mercy" (v. 4), "satisfying with good" (v. 5, cp. Pss 90:14; 91:16), "working vindication and justice" (v. 6), and "making known YHWH's ways and acts" (v. 7).

Moses appears in verse 7, and verse 8 rehearses the self-descriptive words God spoke to Moses on Mount Sinai in Exodus 34:6 after the

18. Adele Berlin, "The Rhetoric of Psalm 145," in *Biblical and Related Studies Presented to Samuel Iwry*, ed. Ann Kort and Scott Morschauser (Winona Lake, IN: Eisenbrauns, 1985), 17–22, at 18.

¹³As a father has compassion for his children,
so the LORD has compassion for those who fear him.
¹⁴For he knows how we were made; he remembers that we are dust.
¹⁵As for mortals, their days are like grass;
they flourish like a flower of the field;
¹⁶for the wind passes over it, and it is gone,
and its place knows it no more.
¹⁷But the steadfast love of the LORD is from everlasting to everlasting
on those who fear him,
and his righteousness to children's children,
¹⁸to those who keep his covenant and remember to do his commandments.
¹⁹The LORD has established his throne in the heavens,
and his kingdom rules over all.
²⁰Bless the LORD, O you his angels, you mighty ones who do his bidding,
obedient to his spoken word.
²¹Bless the LORD, all his hosts, his ministers that do his will.
²²Bless the LORD, all his works, in all places of his dominion.
Bless the LORD, O my soul.

Golden Calf incident. First, YHWH is "merciful" (רחום). The word derives from the noun רחם, which means "womb." References to God's רחום, God's "womb-love," occur no fewer than twenty times in the book of Psalms, three times in Psalm 103 (vv. 4, 8, and 13).[19] Second, YHWH is "gracious" (חנון). The Hebrew verb literally means "to look kindly upon," in many cases where breaches of trust have taken place, as we see in the Golden Calf incident. The attribute is used almost exclusively in descriptions of YHWH in the Hebrew Bible and in concert with other descriptive terms, suggesting the multifaceted character of God.[20] Third, YHWH is "slow to anger." The God who birthed the earth and the habitable world (see Ps 90:2) loves its human inhabitants with the "womb-love" (רחום) of a mother, "looks kindly upon" (חנן) humanity, even when humanity has breached the trust of YHWH, and thus God is "slow to anger."

The source of God's attitude toward God's human creation is the final self-descriptive attribute, "steadfast love" (חסד). Occurring four times in Psalm 103 (vv. 4, 8, 11, and 17), חסד is a difficult word to render into English; it has to do with the relationship between two parties to an

19. See, for example, Pss 25:6; 40:11; 69:16; 77:9; 79:8; 103:13, and the introduction, pp. xliv–xlv.
20. Heinz-Josef Fabry, "חנן *ḥānan*," *TDOT*, 5:23, 30.

agreement, or, in the context of the Hebrew Bible, a covenant. God made a covenant with Abram in Genesis 15:18, and then, in Exodus 19:4-5, God and the people of Israel entered into a covenant relationship at Mount Sinai. God promised that the Israelites would be a treasured possession; they had only to keep God's covenant stipulations. We might say that חסד is about covenant relationship, the sacred agreement between God and God's people.[21] Thus Exodus 34 and Psalm 103 remind us that God is a God of womb-love and a God of covenant promise.

Verses 9-12 offer words of hope in answer to the despair expressed in Psalm 90:7-17. Verse 13 continues with a metaphoric comparison of Yhwh's "compassion" (רחם, "womb-love") to the compassion a "father" (אב) has for his children. This "mixed metaphor" demonstrates well the reason for Melody Knowles's caution about confining ourselves solely to finding biological sex-specific "female attributes and affinities" of God, such as womb-love (רחם).[22]

Verses 14-16 recall Psalm 90:3-6's lament over the transience of human life, with shared language that includes "dust" (עפר, 90:3), "mortals" (אנוש, 90:3), and "grass" (חציר, 90:5). Psalm 103, however, adds a note that God "knows how we were made; he remembers that we are dust" (v. 14). The word translated "made" is from the verbal root יצר, the same verbal root used in the description of the creation work of God in Genesis 2:7 and 19, and the word "dust" (עפר) is the substance out of which human-ity was "made" in Genesis 2:7. The added note in Psalm 103:14 turns the words of lament in Psalm 90:3 and 5 into words of hope—God knows (ידע); God remembers (זכר).

The concluding words of Psalm 103 affirm that hope. They remind the reader or hearer once again of God's "steadfast love" (חסד), the covenant fidelity between Yhwh and the people, and they return to the theme of the enthronement psalms, Yhwh's sovereignty over all creation (v. 19). The psalm ends as it begins, first calling for blessing on Yhwh, this time not by an individual "soul" (vv. 1 and 2) but by both heavenly beings and those who minister to Yhwh here on earth. The closing words in verse 22, however, bring the psalm back to where it began, calling on each individual "soul" (נפש) to join the blessing.

---

21. For an additional discussion of חסד, see the commentary for Psalm 92.

22. See the introduction, p. xlvi, and Melody D. Knowles, "Feminist Interpretation of the Psalms," in *The Oxford Handbook of the Psalms*, ed. William P. Brown (Oxford: Oxford University Press, 2014), 426.

One Day at My Grandmother's House . . . Is Still Today

Psalm 103 is a psalm of praise for a God who heals, redeems, works justice, is compassionate, and remembers our mortal state. But as I look back at the end of apartheid in South Africa in 1994 and the establishment of a democratic government, I can honestly say that nothing much has changed, and I sometimes wonder where God is in South Africa. We black people are not empowered and still live in poverty, in many instances worse poverty than during apartheid. Apartheid brings sad and painful memories for me because I witnessed police brutality at a very early age. I saw tear gas fired out of nowhere in the townships to break up unauthorized social gatherings. I remember one day when there was a gathering at my grandmother's house; she was detained and taken away by a police van together with my little brother whom she was babysitting. I was frightened and sobbing because I didn't know how I could help them and when and if I might see them again.

Well into the twenty-first century a number of issues still divide the white and black communities of South Africa. Basic service delivery is a problem in many black communities, and that lack often results in protests that can lead to violence and damage to infrastructure. Communities are angry, feeling that the government has failed them. Racial inequality is still the main issue facing South Africa, and it is not being addressed adequately. While more and more African students attend university, their graduation rates and prospects upon graduation vary widely. Many African men are unemployed or underemployed and many women labor as housekeepers in white households. Solutions are needed to alleviate poverty by sharing the wealth of our country. A debate that is currently underway in the country is over land reform, a movement to repatriate black Africans to land seized from them by white landowners. For many black people getting the land back is a source of healing for their hearts. I am hopeful that effective and robust engagement will come out of these debates and change our country for the better.

I do not claim to be a feminist, but as an African woman in this country I have the feeling that the words of Psalm 103:2 and 5, "do not forget all his benefits . . . who satisfies you with good as long as you live," seem not to pertain to me. In the current situation in the South African economy white men still dominate. Women, and especially African women, are rarely entrusted with higher positions in the corporate world. Men still earn more than women in the same jobs. Until this changes, South Africa will not be able to move forward.

Another problem facing our country is femicide. Women are emotionally and physically abused by their sexual partners every day in South Africa. Women live in fear. In so many cases brought to the courts, the perpetrators do not receive the sentences they deserve, with the result that women are losing faith in the judicial system. It seems to me that God has not redeemed our lives from the pit; neither did he crown a black woman or man (v. 4) in South Africa. In verse 6 the psalm singer states, "The LORD works vindication and justice for all who are oppressed." In my own life situation I do not know whether to read these words as humor or as irony. There has yet been no justice for black people. As I have said before, we are still oppressed; nothing has changed—or is God not referring to everyone oppressed, including us? This verse makes me question a lot of things about life and God's self. Men should stop feeling superior and instead should protect and care for their partners.

As I read this psalm I find it one-sided, speaking more to men than to women. There is sometimes a notion that men can do better than women. This is not true; we see a lot of women in the corporate world doing sterling work and making meaningful changes in people's lives. Women are the mothers of the nation and the world cannot function without women in it. Verse 22 says I should praise the Lord for all his works everywhere in his dominion. My question is, how I can praise God with all of this going on in South Africa and what am I praising God for?

Most young people have qualifications, yet they can't get jobs; unemployment is high in our country. Lack of growth in the economy means that jobs are not created, and this discourages some of our youth from pursuing their studies. Some cannot go to universities due to lack of funds. "FeesMustFall" protests were undertaken to assist those who cannot afford to pay their fees. Many students were arrested, suspended from their universities, and some are still facing jail time. It seems that I am not supposed to find hope in the Bible; I am not supposed to be empowered by the Scriptures. It is hard to find hope in words you cannot hold on to or even relate to. If this is a God of love, then I ask myself what it is we did as black people so as not to deserve God's love. We pray like everyone else and we do our part to serve our country, yet God does not seem to be pleased. We need to live in peace and harmony. Unity is power, as we are one nation, one love, one South Africa, but I do not find my hope in Psalm 103; rather, I find my hope in women like me who are working very hard to change this nation.

Agnes Besigye (Nkuna)

Psalm 104

Psalm 104 begins and ends just as does Psalm 103, with a call to the "soul" (נַפְשִׁי) to bless Yʜᴡʜ; these are the only places in the Psalter where such a call occurs. The Midrash Tellihim regards them as an overlapping composition, paralleling their fivefold call to "bless Yʜᴡʜ, O my soul" (103:1, 2, 22; 104:1, 35) to the five books of the Torah.[23]

Psalm 104 is characterized variously as an "exuberant poetic reflection,"[24] a "cosmic hymn of praise,"[25] and a "sapiential creation hymn."[26] This commentator characterizes it as a magnificent poetic account of God's sovereignty over all creation, a fitting concluding word for Psalms 93–103 and even to Psalms 90–103. The psalm's "exuberance" makes finding a structure for its thirty-five verses difficult, and scholars have proposed many options.[27] J. Clinton McCann points out shifting foci in the psalm's first twenty-three verses, which move fluidly back and forth as the psalmist sings: the heavens in verses 2-4, the earth in verses 5-6, waters in verses 7-10, wild animals in verse 11, birds in verse 12, the earth again in verse 13, plants to feed the animals and the people in verses 14-15, the trees in verse 16, birds again in verse 17, back to wild animals in verse 18, the heavenly bodies in verses 19-20, a return to the wild animals in verses 20-22, and a focus on humanity in verse 23. All of this culminates in verse 24's concluding statement of wonder and praise.[28]

In verses 25-26, however, we encounter another exuberant outburst, this time with a focus on the sea. Finally, in verses 27-35 the singer sums up the message of the psalm, which is that all of God's creation depends on God, and God alone, for sustenance and for life itself, and that the only proper response by creation is song, praise, meditation, and rejoicing (vv. 33-34).

---

23. William G. Braude, *The Midrash on Psalms*, vol. 2 (New Haven: Yale University Press, 1987), 157.

24. McCann, "The Book of Psalms," 1096.

25. Brown, *Seeing the Psalms*, 158.

26. Erich Zenger, " 'Du kannst das Angesicht der Erde erneuern' (Ps 104,30). Das Schöpferlob des 104. Psalms als Ruf zur ökologischen Umkehr," *BL* 64 (1991): 75–86, at 77.

27. See, for example, Allen, *Psalms 101–150*, 44; Mays, *Psalms*, 331–37; and Frank-Lothar Hossfeld and Erich Zenger, *Psalms 3*, trans. Linda M. Maloney, Hermeneia (Minneapolis: Fortress, 2011), 48.

28. McCann, "The Book of Psalms," 1097.

Psalm 104:1-35

Bless the LORD, O my soul.
   O LORD my God, you are very
      great.
You are clothed with honor and
   majesty,
   ²wrapped in light as with a garment.
You stretch out the heavens like a
   tent,
   ³you set the beams of your
      chambers on the waters,
you make the clouds your chariot,
   you ride on the wings of the wind,
⁴you make the winds your
   messengers,
   fire and flame your ministers.
⁵You set the earth on its foundations,
   so that it shall never be shaken.
⁶You cover it with the deep as with a
   garment;
   the waters stood above the
      mountains.
⁷At your rebuke they flee;

   at the sound of your thunder they
      take to flight.
⁸They rose up to the mountains, ran
   down to the valleys
   to the place that you appointed for
      them.
⁹You set a boundary that they may
   not pass,
   so that they might not again cover
      the earth.
¹⁰You make springs gush forth in the
   valleys;
   they flow between the hills,
¹¹giving drink to every wild animal;
   the wild asses quench their thirst.
¹²By the streams the birds of the air
   have their habitation;
   they sing among the branches.
¹³From your lofty abode you water the
   mountains;
   the earth is satisfied with the fruit
      of your work.

Psalm 104 has many parallels with Psalm 103, including the image of YHWH seated on a royal throne surrounded by "messengers" or "angels" (מלאכים) and "ministers" (משרתים) in 104:4 and 103:19-22, the notice that humans are mere "dust" (עפר) in 104:29 and 103:14, and the designation of creation as the "works" (מעשים) of God in 104:24 and 103:22. Still, their emphases are slightly different. Psalm 103's repeated references to the "mercy" or "compassion" (רחם, vv. 4, 8, 13) and "steadfast love" (חסד, vv. 4, 8, 11, 13, 17) of YHWH indicate that the nature of YHWH is the theme of Psalm 103. Psalm 104's repeated mention of YHWH's "work" or "making" (עשה) in verses 4, 13, 19, 24, and 31 point to YHWH's creative work as its theme. Read together, then, the two psalms remind readers or hearers that the two fundamental characteristics of YHWH are those of creator and sustainer.

As stated earlier, Psalm 104 evinces numerous connections to the psalms in book 4 that precede it (Pss 90–103), confirming its place within

¹⁴You cause the grass to grow for the
cattle,
and plants for people to use,
to bring forth food from the earth,
¹⁵and wine to gladden the human
heart,
oil to make the face shine,
and bread to strengthen the
human heart.
¹⁶The trees of the LORD are watered
abundantly,
the cedars of Lebanon that he
planted.
¹⁷In them the birds build their nests;
the stork has its home in the fir
trees.
¹⁸The high mountains are for the wild
goats;
the rocks are a refuge for the
coneys.
¹⁹You have made the moon to mark
the seasons;

the sun knows its time for setting.
²⁰You make darkness, and it is
night,
when all the animals of the forest
come creeping out.
²¹The young lions roar for their prey,
seeking their food from God.
²²When the sun rises, they withdraw
and lie down in their dens.
²³People go out to their work
and to their labor until the evening.
²⁴O LORD, how manifold are your
works!
In wisdom you have made them all;
the earth is full of your creatures.
²⁵Yonder is the sea, great and wide,
creeping things innumerable are
there,
living things both small and great.
²⁶There go the ships,
and Leviathan that you formed to
sport in it.

the book as a fitting conclusion to this group of psalms. Verse 1's state-ment that YHWH is "clothed with honor [הוד] and majesty [הדר]" is paral-leled in Psalms 93:1 and 96:10, which proclaim that the earth is firmly established and will never be "moved" (מוט). This assurance is reiterated in Psalm 104:5. Verses 6-11 of the psalm, depicting YHWH taming the chaotic waters, confirm the words of Psalms 93:3-4; 95:5; 98:7-8.[29]

In Psalm 90:14 the people ask God to "satisfy" (שבע) them, in 91:16 God promises to satisfy, and in 103:5 the psalm singer characterizes God as one who satisfies. The words of Psalm 104:13, 16, and 28 narrate the fulfillment—God satisfies (שבע) the earth and all of creation.

The words of verses 19-23 recount the rhythm of life God has crafted for the world, the ebb and flow of daily activity, each element finding

29. For a full discussion of the connection between water and chaos, see the com-mentary on Ps 93.

Psalm 104:1-35 (cont.)

²⁷These all look to you
to give them their food in due
season;
²⁸when you give to them, they gather
it up;
when you open your hand, they
are filled with good things.
²⁹When you hide your face, they are
dismayed;
when you take away their breath,
they die
and return to their dust.
³⁰When you send forth your spirit,
they are created;
and you renew the face of the
ground.
³¹May the glory of the Lᴏʀᴅ endure
forever;

may the Lᴏʀᴅ rejoice in his
works—
³²who looks on the earth and it
trembles,
who touches the mountains and
they smoke.
³³I will sing to the Lᴏʀᴅ as long as I
live;
I will sing praise to my God while I
have being.
³⁴May my meditation be pleasing to
him,
for I rejoice in the Lᴏʀᴅ.
³⁵Let sinners be consumed from the
earth,
and let the wicked be no more.
Bless the Lᴏʀᴅ, O my soul.
Praise the Lᴏʀᴅ!

its place within the created order: the "moon," the "sun," "the animals of the forest," the "young lions," and "people" (אדם). Verse 23 confirms humanity's task in the created order, to go out to its "work" (פעל) and "labor" (עבד) each day. These words, heard in conjunction with verses 14-15, affirm God's purpose for humanity at creation. In Genesis 2:15 God put the first human (אדם) in the garden to "till" (עבד, literally "serve," the same Hebrew word as in Ps 104:23) and to "keep" it.

Verses 24-26's words of wonder and praise bring this section of Psalm 104 to a close with the psalm singer celebrating all of God's "works" (עשה, see also vv. 4, 13, 19, and 31). In verse 24 the singer credits "wisdom" (חכמה) as the seed-bed, perhaps even the source, of creation. In Proverbs 8:22-31 Wisdom states that she was present at creation, working alongside God as a "master worker" (אמון), rejoicing in the inhabited world (תבל, see Pss 90:2; 93:1; 96:10, 13; 97:4; 98:7, 9). Verses 24-26 of Psalm 104 are filled with echoes of Genesis 1: the sea (ים, v. 25; Gen 1:6-10); the creeping things and other living creatures (רמש and חיות, v. 25; Gen 1:24); and Leviathan (לויתן, v. 26), called "the great sea monster" in Genesis 1:21 and characterized as a fearsome creature in Job 3:8 and 41:1.

At the end of verse 26 the psalmist says of the sea, according to the NRSV, "There go the ships, and Leviathan that you formed to sport in it [בֹו]." The word translated "sport" is from the Hebrew root שׂחק, the same word used to describe Woman Wisdom's utter delight in creation in Proverbs 8:30. Additionally, the word translated "in" is the Hebrew preposition בְּ, which carries a basic meaning of proximity and thus can be translated "in," "with," or "by." William P. Brown, in an article titled "The Lion, the Wicked, and the Wonder of It All," renders the preposition as "with" and translates the verse as "There go the ships, and Leviathan that you formed to frolic with it." He writes: "God's primordial nemesis is found frolicking [שׂחק, 'sporting'] in the water, and it is not alone. God is also there, splashing away,"[30] suggesting an utter delight by God at the created order, even Leviathan. Such delight seems confirmed by the psalmist's words in verse 31: "may the LORD rejoice [שׂמח] in [בְּ] his works."

The singer of Psalm 104 reflects on myriad elements of God's creation and on their praises—the light, the heavens, the waters, the clouds, the wind, the fire and flame, the mountains, the valleys, the springs of waters, the wild asses, the birds, the cattle, the plants, the wine and oil and bread, the trees, the goats and the rock-badgers, the moon and the sun, the young lions, and humans going forth to work. Psalm 104 counts humanity as one among the many creations of God, who "cause[s] grass to grow for the cattle, and plants for people to use" (v. 14).

Humankind often perceives itself as the pinnacle of creation, with permission to use the rest of it in any way it sees fit. But the words of Psalm 104 remind us that humanity is just one part of God's vast created order, summarized well in the words of verses 20-23. God made the night for the animals of the forest, including the young lions; when the sun rises, the animals withdraw and humanity goes out to "work" (פעל) and "labor" (עבד). Richard Bauckham, in a book titled *The Bible and Ecology*, perhaps sums up best the message of Psalm 104. He writes:

> All God's creatures are first and foremost creatures, ourselves included. All earthly creatures share the same Earth; and all participate in an inter-related and interdependent community. . . . Cosmic humility is a much needed ecological virtue. . . . We need the humility "to walk more lightly upon the Earth, with more regard for the life around us." . . .

---

30. William P. Brown, "The Lion, the Wicked, and the Wonder of It All," *Journal for Preachers* (2006): 15–21, at 16.

We need the humility to know ourselves as creatures within creation, not gods over creation, the humility of knowing that only God is God.[31]

The singer of Psalm 104 expresses the desire that "the Lord rejoice [שׂמח] in his works" (v. 31). If we carefully heed the words of Psalm 104 we can, with the psalm singer, "rejoice [שׂמח] in the Lord" (v. 34).

And God Saw That It Was Good

Psalm 104 starts and ends just like Psalm 103 with the call for the "soul" to bless the Lord. Psalm 103 emphasizes God's good provisions for humanity, while Psalm 104 celebrates God's work in the created world, painting a picture of a psalm singer who is excited and overwhelmed by God's care for humanity and for all of creation. Psalm 104 has a poetic feel that parallels the description of creation in Genesis 1, where God declared each creative act as "good"; Psalm 104 seems to be an exuberant celebration of that "good." In both accounts the elements of creation are named, but whereas Genesis 1 employs more "generic" names for the elements of creation (e.g., plants, v. 11; birds, v. 20; living creatures that move, v. 21), Psalm 104 describes in vivid detail the created things and their place in the created order: "grass to grow for the cattle, and plants for people to use" (v. 14); the high mountains for the wild goats and rocks as a refuge for the coneys (v. 18); "the moon to mark the seasons" (v. 19); and so forth. The psalmist mentions each part of God's creation by name as a reason to praise God, as evidence of the goodness and wisdom of God. In addition, Psalm 104 continues book 4's emphasis on the sovereignty of God. As we learn about God's power and sovereignty over creation we come to realize that we can trust God with the good care of each of our lives. God created us, me, in God's image, and we, I, am good, very good (Gen 1:31).

What the words of Genesis 1 and Psalm 104 tell me is that my existence is no mistake, nothing that can be ignored, tossed aside, or, worse yet, exploited for gratification, financial gain, or conformity to the cultural norms of others. Do we no longer see God's image when we look at each other?

In the society in which I live in South Africa there are many disturbing instances of just such acts against the sanctity of God's creations. A recent news story

---

31. Richard Bauckham, *The Bible and Ecology* (Waco, TX: Baylor University Press, 2010), 64, 46.

told of a man who was found keeping female body parts, including sexual organs, in a storage locker. He killed women, "harvested" their body parts, and supplied them to supposed *sangomas*, traditional healers, who use female organs for *muti*, traditional medications. While legitimate *sangomas* are a group recognized and respected by the South African government and do not engage in such horrific practices, some fraudulent ones do so, apparently to promote their own status and wealth. I wonder what was going through the mind of the man in the news story as he killed those women and removed their body parts one by one—women who were created in the image of God and declared "very good." And I wonder what goes through the minds of the fraudulent *sangomas* who use the body parts for *muti*. Do the lives of women in South Africa matter so little that their body parts can be harvested and used along with plants and minerals?

Another issue in South African society is the murder of infant albinos, more common in sub-Saharan Africa than in other parts of the world. Before hospital births were common in South Africa, home births with the help of midwives (*gogos*) were the norm. If a woman gave birth to an albino baby the *gogo* would smother it immediately and tell the mother that the baby was stillborn. To this day there are some in South Africa who believe that an albino child is a curse and should not be allowed to live. Some fraudulent *sangomas* believe that albinos make the best *muti* ingredients, and so the killing continues. Again, do the lives of these innocent children, also created in the image of God, matter so little?

The psalmist cries out to God in verse 35: "Let sinners be consumed from the earth, and let the wicked be no more." And in verses 1 and 2 she sings to the Lord: "You are clothed with honor and majesty, wrapped in light as with a garment." What that says to me is that even in the midst of the wrong that takes place in the world, God is still somehow in control. Even if others do not see the image of God in these horribly exploited women and these precious albino babies, we know that they are fearfully and wonderfully made in the image of God. It might not be now, but in God's time God will come to protect and ultimately vindicate the abused and vulnerable in South Africa. This assurance helps me to sleep at night; it is my reason to rejoice and bless the Lord.

Lesego Temane

Psalms 105 and 106

Testify and Make Known the Great Acts of the Lord

Psalms 105 and 106, the closing psalms of book 4, recount YHWH's relationship with the people of Israel from the time of the ancestors to the time of their settlement in the land of promise. Both are classified broadly as historical psalms and both open with הודו, translated as "give thanks." Based on the meaning of the verbal root of the word (ידה) a better translation would be "confess" or "testify."[1] A call to confess or testify in the opening words of these psalms provides greater insight into their purpose and their placement at the end of book 4. Psalm 105 calls on the people to "testify" or "confess" to the great acts of YHWH on their behalf from the time of the ancestors to the settlement in the land, and Psalm 106 adjures them to "testify" or "confess" to the disobedience and rebellion of their ancestors against God during that time. Psalm 105 closes with "hallelujah" while Psalm 106 opens and closes with the word. The juxtaposition of the two psalms at the close of book 4, which

---

1. See, for example, Rolf Jacobson's comment in Nancy L. deClaissé-Walford, Rolf A. Jacobson, and Beth LaNeel Tanner, *The Book of Psalms*, NICOT (Grand Rapids: Eerdmans, 2014), 787; John Goldingay, *Psalms*, vol. 3: *Psalms 90–150*, BCOT (Grand Rapids: Baker Academic, 2008), 204, 753. See also Ps 32:5 and Prov 28:13.

according to the storyline of the Psalter is set in the exilic period (see the introduction, pp. liii–liv), is a reminder to the people in exile in Babylon and to readers or hearers in later generations to "testify" to the history of the relationship between Yhwh and the people so that all may know and remember. When read together, Psalms 105 and 106 are a stirring reminder of the complex history of Yhwh's relationship with the Israelite people; in addition, their words were a call to the people in exile in Babylon and those living in the postexilic world to heed the stories of the past and learn from them in order to be able to live again in the land of promise.

Psalm 105

Psalm 105 is a historical psalm, as are Psalms 78, 106, and 136, that recounts the great acts (נפלאות) of God on behalf of the Israelite people from the time of the ancestors, through the exodus and wilderness wanderings, and into the settlement in the land of promise. Its opening words, in verses 1-3, are a call to the people to "give thanks" (הודו) to Yhwh, the source of all goodness to them. The psalm's use of the words "sing" (שיר, v. 2; see Pss 92:1; 98:1; 101:1; 104:33), "sing praises" (זמר, v. 2; see Pss 92:2; 98:4, 5; 101:1; 104:33), "rejoice" (שמח, v. 3; see Pss 90:14, 15; 92:5; 96:11; 97:1, 8, 12; 104:15, 31, 34), and "singing" (רנן, v. 43; see Pss 90:14; 92:5; 95:1; 96:12; 98:4, 8) echoes the celebratory or anticipated celebratory words of the psalms that precede it in book 4.

Moreover, rather than reading the words of Psalm 105 as a recital of the good provisions of Yhwh for the people in the past, a close examination of the word translated "give thanks" (הודו) in the opening verse yields a different understanding of the intent of the psalm. הודו is the *hiphil* imperative form of the verbal root (ידה) that means "to throw, to cast," suggesting a better translation would be "confess" or "testify."[2] A closer examination of the other words of verses 1-3 confirms this understanding. The words in verse 1 translated in the NRSV as "call [קרא] upon [ב] his name" may also be translated "cry out [קרא] in [ב] in his name" while in verse 2 "sing to [שיר ל]" and "sing praises to [זמר ל]" may also be translated "sing of" and "sing praises of."[3] Such a translation refocuses the attention of the psalm singers from words *to* God to words *about*

---

2. deClaissé-Walford, Jacobson, and Tanner, *Psalms*, 787; Goldingay, *Psalms 90–150*, 204, 753; and G. Mayer, "ידה, *ydh*," *TDOT*, 5:427–28, at 428.

3. deClaissé-Walford, Jacobson, and Tanner, *Psalms*, 784, 787.

Psalm 105:1-45

¹O give thanks to the Lᴏʀᴅ, call on his
name,
make known his deeds among the
peoples.
²Sing to him, sing praises to him;
tell of all his wonderful works.
³Glory in his holy name;
let the hearts of those who seek
the Lᴏʀᴅ rejoice.
⁴Seek the Lᴏʀᴅ and his strength;
seek his presence continually.
⁵Remember the wonderful works he
has done,
his miracles, and the judgments
he has uttered,
⁶O offspring of his servant Abraham,
children of Jacob, his chosen ones.
⁷He is the Lᴏʀᴅ our God;
his judgments are in all the earth.

⁸He is mindful of his covenant forever,
of the word that he commanded,
for a thousand generations,
⁹the covenant that he made with
Abraham,
his sworn promise to Isaac,
¹⁰which he confirmed to Jacob as a
statute,
to Israel as an everlasting
covenant,
¹¹saying, "To you I will give the land of
Canaan
as your portion for an inheritance."
¹²When they were few in number,
of little account, and strangers in it,
¹³wandering from nation to nation,
from one kingdom to another
people,
¹⁴he allowed no one to oppress them;

God, suggesting a call to proclaim to others rather than an inward act of praise and reflection.

The focus of Psalm 105, that to which the people are called to "testify" or "confess," is the "covenant" (ברית, v. 8; see Ps 106:45) made with their ancestors and the acts of Yʜᴡʜ that enabled a realization of the covenant promise. References to the land occur no fewer than ten times in the psalm (vv. 7, 11, 16, 23, 27, 30, 32, 35, 36, 44), and the psalmist speaks of God's "deeds" (v. 1), "wonderful works" (vv. 2, 5), "miracles" (vv. 5, 27), and "signs" (v. 27).

The historical recitation in the psalm begins with Abraham in verse 6; he appears again in verses 9 and 42. Verses 6, 9, 10, 17, and 26 name the subsequent patriarchs Isaac, Jacob, Joseph, Moses, and Aaron. Missing in these verses are the names of the matriarchs of the people—Sarah, Rebekah, Rachel and Leah, and especially Miriam.[4] Verses 16-24 tell the story of Israel's sojourn in Egypt; verses 25-43, the escape from Egypt and the time of the wilderness wandering; and verses 44-45, the settlement

---

4. For more on Miriam see especially the commentaries for Pss 90 and 97.

Psalm 105:1-45 (cont.)

he rebuked kings on their account,
[15]saying, "Do not touch my anointed
    ones;
do my prophets no harm."
[16]When he summoned famine against
    the land,
and broke every staff of bread,
[17]he had sent a man ahead of them,
    Joseph, who was sold as a slave.
[18]His feet were hurt with fetters,
    his neck was put in a collar of iron;
[19]until what he had said came to pass,
    the word of the LORD kept testing
    him.
[20]The king sent and released him;
    the ruler of the peoples set him
    free.

[21]He made him lord of his house,
    and ruler of all his possessions,
[22]to instruct his officials at his
    pleasure,
and to teach his elders wisdom.
[23]Then Israel came to Egypt;
    Jacob lived as an alien in the land
    of Ham.
[24]And the LORD made his people very
    fruitful,
and made them stronger than
    their foes,
[25]whose hearts he then turned to hate
    his people,
to deal craftily with his servants.
[26]He sent his servant Moses,
    and Aaron whom he had chosen.

in the land of promise. The historical recitation ends with the people's entry into the land.

A provision of land for the Israelite people is an interwoven focus of Psalm 105 (vv. 11 and 44). J. Clinton McCann maintains that the theme of land is in keeping with the message of book 4. He writes: "Due to the loss of land, possession of the land was a preeminent exilic concern. It was natural, therefore, to look back behind the failed Davidic covenant to the covenant with Abraham."[5] Christopher Wright states, "The covenant is properly conceived as a triangulated relationship among Israel, the land, and YHWH."[6] Leslie C. Allen further maintains that Psalm 105 "takes up a constant OT emphasis in celebrating the interrelatedness of Yahweh, the people, and the land. Here [in Ps 105] it is set in a context of promise and power, of hope and realization."[7]

5. J. Clinton McCann Jr., "The Book of Psalms," *NIB*, vol. 4 (Nashville: Abingdon, 1996), 1104.

6. Christopher J. H. Wright, *God's People in God's Land: Family, Land, and Property in the Old Testament* (Grand Rapids: Eerdmans, 1990), 104–5.

7. Leslie C. Allen, *Psalms 101–150*, WBC 21 (Nashville: Thomas Nelson, 2002), 60.

²⁷They performed his signs among them,
and miracles in the land of Ham.
²⁸He sent darkness, and made the land dark;
they rebelled against his words.
²⁹He turned their waters into blood,
and caused their fish to die.
³⁰Their land swarmed with frogs,
even in the chambers of their kings.
³¹He spoke, and there came swarms of flies,
and gnats throughout their country.
³²He gave them hail for rain,
and lightning that flashed through their land.
³³He struck their vines and fig trees,
and shattered the trees of their country.
³⁴He spoke, and the locusts came,
and young locusts without number;
³⁵they devoured all the vegetation in their land,
and ate up the fruit of their ground.
³⁶He struck down all the firstborn in their land,
the first issue of all their strength.
³⁷Then he brought Israel out with silver and gold,

Richard Clifford suggests that the words of Psalm 105 should not be relegated to a memory of the past, of what God did for the exilic people's and today's ancestors in the faith, but should be read as words of hope for landless people in every time and in every place.[8] How do we appropriate the words of Psalm 105 not only as a historical recitation but as words of hope for the future for all peoples in a situation of exile or displacement?

First, the call by the psalm singers in verses 1-6 is a combined call to any of the faithful who would listen to "testify" (v. 1) and to "remember" (v. 5). Second, while the remembrance of Psalm 105 begins with the promise to Abraham (v. 6), its opening verses suggest a strong connection to the creation language of Psalm 104. Thus the two psalms read in tandem describe a God who, from the time of creation, knew the importance of land, of a place to "be" as a people. Third, the recounting of the "wonderful works" (נפלאות, vv. 2, 5), the "deeds" (עלילות, v. 1), the "miracles" (מופת, vv. 5, 27), and the "signs" (אתות, v. 27) does not mean that they are mere historical memory. Rather, the stories testify to the basic character of God, who has provided in the past and continues to provide.

8. Richard J. Clifford, *Psalms 73–150*, AOTC (Nashville: Abingdon, 2003), 156.

Psalm 105:1-45 (cont.)

and there was no one among their tribes who stumbled. ³⁸Egypt was glad when they departed, for dread of them had fallen upon it. ³⁹He spread a cloud for a covering, and fire to give light by night. ⁴⁰They asked, and he brought quails, and gave them food from heaven in abundance. ⁴¹He opened the rock, and water gushed out; it flowed through the desert like a river.

⁴²For he remembered his holy promise, and Abraham, his servant. ⁴³So he brought his people out with joy, his chosen ones with singing. ⁴⁴He gave them the lands of the nations, and they took possession of the wealth of the peoples, ⁴⁵that they might keep his statutes and observe his laws. Praise the LORD!

The women and men who lived in exile in Babylon must have yearned for their storied, local, rooted place, the land of promise where countless generations were born and raised, lived and died. Their collective memory recalled the "wondrous works," the "miracles" of YHWH that provided the means for them to possess the land. Their words of testimony in Psalm 105 (and again in Pss 106 and 107) give hope to future generations of faithful ones that God continues to provide land, a "storied place" that each of us can call our own.

After the lengthy celebration of God's provisions for the people, including the gift of the land promised to Abraham, verse 45 of Psalm 105 presents the reason for those provisions, "that they might keep his statutes [חק] and observe his laws [תורות]." Ellen Davis reminds us: "The descendants of Israel were given, not a land, but the use of a land, along with precise instructions for its good care."[9] Norman Habel observes: "As a jealous landowner, YHWH desires responsible tenants who will maintain an attitude of reverence and concern for the very soil and soul of the land."[10] Psalm 90:2 reminds us that God birthed (חיל) the earth (ארץ) and the (habitable) world (תבל), and while the creation stories in Genesis

9. Ellen F. Davis, *Scripture, Culture, and Agriculture: An Agrarian Reading of the Bible* (Cambridge: Cambridge University Press, 2009), x.

10. Norman C. Habel, *The Land Is Mine: Six Biblical Land Ideologies*, OBT (Minneapolis: Augsburg, 1993), 110. See, e.g., Lev 19:9-10; 23:9-14; 25:1-7.

1 and 2 tell us that God entrusted the care of the habitable world to humanity, the enthronement psalms in book 4 (Pss 93–100) remind humanity, in the words of Richard Bauckham, that we are "fellow-members of creation with God's other creatures" and that "all earthly creatures share the same Earth; and all participate in an interrelated and interdependent community."[11] In order to possess the land, to have our "storied place," we must be faithful to God's instructions regarding its care.

Where Is My Space, as a Black Woman, in This Land?

Reading Psalm 105 causes deep conflict within me; I can relate to some parts of the psalm while others raise many questions in my mind about my faith and who I am and the God I believe in. The reference to Joseph's slavery in verses 17 and 18 and verse 25's statement that the Israelites who lived in a land of people who hated them reminds me that the Bible contains many stories about slavery and oppression. As a thirty-three-year-old black woman living in the rural area of Mpumalanga in the Gauteng Province of South Africa, I identify more easily with the slaves and oppressed than I do with those in power. Joseph was sold into slavery, and I often feel as though I have been sold into slavery.

I have a matric (high school diploma) and a diploma in computer programming, and for a time I worked in the field and was one of the best. Because of various family situations I am now a domestic worker in three households, the sole source of income for my family that includes my mother, brother, sister, nephew, and my young son. I rise at four o'clock in the morning and travel by bus two hours each way to get to and from the households in which I work. When I began reading this psalm I wanted to praise God as the psalm does; I wanted to thank God for my education and the privilege I had in obtaining it:

O give thanks to the Lord, call
  on his name,
    make known his deeds
      among the peoples.
Sing to him, sing praises to him;
  tell of all his wonderful
    works.
Glory in his holy name;
  let the hearts of those who
    seek the Lord rejoice.
Seek the Lord and his strength;
  seek his presence continually.
Remember the wonderful works
  he has done,
    his miracles, and the
      judgments he has uttered.

11. Richard Bauckham, *The Bible and Ecology* (Waco, TX: Baylor University Press, 2010), 64.

Then I asked: But God, how can I praise you? I am oppressed by my skin color, by the system. I was failed by my government, born and "baptized" into apartheid. Am I doomed to be nothing more than a domestic worker? I have been sold into slavery; I am a Joseph of my time. I feel enslaved in a society where being black brings fewer opportunities than being white, in a culture where being a woman relegates me to the kitchen. Still, I dream endlessly of education and freedom and have a vision for the rights of women and children to live out their dreams.

Psalm 105 mentions by name only men, so where is my space, as a woman, in this "land"? I thank God every day for the end of apartheid, but I sometimes cannot help but think that God punished us black people with apartheid because, despite its end, I feel so often that I am in exile, just as the Israelites were. I think we black people are very strong to have survived apartheid. Women are even stronger, because my mother lived through apartheid and still raised me to love and not to hate the people who created that awful system. Psalm 105 contains many mentions of land (vv. 11, 23, 44); land is a major issue in postapartheid South Africa. I suppose that is why the words about land in Psalm 105 force me to put on the shoes of the Israelites and feel their pain at being outside the land

God promised them:

> For he remembered his holy promise,
>   and Abraham, his servant.
> So he brought his people out with joy,
>   his chosen ones with singing.
> He gave them the lands of the nations,
>   and they took possession of
>   the wealth of the peoples,
> that they might keep his statutes
>   and observe his laws.
> Praise the LORD!

Verse 43 talks about God's chosen ones. In apartheid South Africa the chosen ones were the Afrikaans people. In fact, they used the term "chosen ones" to justify apartheid, and today, twenty-five years after its end, the Afrikaans can still rejoice: "He gave them the lands of the nations, and they took possession of the wealth of the peoples" (v. 44). In my context as a woman in South Africa, who has gone through so much in life, these words raise more questions than feed my soul.

But, perhaps, if I am a Joseph of my time, there is hope for me after all:

> When he summoned famine against the land,
>   and broke every staff of bread,
> he had sent a man ahead of them,
>   Joseph, who was sold as a slave.
> His feet were hurt with fetters,
>   his neck was put in a collar of iron;
> until what he had said came to pass,

the word of the LORD kept
    testing him.
The king sent and released him;
    the ruler of the peoples set him
    free.
He made him lord of his house,
    and ruler of all his
    possessions,
to instruct his officials at his
    pleasure,
    and to teach his elders
    wisdom.

I am a strong believer, and maybe I am naïve as well, but I believe one day God will look down on me and answer my prayers. I am a black woman, and if we black women were given a chance to show our talents, something we have been given so little opportunity to do, this world would be a better place. This psalm was written by and for people of another culture, another time and situation, but I find hope in it because it reminds me that people have always suffered and yet survived. Thus despite all, we black women in South Africa can say *"amandla awethu"* (power is ours). I will strive to be an example to other women of what faith looks like, what equality, equity, diversity, and love look like today in my country. Psalm 105 perplexes my mind but gives hope to my heart and allows my soul to be lifted. And so for now I will "Give thanks to the LORD, for he is good."

Nellie Zania Mahlangu

Psalm 106

Psalm 106 is the last psalm in book 4, which according to its storyline reflects on the time of the Israelites' exile in Babylon (see the introduction, pp. liii–liv). It is categorized as a historical psalm, along with Psalms 78, 136, and its "twin" Psalm 105. Both Psalms 105 and 106 open with the words "give thanks" (הודו); each recounts the history of YHWH's relationship with the people of Israel from the time of the ancestors to the time of the settlement in the land of promise; and while Psalm 105 closes with the word "praise the LORD," Psalm 106 opens and closes with the word. They are, together, a fitting conclusion to the exilic peoples' musing over their lives in Babylon.

As with Psalm 105, the word translated in verse 1 as "give thanks" (הודו) is better rendered "confess" or "testify."[12] Such a rendering refocuses the attention of the psalm singers from words *to* God to words *about* God, suggesting a call to proclaim to others rather than offering

12. See n. 2 above.

Psalm 106:1-48

¹Praise the Lord!
O give thanks to the Lord, for he
is good;
for his steadfast love endures
forever.
²Who can utter the mighty doings of
the Lord,
or declare all his praise?
³Happy are those who observe justice,
who do righteousness at all times.
⁴Remember me, O Lord, when you
show favor to your people;
help me when you deliver them;
⁵that I may see the prosperity of your
chosen ones,
that I may rejoice in the gladness
of your nation,
that I may glory in your heritage.
⁶Both we and our ancestors have
sinned;
we have committed iniquity, have
done wickedly.
⁷Our ancestors, when they were in
Egypt,
did not consider your wonderful
works;
they did not remember the abundance
of your steadfast love,
but rebelled against the Most High
at the Red Sea.
⁸Yet he saved them for his name's
sake,
so that he might make known his
mighty power.
⁹He rebuked the Red Sea, and it
became dry;
he led them through the deep as
through a desert.
¹⁰So he saved them from the hand of
the foe,

and delivered them from the hand
of the enemy.
¹¹The waters covered their
adversaries;
not one of them was left.
¹²Then they believed his words;
they sang his praise.
¹³But they soon forgot his works;
they did not wait for his counsel.
¹⁴But they had a wanton craving in
the wilderness,
and put God to the test in the
desert;
¹⁵he gave them what they asked,
but sent a wasting disease among
them.
¹⁶They were jealous of Moses in the
camp,
and of Aaron, the holy one of the
Lord.
¹⁷The earth opened and swallowed
up Dathan,
and covered the faction of Abiram.
¹⁸Fire also broke out in their
company;
the flame burned up the wicked.
¹⁹They made a calf at Horeb
and worshiped a cast image.
²⁰They exchanged the glory of God
for the image of an ox that eats
grass.
²¹They forgot God, their Savior,
who had done great things in
Egypt,
²²wondrous works in the land of Ham,
and awesome deeds by the Red
Sea.
²³Therefore he said he would destroy
them—
had not Moses, his chosen one,

stood in the breach before him,
to turn away his wrath from
destroying them.
²⁴Then they despised the pleasant
land,
having no faith in his promise.
²⁵They grumbled in their tents,
and did not obey the voice of the
Lord.
²⁶Therefore he raised his hand and
swore to them
that he would make them fall in
the wilderness,
²⁷and would disperse their
descendants among the
nations,
scattering them over the lands.
²⁸Then they attached themselves to
the Baal of Peor,
and ate sacrifices offered to the
dead;
²⁹they provoked the Lord to anger
with their deeds,
and a plague broke out among
them.

³⁰Then Phinehas stood up and
interceded,
and the plague was stopped.
³¹And that has been reckoned to him
as righteousness
from generation to generation
forever.
³²They angered the Lord at the
waters of Meribah,
and it went ill with Moses on their
account;
³³for they made his spirit bitter,
and he spoke words that were
rash.
³⁴They did not destroy the peoples,
as the Lord commanded them,
³⁵but they mingled with the nations
and learned to do as they did.
³⁶They served their idols,
which became a snare to them.
³⁷They sacrificed their sons
and their daughters to the demons;
³⁸they poured out innocent blood,
the blood of their sons and
daughters,

inward praise and reflection. The call is to celebrate the "goodness" (טוב)
and the "steadfast love" (חסד)[13] of Yhwh. Verse 2 asks who is able to
recount the "mighty doings" of Yhwh and declare Yhwh's praise, and
verse 3 provides the answer to the question, introduced by the wisdom
word "happy" (אשרי): those who "observe justice" and "do righteousness," reflecting the call in the closing verse of Psalm 105 to observe the
"statutes" (חקים) and "laws" (תורות).

In verse 6 the focus of the psalm shifts to the history of God's dealing with the people, beginning with a confession of communal sin. The

13. For a full discussion of "steadfast love" (חסד), see the commentaries for Pss 92
and 103.

Psalm 106:1-48 (cont.)

whom they sacrificed to the idols of Canaan;
and the land was polluted with blood.
³⁹Thus they became unclean by their acts,
and prostituted themselves in their doings.
⁴⁰Then the anger of the LORD was kindled against his people,
and he abhorred his heritage;
⁴¹he gave them into the hand of the nations,
so that those who hated them ruled over them.
⁴²Their enemies oppressed them,
and they were brought into subjection under their power.
⁴³Many times he delivered them,
but they were rebellious in their purposes,

and were brought low through their iniquity.
⁴⁴Nevertheless he regarded their distress
when he heard their cry.
⁴⁵For their sake he remembered his covenant,
and showed compassion according to the abundance of his steadfast love.
⁴⁶He caused them to be pitied by all who held them captive.
⁴⁷Save us, O LORD our God,
and gather us from among the nations,
that we may give thanks to your holy name
and glory in your praise.
⁴⁸Blessed be the LORD, the God of Israel,
from everlasting to everlasting.
And let all the people say, "Amen."
Praise the LORD!

words "we and our ancestors" unite the present community with that of the past. Frank-Lothar Hossfeld writes: "The predecessor and progeny have all sinned."[14] Verses 7-46 recount the Israelite people's history with YHWH from the time of the sojourn in Egypt to the Babylonian exile. Much of the history narrated in Psalm 106 overlaps with that narrated in Psalm 105, but the tenor of the two psalms is markedly different.

Psalm 105 celebrates God's goodness to and provision for the people throughout their history. Psalm 106, on the other hand, recounts the people's rebellion against God's good provision for them. They did not consider YHWH's "wonderful works" (נפלאות, v. 7; see Ps 105:2, 5) such as the parting of the Reed Sea (v. 9; Exod 14). They forgot all that YHWH

---

14. Frank-Lothar Hossfeld and Erich Zenger, *Psalms 3*, trans. Linda M. Maloney, Hermeneia (Minneapolis: Fortress, 2011), 94.

did and tested YHWH in the wilderness (vv. 13-15; Exod 16). They were jealous of Moses and Aaron (v. 16; Num 16); they worshiped a golden calf (v. 19; Exod 32); they refused to enter the land of promise (v. 24; Num 13, 14); they worshiped other gods (v. 28; Num 25); they grumbled against YHWH and Moses (v. 32; Num 20); they did not drive out the peoples who occupied the land of promise (v. 35; Judg 1); they worshiped other gods (v. 36; 2 Kgs 21). YHWH delivered the people many times, but they continued to be rebellious (v. 43); nevertheless, God regarded their distress upon hearing their "cry" (v. 44).

The word translated "cry" in verse 44 comes from the verbal root רנן, a word the reader or hearer encounters in numerous psalms in book 4 (see Pss 90:14; 92:4; 95:1; 96:12; 98:4, 8; 105:43). רנן is almost always used in a positive sense in the Hebrew Bible and is connected with joyous outbursts, never with cries of oppression, warfare, etc.[15] Psalm 106:44 contains one of the rare uses of the word in a negative sense.

Despite the history of disobedience and grumbling, verses 45-46 of Psalm 106 detail God's unrelenting care for the people because of God's faithfulness to the "covenant" (ברית, v. 45; see Ps 105:8-10) and to YHWH's "steadfast love" (חסד, v. 45). Verse 45 further speaks of YHWH's "compassion." The root of the word translated "compassion" is נחם, used of both humans and God in the biblical text. When used of humans it is most often translated "comfort."[16] In Job 42:6, however, the word is translated "repent."

The use of the word in reference to God is translated a number of ways in the NRSV. In Genesis 6:6, 7 God is "sorry" (נחם) "that he had made humankind on the earth." God is moved to "pity" (נחם) on the people in Judges 2:18 and provides "comfort" (נחם) in Psalms 23:4 and 71:21. One translation of נחם is particularly interesting in the context of Psalm 106. In Exodus 34:12, 14 (the Golden Calf incident) Moses implores God to "change God's mind" (נחם) and God decides to do so. Psalm 110:4 tells us that God "has sworn and will not change his mind" (נחם), and in Jeremiah 18:8 God says: "If . . . then I will change my mind [נחם] about the disaster I intend to bring on it."

How do the various translations of נחם in the NRSV contribute to an understanding of the meaning of "compassion" that we find in Psalm 106:45?[17] The basic meaning of the Hebrew root is "to decide to do

---

15. Jutta Hausmann, "רנן, *rānān*," *TDOT*, 13:515–22.
16. See, for example, Gen 24:67; 37:35; Ruth 2:13; Job 2:11; Isa 40:1.
17. See also Deut 32:36 and Pss 90:13; 135:14.

something different." The various translations as "be sorry," "comfort," "repent," "pity," and "change the mind" imply a change in character in some way, either inwardly or in outward action. Thus we may connect "compassion" in Psalm 106:45 with a change of heart, a decision to do something different from what would be expected in the given circumstances. The story of Psalm 106 is that of the Israelites' constant rebellion in the face of God's good provisions for them during the wilderness wanderings. Verse 43 says: "Many times he delivered them, but they were rebellious in their purposes, and were brought low through their iniquity." But the psalm continues in verses 44 and 45, "Nevertheless he regarded their distress . . . for their sake . . . and showed compassion [נחם]." Richard Clifford sums up the message of Psalm 106: "The psalm is not primarily about the people's disobedience, but about God. God refuses to let them go."

Psalm 106 closes with a petition to God by the psalm singer: "Save us . . . and gather us from among the nations" (v. 47), voicing the desire of the people of God in exile in Babylon. The second half of verse 47 states the purpose of the saving and gathering—that we may "give thanks" (הדות, see v. 1 and Ps 105:1 and recall that this is better translated as "confess" or "testify") and "praise" (see v. 1; Ps 105:45). The singer of Psalm 106 calls on God to act on the people's behalf so that they might heed the admonishment of the opening verses of the psalm.

Psalm 105 testifies to the good provisions of God for the people, while Psalm 106 recounts the rejection by the people of many of God's provisions. The human community so often tries to set its own course, ignoring or rejecting the good that comes to it from God. When we grumble as we undertake an arduous journey (Exod 15:24; 16:2); when we receive the manna and the quail rather than the "fish . . . the cucumbers, the melons, the leeks, the onions, and the garlic" that we ate in Egypt (Num 11:5); when the fear of change overtakes us (Exod 16:2-4); when we listen to the naysayers and ignore those who speak words of hope (Num 14:1-4), we forget to step back and look at the "big picture." Accepting the good provisions of YHWH, often when they do not make sense to us, is humanity's path to restoration and wholeness.

Book 5 of the Psalter
(Pss 107–150)

Psalm 107

A Place to Call Home

Psalm 107

Psalm 107, a community hymn of praise, opens book 5 of the Psalter. Its opening words, in verses 1-3, voiced in answer to the plea of Psalm 106:47 to "save us and gather us," suggest that the two psalms, though in different books of the Psalter, were purposely juxtaposed. In addition, Psalm 107 continues the theme of "land" addressed in Psalms 105 and 106. Book 5 moves readers or hearers from the exilic to the postexilic period of ancient Israel's life, but the clear ties between Psalms 105 and 106 and Psalm 107 evince a continuity in the life of Israel from the exile in Babylon to the return to the land.

Four groups of people appear in the first thirty-two verses of Psalm 107, representing, perhaps, the "redeemed of the LORD" from the four points of the compass named in verse 3. Verses 4-9 tell of a group of wanderers, lost in the desert, who finally arrive at their destination. East of Palestine is the vast Arabian Desert that separates it from the Fertile Crescent's eastern side in Mesopotamia. Few travelers in the ancient Near East dared to attempt a traverse of this terrain.

Verses 10-16 tell the story of prisoners who are set free. The west is the place where the sun sets, the deathly place of darkness in which, according to ancient Egyptian cosmology, the sun dies every night as it

¹O give thanks to the Lᴏʀᴅ, for he is
good;
  for his steadfast love endures
      forever.
²Let the redeemed of the Lᴏʀᴅ say so,
  those he redeemed from trouble
³and gathered in from the lands,
  from the east and from the west,
  from the north and from the south.
⁴Some wandered in desert wastes,
  finding no way to an inhabited
      town;
⁵hungry and thirsty,
  their soul fainted within them.
⁶Then they cried to the Lᴏʀᴅ in their
      trouble,
  and he delivered them from their
      distress;
⁷he led them by a straight way,
  until they reached an inhabited
      town.
⁸Let them thank the Lᴏʀᴅ for his
      steadfast love,
  for his wonderful works to
      humankind.
⁹For he satisfies the thirsty,
  and the hungry he fills with good
      things.
¹⁰Some sat in darkness and in gloom,
  prisoners in misery and in irons,
¹¹for they had rebelled against the
      words of God,
  and spurned the counsel of the
      Most High.
¹²Their hearts were bowed down with
      hard labor;
  they fell down, with no one to
      help.
¹³Then they cried to the Lᴏʀᴅ in their
      trouble,
  and he saved them from their
      distress;

¹⁴he brought them out of darkness
      and gloom,
  and broke their bonds asunder.
¹⁵Let them thank the Lᴏʀᴅ for his
      steadfast love,
  for his wonderful works to
      humankind.
¹⁶For he shatters the doors of bronze,
  and cuts in two the bars of iron.
¹⁷Some were sick through their sinful
      ways,
  and because of their iniquities
      endured affliction;
¹⁸they loathed any kind of food,
  and they drew near to the gates
      of death.
¹⁹Then they cried to the Lᴏʀᴅ in their
      trouble,
  and he saved them from their
      distress;
²⁰he sent out his word and healed
      them,
  and delivered them from
      destruction.
²¹Let them thank the Lᴏʀᴅ for his
      steadfast love,
  for his wonderful works to
      humankind.
²²And let them offer thanksgiving
      sacrifices,
  and tell of his deeds with songs
      of joy.
²³Some went down to the sea in
      ships,
  doing business on the mighty
      waters;
²⁴they saw the deeds of the Lᴏʀᴅ,
  his wondrous works in the deep.
²⁵For he commanded and raised the
      stormy wind,
  which lifted up the waves of the
      sea.

[26]They mounted up to heaven, they went down to the depths; their courage melted away in their calamity;
[27]they reeled and staggered like drunkards, and were at their wits' end.
[28]Then they cried to the LORD in their trouble, and he brought them out from their distress;
[29]he made the storm be still, and the waves of the sea were hushed.
[30]Then they were glad because they had quiet, and he brought them to their desired haven.
[31]Let them thank the LORD for his steadfast love, for his wonderful works to humankind.
[32]Let them extol him in the congregation of the people, and praise him in the assembly of the elders.
[33]He turns rivers into a desert, springs of water into thirsty ground,
[34]a fruitful land into a salty waste, because of the wickedness of its inhabitants.

makes its journey over the earthly realm.[1] Like the lost ones wandering in the wilderness, the ones dwelling in darkness cry out to God, and God leads them out of darkness and the shadow of death and tears their bonds to pieces.

Verses 17-22 tell of "sick" persons who are healed. The word translated "sick" (עול) actually means "foolish ones." The people of the ancient Near East associated sickness with foolishness or sin and understood it as God's punishment (see Pss 32:1-5; 38:3, 5). In the books of the prophets the north, the third direction mentioned in Psalm 107:3, was often depicted as the direction from which the punishment of God came to the ancient Israelites (see Isa 14:31; Jer 1:13; 6:22; 25:9; Zeph 2:13).

The fourth and final vignette of Psalm 107, verses 23-32, tells the story of a group of sailors who are saved from shipwreck. The compass point connected with the fourth vignette is rendered in the majority of modern English translations as "the south" (v. 3), but in the Masoretic Text the word translated "south" is "sea" (ים). The difference between the Hebrew text and the English translations seems to be a felt need to have the psalmist refer to the four compass directions. In addition, the word for "south" (ימין, literally "right": "south" when one faces the sunrise) is

1. See James B. Pritchard, ed., "The Hymn to the Aton," in *ANET.*

Psalm 107:1-43 (cont.)

35He turns a desert into pools of water,
a parched land into springs of water.

36And there he lets the hungry live,
and they establish a town to live in;

37they sow fields, and plant vineyards,
and get a fruitful yield.

38By his blessing they multiply greatly,
and he does not let their cattle decrease.

39When they are diminished and brought low
through oppression, trouble, and sorrow,

40he pours contempt on princes
and makes them wander in trackless wastes;

41but he raises up the needy out of distress,
and makes their families like flocks.

42The upright see it and are glad;
and all wickedness stops its mouth.

43Let those who are wise give heed to these things,
and consider the steadfast love of the LORD.

an easy emendation from the Hebrew word for "sea" (ים). The sea represented another real threat to those who lived in the ancient Near East. Merchant ships sailing out of the Phoenician ports across the Mediterranean often encountered difficulties in its unpredictable waters (recall the story of Jonah and the dangerous journeys of Paul in the book of Acts). Verses 25-29 depict God as the ruler of the sea, able to command its waters to do the divine bidding (see also Pss 29:34; 65:7; 89:9-10; 95:5).

Each vignette of those "redeemed" by YHWH follows the same format:

a description of the distress (vv. 4-5, 10-12, 17-18, 23-27)

a prayer to YHWH (vv. 6, 13, 19, 28)

details of the delivery (vv. 7, 14, 19-20, 29)

an expression of thanks (vv. 8-9, 15-16, 21-22, 30-32)

Are the four vignettes actual accounts of deliverance by YHWH, or is the psalm purely a literary composition with the four groups representing "all those who have experienced the redemption of the Lord"?[2] Whatever the original *Sitz im Leben* of Psalm 107, its placement in book 5 by the shaping community renders it a hymn celebrating deliverance, and in the story of the Psalter that deliverance is from the exile in Babylon.

2. James L. Mays, *Psalms*, IBC (Louisville: Westminster John Knox, 1994), 345.

In Psalm 107,[3] we read that the Lord makes it possible for the hungry to dwell safely in the land and establish a city; to sow fields, plant vineyards, and gather a harvest; and to have children and increase their cattle (vv. 36-38). In addition, the Lord pours contempt on rulers who oppress the people (vv. 39-40). The actions associated with YHWH in these verses are the actions of the "ideal sovereign" in ancient Israel. Psalm 72, the closing psalm of book 2, is a prayer of blessing that offers a description of such an "ideal sovereign" as one who defends "the cause of the poor," delivers "the needy," and crushes "the oppressor" (v. 4). That person is to be "like showers that water the earth" (v. 6), one who ensures "abundance of grain in the land" so that "people may blossom in the cities like the grass in the field" (v. 16). In the ancient Near East one's ability to live in security and provide for self and family required community. A strong leader who could crush the oppressor, ensure abundance of grain, defend the poor and needy, and such was essential to community life. In their postexilic situation the people of Israel were allowed to return to Jerusalem, to rebuild the temple, and to resume their worship practices, but they were vassals to the Persian government and could not have their own sovereign. Psalm 107 assures them that YHWH can and will be their source of security and provision in the postexilic period.

A sense of belonging, of place, is an essential element of human well-being. Recall the stories of Cain in Genesis 4 and of Hagar and Ishmael in Genesis 21. Cain cries out to God: "My punishment is greater than I can bear" (Gen 4:13); Hagar lifts up her voice and weeps (Gen 21:16). Without place, without landedness, humanity is rendered homeless. How might we understand the greater significance of land, of a physical place to call one's own? Walter Brueggemann writes: "Land is never simply physical dirt but is always physical dirt freighted with social meanings derived from historical experience." It is never "contextless space,"[4] or, perhaps better, it is "storied place." Ellen Davis insightfully adds: "The Bible as we have it could not have been written beside the irrigation canals of Babylon, or the perennially flooding Nile, any more than it could have

---

3. Many commentators maintain that in its original form Psalm 107 consisted of only verses 1-32 and that verses 33-42 were a separate composition added to it at some point in its history. Gerstenberger argues quite convincingly, however, for the unity of Psalm 107. See Erhard S. Gerstenberger, *Psalms, Part 2, and Lamentations*, FOTL 15 (Grand Rapids: Eerdmans, 2001), 246–53.

4. Walter Brueggemann, *The Land: Place as Gift, Promise, and Challenge in Biblical Faith*, 2nd ed. (Minneapolis: Fortress, 2002), 2, 55.

emerged from the vast fertile plains of the North American continent."[5] She goes on to say, quoting American Midwestern writer Scott Russell Sanders, "All enduring literature is local, rooted in place, in landscape or cityscape, in particular ways of speech and climates of mind."[6]

The importance of land, a place to call one's own, is paramount in the words of Psalms 105, 106, and 107; it is a major concern of much of the Hebrew Bible text, and it is a significant issue in the twenty-first-century world. Every person needs a sense of belonging, of groundedness, of knowing where "home" is. For refugees, immigrants, those subject to forced migration, and those abandoned by their families that sense and knowledge of home is shattered. Such people will need a new sense of belonging, of knowing "home," and those who know where "home" is are called on to embrace those who do not and help them find a sense of belonging, thereby allowing them to develop a new story, their new "enduring literature."

Psalm 107 closes with the words:

> Whoever is wise [חכם] will hear these things . . .
> And those keeping the steadfast love [חסד] of the LORD will attend. (v. 43)[7]

While the NRSV translates the first line of verse 43 as "Let those who are wise . . .," the subject is singular ("the one who") in the MT. In the same way that the closing verses of Psalm 106 (vv. 47-48) anticipate the opening verses of Psalm 107 (vv. 1-3), so the closing verse of Psalm 107 (v. 43), addressed to "the one who is wise," anticipates the following psalms, where the character of David returns after being virtually absent in books 3 and 4.[8]

---

5. Ellen F. Davis, *Scripture, Culture, and Agriculture: An Agrarian Reading of the Bible* (Cambridge: Cambridge University Press, 2009), 26.

6. Scott Russell Sanders, "Letter to a Reader," in *Writing from the Center* (Bloomington: Indiana University Press, 1995), 178.

7. Author's translation.

8. David is associated, in their superscriptions, with thirty-nine of the forty-one psalms in book 1, with eighteen of the thirty-one psalms in book 2, but with only one psalm of the seventeen in book 3 and two of the seventeen in book 4. In book 5, David is associated with fourteen of the forty-four psalms. See the introduction, pp. l–lv.

Psalm 107—Ubuntu

Psalm 107 opens with the same words found at the beginning of Psalm 106, "O give thanks to the LORD, for he is good; for his steadfast love endures forever," thereby connecting the closing of book 4 with the opening of book 5 of the Psalter. While the words previously introduced a psalm telling of Israel's disobedience to God throughout its history, in Psalm 107 they begin a psalm that relates God's love and works of salvation in times of distress.

The psalm can be divided into three main sections, each building on the theme of the love, help, and deliverance of YHWH. Verses 1-3, the first section of the psalm, are a hymn of thanksgiving to YHWH for redeeming the people and bringing them back to the land of promise. The redeemed come from the four cardinal directions: the east, the west, the north, and the south.

Verses 4-32, the second section of Psalm 107, recount stories of the salvation of four groups of people whom YHWH delivered out of distressing situations. A description of the distress and a call to YHWH to save is repeated in each of the stories (vv. 6, 13, 19, 28), followed by expressions of praise and thanksgiving to YHWH for deliverance (vv. 8, 15, 21, 31). In the first story, verses 4-9, people experience hunger and thirst in the wilderness and seek YHWH's deliverance from desert places; verses 10-16 tell of prisoners whom YHWH delivers from darkness and gloom; the third story, in verses 17-22, narrates the plight of those sick and near "the gates of death," whom YHWH heals and saves from destruction; the final story, verses 23-32, is one of sailors tossed about on a stormy sea that YHWH commands to be calm, thus delivering the sailors from their distress.

The third and final section of Psalm 107 is verses 33-41 (with vv. 42-43), a hymn celebrating YHWH's ability to reverse and transform people's situations. While YHWH is able to "turn rivers into a desert" and "fruitful land into a salty waste" (v. 33), YHWH instead "turns a desert into pools of water" and "a parched land into springs of water" (v. 35). Thus people can "establish a town to live in" and "sow fields, and plant vineyards, and get a fruitful yield" (vv. 36-37). The psalm ends with two verses of wisdom words that conclude with the theme of YHWH's steadfast love.

Psalm 107 reflects on the Israelites' return from exile in Babylon, recalling that traumatic time by means of imagery of pain and suffering. But the psalm reminds readers or hearers that YHWH is not only a god of judgment but also a god of transformative salvation and love. This is a powerful pastoral message of encouragement to individuals and nations alike. The in-between times, when people are moving from experiences of pain and suffering to salvation and freedom, are perhaps some of the most challenging moments in life. In such times of transition many feel great emotional distress, a loss of identity, and isolation. Reassurance of the presence and continuing love of God are essential elements in overcoming that distress, loss, and isolation.

Psalm 107 provides just such reassurance for individuals in the in-between times as well as for nations. South Africa is known for many things but most significantly perhaps for its history of apartheid and the end to apartheid with a democratic election in 1994. The person most prominently associated with this struggle in his "long walk to freedom" is, of course, Nelson Mandela. After postapartheid South Africa was established, the citizens of the country faced many problems and challenges. Many black South Africans felt they were the victims of apartheid, having been abused by the system, and thus could not overcome the systemic oppression based on their skin color. Many white South Africans feared for the life they had established. All the citizens of South Africa struggled to find their way (and identity) in the newly established democratic society.

In his book *Notes to the Future: Words of Wisdom*, Nelson Mandela wrote: "Disasters will always come and go, leaving their victims either completely broken or steeled and seasoned and better able to face the next crop of challenges that may occur."[9] Out of apartheid a new "rainbow nation" (a common phrase used to describe South Africa) was formed; some of its citizens were broken, some steeled, and some seasoned. In South Africa the Zulu term *Ubuntu* is often used to express hope in this time of rebuilding, of reimagining the future of South Africa. The word may be translated "humanity" or, better, "humanity toward others." Nelson Mandela explained it this way: "A traveller through a country would stop at a village and he didn't have to ask for food or for water. Once he stops, the people give him food, entertain him. That is one aspect of Ubuntu, but it will have various aspects."[10]

Psalm 107 presents an expression of *Ubuntu* for the ancient Israelites, providing hope that in a difficult time of transition YHWH would be among them, hearing their cries of distress and disorientation and delivering them into a good land, a land familiar though changed. And YHWH will turn "deserts into pools of water, a

9. Nelson R. Mandela, *Notes to the Future: Words of Wisdom* (New York: Atria Books, 2012), 92.

10. Claire E. Oppenheim, "Nelson Mandela and the Power of Ubuntu," *Religions* 3 (2012): 369–88, at 369.

parched land into springs of water," so that the people may "establish a town to live in" and "sow fields, and plant vineyards, and get a fruitful yield" (Ps 107:35-37). "Let those who are wise give heed to these things, and consider the steadfast love of the LORD" (v. 43).

Lodewyk Sutton

Psalms 108–110

O God of My Praise, Do Not Be Silent!

Psalms 108–110 are attributed to David in their superscriptions. Seventy-four of the 150 psalms in the Psalter are so attributed, but their occurrence varies greatly from book to book.

According to the storyline of the Psalter, book 5 is set in the postexilic period of ancient Israel (see the introduction, pp. liv–lv). Beginning with Psalm 108, David, who has been virtually absent since his final words in book 2 (Ps 72:20), returns. Psalms 108–110; 122; 124; 131; 138–145 are "of David," and in them David leads the Israelites in praise of God as sovereign. In the center of book 5, with psalms of David (Pss 108–110 and 138–145) forming an *inclusio* around them, are psalms used in various celebrations and commemorations in Jewish life (Pss 113–134). David leads and the people join in to praise and give thanks to the God who created, sustained, and guided them throughout their history.

Psalms 108–110 continue many of the themes found in Psalms 105–107, in particular the theme of land. Psalm 105 celebrates the good provisions of God in delivering the Israelites from Egypt and leading them safely through the wilderness into the land of promise. Its twin psalm, 106, also addresses the escape from Egypt, the wilderness wandering, and the entry into the land, but it focuses on God's good provision despite the rebellion and disobedience of the people. The psalm's closing words ask God to "save" and "gather" the people from among the nations. The opening psalm of book 5, Psalm 107, seems purposely placed in answer to the petition at the end of Psalm 106. And its final verses describe God's provision of a land, a home for the displaced people. What follows in Psalm 108 is a recounting of the fate of the lands within and around ancient Israel.

TRANSLATION MATTERS

Of the 150 psalms in the Hebrew Psalter, 119 have superscriptions, and most of them attribute the psalm to a specific individual or group of individuals— David, the sons of Korah, Asaph, Solomon, Moses, and so forth. Hebrew notes the attribution with the preposition *l*ᵉ (ל) affixed to the beginning of the name. The preposition has a basic meaning of belonging in some manner or other and can be translated as "of," "to," "for," "on behalf of," and even "in the spirit of." The superscriptions of seventy-four of the Hebrew Psalter's psalms include *l*ᵉ David (לדוד). David is remembered as the great song singer of ancient Israel (see 1 Sam 16 and 2 Sam 1 and 22), but we need not maintain that David wrote the psalms. Rather, others wrote them, perhaps "to," "for," "on behalf of," or "in the spirit of" David.

Various books of the Hebrew Bible are attributed to and even bear the names of great leaders in the life of ancient Israel. Moses is connected with the Pentateuch and Job; Samuel and Ezra with the Deuteronomistic History (Joshua, Judges, 1 and 2 Samuel, 1 and 2 Kings); and Solomon with Proverbs, Ecclesiastes (Qoheleth), and Song of Songs.[1] Norman Gottwald reminds us:

> The biblical world was surprisingly devoid of personal pride in authorship and it knew nothing of copyright laws. When the Torah or Pentateuch is assigned to Moses, the psalms to David, and wisdom books to Solomon, we should probably understand Moses as the prototype of lawgiver, David as the prototype of psalmist, and Solomon as the prototype of sage or wise man.[2]

---

1. While some scholars propose that Song of Songs may have been composed by a female sage in answer to the words of Qoheleth and some that the book of Hebrews was written by a woman, no biblical book is ascribed directly to a woman.

2. Norman K. Gottwald, *The Hebrew Bible: A Socio-Literary Introduction* (Philadelphia: Fortress, 1985), 14.

Psalm 108

Psalm 108, the first psalm of David in book 5, is not an original composition. It joins together portions of two psalms found in book 2 of the Psalter: Psalms 57:7-11 (= Ps 108:1-5) and 60:5-12 (= Ps 108:6-13). Psalms 57 and 60 are two of the thirteen psalms in the Psalter whose superscriptions recall specific historical events in the life of David. Psalm 57 recalls the times when David fled from Saul and hid in caves (1 Sam 22:1; 24:3), while Psalm 60's superscription refers to a battle perhaps related in 2 Samuel 8:13-14 and 1 Chronicles 18:12-13.

Scholars disagree about the interpretation of the composite Psalm 108. H.-J. Kraus writes: "It is difficult to understand what the significance is of the combination in Psalm 108 of two completely different pieces," and in his 1993 commentary where one would expect to find an analysis of Psalm 108 readers are simply referred to Psalms 57 and 60.[3] Leslie C. Allen, on the other hand, writes, "The combination of earlier psalms illustrates the vitality of old Scriptures as they were appropriated and applied to new situations in the experience of God's people."[4] We will return to Allen's comment later in this analysis of Psalm 108.

Psalm 108 is classified as a community lament although, not unusually, both the voices of an individual (vv. 1-10) and of the community (vv. 11-13) occur. John Goldingay suggests that Psalm 108, a plea to God to lead in the acquisition of land, is "the other side of the coin" of Psalm 107 in which the psalm singer assures readers or hearers that God does provide a land, a place, a groundedness.[5]

In verses 1-3 of Psalm 108 an individual singer addresses God with words of confidence, stating that she will sing (שׁיר), make melody (זמר) with the harp (נבל) and lyre (כנר), give thanks (ידה) to God among the peoples, and sing praises (זמר) among the nations. These opening words echo the numerous calls to praise God in book 4. "Sing" (שׁיר) occurs in Psalms 92:1; 96:1, 2; 98:1; 101:1; 104:33; 105:2; 106:12. "Make melody/sing praises" (זמר) occurs in Psalms 92:7; 98:4, 5; 104:33; 105:2; "harp" (נבל) in Psalm 92:4; "lyre" (כנר) in Psalms 92:4 and 98:5.

---

3. Hans-Joachim Kraus, *Psalms 60–150: A Commentary*, trans. Hilton C. Oswald, CC (Minneapolis: Fortress, 1993), 333.

4. Leslie C. Allen, *Psalms 101–150*, WBC 21 (Nashville: Thomas Nelson, 2002), 96. See also Erhard S. Gerstenberger, *Psalms, Part 2, and Lamentations*, FOTL 15 (Grand Rapids: Eerdmans, 2001), 255.

5. John Goldingay, *Psalms*, vol. 3: *Psalms 90–150*, BCOT (Grand Rapids: Baker Academic, 2008), 264.

Psalm 108:1-13

A Song. A Psalm of David.

[1]My heart is steadfast, O God, my
   heart is steadfast;
   I will sing and make melody.
   Awake, my soul!
[2]Awake, O harp and lyre!
   I will awake the dawn.
[3]I will give thanks to you, O LORD,
   among the peoples,
   and I will sing praises to you
   among the nations.
[4]For your steadfast love is higher
   than the heavens,
and your faithfulness reaches to
   the clouds.
[5]Be exalted, O God, above the
   heavens,
   and let your glory be over all the
   earth.
[6]Give victory with your right hand,
   and answer me,
   so that those whom you love may
   be rescued.
[7]God has promised in his sanctuary:
   "With exultation I will divide up
   Shechem,

Of particular interest is the psalmist's declaration in verse 3 that she will "give thanks" (ידה). The verb occurs seven times in book 4 and five times in Psalm 107. Readers or hearers first encounter it in Psalm 92:1, where the psalm singer states that it is "good" to "give thanks" to YHWH. The next five occurrences (97:12; 99:3; 100:4; 105:1; 106:1) are imperative calls to readers or hearers to "give thanks." At the end of Psalm 106 the singers plead with God to "save" and "gather" them so that they may "give thanks" (v. 47), and then all five of the instances of the verb in Psalm 107 (vv. 1, 8, 15, 21, and 31) are again imperative calls to "give thanks." In Psalm 108:3 the singer is finally able to state with confidence: "I will give thanks [ידה]," since, as we read in verses 7-9, God has reclaimed as God's own the length and breadth of the land of promise.

The Israelite women and men who returned to Jerusalem in 538 BCE under the rule of the Persian Empire faced much uncertainty. God answered their petition (Ps 106:47); God promised a place to settle and flourish (107:33-41); now the promise is assured in the words "of David" (לדוד) in Psalm 108 (see Translation Matters). Their repatriation was undeserved; it was a gift from God, not earned through the efforts of "human help" (אדם, v. 12).[6] The singers of Psalm 108 can do nothing more than give thanks and learn to rely on their good God. J. Clinton McCann

---

6. See also Ps 146:3.

and portion out the Vale of
Succoth.
⁸Gilead is mine; Manasseh is mine;
Ephraim is my helmet;
Judah is my scepter.
⁹Moab is my washbasin;
on Edom I hurl my shoe;
over Philistia I shout in triumph."
¹⁰Who will bring me to the fortified city?
Who will lead me to Edom?
¹¹Have you not rejected us, O God?
You do not go out, O God, with
our armies.
¹²O grant us help against the foe,
for human help is worthless.
¹³With God we shall do valiantly;
it is he who will tread down our
foes.

writes: "Psalm 108 teaches us that the people of God never live beyond trouble and the need for God's help."⁷

Why include a psalm composed of parts of two other psalms of David at this juncture in book 5, a book that reflects on life in the postexilic period? Psalms 57 and 60 recount episodes in the life of David, and thus Israel, from the distant past. Why not a new psalm of hope for the future? Those who returned to Jerusalem after the Babylonian exile were concerned about the land, their stability in that land, and the provision of the necessities of life in that land. Their collective memory was of the great Davidic empire. The "author" of Psalm 108 was perhaps someone who pored over the traditional songs of the faith and found Psalms 57 and 60, psalms set during other times of uncertainty, continue to celebrate the promise of God's deliverance (Pss 57:1-3; 60:6-8).

Psalm 108 is a borrowing of old words, not newly composed ones. The psalm singer joined them together in a "new song" of confidence in God's ability to deliver and comfort in the exigencies of postexilic life just as God did during the reign of David. James A. Sanders, in an essay titled "Adaptable for Life: The Nature and Function of Canon," reflects on the use of older stories to address the concerns of later generations. He writes:

> One observation that impresses itself time and again in the study of history is that in crisis situations only the old, tried and true has any real authority. Nothing thought up at the last minute . . . can effect the necessary steps of recapitulation and transcendence needed by the threatened community. . . . A new story will not do; only a story with

7. J. Clinton McCann Jr., "The Book of Psalms," *NIB*, vol. 4 (Nashville: Abingdon, 1996), 1122.

old, recognizable elements has the power for life required, because it somehow can pierce beneath the immediate and apparent changes taking place to recover the irreducible core of identity left unthreatened.[8]

Psalm 108 is a reminder of the power of stories, of a community's stories, of individual stories—of the collective memory. A story that had power in one situation is repeated in a later time and situation. The readers or hearers in that later time bring new questions and concerns to the story, yet it is able to speak to the new generation and so it is repeated, handed down, from one generation to the next. With each telling, the story changes ever so subtly, but that change, that slight shift in context and meaning, is crucial to the survival of the story.

America has become a highly mobile, largely disjointed society, and genealogy is a growing interest for many, a quest to know who their ancestors were and to learn something of their stories. In many families women, often older women, the matriarchs of families, are the keepers of the family stories. The biblical text in general, and the book of Psalms in particular, reminds us of the importance of listening to the stories—family stories, faith stories, Bible stories—as we address the issues and concerns of our lives today.

Psalm 109

Psalm 109 is classified as an individual lament in which the psalmist invokes the wrath of God upon a group of foes. The language of the psalm places it within a special category of lament psalms called "imprecatory." The word comes from the Latin word *imprecari*, meaning "pray to, invoke." Many psalms of lament contain imprecatory language in the psalmists' cries to God (see Pss 11:3; 17:13; 31:17; 35:4; 59:11-13; 70:2-3). But in a few psalms the imprecatory language permeates; these include Psalms 12, 58, 83, 94, 109, 137, and 149.[9]

Psalm 109's imprecatory language is vivid and abundant. Because of that the psalm is virtually ignored by the Christian church. It is not included in lectionary readings, and its only reference in the New Testament is in Peter's sermon in Acts 1, where he uses the imprecatory words of Psalm 109:8 in speaking about the fate of Judas Iscariot: "Let another take his position" (Acts 1:20).

---

8. James A. Sanders, "Adaptable for Life: The Nature and Function of Canon," in *From Sacred Story to Sacred Text* (Philadelphia: Fortress, 1987), 21.

9. See Erich Zenger, *A God of Vengeance? Understanding the Psalms of Divine Wrath*, trans. Linda M. Maloney (Louisville: Westminster John Knox, 1996).

Psalm 109:1-31

To the leader. Of David. A Psalm.

¹Do not be silent, O God of my praise.
²For wicked and deceitful mouths are
  opened against me,
  speaking against me with lying
    tongues.
³They beset me with words of hate,
  and attack me without cause.
⁴In return for my love they accuse me,
  even while I make prayer for
    them.
⁵So they reward me evil for good,
  and hatred for my love.
⁶They say, "Appoint a wicked man
  against him;
  let an accuser stand on his right.
⁷When he is tried, let him be found
  guilty;
  let his prayer be counted as sin.

⁸May his days be few;
  may another seize his position.
⁹May his children be orphans,
  and his wife a widow.
¹⁰May his children wander about and
    beg;
  may they be driven out of the
    ruins they inhabit.
¹¹May the creditor seize all that he
    has;
  may strangers plunder the fruits of
    his toil.
¹²May there be no one to do him a
    kindness,
  nor anyone to pity his orphaned
    children.
¹³May his posterity be cut off;
  may his name be blotted out in
    the second generation.

TRANSLATION MATTERS

The Hebrew word translated "accuse" and "accuser" in Psalm 109:4, 6, 20, and 29 is the Hebrew word שָׂטַן, *satan*, which basically means an adversarial opponent. The word occurs twenty-seven times in the Hebrew Bible and is used of human accusers or adversaries as well as "divine" adversaries. In 1 Samuel 29:4 the Philistines fear that David might become "an adversary [שָׂטָן]" to them in battle if he is allowed to fight alongside them. In 1 Kings 11:14 Hadad the Edomite is described as "an adversary [שָׂטָן]" whom God raised up against Solomon.

In the prologue to the book of Job (chaps. 1 and 2) and in Zechariah 3 "the adversary" (הַשָׂטָן) is one of the "heavenly beings" (בני אלהים) who present themselves before YHWH and whose task seems to be to seek out and accuse people who are not faithful to YHWH. The word is not used as a proper name in either of these passages, but rather as a descriptor of one of the heavenly beings. The only instance in the Hebrew Bible where the word could be understood as a proper name is 1 Chronicles 21:1. There *satan* (שָׂטָן without the definite article) stood up against Israel and incited David to "count the people of Israel." Interestingly, the same story in 2 Samuel 24:1 reports that YHWH incited David to "count the people of Israel and Judah." Only in the intertestamental and New Testament periods is the term used as a proper name, denoting a being separate from and in absolute opposition to God and the believing community.

¹⁴May the iniquity of his father be remembered before the Lord, and do not let the sin of his mother be blotted out. ¹⁵Let them be before the Lord continually, and may his memory be cut off from the earth. ¹⁶For he did not remember to show kindness, but pursued the poor and needy and the brokenhearted to their death. ¹⁷He loved to curse; let curses come on him. He did not like blessing; may it be far from him.

¹⁸He clothed himself with cursing as his coat, may it soak into his body like water, like oil into his bones. ¹⁹May it be like a garment that he wraps around himself, like a belt that he wears every day." ²⁰May that be the reward of my accusers from the Lord, of those who speak evil against my life. ²¹But you, O Lord my Lord, act on my behalf for your name's sake; because your steadfast love is good, deliver me.

The first five verses of Psalm 109 are words of the psalm singer directed to God, asking that God "not be silent" in the face of what the psalmist is enduring from the "wicked [רשע] and deceitful mouths" surrounding her. In verses 6-20 words of imprecation are piled one on another. A major issue in reading Psalm 109 is identifying the voices in this portion of the psalm. Although the NRSV translation adds "they say" to the beginning of verse 6, the MT simply begins, "Appoint a wicked man [רשע] against him."[10] Are the imprecatory words in these verses those of the pray-er against a group of foes, or are they a direct quote by the pray-er of the words of the foes? In other words, is the psalmist imprecating the judgment of God upon the foes or recounting to God the unjust words spoken by her foes?

The use of singular nouns and verbs in verses 6-20 suggests that the psalm singer is quoting the words of the oppressors, but using singular forms may be the psalm singer's way of personalizing and emphasizing the words of indictment against those oppressing her. The imprecation ends in verse 20 with "May that be the reward of my accusers [שטן] from

10. The NIV, the NASB, and the KJV do not add "They say" to the text. The CEB agrees with the translation of the NRSV.

²²For I am poor and needy,
and my heart is pierced within me.
²³I am gone like a shadow at evening;
I am shaken off like a locust.
²⁴My knees are weak through fasting;
my body has become gaunt.
²⁵I am an object of scorn to my
accusers;
when they see me, they shake
their heads.
²⁶Help me, O LORD my God!
Save me according to your
steadfast love.
²⁷Let them know that this is your hand;
you, O LORD, have done it.
²⁸Let them curse, but you will bless.
Let my assailants be put to
shame; may your servant
be glad.
²⁹May my accusers be clothed with
dishonor;
may they be wrapped in their own
shame as in a mantle.
³⁰With my mouth I will give great
thanks to the LORD;
I will praise him in the midst of the
throng.
³¹For he stands at the right hand of
the needy,
to save them from those who
would condemn them to
death.

the LORD," again inviting the question: "Are we reading in verse 6-20 the words of the accusers against the psalm singer or the words of the psalm singer against the accusers?" Psalm 109 contains no clear answer to the question; it leaves the reader or hearer to struggle for herself with the ambiguity.

In verses 21-31 the psalm singer turns her attention directly to YHWH as her deliverer (v. 21, יצל). In verse 22 she states that she is "poor [עני] and needy [אביון]," the same words used in verse 16's condemnation against either the psalm singer or the accusers. In the final words of imprecation in verse 29 the psalm singer asks that the accusers be "clothed" (לבש) and "wrapped" (עטה) in dishonor and shame, echoing the words of verses 18 and 19. The psalm closes in verse 31 with words of confidence that YHWH is on the side of the needy (אביון) and will save them.

Compared to Psalms 108 and 110, the psalms surrounding it, Psalm 109 is a lengthy thirty-one verses. It is difficult to incorporate it into the storyline of the Psalter. Erhard Gerstenberger writes of it, "This clear-cut individual complaint voices overwhelming disgust for and aggression against enemies. There is no other example of individual complaint with an equal share of imprecative and ill-wishing affirmations."[11] In A. F.

11. Gerstenberger, *Psalms, Part 2, and Lamentations,* 257.

Kirkpatrick's 1910 commentary on the Psalms he writes that psalms such as 109 "startle and shock the Christian reader" and are "the very opposite of the spirit of the Gospel."[12]

In *A God of Vengeance: Understanding the Psalms of Divine Wrath*, Erich Zenger relates the attitude to the imprecatory psalms recited in the mid-twentieth century by the prioress of the Carmelite convent in Dachau, Germany. When the nuns were given permission to conduct services in German rather than in Latin, services attended by many tourists, she wondered if it might be best to return to Latin since, as she writes,

> No matter how much the vernacular brought home to us the riches of the psalms, the Latin had at least covered up the weaknesses of the psalms as prayer. In the immediate *vicinity of the concentration camp*, we felt ourselves unable to say out loud psalms that spoke of a punishing, angry God and of the destruction of enemies, often in hideous images . . . in the presence of people who came into our church agitated and mentally distressed by their visit to the camp. . . . It is a different matter when one prays [the psalms] privately or in community.[13]

How does the reader or hearer in the twenty-first century incorporate Psalm 109 into an understanding of God? John Goldingay reminds readers: "Retribution is not *the* fundamental principle, in OT or NT; in both, God's wrath is less central to God's character and activity than God's love. But it is *a* fundamental principle."[14] In the act of protesting vehemently to God, the psalmist points out the acts of violence that so often accompany injustice and unexplainable suffering. J. Clinton McCann writes this of Psalm 109:

> It suggests that evil, injustice, and oppression must be confronted, opposed, hated because God hates them. From this perspective, the psalmist's desire for vengeance amounts to a desire for justice and righteousness in self and society. . . . The anger is expressed, but it is expressed in prayer and thereby submitted to God.[15]

We live, and always have lived, in a world of unspeakable injustices. In the twentieth and twenty-first centuries alone Jim Crow laws, the *sho'ah*, issues of women's rights, racial injustice, forced migrations of peoples, human

---

12. A. F. Kirkpatrick, *The Book of Psalms* (Cambridge: Cambridge University Press, 1910), 652.

13. Zenger, *A God of Vengeance?*, 21.

14. Goldingay, *Psalms 90–150*, 288–89.

15. McCann, "The Book of Psalms," 1127.

trafficking, political oppression, food deserts, economic inequalities, and many issues and events are stark reminders that psalms of vengeance are still relevant today. We must speak out against injustice, inequality, and acts of violence. The words of Psalm 109 teach us, though, that anger and action exist in a delicate dance. When and to what extent do we ourselves act, and what do we commit to the safekeeping of the God of all creation? "O God of my praise, do not be silent!"[16]

Years of Discrimination and Inequality

After completing school I studied law and became an advocate in South Africa. One of the first rules you are taught as a law student is the Latin phrase *nemo iudex in sua causa* (literally, "None should be a judge in his or her own case"). Such an axiom can be a problem, though, when you live in a country that is well known for its corruption. To be given a fair trial is a basic fundamental right of every person, especially if one is accused of a crime and even more so if one finds oneself being falsely accused. Being your own judge, then, may seem a better alternative than finding yourself the victim of an unfair trial. Just such a situation seems to be the case for the singer of Psalm 109.

Psalm 109 is classified as one of the "imprecatory psalms" because of its use of curses or condemnatory words toward the ones persecuting the psalmist. The setting of the psalm seems to be some sort of judicial redress, perhaps in a religious court. There an individual is launching a defense against those who are accusing her or him of some form of evildoing (vv. 6-20). Whether the words uttered by the psalmist in verses 6-20 are hurled by the accused against her accusers or spoken by the accusers against her and now quoted by the psalmist is not made clear in the psalm. But the whole seems clearly to be a juridical appeal to Yhwh (vv. 1-5) to provide protection for the psalm singer against unjustified accusers.

If we accept that the words uttered by the psalmist in verses 6-20 are words of imprecation spoken against her by her accusers and then hurled back against them by the psalmist, then the psalm singer outlines the tactics of the accusers in vivid detail: they bring false charges before a presumably corrupt judge or presiding officer in verses 6 and 7, calling for the death of the psalmist and

---

16. For further discussion, see the commentary on Psalm 129.

her family in verses 8-13 and the total obliteration of her memory in verses 14-19. In verses 20-29 the psalm singer pleads for Yнwн to intervene and "put to shame" those speaking false words of accusation against her, thereby relinquishing to Yнwн her own felt need to act against her accusers. The psalmist does not become the judge in her own case. The psalm ends with a declaration of trust and thanks to Yнwн as the God who protects the poor and needy (vv. 30-31).

After the end of apartheid in 1994, when South Africa became a democracy, one of the nation's first priorities was to protect and guarantee the individual rights of each of its citizens. Recognizing every person as an individual with equal rights was so important because of the many years of discrimination and inequality that preceded the beginning of democracy in South Africa. Discrimination and unjust treatment existed on many levels—white on white, white on black and colored, black on white and colored, black on black. In so many instances people were treated as objects or as nonexistent in other people's eyes, saying perhaps along with those who oppress the singer of Psalm 109, "May there be no one to do him a kindness. . . . May his posterity be cut off; may his name be blotted out in the second generation" (vv. 12-13).

Unfortunately, such discrimination and unjust treatment was reflected in the South African juridical system even after the end of apartheid. The issue was addressed with the acceptance of the Constitution of South Africa in 1996 (Law 108 of 1996) and even more so in chapter 2 of the Constitution, the "Bill of Rights." The preamble of the Constitution of South Africa reads:

> We, the people of South Africa, Recognise the injustices of our past;
> Honour those who suffered for justice and freedom in our land;
> Respect those who have worked to build and develop our country; and
> Believe that South Africa belongs to all who live in it, united in our diversity.
> We therefore, through our freely elected representatives, adopt this Constitution as the supreme law of the Republic so as to—
> Heal the divisions of the past and establish a society based on democratic values, social justice and fundamental human rights;
> Lay the foundations for a democratic and open society in which government is based on the will of the people and every citizen is equally protected by law; Improve the quality of life of all citizens and free the potential of each person;

and Build a united and democratic South Africa able to take its rightful place as a sovereign state in the family of nations.

The Constitution of South Africa mandates that citizens are not to take justice or vengeance into their own hands but leave such matters to the juridical system. A democratic South Africa can exist only as long as its people do not become the judges in their own cases, even as regards vengeance, for in the words of the singer of Psalm 109, God "stands at the right hand of the needy, to save them from those who would condemn them to death" (v. 31).

Lodewyk Sutton

Psalm 110

Psalm 110 is the last of the three psalms "of David" that open book 5. It is classified as a royal psalm, words most likely spoken during an enthronement ceremony for one of ancient Israel's kings.[17] Its placement in book 5 can be puzzling since, according to the storyline of the Psalter (see the introduction, pp. liv–lv), the book recounts the postexilic period of ancient Israel's history, when the people had returned from exile in Babylon and were under the rule of the Persian Empire; thus they could not have a sovereign of their own ruling over them.

TRANSLATION MATTERS

Verses 1, 4, and 5: Three words are translated as "Lord" in verses 1, 4, and 5 of Psalm 110, but they are, in fact, three different Hebrew words. In verses 1 and 4 the word rendered "Lord" in the NRSV translates the Hebrew tetragrammaton Yhwh; "my lord" in verse 1 translates אדני, *'adoniy*, a term used by one person to address a human being who is in some way superior to that person. Verse 5's "the Lord" translates the Hebrew word אדני, *'adonay*, which is used in the Hebrew Bible only when addressing God. In verse 1, then, "the Lord" (יהוה) assures "my lord" (אדני, *adoniy*), the king, of a favored position: "Sit at my right hand." In verse 5 the psalm singer assures the newly enthroned king that "the Lord" (אדני, *'adonay*, God) will provide defense against enemies: "The Lord is at your right hand."

17. The other royal psalms in the Psalter are Pss 2, 18, 20, 21, 45, 72, 89, 101, 132, and 144.

Psalm 110:1-7

Of David. A Psalm.
[1]The LORD says to my lord,
  "Sit at my right hand
until I make your enemies your
    footstool."
[2]The LORD sends out from Zion
  your mighty scepter.
  Rule in the midst of your foes.
[3]Your people will offer themselves
    willingly
  on the day you lead your forces
  on the holy mountains.
From the womb of the morning,
  like dew, your youth will come to
    you.

[4]The LORD has sworn and will not
    change his mind,
  "You are a priest forever according
    to the order of Melchizedek."
[5]The Lord is at your right hand;
  he will shatter kings on the day of
    his wrath.
[6]He will execute judgment among the
    nations,
  filling them with corpses;
he will shatter heads
  over the wide earth.
[7]He will drink from the stream by the
    path;
  therefore he will lift up his head.

In addition to the question of its placement in book 5, Psalm 110 presents a number of textual and interpretational difficulties. The rendering of verse 3 varies widely in modern English translations, but the intent seems to be to convey "an elevated description of the newly enthroned monarch who is obeyed willingly by the people and endowed with strength and stamina."[18] The reference to Melchizedek in verse 4 poses another difficulty in interpretation. Melchizedek is mentioned in only one other place in the Hebrew Bible, Genesis 14:18-20. There he is described as king of Salem and "priest of the God Most High [אל עליון]." "Salem" is most likely the city of Jerusalem, in the territory of the Jebusites, which David captured and made his capital and the dwelling place of YHWH according to 2 Samuel 5:6-9; 6:1-15.[19] Psalm 110 implies, based on the comparison of the Israelite monarch with Melchizedek, that the king being enthroned in Psalm 110 is both king and priest.

The blending of kingly and priestly duties in Psalm 110 speaks of the hope of a future priestly king—a messiah—who will free the people from

---

18. Nancy L. deClaissé-Walford, Rolf A. Jacobson, and Beth LaNeel Tanner, *The Book of Psalms*, NICOT (Grand Rapids: Eerdmans, 2014), 836. See the various translations in the NIV, NASB, CEB, and ESV, for example.

19. In Ps 76:2 "Salem" is used in poetic parallelism with "Zion" as a designation for Jerusalem, the dwelling place of God.

foreign rule and oppression. Erhard Gerstenberger maintains that "Messianic promises typically arise in downtrodden groups or nations."[20] He goes on to say, concerning the reference to Melchizedek,

> The Jewish community of the Second Temple periodically developed fervent expectations for a restitution of the Davidic empire . . . or, more generally, hopes for a thorough change of all political, social, and economic affairs. . . . There is a cryptic air about Psalm 110. Very likely, songs like this had to use veiled language, in order not to arouse distrust and draw the attention of Persian officials.[21]

Erich Zenger suggests that Psalm 110 is a song of confidence by the postexilic community of a restoration of the territory outlined in Psalm 108:7-9 and a promised hope of retribution for the singer of Psalm 109.[22]

But perhaps there is more to Psalm 110 than immediately "meets the eye" of the reader or hearer. Many commentators point out the marked theocentric emphasis of Psalm 110. W. Dennis Tucker Jr. maintains that the chief theme of Psalm 110 is Yhwh's rule over enemy kings and nations.[23] Erich Zenger writes: "Psalm 110 is consistently theocentric. . . . On the one hand, the king is incorporated into God's own sphere of power and so is 'divinized,' but, on the other hand, he is disempowered as an independent figure insofar as he is ultimately a function of God."[24] Richard Clifford adds an interesting tie to the enthronement psalms of book 4 (Pss 93–100): "Davidic kingship was rooted in the kingship of Yahweh, the patron of the dynasty. Kingship was understood as leadership over the creatures of heaven and earth achieved by victory over malicious forces."[25] And J. Clinton McCann summarizes well the intent of Psalm 110 when he states that it is a threat to "politics as usual": "[It] is no mere artifact of ancient political propaganda. Rather . . . it is a world-transforming challenge to every form of politics and power that does not begin with submission of the self to God's claim."[26]

---

20. Gerstenberger, *Psalms, Part 2, and Lamentations*, 267.

21. Ibid., 267.

22. Frank-Lothar Hossfeld and Erich Zenger, *Psalms 3*, trans. Linda M. Maloney, Hermeneia (Minneapolis: Fortress, 2011), 146.

23. W. Dennis Tucker Jr., *Constructing and Deconstructing Power in Psalms 107–150* (Atlanta: SBL Press, 2014), 79.

24. Hossfeld and Zenger, *Psalms 3*, 154.

25. Richard J. Clifford, *Psalms 73–150*, AOTC (Nashville: Abingdon, 2003), 177.

26. McCann, "The Book of Psalms," 1131.

The writers of the New Testament quote Psalm 110 some fourteen times, more than any other psalm in the Psalter.[27] For them the words of this psalm were brought to life in the ministry of Jesus, who indeed challenged the forms of politics and powers of his time and thus those of all times. The words of Psalm 110, read in the context of subversion of political power, are a powerful source of hope to those who live in circumstances of oppression brought about by corrupt or misguided politics. In so many instances such oppression is felt most by women, children, and the elderly in society. In the transformative words of Psalm 110, may such find hope that Yhwh will indeed "execute judgment among the nations" (v. 6).

27. Matt 22:44; Mark 14:62; 16:19; Luke 22:69; Acts 2:34-35; 7:55; Rom 8:34; Eph 1:20; Col 3:1; Heb 1:3, 13; 8:1; 10:12; 1 Pet 3:22.

Psalms 111 and 112

The Reverence of the Lord Is the Beginning of Wisdom

Beginning with Psalm 111 the reader or hearer encounters a series of psalms that share a common introduction and/or conclusion. Psalm 111, along with Psalms 112 and 113, opens with the words "praise the LORD" (הללו יה). Psalms 112 and 113 close with the same words, as do Psalms 115–117. Only Psalm 114 in this series does not contain the characteristic opening or closing, but some scholars suggest that the closing "praise the LORD" of Psalm 113 (v. 9) may actually belong to the beginning of Psalm 114.[1]

Psalms 111 and 112 are alphabetic acrostics, as is the massive Psalm 119, in which each colon, verse, or group of verses of the psalm begins with a successive letter of the Hebrew alphabet.[2] Acrostic poems were the work of highly skilled literary artists and functioned in ancient Israelite literature in a number of ways. First, they were most probably memory devices to aid in private and public—individual and corporate—recitation; second, literarily they summarized all that could be said or needed to be said about a particular subject from *aleph* to *tav*, from A to Z. And

---

1. See the commentary for Ps 114.
2. The other alphabetic acrostics in the Psalter are Pss 25, 34, and 145.

third, as Adele Berlin writes, commenting on the structure of another alphabetic acrostic, Psalm 145:

> The poet praises God with everything from A to Z: his praise is all inclusive. More than that, the entire alphabet, the source of all words, is marshaled in praise of God. One cannot actually use all of the words in a language, but by using the alphabet one uses all potential words.[3]

Psalms 111, 112, and 119 share a common theme of reverence for the Torah, the instruction given by God to the ancient Israelites at Sinai. But in contrast to Psalm 119's 176 verses, Psalms 111 and 112 each consist of only ten verses. Psalm 111 contains seventy-two words, and Psalm 112 has seventy-nine words, making them succinct and masterful acrostic compositions.

In addition, these two brief psalms share no fewer than twelve key terms, including "fear" (ירא), 111:5, 9, 10; 112:1, 5, 7, 8; "delight in" (חפץ), 111:2; 112:1; "the upright" (ישר), 111:1, 8; 112:2, 4; "good" (טוב), 111:10; 112:5; "gracious" (חנון), 111:4; 112:4; "merciful" (רחום), 111:4; 112:4; "righteousness, righteous" (צדיק, צדקה), 111:3; 112:3, 4, 6, 9; "just, justice" (משפט), 111:7; 112:5; "remember (renown)" (זכר), 111:4, 5; 112:6; "established, steady" (סמך), 111:8; 112:8; "provide, give, distribute" (נתן), 111:5, 6; 112:9; and "forever, ever mindful," (לעולם, לעד), 111:3, 5, 9, 10; 112:3, 6, 9.

Psalm 111 is classified as an individual hymn of thanksgiving, while Psalm 112 is designated a wisdom psalm. Verse 10 of Psalm 111 acts as the bridge linking them: "The fear of the Lord is the beginning of wisdom; all those who practice it have a good understanding." The two psalms together are a celebration of God's mighty deeds on behalf of the people and instructions for the proper response by the people. Klaus Seybold observes that Psalm 111 is "theology" while Psalm 112 is "anthropology."[4]

Psalm 111

The opening words of Psalm 111, "I will give thanks to the Lord" (אודה יהוה), tie it to the preceding psalms of book 5. Psalm 107 called on those redeemed by Yhwh to "give thanks to the Lord [הדו ליהוה]"

---

3. Adele Berlin, "The Rhetoric of Psalm 145," in *Biblical and Related Studies Presented to Samuel S. Iwry*, ed. Ann Kort and Scott Morschauser (Winona Lake, IN: Eisenbrauns, 1985), 18. Kathleen O'Connor in *Lamentations and the Tears of the World* (Maryknoll, NY: Orbis Books, 2003), 12, adds, "Alphabetic devices embody struggles of survivors to contain and control the chaos of unstructured pain. . . . The poems are not spontaneous outbursts but carefully composed works."

4. Klaus Seybold, *Die Psalmen*, HAT (Tubingen: Mohr, 1996), 440.

Psalm 111:1-10

א ¹Praise the LORD!
I will give thanks to the LORD with
my whole heart,

ב in the company of the upright,
in the congregation.

ג ²Great are the works of the LORD,

ד studied by all who delight in
them.

ה ³Full of honor and majesty is his
work,

ו and his righteousness endures
forever.

ז ⁴He has gained renown by his
wonderful deeds;

ח the LORD is gracious and
merciful.

ט ⁵He provides food for those who
fear him;

י he is ever mindful of his
covenant.

כ ⁶He has shown his people the
power of his works,

ל in giving them the heritage of
the nations.

מ ⁷The works of his hands are
faithful and just;

נ all his precepts are
trustworthy.

ס ⁸They are established forever and
ever,

ע to be performed with faithfulness
and uprightness.

פ ⁹He sent redemption to his
people;

צ he has commanded his
covenant forever.

ק Holy and awesome is his
name.

ר ¹⁰The fear of the LORD is the
beginning of wisdom;

ש all those who practice it have a
good understanding.

ת His praise endures
forever.

in verses 1, 8, 15, 21, and 31. The words occur also in Psalms 108:3 and 109:30. The words of thanks in Psalm 111, however, are more general than specific in comparison with those in Psalms 107–109. In verses 2, 3, 4, 6, and 7 of Psalm 111 the psalmist speaks of YHWH's "works" (מעשים, vv. 2, 6 and 7), "work" (פעל), and "wonderful deeds" (נפלאות), with no overt historical or situational references. Perhaps, though, we may find a more specific reference lurking behind the generalized words of the psalm.

Verse 4 states that YHWH is "gracious" (חנון) and "merciful" (רחום), two of God's self-declarative attributes given to Moses on Mount Sinai in Exodus 34:6. The Hebrew root of "gracious" is חנן and means "to look kindly upon" in many cases where breaches of trust have taken place, as we see in the Golden Calf incident (Exod 32). חנן is used almost exclusively of YHWH in the Hebrew Bible and often in concert with other descriptive terms, suggesting the multifaceted character of God.[5] The

5. Heinz-Josef Fabry, "חנן ḥānan," *TDOT*, 5:23, 30.

word translated "merciful" derives from the noun רחם, whose literal meaning is "womb." References to God's רחום and רחמים, God's "womb-love," occur no fewer than twenty times in the book of Psalms.[6] In verse 5 God gives "food" (טרף), a reference perhaps to the giving of the manna and quail in the wilderness (Exod 16 and Num 11). The notice that God "gives food" can also be understood as a reference to another feminine attribute of God, that of preparing and providing the necessary nourishment for one's household, in this case the faithful people of God.[7]

Verse 6's "the inheritance of the nations" (נחלי גוים) suggests God's giving of the promised land to the Israelites (Deut 6–7). The "precepts" (פקודים) of verse 7 are part of the Torah, YHWH's instruction given at Sinai (see Pss 119:27, 104, 173, etc.), while the references to the "covenant" (ברית) in verses 5 and 9 remind the reader or hearer of the unconditional covenant with Abram in Genesis 15 and the reciprocal covenant with the Israelites at Sinai in Exodus 19. Finally, verse 9's reference to "redemption" (פדות) summarizes the actions of God in the exodus from Egypt.[8]

Verse 10 promises "wisdom" (חכמה) to all who "fear" (ירא) YHWH. The word translated by NRSV as "fear" in verse 10 is the same one rendered as "awesome" in verse 9. The choice of translation for ירא in these two verses is an interesting study in the meaning of the Hebrew root. "Fear" is a good translation of the word, but in today's culture the idea of fear is usually connected with the basic human instincts to run, defend, or retaliate. ירא encompasses a larger meaning of "awe, reverent respect, honor." It appears in the Hebrew Bible as a synonym for "love" (אהב, Deut 10:12), "cling to" (דבק, Deut 10:20), and "serve" (עבד, Deut 6:13; Josh 24:14). At its root the word denotes obedience to the divine will. The one who "fears" YHWH will receive wisdom (חכמה). As with "fear," "wisdom" is a word with multiple nuances of meaning, both in the biblical text and in the twenty-first-century world. The word occurs over one hundred times in the wisdom literature of the Hebrew Bible (Job, Proverbs, and Qoheleth). Two Hebrew words frequently used synonymously with חכמה are בין (meaning "to discern") and ידע (meaning "to know").[9] Wisdom is further personified as a woman in Proverbs and the Deuterocanonical books of the Wisdom of Solomon,

6. See, for example, Pss 25:6; 40:11; 69:16; 77:9; 79:8; 103:4, 8, and 13, and see the introduction, pp. xliv–xlv.

7. See Carol Meyers, *Rediscovering Eve: Ancient Israelite Women in Context* (Oxford: Oxford University Press, 2013), 123–32.

8. See Exod 8:23 and Isa 50:2.

9. See Gen 41:33 and 39; 2 Sam 14:20; Job 15:2; Prov 1:5; 17:28; Qoh 8:5; Isa 5:21; Jer 4:22.

Ben Sirach, and Baruch. The sexually evocative language of Ben Sirach equates the pleasures of knowing Woman Wisdom with the pleasures of knowing the Torah (Sir 24:19-22). Ben Sirach 24:23 states, in fact, "All this is the book of the covenant of the Most High God, the law [νόμον] that Moses commanded us," and Baruch 4:1 says, "She is the book of the commandments of God, the law [νόμος] that endures forever." The book of Psalms equates wisdom with Torah, specifically in Psalms 1 and 119, thereby inviting the reader to hear in the wisdom psalms and the wisdom elements of the psalms the voice of Woman Wisdom, the feminine iteration of YHWH, calling humankind to search out the path to a right relationship with YHWH through obedience to the Torah, expressed in Psalm 111 as "the fear of the LORD."[10]

Martin Luther writes of Psalm 111: "The words of this psalm are big with meaning."[11] While the psalm makes no direct reference to the redeeming acts of God during the Exodus and wilderness wandering, its words cannot but call to mind the great deeds and wondrous acts of God at that time. Thus it is a celebration of the foundational work of YHWH on behalf of the people of Israel. Its words of celebration preface the human response to YHWH called for in Psalm 112, and the wisdom words at the end of Psalm 111 provide the link to move the reader or hearer from celebration to action.

Why Should I Praise the Lord?

Writing this reflection on Psalm 111 at the end of a very tumultuous year in my life has helped me remember God's sovereignty over and continued presence to me. In the space of one year, three of my family members died. It seemed that just when the sting of one death was subsiding a little, another death opened the wounds that were beginning to heal.

What made the deaths even more traumatic is that these were three male members of my family. In my South African culture the men are expected to be the shepherds of the family. Women are not viewed as being competent heads of household, so these deaths left my family feeling anxious and vulnerable. Our questions were many. "Who will lead the family? Where will provision come from? Who will protect us?"

---

10. For further commentary on wisdom, see the introduction, pp. xlv–xlvi.

11. Martin Luther, *First Lectures on the Psalms 2*, Luther's Works, vol. 13 (St. Louis: Concordia, 1976), 371.

A little personal background may help the reader to understand the anxiety attached to the grief of losing these three male family members. I come from a poverty-stricken area of rural South Africa where many of the villages lack basic infrastructure and sanitation systems. The majority of the households survive on social welfare payments and their seasonal work in agriculture. There is great need; poverty is the norm, often in extreme forms. This is where I come from; I have lost three male family members. Given the world in which I grew up and all that has happened to my family during the last year, what reasons do I have to praise the Lord as Psalm 111 demands (v. 1)?

Reading Psalm 111 reminded me, however, that God always seems to make a way. Let's go exploring. The psalm singer begins with a declaration of praise to the Lord, alerting the reader to the intent of the psalm, which is to praise and offer gratitude to God. But I ask again, with all that has happened in my life, why should I praise the Lord? What possible reasons do I have to offer such in the world in which I live?

Psalm 111 tells me there are many. In verse 1 the psalm singer gives thanks to the Lord "with my whole heart," suggesting that it is possible for every part of our being to be thankful without reservation, without consideration of what we lack. Taking into account everything that I lack, everything that I have

lost, is it possible for every part of my being to thank God? Further, the verse tells us that we are to thank the Lord not just privately but in the company of the upright in the congregation. Even though elsewhere women are instructed to remain quiet in church (1 Cor 14:34), the psalm singer says we should not remain silent when it comes to exalting God.

Verses 2-4 describe the works of the Lord as "great," "full of honor," "majestic," and "wonderful." Humans are part of the creative "works" of the Lord (Eph 2:10), and so all of us—men, women, poor, rich, young, and old—are "full of honor" and "majestic." That includes my family and me. Moreover, the saving "works" of God, God's deeds, are "great" and "wonderful." Verse 5 reminds us that even in his grandeur God is mindful of the immediate needs of creation. The text speaks of "food," but we can presume that God is mindful of all our needs—water, clothing, shelter (Matt 6:25)—especially for the vulnerable in society: the helpless, the widows, and the orphans. And as a woman who, in her culture, often feels inadequate, I am also assured that God will provide me with my needs. I do not have to look to a man for provision but to the God who is able to provide.

Verses 6-8 celebrate the works of God's hands, works that are not metaphorical but tangible and powerful. God has "shown his people" the power of his works. "His people" in verse 6 refers not only to men but to women as well, and so all humanity is given "the heritage of the nations." The "faithful and just" works of God's hands are for all people, including me!

Verse 9 reminds us that God has sent redemption to his people. While we often think of redemption as being "saved from sin," marginalized people also cry out for redemption from centuries of oppression, abuse, neglect, and injustices. Women from impoverished areas like the one in which I grew up often despair of ever finding such redemption and cling to Psalm 111's words, which remind us that God has commanded his covenant forever, assuring readers that redemption is not an event but a continual process.

Verse 10 tells us that the fear of the Lord is the beginning of wisdom and those who practice it will have a good understanding. I believe that the fear of the Lord is what makes people consider others as equals rather than inferior in one way or another based on social status or position. These final words of Psalm 111 summarize well the message of the psalm and assure me that God, in his intentional work, deliberately created the women in my family and me female! God created us in God's image, and no matter the struggle we are sufficient human beings with great purpose and a stronghold in God. Thus, with the psalm singer, we—I—can "praise the Lord!"

Siphokazi Dlwati

Psalm 112

Psalm 112 is, like Psalm 111, a brief alphabetic acrostic consisting of seventy-nine words. (Psalm 111 contains seventy-two.) The two psalms are linked by verse 10 of Psalm 111: "The fear[12] of the Lord is the beginning of wisdom; all those who practice it have a good understanding."

Psalm 112 opens with "happy" (אשרי), a word used twenty-six times in the book of Psalms.[13] It signals that the reader or hearer is entering the sphere of Israelite wisdom teachings. The verbal root of the word is most likely אשר, which means "go straight, advance, follow a track," suggesting that the "happy" person is one who follows a well-planned path. The second half of verse 1 describes the well-planned path that

12. For a discussion of the Hebrew word translated here as "fear," see the commentary for Ps 111:10.

13. Pss 1:1; 2:12; 32:1-2; 33:12; 34:8; 40:4; 41:1; 65:4; 84:4, 5, 12; 89:15; 94:12; 106:3; 112:1; 119:1-2; 127:5; 128:1-2; 137:8, 9; 144:15; 146:5.

Psalm 112:1-10

[1]Praise the Lord!

א   Happy are those who fear the
Lord,

ב   who greatly delight in his
commandments.

ג   [2]Their descendants will be mighty
in the land;

ד   the generation of the upright
will be blessed.

ה   [3]Wealth and riches are in their
houses,

ו   and their righteousness
endures forever.

ז   [4]They rise in the darkness as a
light for the upright;

ח   they are gracious, merciful,
and righteous.

ט   [5]It is well with those who deal
generously and lend,

י   who conduct their affairs with
justice.

כ   [6]For the righteous will never be
moved;

ל   they will be remembered
forever.

מ   [7]They are not afraid of evil tidings;

נ   their hearts are firm, secure in
the Lord.

ס   [8]Their hearts are steady, they will
not be afraid;

ע   in the end they will look in
triumph on their foes.

פ   [9]They have distributed freely, they
have given to the poor;

צ   their righteousness endures
forever;

ק   their horn is exalted in honor.

ר   [10]The wicked see it and are angry;

ש   they gnash their teeth and melt
away;

ת   the desire of the wicked comes
to nothing.

---

the "happy" person follows. Such a one greatly "delights" (חפץ) in the "commandments" (מצות). The words of Psalm 112:1 call to mind Psalm 1, which says that the "happy" (אשרי) person is one who "delights" (חפץ) in the "law" (תורה) of Yhwh (Ps 1:1-2).[14]

Verses 2 and 3 outline the rewards for those who "fear the Lord" and "delight in the commandments." They will have "mighty," "upright," and "blessed" descendants and a "house" (בית) in which are "wealth" (הון) and "riches" (עשר).[15] The words translated in the NRSV as "wealth" and "riches" occur extensively in the wisdom literature of the Old Testament. The primary message regarding wealth and riches is first that they

---

14. In Ps 119, "commandment" (מצוה) and "law" (תורה) are two of the eight terms used interchangeably to refer to the instructions given by God to the Israelites at Sinai during the wilderness wanderings.

15. The words of these verses echo in many ways the promises given by God to Abram in Gen 12, 13, and 15—descendants, land, house, and blessing.

come from God. In Proverbs 8:18, Woman Wisdom states, "Riches [עשֶׁר] and honor are with me, enduring wealth [הוֹן] and prosperity."

Second, wealth and riches are the result of diligence and hard work. Proverbs 13:11 states: "Wealth [הוֹן] hastily gotten will dwindle, but those who gather little by little will increase it." In Proverbs 10:4 we read: "A slack hand causes poverty, but the hand of the diligent makes rich [עשֶׁר]." Third, though, in many instances people have little control over their own ability to achieve wealth and riches. Proverbs 22:2 states: "The rich [עשִׁיר] and the poor have this in common: the Lord is the maker of them all." Hannah sings in 1 Samuel 2:7-8:

> The Lord makes poor and makes rich [מעשִׁיר];
>> he brings low, he also exalts.
> He raises up the poor from the dust;
>> he lifts the needy from the ash heap,
> to make them sit with princes
> and inherit a seat of honor.

Fourth, the pursuit of wealth and riches can be detrimental to true happiness. In Proverbs 22:1 we read, "A good name is to be chosen rather than great riches [עשֶׁר]; and favor is better than silver or gold"; in Proverbs 23:4, "Do not wear yourself out to get rich [עשֶׁר]; be wise enough to desist." Further, wealth and riches are often depicted negatively in the pages of the Hebrew Bible, as we see in Qoheleth 5:13: "There is a grievous ill that I have seen under the sun: riches [עשֶׁר] were kept by their owners to their hurt." In Proverbs 28:6 we read, "Better to be poor and walk in integrity than to be crooked in one's ways even though rich [עשִׁיר]," and in Proverbs 11:28, "Those who trust in their riches [עשֶׁר] will wither, but the righteous will flourish like green leaves."

Fifth, the Hebrew Bible wisdom writers condemned amassing wealth at the expense of the poor. Thus we find in Proverbs 22:16: "Oppressing the poor in order to enrich oneself, and giving to the rich [עשֶׁר], will lead only to loss," and in Proverbs 22:7: "The rich [עשִׁיר] rule over the poor, and the borrower is the slave of the lender." In the prophetic literature the book of Amos condemns those "who sell the righteous for silver, and the needy for a pair of sandals" (2:6) and those "who oppress the poor, who crush the needy" (4:1). The Hebrew Bible thus presents a conflicted picture of wealth. It is a gift from God that comes about as a result of diligent hard work, but when amassed without thought for or at the expense of others it becomes a perversion, a false basis for happiness.

Verses 3 and 4 of Psalm 112 parallel verses 3 and 4 of Psalm 111, suggesting that the "happy" person is focused on things that concern Yhwh.

YHWH's "righteousness" (צְדָקָה) endures for all time (Ps 111:3) as does that of the "happy" person (Ps 112:3). Words derived from the Hebrew root "righteous" (צדק) occur some 523 times in the Hebrew Bible, and its basic meaning is "doing what is right or just." Righteousness has less to do with a pious mind-set than with a sense of what is right. A striking story of righteousness in the Hebrew Bible is found in Genesis 38. Tamar, Judah's daughter-in-law, in an act of deception conceives twins by Judah in order to fulfill the Levirate marriage requirements of the Torah (Deut 25:5-10). Though she deceives him, Judah declares at the end of the story: "She is more in the right [צדקה] than I" (Gen 38:26). Delighting in the commandments of YHWH renders the "happy" person of Psalm 112 "righteous," that is, "knowing and doing what is right."

The outworking of that "righteousness" is outlined in verses 4-9 of Psalm 112. The "happy" person is a light in the darkness, being "gracious [חנון] and merciful [רחום]," just as YHWH is in Psalm 111:4.[16] That person generously lends, conducts her affairs with justice, is not afraid of evil tidings, has a firm heart, distributes freely, and gives to the poor.[17]

Verse 6 acts as something of an interlude for Psalm 112, stating that the righteous will not be moved (מוט)[18] and will for all time be remembered (זכר). The verse is strikingly parallel to Psalm 111:4's words: YHWH has "gained renown" (זכר) because of "his wonderful deeds" (נפלאות). The ending of Psalm 112 in verse 10 offers a summary statement of the contrasting fates of the righteous and the wicked, typical of the wisdom tradition of ancient Israel. The wicked come to nothing; they are angry, gnash their teeth, and melt away (Ps 112:10) while the righteous are a light to the upright (Ps 112:4).

Two major issues confront twenty-first-century readers or hearers of Psalm 112. First and most important is the profound degree of economic, social, and political inequality in the world, seemingly a given in our world today. Many people are, like this writer, are part of a privileged elite who have had opportunities for education, have enough to eat each

---

16. For a full discussion of "gracious" (חנון) and "merciful" (רחום), see the commentary on Ps 111.

17. When the apostle Paul wants to encourage the church at Corinth to contribute financially to the impoverished church in Jerusalem he quotes Ps 112:9 as an example of a cheerful giver (2 Cor 9:9).

18. מוט occurs numerous times in descriptions of the "habitable" world (תבל) in the enthronement psalms: it will not be moved. See Pss 93:1 and 96:10. In 94:18 the psalm singer states that when her foot was slipping (מוט) YHWH's "steadfast love" held her up.

day, have access to adequate health care, trust the quality of their drinking water, and have the freedom and means to travel from one place to another. But we live in societies in which the rich continue to manipulate power to their own ends and marginalize those less able to contend for themselves. Many more women than men live in an oppression of inequality, even in so-called developed countries. Their roles, particularly when they are also single parents, contribute to their plight of low wages, lack of affordable housing and slum landlords, lack of affordable childcare, no sick leave time from work, no employer-provided health care, and no time or opportunity for education and job training.

Second, in the global world in which we live "benevolent mission work" is an increasing phenomenon. The "haves" swoop in to temporarily rescue and provide for the "have nots." While the benefits of such "mission work" are important, the greater need is for an end to the economic and social disparity that leads to the need for such "mission work" in the first place.

Psalms 111 and 112 are a summary statement of what faith is all about: who God is and what humans must do in response to God. In a rich intertwining of language and metaphor, the "happy" person of Psalm 112 partners with the God of Psalm 111 and together they work to achieve righteousness—right living, correct order, and truth—in the world.

Psalms 113–118

From a Narrow Place to a Broad Place—Celebrating Deliverance from Oppression

Psalms 113–118 are a group of psalms in book 5 known as the Egyptian Hallel (הלל) because of their frequent references to the exodus from Egypt (Pss 114:1; 116:3-4, 16; 118:5) and the wilderness wanderings (Pss 114:3-8; 116:5; 118:10-13).[1] These psalms were used at all three of the Jewish pilgrimage festivals—Passover, Weeks (Pentecost), and Tabernacles (Sukkoth, Booths)—but in particular at the spring celebration of Passover (Pesach, פסח). The Egyptian Hallel is the first of a group of pilgrimage psalms in book 5; Psalm 119 is also read at the feast of Weeks, which commemorates the giving of the Torah at Sinai, and Psalms 120–134, the Songs of Ascents, are sung at the festival of Tabernacles, which celebrates God's provision for the Israelites during the wilderness wanderings.

The Mishnah describes how Passover was celebrated in Jerusalem, at least in later times. When the court of the temple was filled with people the gates were closed, individual sacrifices were offered, and Psalms

---

1. See The Babylonian Talmud Tractate Ber. 56a.

113–118 were sung. The priests took portions of the sacrifices for burnt offerings and returned the rest to the people. After nightfall the people left the court of the temple and roasted their offering for the Passover meal.[2] In modern Jewish life the Egyptian Hallel is part of the Passover Seder, with Psalms 113–114 recited before the Passover meal and Psalms 115–118 at its conclusion. Passover is one of the three celebrations in Jewish life, including Weeks and Tabernacles, that are best celebrated in Jerusalem. At the conclusion of the modern Passover Seder meal, as participants raise the last cup of wine, they say, "Next year in Jerusalem!"

Psalms 113–118, except for their references to the exodus and wilderness wanderings, can seem a fairly disjointed collection. With Elizabeth Hayes, however, we see that they flow in a cohesive manner from a call to praise Yhwh (113:1-3) to a vow to praise and exalt Yhwh (118:28-29).[3] Her outline is as follows:

113:4–114:8	A narrative of God at work in the lives of the people—the poor and needy, the barren one, and the captives in Egypt
115:1–116:19	A declaration that the name of Yhwh is to be glorified because of Yhwh's steadfast love and faithfulness, in contrast to the idols of the nations
117:1-2	Therefore Yhwh is to be praised and extolled by all nations and all peoples
118:1-27	Yhwh is to be thanked for his goodness and steadfast love by Israel, by Aaron, and by all who fear him
118:28-29	A vow to thank and extol Yhwh for his goodness and steadfast love

Psalm 113

Psalm 113 is the first psalm in the Egyptian Hallel. In modern Jewish life Psalms 113–114 are recited before the Passover meal and Psalms 115–118 at its conclusion. Psalm 113 is sung at the blessing of the first Passover cup of wine. It calls its hearers to praise the name of the Lord

2. See m. Pesaḥ. 5:5-10.
3. Elizabeth Hayes, "The Unity of the Egyptian Hallel Psalms 113–18," *BBR* 9 (1999): 145–56.

Psalm 113:1-9

¹Praise the LORD!
Praise, O servants of the LORD;
    praise the name of the LORD.
²Blessed be the name of the LORD
    from this time on and forevermore.
³From the rising of the sun to its setting
    the name of the LORD is to be
        praised.
⁴The LORD is high above all nations,
    and his glory above the heavens.
⁵Who is like the LORD our God,
    who is seated on high,
⁶who looks far down
    on the heavens and the earth?
⁷He raises the poor from the dust,
    and lifts the needy from the ash
        heap,
⁸to make them sit with princes,
    with the princes of his people.
⁹He gives the barren woman a
        home,
    making her the joyous mother of
        children.
Praise the LORD!

for all of the Lord's goodness to the people and is an apt introduction to the Passover story, which is then recounted in the following Psalm 114.

Two evenly divided stanzas make up Psalm 113, verses 1-4 and 5-9, with verse 5a as the centerpiece connecting the two parts. In verses 1-4 the phrase "the name [שׁם] of the LORD" appears three times, followed by the rhetorical question in 5a, "Who is like the LORD?" In verses 5b-9a God's activity is described with participial phrases, indicating the active and ongoing work of God in the world. Verse 9b frames the psalm with a closing hallelujah. The psalm may have been used antiphonally, sung by two choirs in a worship setting.[4]

The psalm opens with "hallelujah" (הללו יה), a call to praise YHWH. Twice more in the opening verse the call to praise is issued, first naming the subject of the command, "O servants of the LORD," and then further identifying the object of praise, "the name [שׁם] of the LORD." The phrase "the name of the LORD" appears again in verses 2 and 3, where hearers are called to praise it "from this time on and forevermore" and "from the rising of the sun to its setting."

"Name" was an important concept in the ancient Near East. Names reflected the natures and characters of the persons who bore them and were conceptually equal to the very essence of being. To know someone's name was to possess some part of that person; to speak a name

4. Hans-Joachim Kraus, *Psalms 60–150*, trans. Hilton C. Oswald, CC (Minneapolis: Fortress, 1993), 367.

was to speak into being. In the creation story in Genesis 2, God brings the animals one by one to the first human and we read, "and whatever the [human] called every living creature, that was its name" (Gen 2:19). Here we have a wonderful picture of humanity working together with God as co-creator. The name "Jacob" means "he usurps," because he grabs Esau's heel at their birth, attempting to be the firstborn twin (Gen 25:26). He indeed usurps his brother's lot later in life when he coerces Esau into selling him his birthright and tricks Isaac into giving him the blessing. After the incident at the Jabbok, God changes Jacob's name to "Israel," which means "he has struggled with God" (Gen 32:28). In Exodus 3, Moses encounters God at the burning bush. In that encounter Moses replies to God's command to return to Egypt with a seemingly simple request. "If I come to the Israelites and say to them, 'The God of your ancestors has sent me to you,' and they ask me, 'What is his name?' what shall I say to them?" (3:13). Moses asks for God's name. What is the nature and character of the God who is requesting such a thing? God replies with self-naming words of existence, "I am that I am" (אהיה אשר אהיה), from which the ancient Israelites derived the name Yhwh (יהוה). The book of Deuteronomy tells us that God's name (שם) will dwell in the place of God's choosing in the land (Deut 12:5; 14:23-24; 16:2), and Psalm 8:1 cries, "O Lord, our sovereign, how majestic is your name [שם] in all the earth." Verse 4 of Psalm 113 echoes Psalm 8. The name of Yhwh is exalted over the nations; God's glory is over the heavens.

Name remains an important concept in our world today. When we meet others for the first time we learn their names. They are markers of identity, of ties to family and home. But what happens when that identity is altered—voluntarily or involuntarily? When women marry they often change their surnames to that of their spouses. When people want to leave the past behind and begin anew they sometimes change their name. When Africans were brought to America as slaves in the eighteenth and nineteenth centuries their names were changed or Anglicized. When immigrants came to America in the nineteenth and twentieth centuries their sometimes seemingly complicated names were simplified by immigration authorities. How do such changes affect a person's sense of identity, of belonging, of family and home? The quest to know one's ancestors and to participate in a collective family memory is a growing interest in our mobile and disjointed society today. Women, especially the matriarchs of families, are often the keepers of collective family memories. They are living models of Woman Wisdom who takes her stand in the busiest corner of the city and admonishes those who would listen to heed her wise words (Prov 1–3).

The question of verse 5 is the center of Psalm 113, connecting the call to praise in the first four verses with the reasons to praise found in verses 6-9. The answer to the question "who is like the Lord our God?" is obvious, based on the description of Yhwh that follows. Verse 6 states that God "is seated [שׁב] on high," yet God "looks down on the heavens and the earth." In verses 7 and 8 God "raises up from the dust [עפר]" and "lifts up from the ash heap [אשׁפת]" the poor (דל) and the needy (אביון) and causes them to sit (שׁב) with princes. And in verse 9 God "gives a home [מושׁיבי הבית]" to "the barren woman [עקרה]," making her the joyous mother of children.

In the context of the Egyptian Hallel psalms, the needy and the poor in Psalm 113 can be understood as the Israelites in slavery in Egypt and the barren woman as Israel. The repetition of the verb "to dwell, to sit (שׁב)" in verses 6, 8, and 9 is striking. God, who dwells in heaven, elevates the poor and needy to dwell with princes and the barren one to dwell in her own home.

In addition, Psalm 113:5, 7-8, 9 can be connected with verses 2, 5, and 8 of Hannah's Song in 1 Samuel 2, in which Hannah sings to the "Holy One," the "Rock" (v. 2), because "the barren [עקרה] has born seven" (v. 5) and because Yhwh "raises up the poor [דל] from the dust [עפר]; he lifts the needy [אביון] from the ash heap [אשׁפת], to make them sit [שׁב] with princes" (v. 8). The story of God's care for Hannah thus becomes a model for God's care for Israel. The barren woman is a common theme in the Hebrew Bible—Sarah, Rebekah, Rachel, Tamar, and Hannah.[5] Each of their stories has to do with the future of God's covenant relationship with Israel.

In the twenty-first century the meaning of Psalm 113's phrase "the joyous mother of children" encompasses much more than the biological function of birthing and rearing children. The world in which we live needs "mothers" living out their lives in myriad ways in order to ensure the future of God's covenant relationship with humanity. The neighborhood child whose only real sense of belonging comes from having a snack and a chat at your house; the elderly relative who counts on you to shop, cook, clean, and call to check on her or him; the smile and brief chat with the clerk at the grocery store; the teen you mentor through educational struggles; the hug given to the widow, the widower, the lonely person whom you meet; genuine care for humanity—these are

5. For Sarah, see Gen 16; for Rebekah, see Gen 25; for Rachel, see Gen 30; for Tamar, see Gen 38; and for Hannah, see 1 Sam 1.

the makings of the "joyous mother of children," those who ensure the future of God's covenant relationship with humanity.

Psalm 113 ends with the same word with which it begins—hallelujah—framing the psalm with words of praise. The psalm is a call to a community of believers to praise a transcendent God who cares enough for humankind to look down, reach down, and raise up the poor and needy of the earth. The answer to the question "Who is like the LORD our God?" can be nothing more and nothing less than "No one."

The Lord Lifts the Needy and Gives the Barren Woman a Home

One of the moral guidelines by which I live my life is that "the last book I have read must not become my newest viewpoint." That means every time I read, hear, or learn something I need to compare and critically evaluate it before I express or conform to its statement or viewpoint. Psalm 113 is one of those psalms that challenges one's understanding of life. Just when you think you have a full understanding of God and the nature of human life, something in the psalm triggers a new thought and you have to reconsider what you understand. One of these triggers is the imagery of the man and the woman in verses 7-9, especially that of the barren woman.

In the Old Testament world the man's domain was the public sphere and the woman's was the household. In public the man strove to support his and his family's honor and status, and it was the woman's role to manage the household and bear children for her husband. Verses 7-9 of Psalm 113 present, in my reading, a scene in which both the man and the woman seem to somehow fail in their designated functions. The man is poor and needy and sits in dust and ashes; the woman is barren. The fate of both is reversed when YHWH lifts up the man and provides children for the woman, restoring the honor and purpose of both.

There are many examples of women in the Old Testament who are barren and thus cannot fulfill their purpose in life. In most of the stories YHWH intervenes, whether by giving the woman her own child or the child of another woman to care for (Sarai in Gen 16:15; Rebekah in Gen 25:21; Rachel in Gen 30:5; Samson's mother in Judg 12:2-3; Hannah in 1 Sam 1–2), thereby restoring her status.

But what about women (and men) who are never able to have children for one reason or another? How might they read and interpret verses 7-9 of Psalm 113? One helpful way would be to understand the man and woman in these verses as a metaphor for the people of Israel who in so many instances in their history lived in situations in which a sense of honor and self-worth seemed out of reach. The words of Psalm 113, a psalm that opens and closes with the words "Praise the LORD" and is one of the psalms recited at Passover, the celebration of God's deliverance of the Israelites from captivity in Egypt, offers hope in the midst of despair for the poor, the needy, and the barren.

Is it possible for a woman and a man who have recently suffered a miscarriage and despair of being able to have children to find words of hope in Psalm 113? How do those who feel poor, needy, and barren embrace its words? My wife and I went through the pain and sorrow of a miscarriage. We together experienced the grief that comes when the doctor says there is no life remaining, the painful changes in the woman's body in the aftermath of a miscarriage, the self-blaming and self-questioning.

A few years after that painful experience we had our first child, and it was another five years before the birth of our second. We experienced the redemption promised in Psalm 113, but there are many others who are never able to have children and thus sense the redemption that Psalm 113 offers. How do they read the psalm, especially in the context of so many societies in which people expect that the natural result of marriage is offspring? The questions, the looks, the side conversations can be devastating and evoke a sense of inequality or inadequacy.

Reading Psalm 113 from its beginning can help the reader focus on the message of the whole psalm rather than solely on verses 7-9. Verses 1-6 remind us of the one who is to be praised—YHWH—and that the "name" of YHWH is essential to our praise "from the rising of the sun to its setting" (v. 3). The psalm further states that YHWH is "high above all nations" (v. 4), his "glory [is] above the heavens" (v. 4). YHWH is "seated on high" (v. 5), but "looks far down on the heavens and the earth" (v. 6). But the words of verse 1 are the great equalizer— we are all servants of YHWH who is "seated on high" and "looks far down." No one is higher than I, than any of us, except YHWH. Those who look down on me, consider themselves greater or better than me, pass judgment on me or question my faith cannot dominate or oppress me because we are all servants of YHWH and we stand equally before the God who is seated on high over the earth and all creation. This is the space in which all in the world come to bow down as equals and exclaim the opening and closing words of the psalm: "Praise the LORD— Hallelujah!" This is the space where we all are recognized by the one who sees us (Gen 16:13-14), the one who hears us (Ps 66:19), the one who feels the pain of human selfishness (Gen 6:6).

For those who read verses 7-9 of Psalm 113 and yet despair of having children, so much an expectation in some modern societies, the words of verses 1-6 may provide a measure of comfort that, in the end, God is "high above all" (v. 4) and God "looks far down" (v. 6), "raises" and "lifts" (v. 7), and makes the barren woman "the joyous mother of children" (v. 9). Biological children may not come as expected for a woman and man, but children, offspring, come in many iterations—nieces and nephews, students and parishioners, neighbors and the elderly. That, I maintain, is the message of Psalm 113. But for the questioning and self-blame of the childless couple there are no easy answers. Only God on high (v. 5) can give true joy (v. 9) and redirect our understanding of what gives honor and joy. Only then can we experience the true joy that comes from and results in praise to Yhwh.

Lodewyk Sutton

Psalm 114

Psalm 114 is the second psalm in the Egyptian Hallel. Psalm 113 is sung at the blessing of the first Passover cup of wine. It calls its hearers to praise the name of Yhwh for all of Yhwh's goodness to the people and is an apt introduction to the Passover story, which is then recounted in Psalm 114.

Psalm 114 is somewhat unusual in the Egyptian Hallel collection. It does not include the "hallelujah" (הלל יה) that is characteristic of this group of psalms. Since Psalm 113 both begins and ends with "hallelujah" and Psalms 115–117 end with it, some suggest that the final "hallelujah" of Psalm 113 be transferred to the beginning of Psalm 114. The final psalm in this collection, however, Psalm 118, also does not have "hallelujah" either at its beginning or end, so the seemingly missing "hallelujah" in Psalm 114 need not be viewed as problematic.

The opening words of the psalm place the reader or hearer in the midst of the story of the great saving act of God on behalf of Israel, the exodus from Egypt. Verses 1 and 2 are parallel expressions: Israel and house of Jacob, Egypt and a people of a strange language (לעז) in verse 1; and Judah and Israel, holy place and dominion in verse 2. The word translated "strange language [לעז]" in verse 1 is a *hapax legomenon*; it appears nowhere else in the text of the Hebrew Bible, though the prophetic books refer to peoples of different languages. Isaiah 28:11 speaks

Psalm 114:1-8

¹When Israel went out from Egypt,
the house of Jacob from a people
of strange language,
²Judah became God's sanctuary,
Israel his dominion.
³The sea looked and fled;
Jordan turned back.
⁴The mountains skipped like rams,
the hills like lambs.
⁵Why is it, O sea, that you flee?
O Jordan, that you turn back?
⁶O mountains, that you skip like rams?
O hills, like lambs?
⁷Tremble, O earth, at the presence of
the LORD,
at the presence of the God of
Jacob,
⁸who turns the rock into a pool of
water,
the flint into a spring of water.

of people with a "stammering lip" and "alien tongue," Isaiah 33:19 of "obscure speech," and Ezekiel 3:5-6 of people of "obscure speech" and "difficult language." In each of these references to unintelligible language the context connotes a sense of "the other," of "those who are different." One commentator likens the experience of the Israelites living among those of a "strange language" to that of immigrants, displaced persons, and refugees who daily struggle to understand and communicate and thus incur a sense of "loss and inferiority."[6]

The word translated in verse 2 as "holy place [קֹדֶשׁ]" is from a root that means "to be devoted, set apart," while the word translated "dominion [מִשֶׁל]" means "to rule over, reign." The two words convey two important characteristics of God as the Holy One in the midst of the people (see Hos 11:9) and the one ruling over the people (see Deut 33:5). Interestingly, neither of the names for Israel's God, Elohim (אֱלֹהִים) or YHWH (יהוה), appear in the first verses of Psalm 114, perhaps further strengthening the idea that Psalm 113, where we encounter the divine name nine times, is to be read as an introduction to Psalm 114.

Verses 3 and 4 introduce the major themes of Psalm 114. They complete the temporal clause begun with verse 1, "When Israel went out from Egypt." As with verses 1 and 2, verses 3 and 4 are parallel expressions: the sea and the Jordan, fled and turned back in verse 3; mountains and hills, rams and the young of the flock in verse 4. "The sea" in verse 3 probably refers to the Reed Sea that God parted in Exodus 14, and "the Jordan" to the stopping of the river's flow in Joshua 3.

6. Richard D. Nelson, "Psalm 114," *Int* 63 (April 2009): 172–74, at 174.

"The mountains" of verse 4 may be understood as Mount Sinai, while "the hills" are perhaps the central hill country of Syria/Palestine, where the Israelites first settled in the land of promise.[7] In these two verses an entire historical narrative is encapsulated: the escape from Egypt, the time in the wilderness, the crossing of the Jordan, and the settlement in the land of promise, the single most formative period in the life of ancient Israel.

Verses 5 and 6 repeat verses 3 and 4, but this time in question form. "Why is it, O sea . . . O Jordan . . . O mountains . . . O hills?" The psalm singer calls on nature to explain its behavior, but without waiting for an answer the singer commands the earth to "tremble [חיל, חול]" in the presence of the Lord, the God of Jacob. The verb חיל, חול is a powerful verb with a range of meanings that include "writhe, whirl about, dance, be in labor (as an expectant mother), tremble." In its context in Psalm 114 it recalls the opening psalm of book 4 (Ps 90), where we read in verse 2 that God "birthed" (חיל) the earth and world. In the enthronement psalms of book 4 (Pss 93–100) the reader or hearer encounters חיל, חול in Psalms 96:9 and 97:4, where the call to the earth to "tremble" in 96:9 is realized in 97:4. While the NRSV translates Psalm 96:9 as "tremble before him, all the earth," Arthur Walker-Jones, in *The Green Psalter*, translates the verse as "Worship the Lord in sacred glory; Dance [חיל, חול] before him all Earth."[8]

This commentator pondered the words of Psalm 96:9: Is God calling the earth that God "birthed" in Psalm 90 to joyously "dance" in God's presence? Or is the earth to "tremble—writhe along with God" at God's wondrous "birthing" of the earth?[9] We may ask the same question of Psalm 114. Is verse 7 calling on the earth to "tremble" or to "dance" at the presence of Yhwh?[10] As with Psalm 96, whatever meaning we choose for חול/חיו, the singer of Psalm 114 calls on the earth to respond in one way or another to the presence of Yhwh.

Continuing the storyline of verses 3 and 4, verse 8 reminds the reader or hearer that Yhwh provided for the people during the wilderness

---

7. Other psalms narrate the leaping of the mountains and hills. In Ps 29:6 God causes Lebanon to "skip like a calf, and Sirion like the son of a wild ox." See also Judg 5:5; Ps 18:7; Hab 6:6.

8. Arthur Walker-Jones, *The Green Psalter* (Louisville: Westminster John Knox, 2009), 136.

9. See the commentary for Ps 96.

10. See Frank-Lothar Hossfeld and Erich Zenger, *Psalms 3*, trans. Linda M. Maloney, Hermeneia (Minneapolis: Fortress, 2011), 197–98.

wandering by turning rocks into pools of water and flint into springs of water. Numerous times in the wilderness Israel cried out in thirst, and God provided water for them.[11]

Psalms 113 and 114 are recited on the eighth day of Passover, just before the Passover meal is eaten. Psalm 113:5-6 asks: "Who is like the LORD our God, who is seated on high; who looks far down on the heavens and the earth?" Psalm 114:5-6 questions: "Why is it, O sea, that you flee? O Jordan, that you turn back? O mountains, that you skip like rams? O hills, like lambs?" An important tradition of the Passover celebration is the asking of questions. Traditionally the youngest person at the Passover table asks: (1) Why is this night different from all the other nights? (2) Why on all other nights do we eat either leavened bread or *matzah*, but on this night only *matzah*? (3) Why on all other nights do we not dip herbs at all, but on this night we dip them twice? and (4) Why on all other nights do we eat in an ordinary manner, but tonight we dine with special ceremony?

In answer to the questions the story of the exodus and wilderness wandering is repeated, and each participant in the Passover celebration becomes a part of the community of Israelites who made their way from slavery to freedom under the powerful leading of the God of Abraham and Sarah, Rebekah and Isaac, Jacob and Leah and Rachel. Psalms 113 and 114 introduce that story and emphasize the importance of asking and finding answers to questions.

Psalm 115

Psalm 115 is third in the collection of the Egyptian Hallel psalms, the first of four (Pss 115–118) that are read after the Passover meal's concluding prayer.

Psalms 113–118 are called the Egyptian Hallel because of the introductory and/or concluding "hallelujah [הללו יה]" common to them. But since Psalm 115 ends with but does not begin with "hallelujah," a number of ancient Hebrew manuscripts, along with the Vulgate and the Septuagint, join Psalms 114 and 115 together as a single psalm. Psalms 116 and 117, however, have "hallelujah" only at their ends, not at their beginnings, while Psalms 114 and 118 do not contain the word at all. Therefore we can conclude that "hallelujah" is common to but in no way an elemen-

---

11. See Exod 15:22-25; 17:1-7; Num 20:2-13; 21:16-18; Deut 8:15.

Psalm 115:1-18

¹Not to us, O LORD, not to us, but to
 your name give glory,
  for the sake of your steadfast love
   and your faithfulness.
²Why should the nations say,
 "Where is their God?"
³Our God is in the heavens;
 he does whatever he pleases.
⁴Their idols are silver and gold,
 the work of human hands.
⁵They have mouths, but do not
  speak;
 eyes, but do not see.

⁶They have ears, but do not hear;
 noses, but do not smell.
⁷They have hands, but do not feel;
 feet, but do not walk;
 they make no sound in their
  throats.
⁸Those who make them are like
  them;
 so are all who trust in them.
⁹O Israel, trust in the LORD!
 He is their help and their shield.
¹⁰O house of Aaron, trust in the LORD!
 He is their help and their shield.

tary characteristic of this collection of psalms, and we are justified in accepting the integrity of the MT, which renders Psalms 114 and 115 as two separate compositions.

The NRSV translates the opening words of Psalm 115 as "Not [לֹא] to us [לָנוּ], O LORD, not to us, but to your name [לְשִׁמְךָ] give glory." The question readers or hearers may ask is: "Were the people concerned that the 'glory' usually ascribed to the name of YHWH was being credited to them?" A better way to understand the opening words of the psalm may be to render the preposition "to [לְ]," used in conjunction with "us" and "your name," as "on account of." Thus we may read, "Not on account of us . . . but on account of your name [שֵׁם] give glory."[12]

The psalm singer states the reason for YHWH's glory in the second half of verse 1: "for the sake of your steadfast love and your faithfulness." As with the preposition "to [לְ]" in the first portion of the verse, the preposition "for the sake of [עַל]" in the second portion might better be rendered "because of": "because of your steadfast love [חֶסֶד] and your faithfulness [אֱמֶת]." These are two of the self-descriptive words YHWH spoke to Moses in Exodus 34:6.

In verse 2 the reader or hearer encounters a question that those who taunt Israel ask over and over in the Psalter: "Where is their God?"[13] Further, in this verse we find another instance, like those in Psalms 113:5-6

---

12. For a discussion of the importance of name, see the commentary on Ps 113.
13. See, for example, Pss 42:3, 10 and 79:10.

¹¹You who fear the L<small>ORD</small>, trust in the L<small>ORD</small>!
He is their help and their shield.
¹²The L<small>ORD</small> has been mindful of us;
he will bless us;
he will bless the house of Israel;
he will bless the house of Aaron;
¹³he will bless those who fear the L<small>ORD</small>,
both small and great.
¹⁴May the L<small>ORD</small> give you increase,
both you and your children.
¹⁵May you be blessed by the L<small>ORD</small>,
who made heaven and earth.
¹⁶The heavens are the L<small>ORD</small>'s heavens,
but the earth he has given to human beings.
¹⁷The dead do not praise the L<small>ORD</small>,
nor do any that go down into silence.
¹⁸But we will bless the L<small>ORD</small>
from this time on and forevermore.
Praise the L<small>ORD</small>!

and 114:5-6, of the questioning that constitutes an important element of the Passover Seder. Verse 3 provides the answer to the question posed in verse 2 and introduces the major theme of Psalm 115: "Our God is in the heavens."

Verses 4-8 contrast human-made idols and Y<small>HWH</small>, who "is in the heavens." Their words share many elements of other diatribes against the idols of the people such as those we read in Isaiah 44:9-20 and Psalm 135:15-18. Verse 4 offers an introductory summary statement—"Their idols are silver and gold, the work of human hands"—and verses 5-7 pose statement-questions to the nations concerning their gods: "They have mouths, but do not speak; eyes, but do not see. They have ears, but do not hear; noses, but do not smell. They have hands and feet, but do not feel . . . or walk; they make no sound in their throats." Verse 8 then compares those who make and those who trust in idols to the idols themselves.

Y<small>HWH</small> commanded the people at Sinai not to make for themselves an idol, "whether in the form of anything that is in heaven above, or that is on the earth beneath, or that is in the water under the earth" (Exod 20:4). In the ancient Near East, where the gods of cities and nations were monumental figures set up in prominent places and where household gods were commonplace, the concept of a God who had no physical characteristics was difficult to comprehend and embrace as an active entity in the world. Thus in verses 9-11 the singer of Psalm 115 calls on the people—Israel, the house of Aaron, and the ones who fear Y<small>HWH</small>—to trust in Y<small>HWH</small>, because Y<small>HWH</small> is their "help" and "shield."

The same three groups are called on in Psalm 118:2-4 to celebrate Yнwн's steadfast love.

Commentators present varying positions with regard to the identities of the three groups. Many maintain that these are distinct groups: the Israelite community as a whole, the priests and the Levites of the temple (house of Aaron),[14] and those from other places who joined with Israel and adopted its faith.[15] Others suggest that the verses refer to two groups: the Israelite community and the priests and Levites of the temple, with the phrase "you who fear the Lord" as a summary naming of the two.[16] Another proposal is to understand the three terms as parallel descriptors for the whole people of ancient Israel.[17] Whatever the identities of the groups, verses 9-11 of Psalm 115 state that all of them are to "trust in the Lord" as "their help [עֵזֶר] and their shield."

The word "help [עֵזֶר]" in reference to Yнwн occurs some twenty-eight times in the Psalter and no fewer than twenty-five times in reference to Yнwн elsewhere in the Hebrew Bible.[18] Except where עֵזֶר appears as part of a proper name, in the Psalms and the remainder of the Hebrew Bible the term almost always occurs in reference to the "help" one gives or receives in warfare.[19]

An interesting occurrence of the word, giving further insight into the nuances of its meaning, is found in the creation story in Genesis 2. In verses 7 and 15 we read that Yнwн forms the first human from the ground and places the human in the garden to "till" and to "keep" it.

---

14. Psalm 135:19-20 names four groups of worshipers in contrast to Ps 115's three: "the house of Israel, the house of Aaron, the house of Levi, and you that fear the Lord." Psalm 135 may reflect the strong distinction between the houses of Aaron and Levi that is prevalent in the books of Numbers and Chronicles.

15. See Exod 12:38; Josh 6:25; 9:21; Kraus, *Psalms 60–150*, 381; Erhard S. Gerstenberger, *Psalms, Part 2, and Lamentations*, FOTL 15 (Grand Rapids: Eerdmans, 2001), 288; Robert Davidson, *The Vitality of Worship: A Commentary on the Book of Psalms* (Grand Rapids: Eerdmans, 1998), 378; James Limburg, *Psalms*, WBiC (Louisville: Westminster John Knox, 2000), 395.

16. Leslie C. Allen, *Psalms 101–150*, WBC 21 (Nashville: Thomas Nelson, 2002), 110; Samuel Terrien, *The Psalms: Strophic Structure and Theological Commentary*, ECC (Grand Rapids: Eerdmans, 2003), 773.

17. Richard J. Clifford, *Psalms 73–150*, AOTC (Nashville: Abingdon, 2003), 196.

18. See, for example, Pss 10:14; 30:11; 46:6; 86:17; 119:175; 124:8; 146:5; Gen 49:25; Deut 33:26; 1 Sam 7:12; Isa 41:10; Hos 13:9.

19. See, for example, Deut 32:38; Josh 1:14; 10:6; 2 Sam 18:3; 1 Kgs 20:16; 2 Chr 19:2; Ezra 8:22; Isa 30:7; Lam 1:7; Ezek 12:14.

In verse 18 YHWH sees that "it is not good for the man [אדם, human] to be alone" and says, "I will make him a helper [עזר] as his partner." The "helper" God creates is the first woman, and the words of Genesis 2:18 are often interpreted as describing someone subordinate to the first human, a "helper." But the use of the word in the Hebrew Bible context reveals that it does not imply a subordinate status; rather, it conveys a sense of strength, of presence, and of defense.[20] The role of the partner for the first human was to be a strong "other" and a "defending presence" in the world in which the humans found themselves, because it was "not good for the human to be alone."

Verses 12-14 of Psalm 115 affirm that YHWH, who is the "help" and "shield" of Israel, of the house of Aaron, and of all who fear YHWH, is mindful of and blesses them, with a summary statement that the blessing includes all, "both small and great," and extends to the children of those who fear YHWH. Verses 15-16 remind those who fear YHWH that the God who, we are told in verse 3, "is in the heavens" is also the one "who made heaven and earth." Heaven is the realm of YHWH, and the earth is a gift to human beings (בני אדם). God, who created heaven and earth, is the maker of the very elements—the gold and the silver (v. 4)—out of which the gods of the nations are crafted by human beings.

Psalm 115's declaration that YHWH has given the earth to human beings echoes the sentiments of Genesis 2 and Psalm 8, which tell us that humankind is to have "dominion" and "subdue" the earth. But the words stand in stark contrast to the sentiments of the enthronement psalms (93–100) and Psalm 104, where we read of humanity's place as part and parcel of God's created order. In his book *The Bible and Ecology*, Richard Bauckham reminds humanity that "all God's creatures are first and foremost creatures" and urges humanity to embrace a concept he calls "cosmic humility."[21]

The "dead" (מתים) and "any that go down into silence" in verse 17 may refer to the idols in verses 4-7, who cannot feel or see or smell and who cannot speak. Idols fashioned with human hands cannot praise the God of the heavens. But those who fear YHWH are able to and will bless YHWH "from this time on and forevermore."

---

20. עזר occurs twenty-eight times in the Psalter, twenty-two times in reference to God. See Pss 10:14; 30:11; 54:6; 70:6.

21. Richard Bauckham, *The Bible and Ecology* (Waco, TX: Baylor University Press, 2010), 64, 46.

We Bless the Lord, but What about Our Ancestors?

Verse 1 of Psalm 115 appeals: "Not to us, O LORD, not to us, but to your name give glory." For many African people giving glory to what is viewed by many as the foreigners' "God" is something of a problem. I am a first-generation college student; my homeland is in the Eastern Cape of South Africa where the predominant language is IsiXhosa and most of the people there maintain very traditional ways of life. When we IsiXhosa people give praise, a major element of that praise is acknowledgment of our ancestors, but we can and will add God to the mix. In a recent visit to my homeland I read this verse from Psalm 115 to a young man I encountered and his immediate question was: "But what about my ancestors, because they have never left me? And I believe that as much as God has to receive glory to his name, so do they. Our ancestors are a part of us, so when this psalm says 'not to us' it says that we should not give glory to our ancestors who are a part of us."

Verse 2 of the psalm asks: "Why should the nations say, 'Where is their God?'" This question is one that is a constant topic of discussion when I meet with family and friends. During a school break I met with friends and a family friend told us about a sacrificial ceremony they observed called in the Setswana language *mpho ya badimo*, translated as "gift to the gods." It is a ceremony performed to thank the ancestors for good health, fortune, fertility, and so forth, as well as to ask forgiveness for any wrongdoing that might have prevented one from having a good quality of life. After the ceremony I mentioned to this family friend that I wasn't sure where my next semester's tuition fees would come from, and he replied: "Where is your God? You can see my ancestors are taking care of me. You, with your 'I believe in Jesus,' are not even sure about tomorrow. Why don't you go back to your roots and stop following the 'white man's' mind-control game?"

The singers of Psalm 115 answer the question posed in verse 2, I think, with the simple words of verse 3: "Our God is in the heavens; he does whatever he pleases." Such a response should silence the voices of doubt and worry about the present and the future. But my family friend could say, "Your God is somewhere and we don't know where that is, and he does whatever he pleases? And yet you Christians want me to pray to this selfish God? You are wasting your time praying to him." Verses 4-7 describe the idols of the peoples who are taunting the psalm singers. "They have mouths, eyes, ears, noses, hands, feet, throats, but. . . ." The psalm singers name all five of the human senses, emphasizing the powerlessness of idols and the intimate relationship God has with humanity. While the IsiXhosa people do not have idols made of silver and gold, they do make use of animals and mediums to communicate with and make contact with the ancestral world. Comparison of attributes and powers among various gods is common, but what makes a god "good"? Is it a god who gives material blessings, who unfailingly provides for our material needs, who will never let bad things happen to us?

Verses 9-11 are a call to all of Israel to trust in God. Christians in my culture are taught that God is a father, and in my culture one does not disturb or question a father or an older male member of society. You do not even look them in the eye; you are totally out of their sight or concern unless you transgress cultural norms and rules. Thus we try to live our best, and if we don't succeed we are first instructed to call on our ancestors, and if they cannot help, only then do we call on the Christian God. To do otherwise would show disrespect to the "father," elder males, and the ancestors. So how do I, how should I "trust" in God? The words of verses 12-15 only add to my questioning. They say that God will bless us, but why do the blessings of God not come when I need them most? How can I be faithful to the Christian God when my culture constantly reminds me that my God seems so often not to care about what is happening to me.

Perhaps the words of verse 16 can help me understand. "The heavens are the LORD's, but the earth he has given to human beings." In South Africa the reality is that two groups seem to "have" the earth: the educated elite and the criminals. The rest of the country's population simply survives and lives every day as it comes. So the reason God does not care about what is happening to me is that I am not among those to whom the earth has been "given"? I wonder if that is why the prosperity gospel, preaching and teaching that the poor and underprivileged can claim the wealth and dominion that seems to elude them, is so attractive to these groups. But the words of verses 17 and 18 bring me back to reality. We faithful believers will ultimately bless God for God's goodness to us.

In my IsiXhosa culture, ancestors are very important. They are gone in the flesh but still with us in spirit and are very active in our lives. My people are not unbelievers; they simply believe that God has given us our ancestors to deal with the issues of everyday life. For those matters they deem less important than some of the big issues that face humanity they begin with the ancestors. After all, the fathers and elder men of the tribe cannot be bothered with the seemingly trivial. Only when we cannot find an answer from the ancestors should we go to father God. God is always there; but as God is seen as "the white man's God," we don't bother him so often. Still, in the end, I believe we can bless God for God's goodness to us "from this time on and forevermore."

Gweneth Ntamo

Psalm 116

Psalm 116 is the fourth of the Egyptian Hallel psalms, one of those read while drinking the fourth cup of wine at the conclusion of the Passover Seder. It echoes many of the themes the reader or hearer encounters in Psalm 115, suggesting that the two should be considered "twin" psalms, with Psalm 116 responding to questions and/or statements posed in Psalm 115 (see especially 115:6 and 116:2; 115:1 and 116:5; 115:17 and 116:8, 17). Psalm 115 is a call to trust (see vv. 9-11). Psalm 116 is an individual hymn of thanksgiving, in which a psalm singer praises God for deliverance from some trying situation (oppression, war, sickness, etc.). Individual hymns of thanksgiving typically consist of three elements:

- an introduction, in which the psalmist declares the intention of giving thanks and praising God (see vv. 1-2)

- a narrative, in which the psalmist tells what has happened to the psalmist and what has prompted the words of praise (see vv. 3-11)

- a conclusion, in which the psalmist praises God for all that God has done on the psalmist's behalf (see vv. 12-19)

Verse 1 presents an interpretational difficulty that has led many translators to emend the text for supposed greater clarity. The MT reads, "I love because Yʜwʜ has heard my voice." The NRSV translators, along with English translations such as the KJV, the NASB, the NIV, and the CEB, render the verse as "I love the Lᴏʀᴅ because he has heard my voice." This follows the MT's suggested emendation of the phrase from אהבתי יהוה כי־ישמע יהוה to אהבתי כי־ישמע יהוה.[22]

The question for interpreters is: "Does the psalm singer love (in general) because God has heard the singer's voice or does the singer love God because God has heard the singer's voice?" Leslie Allen observes that the unemended structure of verse 1 parallels the structure of verse 10, both of which have an initial first singular perfect verb with no direct object, followed by the conjunction *ki* (כי).[23] Samuel Terrien writes: "The cry 'I love' without a direct object reveals the absolute degree of the psalmist's passion for his God."[24] This commentator opts to leave the MT as it stands and translates the phrase as: "I love [in general] because . . ."

---

22. The emendation of the text to "I love the Lᴏʀᴅ because . . ." harmonizes it with Pss 18:1 and 31:23.

23. Allen, *Psalms 101–150*, 112.

24. Terrien, *The Psalms*, 777.

Psalm 116:1-19

¹I love the LORD, because he has heard
my voice and my supplications.
²Because he inclined his ear to me,
therefore I will call on him as long
as I live.
³The snares of death encompassed
me;
the pangs of Sheol laid hold on me;
I suffered distress and anguish.
⁴Then I called on the name of the
LORD:
"O LORD, I pray, save my life!"

⁵Gracious is the LORD, and righteous;
our God is merciful.
⁶The LORD protects the simple;
when I was brought low, he saved
me.
⁷Return, O my soul, to your rest,
for the LORD has dealt bountifully
with you.
⁸For you have delivered my soul from
death,
my eyes from tears,
my feet from stumbling.

TRANSLATION MATTERS

The word שְׁאוֹל (*sheol*) occurs some sixty-five times in the Hebrew Bible. It comes from the root שאל, which means "to be extinguished." The biblical text identifies it as the abode of the dead to which all went, regardless of whether they had been righteous or wicked in life, and generally locates it in the depths of the earth.[25] Psalm 116:3 uses it in parallel poetic construction with "death" and further identifies it as a place of "distress and anguish."[26]

Sheol is invariably depicted negatively in the biblical text.[27] It signaled the end of life and thus the end of a relationship with YHWH, since Israel's God is the God of the living, not of the dead. Life was a precious commodity, the time in which one sought to be righteous and just, to live in the presence of God. Psalm 115:17 states: "The dead do not praise the LORD, nor do any that go down into silence." The psalms speak of God delivering or rescuing the psalm singer from *sheol* (see Pss 16:9-10; 30:3; 49:15), which meant that the person would be alive and would still have available the goodness of life lived in the presence of God.

Verse 1 continues, stating the reason why the psalmist "loves." God hears the psalmist's voice and her "supplications" (תחנון). The verbal root of the word translated "supplications" is חנן, one of the self-descriptive terms God speaks to Moses in Exodus 34. חנן means literally "to look kindly upon." The notice in verse 2 that God has "inclined [נטה, literally

25. See Gen 37:35; Deut 32:22; 1 Kgs 2:6; Isa 38:10; Ps 86:13; Prov 9:18.
26. See also Pss 6:6; 18:5; 89:48; Prov 5:5.
27. See Pss 88:3-5; Prov 9:18; Isa 38:10; 57:9; Hos 13:14.

Psalm 116:1-19 (cont.)

⁹I walk before the LORD
   in the land of the living.
¹⁰I kept my faith, even when I said,
   "I am greatly afflicted";
¹¹I said in my consternation,
   "Everyone is a liar."
¹²What shall I return to the LORD
   for all his bounty to me?
¹³I will lift up the cup of salvation
   and call on the name of the LORD.
¹⁴I will pay my vows to the LORD
   in the presence of all his people.
¹⁵Precious in the sight of the LORD

is the death of his faithful ones.
¹⁶O LORD, I am your servant;
   I am your servant, the child of
      your serving girl.
   You have loosed my bonds.
¹⁷I will offer to you a thanksgiving
      sacrifice
   and call on the name of the LORD.
¹⁸I will pay my vows to the LORD
   in the presence of all his people,
¹⁹in the courts of the house of the LORD,
   in your midst, O Jerusalem.
Praise the LORD!

'stretched out']" an ear to the psalm singer is a wonderful picture that confirms the basic meaning of חזק. It also echoes the words of Psalm 115 concerning idols made by human hands: "They have ears, but do not hear" (v. 6). But YHWH "stretches out the ear" to the supplications of the singer of Psalm 116.

Verses 3-11 describe the events in the psalmist's life that precipitated the hymn of thanksgiving. Verse 3 tells us that the psalmist was inflicted with great distress, including the threat of death. Again the reader or hearer is reminded of Psalm 115's notice concerning the idols of humanity that "The dead do not praise the LORD" (v. 17). But in Psalm 116 the psalmist states confidently that YHWH has delivered the psalmist's "soul" (נפש, literally "whole being" or "inmost being") from death, her eyes from tears, and her feet from stumbling. Thus she will walk in the presence of YHWH in the land of the living.[28]

Verse 5 opens with the word "gracious" (חנון), from the same root word translated "supplications" in verse 1. God is gracious; thus the cries of the psalmist do not fall on deaf ears. The verse continues with two other descriptive terms for God found in Exodus 34:6—"righteous" (צדיק) and "merciful" (רחם).

The word "merciful" (רחם, also translated in the NRSV as "compassion") derives from the noun רחם, literally "womb," and thus we may

---

28. See Pss 56:13 and 118:17.

understand it as a reference to "God's womb-love" for the earth that God painstakingly birthed (see Ps 90:2). The noun רחם and derivations of it referring to God's "womb-love" occur no fewer than twenty times in the book of Psalms.[29] In an interesting juxtaposition of metaphors, Psalm 103:13 says, "As a father has compassion [כרחם אב] for his children, so the LORD has compassion [יהוה רחם] for those who fear him," and in Psalm 77:9 the psalm singer cries out, "Has God forgotten to be gracious? Has he in anger shut up his compassion [רחמיו]?" bringing to mind the words of 1 Samuel 1:6, a notice that YHWH had "closed" Hannah's womb (רחם).

The final section of Psalm 116, verses 12-19, contains the psalmist's praise to God for deliverance and protection. Two refrains divide it at verses 14 and 18: "I will pay my vows to the LORD in the presence of all his people." In verse 12 the psalmist asks what may be given to YHWH for all the goodness YHWH bestows. Verses 13 and 14 answer the question: "a cup of salvation" and completion of vows. While in the context of the Egyptian Hallel psalms the "cup of salvation" refers to the fourth cup of celebratory wine drunk at the Passover meal, it was originally most likely some form of sacrificial offering to God such as we see in Exodus 29:40 and Numbers 28:7. In the New Testament, Jesus infuses the fourth cup of the Passover meal with a new meaning.[30] J. Clinton McCann writes: "Jesus' lifting of the cup and new interpretation of it point to his own death as the sacrifice (116:7) and to a new dimension of the affirmation of what it means for him and for his followers to be delivered from death into 'the land of the living' (116:9)."[31]

Verse 15 has puzzled interpreters for millennia. The NRSV renders it as "Precious in the sight of the LORD is the death of his faithful ones," following closely the traditional translation of the Authorized Version. The word usually translated "precious" comes from the Hebrew root יקר, which means "be dignified, honorable, heavy, valuable." It occurs nine times in the book of Psalms and is translated variously in the NRSV as "precious," "glory," "honor," "costly," "pomp," and "weighty."[32] The use of יקר to describe the death of YHWH's faithful ones indicates that God does not happily accept the death of any faithful one but considers life

29. See, for example, Pss 25:6; 40:11; 69:16; 77:9; 79:8; 103:13; 119:156.
30. See Matt 26:47-28; Mark 14:23-24; Luke 22:20.
31. J. Clinton McCann Jr., "The Book of Psalms," *NIB*, vol. 4 (Nashville: Abingdon, 1996), 1149.
32. See Pss 36:8; 37:20; 45:10; 49:9, 13, 21; 72:14; 116:15; 139:17.

the better alternative and counts each death as costly and weighty (see "Translation Matters" at the beginning of the commentary for this psalm).

Verse 16 returns to the praise of Yʜwʜ for deliverance and protection, as we see in verses 3-4. The psalmist writes: "O Lord, I am your servant . . . the child of your serving girl; You have loosed my bonds." Echoing the words of verse 14, the psalm singer says in verses 17 and 18: "I will offer to you a thanksgiving sacrifice. . . . I will pay my vows to the Lord." Here there is no question posed as was the case in verse 12, but nonetheless the psalm singer responds in verses 17 and 18 in much the same way as in verses 13 and 14; the psalmist will offer a "thanksgiving sacrifice" and "pay my vows," this time not only in the presence of God's people but "in the courts of the house of the Lord, in your midst, O Jerusalem."

The Passover celebrants raise the fourth cup of wine while Psalm 116 is recited as a closing remembrance of God's goodness to their ancestors and to each of them individually in the exodus from Egypt. Psalm 116 is also recited in Christian tradition during the celebration of communion on Holy Thursday. As in the Passover celebration, so Christians raise a cup of wine in remembrance of God's goodness to their ancestors in the faith and to them individually.

Psalm 117

Psalm 117 is the fifth of the Egyptian Hallel psalms. Only two verses comprise this hymn of praise, making it the shortest psalm in the Psalter. A number of Hebrew manuscripts and modern scholars connect it to Psalm 116, but the consensus of the textual evidence is that Psalm 117 should be read as a discrete psalm with a simple yet powerful statement about the relationship between a believing community and its God.[33]

The psalm opens with the psalm singers inviting all nations (גוים) and all peoples (אמים) to join with them in their praise and extolling of Yʜwʜ. Verse 2 begins with the conjunction "for" (כי), a common introduction to a hymnic narrative in the Psalter that states why "all nations" and "all peoples" are called to praise Yʜwʜ.[34] The singers remember God's great steadfast love (חסד) and enduring faithfulness (אמת), two of God's self-descriptive characteristics spoken to Moses in Exodus 34. The brief

---

33. Allen, *Psalms 101–150*, 158.
34. See also Pss 33:4; 135:4, 5, 14; 136:1.

Psalm 117:1-2

¹Praise the Lᴏʀᴅ, all you nations!
   Extol him, all you peoples!
²For great is his steadfast love
   toward us,

and the faithfulness of the Lᴏʀᴅ
   endures forever.
Praise the Lᴏʀᴅ!

psalm closes with words that occur often in the Egyptian Hallel psalms, hallelujah (הללו יה).³⁵

Psalm 117 was most likely used as a refrain by the ancient Israelites in cultic settings of worship. The apostle Paul wove the opening words of the psalm into his exhortation in Romans 15:11: "Praise the Lord, all you Gentiles [ἔθνη], and let all the peoples [λαοί] praise him." God is indeed the God of all, a God of steadfast love and faithfulness, and Psalm 117 is certainly an apt refrain in worship settings today.

Psalm 118

Psalm 118 is the final Egyptian Hallel psalm. It is an interesting and rather lengthy composition with a significant history of transmission and use in Jewish and Christian religious life. Erhard Gerstenberger writes that the psalm "abounds in liturgical forms and rhythmic, repetitious, formulaic phrases and shouts."³⁶ Samuel Terrien adds: "The psalm appears to be a conglomeration of independent fragments,"³⁷ and Michael Goulder calls it "a paean of joy."³⁸

The consensus of most scholars is that Psalm 118 was used in early Jewish life in liturgical processions, perhaps as an entrance liturgy into the temple in Jerusalem, in much the same way that Psalms 15 and 24 may have been used.³⁹ According to the Mishnah the procession around the altar that took place on seven successive days during the feast of Tabernacles was accompanied by the recitation of Psalm 118:27.⁴⁰ In the New Testament, Psalm 118 is the most quoted and referenced psalm

35. הללו יה occurs in Pss 113:1, 9; 115:18; 116:19; and 117:2.

36. Gerstenberger, *Psalms, Part 2 and Lamentations*, 307.

37. Terrien, *The Psalms*, 783.

38. Michael D. Goulder, *The Psalms of the Return (Book V, Psalms 107–150)*, JSOTSup 258 (Sheffield: Sheffield Academic, 1998), 182.

39. See esp. the commentary on Psalm 118 in Kraus, *Psalms 60–150*, 392–401.

40. m.Sukkah 4:5; 5:1-4. See Clifford, *Psalms 73–150*, 208.

Psalm 118:1-29

¹O give thanks to the LORD, for he is
    good;
    his steadfast love endures forever!
²Let Israel say,
    "His steadfast love endures
      forever."
³Let the house of Aaron say,
    "His steadfast love endures
      forever."
⁴Let those who fear the LORD say,
    "His steadfast love endures
      forever."
⁵Out of my distress I called on the
    LORD;
    the LORD answered me and set
    me in a broad place.
⁶With the LORD on my side I do not
    fear.
    What can mortals do to me?
⁷The LORD is on my side to help me;

    I shall look in triumph on those
      who hate me.
⁸It is better to take refuge in the LORD
    than to put confidence in mortals.
⁹It is better to take refuge in the LORD
    than to put confidence in princes.
¹⁰All nations surrounded me;
    in the name of the LORD I cut them
      off!
¹¹They surrounded me, surrounded
    me on every side;
    in the name of the LORD I cut them
      off!
¹²They surrounded me like bees;
    they blazed like a fire of thorns;
    in the name of the LORD I cut them
      off!
¹³I was pushed hard, so that I was
    falling,
    but the LORD helped me.

from the Hebrew Bible. The citations and references number anywhere between twenty and sixty, "depending on the judgement of individual exegetes."[41]

All four of the gospel writers use the words of Psalm 118:26, "Blessed is the one who comes in the name of the LORD," in their Palm Sunday narratives.[42] In Mark 12, Jesus quotes Psalm 118:22, "The stone that the builders rejected has become the chief cornerstone," as the explanation for the Parable of the Vineyard. Peter quotes the same verse in Acts 4:11 in reference to Jesus, and the author of Ephesians alludes to it in Ephesians 2:20-21. The words of Psalm 118:6, "With the LORD on my side I do not fear," echo in Romans 8:3 and Hebrews 13:6. In modern lectionary use Psalm 118:1-2, 14-24 is the psalm reading for Easter Sunday in all three years; Psalm 118:1-2, 19-29 is the reading for the Liturgy of the

41. Hossfeld and Zenger, *Psalms 3*, 245.
42. Matt 21:9; Mark 11:9-10; Luke 19:38; John 12:13.

¹⁴The L<small>ORD</small> is my strength and my
  might;
he has become my salvation.
¹⁵There are glad songs of victory in
    the tents of the righteous:
  "The right hand of the L<small>ORD</small> does
    valiantly;
¹⁶the right hand of the L<small>ORD</small> is exalted;
  the right hand of the L<small>ORD</small> does
    valiantly."
¹⁷I shall not die, but I shall live,
  and recount the deeds of the L<small>ORD</small>.
¹⁸The L<small>ORD</small> has punished me severely,
  but he did not give me over to
    death.
¹⁹Open to me the gates of
    righteousness,
  that I may enter through them
  and give thanks to the L<small>ORD</small>.
²⁰This is the gate of the L<small>ORD</small>;

the righteous shall enter through it.
²¹I thank you that you have answered
    me
  and have become my salvation.
²²The stone that the builders rejected
  has become the chief cornerstone.
²³This is the L<small>ORD</small>'s doing;
  it is marvelous in our eyes.
²⁴This is the day that the L<small>ORD</small> has
    made;
  let us rejoice and be glad in it.
²⁵Save us, we beseech you, O L<small>ORD</small>!
  O L<small>ORD</small>, we beseech you, give us
    success!
²⁶Blessed is the one who comes in
    the name of the L<small>ORD</small>.
  We bless you from the house of
    the L<small>ORD</small>.
²⁷The L<small>ORD</small> is God,
  and he has given us light.

Palms in all three years; and Psalm 118:14-29 is the psalm reading for the Second Sunday of Easter in Year C. Erich Zenger adds that "when the liturgy of the Mass quotes in the *sanctus* both 118:25 (*'hosanna'*) and 118:26 (*'benedictus qui venit in nomine domini'*),[43] it places the celebration of the Eucharist within a magnificent horizon."[44]

Psalm 118 is presented as the voice of an individual psalm singer, but that individual voice is woven into and "anchored in"[45] the liturgy of the gathered worshiping community. We hear the individual in the first twenty-three verses of the psalm thanking Y<small>HWH</small> for deliverance from a situation of personal peril, and then, beginning in verse 24, the community adds its voice to that of the individual in a context of corporate worship.

43. "Blessed is he who comes in the name of the Lord."
44. Hossfeld and Zenger, *Psalms 3*, 246.
45. Kraus, *Psalms 60–150*, 401.

Psalm 118:1-29 (cont.)

Bind the festal procession with
branches,
up to the horns of the altar.
[28]You are my God, and I will give
thanks to you;

you are my God, I will extol you.
[29]O give thanks to the LORD, for he is
good,
for his steadfast love endures
forever.

In verses 1-4 worshipers are called to "give thanks to the LORD" because of YHWH's goodness and steadfast love (חסד). The words of verse 1 are typical gathering words, used in many calls to worship in the Hebrew Bible.[46] In verses 2-4 three groups of people are singled out to join in the words of thanks: Israel, the house of Aaron, and the ones who fear YHWH—the same three groups who are called on in Psalm 115:9-11. Whereas the groups are called in Psalm 115 to "trust in the LORD" as their "help and shield," in Psalm 118 they are called to "say" that "YHWH's steadfast love [חסד] endures forever." For a full discussion of the three groups see the commentary for Psalm 115.[47] Whatever the identities of the groups, we can conclude with Psalm 115 that "all" are called to celebrate YHWH's abundant help and love.

After verse 4, חסד does not appear again in the psalm until its closing, at verse 29. Therefore we may be permitted to understand verses 5-28 of the psalm as a description, an example story, of חסד, of what God is and does in the world and what humanity is expected to be and do in the world. In verse 5 the psalm singer says that she was in "distress" (מצר, literally "a narrow place") and God answered the cry for help by providing "a broad place."[48] The psalmist then declares in verses 6 and 7:

> With the LORD on my side I do not fear.
> What can mortals [אדם] do to me?
> The LORD is on my side to help me;
> I shall look in triumph on those who hate me.

---

46. See Pss 106:1; 107:1; 136:1; 1 Chr 16:34; 2 Chr 5:13; 7:3; 20:21.

47. Psalm 135:19-20 names four groups of worshipers in contrast to Psalm 115's three: "the house of Israel, the house of Aaron, the house of Levi," and "you that fear the LORD." Psalm 135 may reflect the strong distinction between the houses of Aaron and Levi that is prevalent in the books of Numbers and Chronicles.

48. For the same phrase see Pss 18:19 and 31:8.

The Hebrew of verse 7b is literally "I, I will look [אֲנִי אֶרְאֶה] at those who hate me," indicating with its emphatic use of the personal pronoun אֲנִי that the psalmist will be able to confidently face those who hate her since Yhwh is on her side. A striking feature of verses 5-7 is the repetition of the first-person pronoun. The words "I" and "me" ring out, emphasizing God's individual, intimate care for the psalmist.

The "it is better . . . than" sayings of verses 8 and 9 are perhaps best understood as proverbial aphorisms on the model of the מָשָׁל sayings of the book of Proverbs.[49] The psalm singer has experienced the goodness of Yhwh in her deliverance from "narrow straits" to "a broad place" and reflects on the experience with traditional proverbial sayings about Yhwh. The word translated "take refuge" in these verses comes from the verbal root בָּטַח, which means "to attach oneself to, to confide in, to feel secure."[50]

The word "surround" occurs three times in verses 10-12 in reference to "all the nations" (גּוֹיִם). In each verse the psalm singer cries out: "In the name of the Lord I cut them off." Thus she no longer fears the "distress" of verse 5 that seems to be brought on by the encircling enemy; she is able to cut them off and dwell in a "broad place."

Many English translations of verse 13 follow the emendation of the Septuagint, Syriac, and Vulgate translators and render the active verb דְּחָה ("you pushed me") as passive ("I was pushed"),[51] but such an emendation is not necessary to grasp the felt imagery of the verse. The psalm singer nearly fell, but Yhwh helped her, and in verse 14 she celebrates with words of praise, affirming that Yhwh is "my strength and my might" and "my salvation." The words of verse 14 repeat exactly the words that Moses, Miriam, and the children of Israel sing in Exodus 15:2 after they have crossed the Reed Sea; likewise the words of verses 15b and 16 echo those of Exodus 15:6 and 12 in a threefold summary of the might of the right hand of Yhwh. The singer of Psalm 118 likens the help rendered in the present situation to the help God gave the Israelites in the Exodus from Egypt, and in verse 17 the psalmist affirms, "I shall not die, but I shall live, and recount the deeds of the Lord." The psalm singer has escaped; the enemy has perished; a new life lies ahead. Martin

---

49. See Prov 15:16, 17; 16:8, 19; 17:1; 19:1.

50. In Psalm 115's call to "Israel," the "house of Aaron," and those "who fear Yhwh" in verses 9-11, however, the NRSV translates בָּטַח as "trust," rather than "take refuge."

51. See, for example, the NIV, NRSV, and CEB.

Luther inscribed Psalm 118:17 on a wall of Coburg Castle in Bavaria dur-ing his 165 days of hiding during the Diet of Augsburg.

In verse 19 the gates of righteousness are opened and the psalm singer enters with thanks. These verses in particular mark Psalm 118 as an en-trance liturgy, words recited as worshipers enter the gates of Jerusalem and make their way to the temple to worship with sacrifice and celebra-tion. As stated above, the words of verse 22 are quoted and alluded to in many places in the New Testament. In the ancient Israelite context of Psalm 118 we may understand the "stone the builders rejected" as the psalm singer, who has not been rejected but has become a chief corner-stone, an essential element in the construction of the life of the ancient Israelite faithful. Erich Zenger calls verse 22 a proverb and describes it in this way: "[It] evokes the imagery of building a house, when the builders test each individual stone and sort out some stones that are of no use, throwing them aside. . . . A stone thrown away by the builders is taken by YHWH . . . and is even placed as a very important stone in *his* building."[52]

A student in a Psalms class I taught a few years ago offered an apt illustration of "the stone that the builders rejected." He told the story of Ishmael Beah, who at the age of thirteen was "recruited" by a rebel government in West Africa to be a child soldier. The rebels desensitized the children to violence, made them feel like outcasts from their families, and gave them little hope for any future outside of the rebel groups for whom they worked. But Ishmael's story ended differently than for the majority of the children. The United Nations International Children's Emergency Fund (UNICEF) rescued him and taught him to forgive himself, to regain his humanity, and to heal. Ishmael has since commit-ted his life to helping other child soldiers as an advocate, activist, and author. Imagine the words of Psalm 118:21-24—"I thank you that you have answered me . . . the stone that the builders rejected . . . this is the Lord's doing"— spoken by Ishmael Beah![53]

In verse 24 the voice of the community appears clearly for the first time in the psalm and is mingled with the voice of the individual psalm singer for the remainder of the psalm. The community declares, "This is the day that the LORD has made; let us rejoice and be glad in it." The Mishnah associates the words of verse 27 with the feast of Tabernacles,

---

52. Hossfeld and Zenger, *Psalms 3*, 241.
53. See Ishmael Beah, *A Long Way Gone: Memoirs of a Boy Soldier* (New York: Mac-millan, 2008).

the autumn celebration commemorating the wilderness wanderings and the giving of the Torah to Moses on Sinai. The procession around the altar took place on seven successive days during the feast of Tabernacles and was accompanied by the recitation of Psalm 118:27. The words "Bind the festal procession with branches, up to the horns of the altar" are explained in the Mishnah as follows:

> What was the rite of the willow branch? There was a place below Jerusalem called Motsa. They went down there and collected young willow branches, and they came and set them up right along the sides of the Altar with their tops bent over the top of the Altar. They then sounded a prolonged blast, a quavering note, and a prolonged blast. Each day [for the seven days of the festival] they walked in procession once around the Altar. (m.Sukkah 4:5)

The final verse of Psalm 118—"O give thanks to the LORD, for he is good"—repeats the "gathering words" of verse 1, calling worshipers to praise God because of God's "goodness" and "steadfast love" (חסד) and providing a closing envelope structure to this individual hymn of thanksgiving.

Psalm 118 is a rich composition, sung first as an individual hymn of thanksgiving in a corporate worship setting, adopted by the ancient Israelites as a song of celebration for the feast of Tabernacles, and for Christians many of its verses suggest the life and times of Jesus. Erich Zenger says this about Psalm 118: "As a voice in opposition to the threatening power of hatred and violence, the psalm evokes the experience of Israel and the church that the 'true' God is 'good,' . . . and that his 'love,' that is, his mercy, endures forever."[54]

---

54. Hossfeld and Zenger, *Psalms 3*, 246.

Psalm 119

Words from Woman Wisdom

Psalm 119

The acrostic structure of Psalm 119 marks it as a wisdom composition, as do its content and message.[1] Wisdom writers attempted to categorize the world, measure human actions, evaluate the relative status of events and movements of life, and prescribe paths of life. Their writings thereby created a *mythos*, a particular view of reality around which human society could organize and order itself. In the case of psalmic wisdom one way in which this concern for order expresses itself concretely, indeed visually, is in its employment of the acrostic, underlining the sense of order and symmetry the psalmist attempts to bring to the subject matter of the poem.[2]

The wisdom tradition of the Hebrew Bible as we find it in Proverbs, Job, Ecclesiastes, and the wisdom psalms reflects a particular view of

---

1. For a full discussion of the acrostic form, see the commentary on Psalms 111 and 112.

2. Anthony R. Ceresko, "The Sage in the Psalms," in *The Sage in Israel and the Ancient Near East*, ed. John G. Gammie and Leo G. Perdue (Winona Lake, IN: Eisenbrauns, 1990), 217–30, at 224–25.

א ¹Happy are those whose way is
blameless,
who walk in the law of the LORD.
²Happy are those who keep his
decrees,
who seek him with their whole
heart,
³who also do no wrong,
but walk in his ways.
⁴You have commanded your
precepts
to be kept diligently.
⁵O that my ways may be steadfast
in keeping your statutes!
⁶Then I shall not be put to shame,
having my eyes fixed on all your
commandments.
⁷I will praise you with an upright
heart,
when I learn your righteous
ordinances.
⁸I will observe your statutes;
do not utterly forsake me.

ב ⁹How can young people keep their
way pure?
By guarding it according to your
word.
¹⁰With my whole heart I seek you;
do not let me stray from your
commandments.
¹¹I treasure your word in my heart,
so that I may not sin against you.
¹²Blessed are you, O LORD;
teach me your statutes.
¹³With my lips I declare
all the ordinances of your mouth.
¹⁴I delight in the way of your decrees
as much as in all riches.
¹⁵I will meditate on your precepts,
and fix my eyes on your ways.
¹⁶I will delight in your statutes;
I will not forget your word.

ג ¹⁷Deal bountifully with your servant,
so that I may live and observe
your word.
¹⁸Open my eyes, so that I may
behold
wondrous things out of your law.
¹⁹I live as an alien in the land;
do not hide your commandments
from me.
²⁰My soul is consumed with longing
for your ordinances at all times.
²¹You rebuke the insolent, accursed
ones,
who wander from your
commandments;
²²take away from me their scorn
and contempt,
for I have kept your decrees.
²³Even though princes sit plotting
against me,
your servant will meditate on
your statutes.
²⁴Your decrees are my delight,
they are my counselors.

ד ²⁵My soul clings to the dust;
revive me according to your word.
²⁶When I told of my ways, you
answered me;
teach me your statutes.
²⁷Make me understand the way of
your precepts,
and I will meditate on your
wondrous works.
²⁸My soul melts away for sorrow;
strengthen me according to your
word.
²⁹Put false ways far from me;
and graciously teach me your law.
³⁰I have chosen the way of
faithfulness;
I set your ordinances before me.
³¹I cling to your decrees, O LORD;

let me not be put to shame.

ד ³²I run the way of your
commandments,
for you enlarge my understanding.

ה ³³Teach me, O Lord, the way of
your statutes,
and I will observe it to the end.
³⁴Give me understanding, that I
may keep your law
and observe it with my whole
heart.
³⁵Lead me in the path of your
commandments,
for I delight in it.
³⁶Turn my heart to your decrees,
and not to selfish gain.
³⁷Turn my eyes from looking at
vanities;
give me life in your ways.
³⁸Confirm to your servant your
promise,
which is for those who fear you.
³⁹Turn away the disgrace that I
dread,
for your ordinances are good.
⁴⁰See, I have longed for your
precepts;
in your righteousness give me life.

ו ⁴¹Let your steadfast love come to
me, O Lord,
your salvation according to your
promise.
⁴²Then I shall have an answer for
those who taunt me,
for I trust in your word.
⁴³Do not take the word of truth
utterly out of my mouth,
for my hope is in your ordinances.
⁴⁴I will keep your law continually,
forever and ever.
⁴⁵I shall walk at liberty,
for I have sought your precepts.

⁴⁶I will also speak of your decrees
before kings,
and shall not be put to shame;
⁴⁷I find my delight in your
commandments,
because I love them.
⁴⁸I revere your commandments,
which I love,
and I will meditate on your statutes.

ז ⁴⁹Remember your word to your
servant,
in which you have made me hope.
⁵⁰This is my comfort in my distress,
that your promise gives me life.
⁵¹The arrogant utterly deride me,
but I do not turn away from your
law.
⁵²When I think of your ordinances
from of old,
I take comfort, O Lord.
⁵³Hot indignation seizes me
because of the wicked,
those who forsake your law.
⁵⁴Your statutes have been my songs
wherever I make my home.
⁵⁵I remember your name in the
night, O Lord,
and keep your law.
⁵⁶This blessing has fallen to me,
for I have kept your precepts.

ח ⁵⁷The Lord is my portion;
I promise to keep your words.
⁵⁸I implore your favor with all my
heart;
be gracious to me according to
your promise.
⁵⁹When I think of your ways,
I turn my feet to your decrees;
⁶⁰I hurry and do not delay
to keep your commandments.
⁶¹Though the cords of the wicked
ensnare me,

I do not forget your law.

ח ⁶²At midnight I rise to praise you,
because of your righteous
ordinances.
⁶³I am a companion of all who fear
you,
of those who keep your precepts.
⁶⁴The earth, O Lᴏʀᴅ, is full of your
steadfast love;
teach me your statutes.

ט ⁶⁵You have dealt well with your
servant,
O Lᴏʀᴅ, according to your word.
⁶⁶Teach me good judgment and
knowledge,
for I believe in your
commandments.
⁶⁷Before I was humbled I went
astray,
but now I keep your word.
⁶⁸You are good and do good;
teach me your statutes.
⁶⁹The arrogant smear me with lies,
but with my whole heart I keep
your precepts.
⁷⁰Their hearts are fat and gross,
but I delight in your law.
⁷¹It is good for me that I was
humbled,
so that I might learn your statutes.
⁷²The law of your mouth is better
to me
than thousands of gold and silver
pieces.

י ⁷³Your hands have made and
fashioned me;
give me understanding that I may
learn your commandments.
⁷⁴Those who fear you shall see me
and rejoice,
because I have hoped in your
word.

⁷⁵I know, O Lᴏʀᴅ, that your
judgments are right,
and that in faithfulness you have
humbled me.
⁷⁶Let your steadfast love become
my comfort
according to your promise to your
servant.
⁷⁷Let your mercy come to me, that I
may live;
for your law is my delight.
⁷⁸Let the arrogant be put to shame,
because they have subverted me
with guile;
as for me, I will meditate on your
precepts.
⁷⁹Let those who fear you turn to me,
so that they may know your
decrees.
⁸⁰May my heart be blameless in
your statutes,
so that I may not be put to shame.

כ ⁸¹My soul languishes for your
salvation;
I hope in your word.
⁸²My eyes fail with watching for your
promise;
I ask, "When will you comfort
me?"
⁸³For I have become like a wineskin
in the smoke,
yet I have not forgotten your
statutes.
⁸⁴How long must your servant
endure?
When will you judge those who
persecute me?
⁸⁵The arrogant have dug pitfalls for
me;
they flout your law.
⁸⁶All your commandments are
enduring;

I am persecuted without cause;
    help me!
ב   ⁸⁷They have almost made an end of
    me on earth;
    but I have not forsaken your
        precepts.
⁸⁸In your steadfast love spare my life,
    so that I may keep the decrees of
    your mouth.
ל   ⁸⁹The Lord exists forever;
    your word is firmly fixed in heaven.
⁹⁰Your faithfulness endures to all
        generations;
    you have established the earth,
        and it stands fast.
⁹¹By your appointment they stand
        today,
    for all things are your servants.
⁹²If your law had not been my delight,
    I would have perished in my
        misery.
⁹³I will never forget your precepts,
    for by them you have given me life.
⁹⁴I am yours; save me,
    for I have sought your precepts.
⁹⁵The wicked lie in wait to destroy
        me,
    but I consider your decrees.
⁹⁶I have seen a limit to all perfection,
    but your commandment is
        exceedingly broad.
מ   ⁹⁷Oh, how I love your law!
    It is my meditation all day long.
⁹⁸Your commandment makes me
        wiser than my enemies,
    for it is always with me.
⁹⁹I have more understanding than
        all my teachers,
    for your decrees are my
        meditation.
¹⁰⁰I understand more than the aged,
    for I keep your precepts.

¹⁰¹I hold back my feet from every
        evil way,
    in order to keep your word.
¹⁰²I do not turn away from your
        ordinances,
    for you have taught me.
¹⁰³How sweet are your words to my
        taste,
    sweeter than honey to my mouth!
¹⁰⁴Through your precepts I get
        understanding;
    therefore I hate every false way.
נ   ¹⁰⁵Your word is a lamp to my feet
    and a light to my path.
¹⁰⁶I have sworn an oath and
        confirmed it,
    to observe your righteous
        ordinances.
¹⁰⁷I am severely afflicted;
    give me life, O Lord, according to
        your word.
¹⁰⁸Accept my offerings of praise,
        O Lord,
    and teach me your ordinances.
¹⁰⁹I hold my life in my hand
        continually,
    but I do not forget your law.
¹¹⁰The wicked have laid a snare for
        me,
    but I do not stray from your
        precepts.
¹¹¹Your decrees are my heritage
        forever;
    they are the joy of my heart.
¹¹²I incline my heart to perform your
        statutes
    forever, to the end.
ס   ¹¹³I hate the double-minded,
    but I love your law.
¹¹⁴You are my hiding place and my
        shield;
    I hope in your word.

ס ¹¹⁵Go away from me, you evildoers,
that I may keep the
commandments of my God.
¹¹⁶Uphold me according to your
promise, that I may live,
and let me not be put to shame in
my hope.
¹¹⁷Hold me up, that I may be safe
and have regard for your statutes
continually.
¹¹⁸You spurn all who go astray from
your statutes;
for their cunning is in vain.
¹¹⁹All the wicked of the earth you
count as dross;
therefore I love your decrees.
¹²⁰My flesh trembles for fear of you,
and I am afraid of your judgments.

ע ¹²¹I have done what is just and right;
do not leave me to my oppressors.
¹²²Guarantee your servant's well-
being;
do not let the godless oppress me.
¹²³My eyes fail from watching for
your salvation,
and for the fulfillment of your
righteous promise.
¹²⁴Deal with your servant according
to your steadfast love,
and teach me your statutes.
¹²⁵I am your servant; give me
understanding,
so that I may know your decrees.
¹²⁶It is time for the Lord to act,
for your law has been broken.
¹²⁷Truly I love your commandments
more than gold, more than fine
gold.
¹²⁸Truly I direct my steps by all your
precepts;
I hate every false way.

פ ¹²⁹Your decrees are wonderful;

therefore my soul keeps them.
¹³⁰The unfolding of your words gives
light;
it imparts understanding to the
simple.
¹³¹With open mouth I pant,
because I long for your
commandments.
¹³²Turn to me and be gracious to me,
as is your custom toward those
who love your name.
¹³³Keep my steps steady according
to your promise,
and never let iniquity have
dominion over me.
¹³⁴Redeem me from human
oppression,
that I may keep your precepts.
¹³⁵Make your face shine upon your
servant,
and teach me your statutes.
¹³⁶My eyes shed streams of tears
because your law is not kept.

צ ¹³⁷You are righteous, O Lord,
and your judgments are right.
¹³⁸You have appointed your decrees
in righteousness
and in all faithfulness.
¹³⁹My zeal consumes me
because my foes forget your
words.
¹⁴⁰Your promise is well tried,
and your servant loves it.
¹⁴¹I am small and despised,
yet I do not forget your precepts.
¹⁴²Your righteousness is an
everlasting righteousness,
and your law is the truth.
¹⁴³Trouble and anguish have come
upon me,
but your commandments are my
delight.

צ ¹⁴⁴Your decrees are righteous
forever;
> give me understanding that I may
> live.

ק ¹⁴⁵With my whole heart I cry;
> answer me, O Lord.
> I will keep your statutes.
¹⁴⁶I cry to you; save me,
> that I may observe your decrees.
¹⁴⁷I rise before dawn and cry for help;
> I put my hope in your words.
¹⁴⁸My eyes are awake before each
watch of the night,
> that I may meditate on your
> promise.
¹⁴⁹In your steadfast love hear my
voice;
> O Lord, in your justice preserve
> my life.
¹⁵⁰Those who persecute me with
evil purpose draw near;
> they are far from your law.
¹⁵¹Yet you are near, O Lord,
> and all your commandments are
> true.
¹⁵²Long ago I learned from your
decrees
> that you have established them
> forever.

ר ¹⁵³Look on my misery and rescue
me,
> for I do not forget your law.
¹⁵⁴Plead my cause and redeem me;
> give me life according to your
> promise.
¹⁵⁵Salvation is far from the wicked,
> for they do not seek your statutes.
¹⁵⁶Great is your mercy, O Lord;
> give me life according to your
> justice.
¹⁵⁷Many are my persecutors and my
adversaries,

> yet I do not swerve from your
> decrees.
¹⁵⁸I look at the faithless with disgust,
> because they do not keep your
> commands.
¹⁵⁹Consider how I love your
precepts;
> preserve my life according to your
> steadfast love.
¹⁶⁰The sum of your word is truth;
> and every one of your righteous
> ordinances endures forever.

שׁ ¹⁶¹Princes persecute me without
cause,
> but my heart stands in awe of
> your words.
¹⁶²I rejoice at your word
> like one who finds great spoil.
¹⁶³I hate and abhor falsehood,
> but I love your law.
¹⁶⁴Seven times a day I praise you
> for your righteous ordinances.
¹⁶⁵Great peace have those who love
your law;
> nothing can make them stumble.
¹⁶⁶I hope for your salvation, O Lord,
> and I fulfill your commandments.
¹⁶⁷My soul keeps your decrees;
> I love them exceedingly.
¹⁶⁸I keep your precepts and decrees,
> for all my ways are before you.

ת ¹⁶⁹Let my cry come before you,
O Lord;
> give me understanding according
> to your word.
¹⁷⁰Let my supplication come before
you;
> deliver me according to your
> promise.
¹⁷¹My lips will pour forth praise,
> because you teach me your
> statutes.

Psalm 119:1-178 (cont.)

ה 172My tongue will sing of your promise,
   for all your commandments are right.
173Let your hand be ready to help me,
   for I have chosen your precepts.
174I long for your salvation, O LORD,

and your law is my delight.
175Let me live that I may praise you,
   and let your ordinances help me.
176I have gone astray like a lost sheep; seek out your servant,
   for I do not forget your commandments.

reality that incorporates the faith traditions of the Israelites.[3] In a number of the wisdom psalms, such as Psalms 1, 112, and 119, the path to wisdom is through adherence to the law, the instruction of YHWH. In the Hebrew Bible and in the Deuterocanonical literature a character called "Woman Wisdom" (חכמה) provides the way to discovering wisdom in the instruction of YHWH.

We find Woman Wisdom in the books of Job and Proverbs in the Hebrew Bible and in the Deuterocanonical books of Wisdom of Solomon, Baruch, and Sirach, all of which are poetic compositions. Kathleen O'Connor reminds us: "That the Wisdom Woman is a figure of poetry means that she can and should be understood on many intertwined levels of meaning rather than in a linear, flat way."[4]

The Hebrew Bible and Deuterocanonical literature confirm O'Connor's characterization of Woman Wisdom since they present a consistent yet varied view of the figure. Her representation is consistent in that, except in Job 28, wisdom is depicted as a woman, a divine consort or feminine counterpart to God. Wisdom is described, however, in varied roles. In Job 28, Wisdom is hidden from and inaccessible to humanity; only God knows where Wisdom dwells (28:33). In Proverbs, in contrast, Woman Wisdom dwells in the midst of humanity, crying out in the streets and at the entrance to the city gates, calling on passersby to listen to her words (Prov 2:5). She claims, in Proverbs 8:22-31, to have an intimate acquaintance with God; she was there at creation, working beside God and "delighting [שעשע, see Ps 119:24, 77, 92, 143, 174] in the human race."

3. Nancy L. deClaissé-Walford, *Introduction to the Psalms: A Song from Ancient Israel* (St. Louis: Chalice Press, 2004), 25–26. This author includes Pss 1, 32, 37, 49, 73, 78, 112, 119, 127, 128, 133, and 145 in the *Gattung* "wisdom psalm."

4. Kathleen M. O'Connor, *The Wisdom Literature* (Collegeville, MN: Liturgical Press, 1988), 64.

While Psalms 1 and 119 link wisdom with adherence to the Torah, the Deuterocanonical books equate wisdom and Torah. In the Wisdom of Solomon she is sought after as the desired spouse of the book's writer, a pseudonymous "Solomon"; she has "knowledge of things of old," gives "good counsel," and teaches "self-control and prudence, justice and courage" (7:22–8:9). In Sirach 24, Wisdom states that she "came forth from the mouth of the Most High" at creation and was destined to dwell in Israel. The sexually evocative language of Sirach 24:19-34 and 51:13-28 equates the pleasures of knowing Woman Wisdom with the pleasures of knowing the Torah: "All this is the book of the covenant of the Most High God, the law that Moses commanded us" (24:23). Baruch 4:1 says of Wisdom: "She is the book of the commandments of God, the law that endures forever."

Thus while Wisdom is a consistent presence in the biblical texts, they present a varied view of her as (1) present with God at creation (Prov 8); hidden and known only to God (Job 28); (2) an active participant in human life (Prov 2 and 8); (3) discovered by adherence to the Torah (Pss 1 and 119); (4) a sought-after intimate companion of humanity (Wis 7–8); (5) created by God to dwell in Israel (Sir 24); and (6) the embodiment of Torah (Sir 24; Bar 4).[5] Kathleen O'Connor provides these summary words about Wisdom: "The Wisdom Woman exists in human reality as if it were a tapestry of connected threads, patterned into an intricate whole of which she is the center."[6]

In Psalm 119 the law (תורה), in its eight synonymous renderings, is the central focus. But, interestingly, the psalm itself does not mention Moses or Sinai and it does not contain the actual content of any of the laws given to the ancient Israelites. David Noel Freedman writes this about the psalm:

> In Psalm 119 *tôrâ* is a monolithic presence, consisting of individual laws and teachings to be sure, but described in only the most general terms, namely the 8 interchangeable *tôrâ*-words. . . . *Tôrâ* has become for the psalmist much more than the laws by which Israel should live, as given in the Pentateuch; *tôrâ* has become a personal way to God.[7]

He suggests: "In short, Psalm 119 gives *tôrâ* virtually the status of a divine

---

5. See also Roland E. Murphy's comments on Woman Wisdom in *The Tree of Life: An Exploration of Biblical Wisdom Literature*, 2nd ed. (Grand Rapids: Eerdmans, 1996), 145–46.

6. O'Connor, *Wisdom Literature*, 59.

7. David Noel Freedman, *Psalm 119: The Exaltation of Torah*, BJSUCSD 6 (Winona Lake, IN: Eisenbrauns, 1999), 89.

hypostasis, like wisdom (*ḥokmâ*) in Proverbs 8."[8] In Psalm 119, then, the law of Yhwh is not presented as a strict set of rules and regulations but as a way of life or approach to being that brings one closer to God, and in the Deuterocanonical literature that way of life is identified with Woman Wisdom (see Sir 24 and Bar 4).

Psalm 119, an expansive 176-verse alphabetic acrostic, follows the Egyptian Hallel psalms (Pss 113–118) in book 5. It is recited at the feast of Pentecost, a spring festival observed fifty days after Passover celebrating the giving of the Torah to Moses at Sinai during the wilderness wanderings. It contrasts dramatically in length with the two alphabetic acrostics that precede the Egyptian Hallel, Psalms 111 and 112. Psalm 111 consists of only seventy-two words and Psalm 112 of seventy-nine words. Psalm 119's 176 verses are divided into strophes of eight verses, each of which begins with a successive letter of the Hebrew alphabet. The three psalms, however, share a common theme of reverence for the Torah (תורה), as do Psalms 1 and 19.

Leslie Allen describes Psalm 119 as "the most developed instance [of the acrostic form] in the Old Testament."[9] Hans-Joachim Kraus writes, "The art of alphabetic organization has produced an unusual opus which in schematism and compulsion of form has no parallel in the OT."[10] Acrostic poems were the works of highly skilled literary artists and functioned in ancient Israelite literature in a number of ways—perhaps as a memory device to aid in public recitation and as a summary statement of all that can be said about a topic, from *aleph* to *tav*, from A to Z.[11] Erich Zenger adds that Psalm 119's acrostic structure (using all the letters of the Hebrew alphabet) perhaps "spells out" the whole of the content of the Torah and equates it with "an order that underlies the world."[12]

The singer of Psalm 119 weaves together words of lament, petition, trust, and exuberant joy in this marvelous ode to the Torah. J. Clinton McCann writes: "As a literary artist, the psalmist intended the structure of the poem to reinforce its theological content. In short, *torah*—God's

---

8. Freedman, *Psalm 119*, 89.

9. Leslie C. Allen, *Psalms 101–150*, WBC 21 (Nashville: Thomas Nelson, 2002), 180. He adds that the closest parallel is Lamentations 3.

10. Hans-Joachim Kraus, *Psalms 60–150*, trans. Hilton C. Oswald, CC (Minneapolis: Fortress, 1993), 411.

11. For a full discussion of the acrostic form, see the commentary for Psalms 111 and 112.

12. Frank-Lothar Hossfeld and Erich Zenger, *Psalms 3*, trans. Linda M. Maloney, Hermeneia (Minneapolis: Fortress, 2011), 257.

revelatory instruction—is pervasive and all-encompassing."[13] Claus
Westermann writes: "If a person succeeds in reading this psalm's 176
verses one after the other at one sitting, the effect is overwhelming. In its
extent the psalm has the effect of a massive mountain range. One has the
feeling that it represents the boundary between the world of the Psalms
and a different world, that of law piety."[14]

In Psalm 119 seven Hebrew words are used in synonymous inter-
change with the word "law" (תורה), which itself is used twenty-five times
(see, e.g., vv. 1, 18, 53, 97, 163).[15] The words are:

"decree," עדה (used twenty-three times: e.g., vv. 2, 31, 46, 88, 111)

"precept," פקוד (used twenty-one times: e.g., vv. 4, 45, 87, 110, 168)

"statute," חק (used twenty-two times: e.g., vv. 5, 26, 54, 118, 171)

"commandment(s)," מצוה (used twenty-two times: e.g., vv. 6, 32, 80,
151, 176)

"ordinance," משפט (used twenty-three times: e.g., vv. 7, 13, 91, 120, 164)

"word" or "promise," אמרה (used nineteen times: e.g., vv. 11, 41, 67,
82, 148)

"word," דבר (used twenty-two times: e.g., vv. 16, 25, 65, 101, 130)

Five of the eight synonyms (תורה, עדה, פקוד, מצוה, and משפט) occur also
in Psalm 19:7-14, leading some scholars to suggest that Psalm 119 may
be dependent on Psalm 19.[16] While each of the seven synonyms for
"law" carries a slightly different nuance of meaning, little is gained by
attempting to distinguish a separate meaning, theological or otherwise,
for each. Below I will give a brief explication of each strophe and then
offer some general comments on the message of the psalm as a whole.

The א strophe (vv. 1-8): The first two verses of Psalm 119 begin with
the wisdom word "happy" (אשרי), the same word that opens the Psalter
in Psalm 1:1 and appears twenty-six times in the book, often at key

---

13. J. Clinton McCann, Jr., "The Book of Psalms," *NIB*, vol. 4 (Nashville: Abingdon,
1996), 1166.

14. Claus Westermann, *The Psalms: Structure, Content & Message*, trans. Ralph D.
Gehrke (Minneapolis: Augsburg, 1980), 117.

15. Only the second strophe of Ps 119, vv. 9-16, does not contain the word "torah"
(תורה).

16. Allen, *Psalms 101–150*, 139.

junctures.[17] For a full discussion of the meaning of אשרי, see the commentary on Ps 112. The source of happiness in Psalm 119 is the same as in Psalms 1 and 112: the "law [תורה] of the LORD."

The ב strophe (vv. 9-16): Verse 9 poses a wisdom-like question: "How can young people keep their way pure?" The question echoes those found in Psalm 73:13 and Proverbs 20:9, but while neither Psalm 73 nor Proverbs 20 provides an answer to the question, Psalm 119:9 advises: "By guarding it according to your word" (דבר). While all the synonyms for תורה are used in this strophe of Psalm 119 ("word," דבר, v. 9; "commandment," מצוה, v. 10; "word," אמרה, v. 11; "statute," חק, vv. 12, 16; "ordinance," משפט, v. 13; "decree," עדה, v. 14; and "precept," פקוד, v. 15), it is the only strophe in which the word "law" (תורה) does not occur.

The ג strophe (vv. 17-24): Despite its general classification as a wisdom psalm, lament elements are prominent in many portions of Psalm 119, particularly verses 17-24.[18] In this strophe words of petition (vv. 17-18) give way to complaint (v. 19), move on to a description of the oppressors (vv. 21-23), and end with trust (v. 24).

The ד strophe (vv. 25-32): The lament continues in this strophe, with the psalmist's words moving quickly back and forth from complaint ("My soul clings to the dust," v. 25) to trust ("you answered me," v. 26) to petition ("Make me understand the way of your precepts," v. 27) to complaint ("My soul melts away for sorrow," v. 28) to petition ("strengthen me . . . teach me your law," vv. 28, 29) to trust ("I set your ordinances before me. I cling to your decrees," vv. 30, 31) and, finally, to petition ("let me not be put to shame," v. 31).

The ה strophe (vv. 33-40): Petition dominates this strophe, with a series of *hiphil*-causative verbs driving the plea of the psalm singer. She says, "teach me . . . your statutes" (v. 33); "give me understanding" (v. 34); "lead me in the path of your commandments" (v. 35); "turn my heart to your decrees" (v. 37); "turn my eye from looking at vanities" (v. 37); "confirm . . . your promise" (v. 38); "turn away the disgrace" (v. 39).

---

17. See, for example, Pss 1:1; 2:12; 41:1; 106:3; 112:1; 146:5. In addition, אשרי occurs thirty-five times in the Psalms and wisdom literature of the Hebrew Bible but only eight times in the remainder of the books.

18. See deClaissé-Walford, *Introduction to the Psalms*, 23–25, for a form-critical analysis of lament psalms. Psalm 119 incorporates many psalmic types, including, among others, questions (v. 9), laments (vv. 17-24), words of trust (vv. 41-48), praise and rejoicing (vv. 65-72, 129-136), and, perhaps most prevalent, petitions to God (vv. 33-40, 49-56, 145-152).

The ו strophe (vv. 41-48): The psalm singer begins with additional words of petition in verses 41 and 43—"Let your steadfast love come to me" (v. 41); "Do not take the word of truth utterly out of my mouth" (v. 43). Words of trust, though, dominate the strophe. In verse 42 the psalmist proclaims, "Then I shall have an answer for those who taunt me"; in verse 45, "I shall walk at liberty"; in verse 46, "I shall not be put to shame"; and in verse 48, "I revere your commandments, which I love, and I will meditate on your statutes."

The ז strophe (vv. 49-56): The word "remember" (זכר) occurs three times in this strophe—in verses 49, 52 (translated "think" in the NRSV), and 55. The word "remember" is powerful and pervasive in the Hebrew Bible. In Genesis 9:16 God says to Noah: "When the bow is in the clouds, I will see it and remember [זכר] the everlasting covenant between God and every living creature of all flesh that is on the earth." When the Israelites are in slavery in Egypt "God heard their groaning, and God remembered [זכר] his covenant with Abraham, Isaac, and Jacob" (Exod 2:24). In the Decalogue, God calls the Israelites to "remember [זכר] the sabbath day, and keep it holy" (Exod 20:8). The word "remember" occurs nearly two hundred times in the Hebrew Bible and generally conveys the idea of "the presence and acceptance of something in the mind."[19] Interestingly, the word "law" (תורה) occurs three times in this strophe as well (vv. 51, 53, and 55).

The ח strophe (vv. 57-64): This strophe begins with the word "portion" (חלק), calling to mind God's division of the land of promise among the Israelites in the book of Joshua (see, for instance, Josh 12:7; 15:13; 18:7; 19:9), but here the psalmist states that her "portion" (חלק) is YHWH (see also Pss 16:5; 73:26; 142:6). As if to emphasize the statement, each of the strophe's eight verses contains one of the תורה-synonyms: "word" (דבר) in verse 57; "promise" (אמרה) in verse 58; "decree" (עדה) in verse 59; "commandment" (מצוה) in verse 60; "law" (תורה) in verse 61; "ordinance" (משפט) in verse 62; "precept" (פקוד) in verse 63; and "statute" (חק) in verse 64. The strophe ends with verse 64's declaration that YHWH's "steadfast love" (חסד) "fills the earth."

The ט strophe (vv. 65-72): The word "good" (טוב) occurs six times in this strophe, even in the midst of the psalmist's despair (vv. 67, 69, 71). In verse 72 "good" (טוב) is the basis of a "better than" (טוב . . . מן) saying

---

19. Hermann Eising, "זכר, *zākār*," *TDOT*, 4:64–82, at 65.

typical of biblical wisdom literature, stating that God's "law" (תורה) is better "than thousands of gold and silver pieces."[20]

The י strophe (vv. 73-80): In verse 73 the psalmist affirms that God's hands "made" and "fashioned" her and asks that God's "mercy" (רחם, v. 77) may allow her to live. The word translated in verse 77 as "mercy" is one of the four self-descriptive words YHWH uses in his declaration to Moses on Mount Sinai after the Golden Calf incident (see Exod 34:6). The Hebrew root of the word is literally "womb," suggesting the kind of love a mother gives to her yet-to-be-born child as it is formed and fashioned in the womb. The psalmist thus celebrates the creator God whose hands "made" and "fashioned" her in the womb.

The כ strophe (vv. 81-88): The word כלה occurs three times in this strophe, translated in the NRSV in three different ways. In verse 81 the psalmist's soul "languishes" (כלה), in verse 82 her eyes "fail" (כלה), and in verses 84-87 those who persecute her and the arrogant have almost "made an end [כלה]" of her. The basic meaning of כלה is "bring to an end, cease," especially prematurely.[21]

The psalm singer states in verse 83 that she has become "like a wineskin in the smoke." This phrase occurs nowhere else in the Hebrew Bible and commentators have puzzled over its meaning. Erich Zenger suggests that we might have here the image of a worn-out wineskin hung in the chimney or of an empty wineskin hung above the fireplace until it is needed again, reflective of the psalmist's feeling that YHWH has forgotten her.[22] But for her part, "I have not forgotten your statutes."

The ל strophe (vv. 89-96): Perhaps in answer to the cries of the psalm singer in the previous strophe, verses 89-91 are an exuberant proclamation that God's word (דבר) is "firmly fixed" in heaven and that God established the earth and it "stands firm." Thus, despite those who persecute (vv. 84, 86) and who are arrogant (v. 85), the psalmist declares in verses 92-96 that she "delights" (שעשעים) in God's "law" (תורה) and finds "life" in God's "precepts" (פקוד).[23]

The מ strophe (vv. 97-104): In these verses the psalm singer employs a number of "wisdom" terms in her expression of love for God's "law" (תורה). She states that it makes her "wise" (חכמה, v. 98) and that she has more "understanding" (שׂכל, v. 99; בין, vv. 100 and 104). Verses 101 and

---

20. See Prov 12:9; 15:16, 17; 16:8; 17:1, 12; 19:1; 22:1; 25:7, 24; 27:5, 10; 28:6.

21. F. J. Helfmeyer, "כלה, *kālāh*," *TDOT*, 7:157–64, at 157.

22. Hossfeld and Zenger, *Psalms 3*, 275.

23. The word שעשעים occurs only nine times in the Hebrew Bible: five times in Ps 119 and twice in Prov 8 (the other instances are Isa 5:7 and Jer 31:20).

104 speak of the "way" (ארח), a wisdom metaphor found throughout the book of Proverbs.[24]

The כ strophe (vv. 105-112): Just as verse 57's use of the word "portion" (חלק) calls to mind the division of land among the Israelites in the book of Joshua (15:13; 18:7; 19:9), so does verse 111's use of "heritage" (נחלה).[25] But as in verse 57, in verse 111 the psalmist's "portion" is not the land; the "decrees" (עדה) of YHWH are her "heritage."

The ס strophe (vv. 113-120): Here the psalm singer declares her "hate" (שׂנא) for the "double-minded" (v. 113), "evildoers" (v. 115), and the "wicked" (v. 119) and her "love" for the "law" (תורה, v. 113) and the "decrees" (עדה, v. 119). The word "hate" (שׂנא) in Hebrew refers to an emotional reaction of aversion to someone or something; the aversion does not necessarily invoke a desire for harm to come to the other but rather a desire to distance oneself from the other. In Proverbs 19:7 we read: "If the poor are hated even by their kin, how much more are they shunned by their friends!" In the Hebrew Bible, God "hates" particular actions and behaviors rather than particular people. Moses says to the Israelites in Deuteronomy 16:21-22, "You shall not plant any tree as an Asherah beside the altar that you make for the LORD your God; nor shall you set up a stone pillar—things that the LORD your God hates." And in the Psalter the psalm singers affirm that God hates "evildoers" (Ps 5:5), "lovers of violence" (Ps 11:5), and "wickedness" (Ps 45:7).[26]

The ע strophe (vv. 121-128): In this strophe the psalmist implores God to guarantee her well-being (טוב, v. 122), to deal with her according to God's steadfast love (חסד, v. 124), to teach her the statutes (חק, v. 124), and to give her understanding (בין, v. 125) because she loves the commandments more than gold, more than fine gold, and hates every false way (vv. 127-128).

The פ strophe (vv. 129-136): The strophe begins with the psalmist praising God for God's "wonderful [פלא] decrees."[27] The word פלא occurs in its various forms some thirty-three times in the book of Psalms, often in reference to the deliverance of the Israelites from Egypt.[28] It is used most often in biblical Hebrew to describe "extraordinary phenomena,

---

24. See, e.g., Prov 1:10; 2:8, 13, 15, 19, 20; 3:6; 8:20; 10:17; 17:23.

25. For "portion" (חלק) see, e.g., Josh 15:13; 18:7; 19:9. "Heritage/inheritance" (נחלה) occurs some forty-nine times in the book of Joshua. See, e.g., Josh 11:23; 13:8; 19:39; 24:28.

26. Edward Lipiński, "שׂנא, śānēʾ," *TDOT*, 14:164–74.

27. פלא occurs also in Ps 119:18, 27.

28. See Pss 105:2, 5; 106:7, 22; 136:4.

transcending the power of human knowledge and imagination"[29] and finds perhaps its best parallel in the word "miracle." For a full discussion of the concept of "miracle" in the Hebrew Bible, see the commentary for Psalm 105. Thus the singer of Psalm 119 equates the decrees of Yнwн with Yнwн's wondrous acts of deliverance on behalf of the people of Israel.

In verse 130 the psalmist, using wisdom language once again, states that the opening of Yнwн's words (דבר) gives light and understanding to the simple (פתי). The word translated "simple" occurs only eighteen times in the Hebrew Bible, with fifteen occurrences in the book of Proverbs.[30]

The צ strophe (vv. 137-144): Words derived from the root צדק occur five times in this strophe in reference to Yнwн ("righteous" in vv. 137 and 144; "righteousness" in vv. 138 and 142 [2x]). Paralleling verse 92, the psalm singer says in verse 143 that Yнwн's commandments are her delight (שעשע) and then offers familiar words of petition in verse 144: "give me understanding that I may live" (see vv. 17, 25, 27, 34, 37, 40, 73, 77, 88, 93, 107, 125, 149).

The ק strophe (vv. 145-152): In this strophe the psalmist cries out to Yнwн for an answer and for rescue from those who persecute her with evil (vv. 145-146; 150). Her persecutors are nearby, but she knows that Yнwн is as well (vv. 150-151) because she has learned from the decrees (עדה) that Yнwн established them forever (v. 152).

The ר strophe (vv. 153-160): The familiar petition "give me life/preserve my life" that pervades Psalm 119 (see also vv. 15, 37, 50, 93, 107, 117, 144, 149) occurs repeatedly in this strophe, in verses 154, 156, and 159. Continuing the theme of the previous strophe, the psalmist maintains that while she "does not forget" (v. 153) and "has not swerved" (v. 157) from God's law and decrees, the wicked (v. 155), her persecutors and adversaries (v. 157), and the faithless (v. 158) "do not seek" (v. 155) and "do not keep" (v. 158) Yнwн's statutes (חק) and commands (אמרה).

The ש strophe (vv. 161-168): As if in answer to the two previous strophes, verses 161-168 voice the sense of peace the psalm singer finds in the law of God, despite being persecuted (see vv. 150 and 157). Verse 164 states that the psalmist praises (הלל) God seven times a day. While the verbal root הלל is found frequently in book 5 (more than sixty times), its first occurrence in Psalm 119 is in verse 164. We may perhaps read it as a concluding word of response to the sureness of Yнwн's law.

---

29. J. Conrad, "פלא, *pl'*, *pele'*," *TDOT*, 11:533–46, at 534.
30. See Prov 7:7; 9:4; 14:18; 21:11; 27:12.

The ת strophe (vv. 169-176): In verse 169, the opening verse of the final strophe of Psalm 119, the NRSV reads that the psalm singer "cries" (רִן) to YHWH to give her understanding. The verbal root רנן is almost always used in a positive sense in the Hebrew Bible and is connected with joyous outbursts: never with cries of oppression, persecution, etc.[31] Further, in verse 171 the psalm singer says that she will pour forth "praise" (הלל) and in verse 172 that she will "sing" (ענה), because (v. 174) YHWH's law is her "delight" (שעשע).[32] The final strophe of Psalm 119 may be read as the words of praise the psalm singer offers to YHWH seven times a day (v. 164).

Just as the first verse of Psalm 119 echoes the first verse of Psalm 1 with the introductory wisdom word אשרי, so the final verse of Psalm 119 echoes Psalm 1's final verse. In Psalm 119:176 the psalmist confesses to having gone astray like a "lost" (אבד) sheep and implores God to "seek out your servant, for I do not forget your commandments." Psalm 1:6 reads, "for YHWH watches over the way of the righteous, but the way of the wicked will perish [אבד)]."

Finding Redemption in a Painful Past

In an initial reading of Psalm 119 from my limited knowledge of the Old Testament I noticed two things. First, the psalm is structured around the sequential letters of the Hebrew alphabet and the repetition of words such as "statutes," "law," "precept," "word," and "judgment."

I further noticed that the psalm singer moves from proclaiming her devotion to the "law," (vv. 10-11, 59-60, 92-93, 164) to lamenting those who oppress her (vv. 23, 51, 85, 107, 110, 150) to imploring God for help in adversity (vv. 22, 41-42, 81-83, 153-154). Yet God is silent in Psalm 119. No words from God come to the psalmist in the midst of her declaration of devotion, her laments of oppression, and her cries for help.

I grew up in, and in many ways still live in, an oppressive patriarchal society. As a colored (biracial) female South African I have a different story from the familiar one of the divide between whites and blacks in our country. Being colored during the apartheid regime was different from just being racially black, white, or Indian; we were illegal hybrids labeled *amperpass*, an Afrikaans term meaning

---

31. Jutta Hausmann, "רנן, *rānan*," *TDOT*, 13:515–22. For a full treatment of רנן, see the commentary for Ps 95.

32. For שעשעים see n. 23 above.

"almost like the master" because of our fair complexion.

In the early days of apartheid poor white adolescents were sent to "industrial" schools to learn a trade so that they would not be subject to the same kinds of demeaning labor as were blacks. Colored adolescents were eventually also admitted to these schools, which then became known as "reformatory" schools. Reformatory schools were instituted and managed by a cooperation between the departments of education and prisons in South Africa. As the number of colored students increased in the reformatory schools they moved away from skilled training toward educational and discipline tactics that fostered social isolation and psychological slavery, tactics that in some cases led students to commit suicide.

I was sent to a reformatory school because my mother was not able to keep and raise me as a biracial child. I thus grew up in a segregated and isolated world that seemed normal to me until I discovered the true history of the treatment of colored people during the apartheid regime. Even after the end of apartheid, though, little has changed for colored people in South Africa. South Africa's motto, "the rainbow nation," seems not to include the marginalized colored population. I am neither black nor white, and thus I feel so often that I do not belong in either the "black world" or the "white world" in South Africa.

When I read Psalm 119 I am particularly drawn to verses 57-72. In verse 61 the psalm singer cries, "the cords of the wicked ensnare me," picturing for me a person lamenting a sense of loss and being robbed. As a colored female I was sent to a reformatory school without understanding why. I did not know that my mother was black and my father was white. I only discovered my heritage when my mother told me when I was twenty-two years old. But I was not alone; I was only one of many colored children who ended up in reformatory schools because their parents knew they could not raise them, and thus we became wards of the state.

In verse 62 of Psalm 119 the psalm singer states that she rises at midnight to give praise to God. I ask: "Is her rising a sign of joyfulness or of restlessness?" For me as a female who was caught up in the bonds of an oppressive political structure, not trained for any skill that would afford her the ability to survive in my society and deprived of the traditions and culture of my two heritages, my rising at midnight is because of a restlessness about my life as a colored woman in South Africa. I don't look like most of the people around me; I can't identify culturally with any particular group in South Africa, a country in which such identity is so culturally crucial; I so often feel disconnected from so many and so much around me. And yet I resonate with the words of the psalm singer in verse 63 who says to God, "I am a companion of all who fear you, of those who keep your precepts." The words of the psalms remind me that God is the equalizer and final judge of the oppressed and oppressor in all things, and the words of the singer of Psalm 119 remind me that God invites our crying out in joy and sorrow and petition.

This reflection has allowed me to express my frustrations, anguish, and deep sense of pain and brokenness in the presence of God without feelings of guilt. The words of verse 71, "It is good for me that I was humbled, so that I might learn your statutes," help me despite all I have been through in my life. Like the singer of the psalm, I yearn more for God's salvation of me as an individual and to be fully equipped from a spiritual and social perspective to help my fellow colored South Africans who have experienced the same marginalization as I.

Belinda Crawford

Psalms 120–134

I Lift My Eyes to the Hills and Seek Peace

Psalms 120–134: The Songs of Ascents

Psalms 120–134 make up a lengthy collection in the middle of Book Five. Each of these fifteen psalms has a superscription identifying it as "A Song of Ascents" (שיר המעלות).[1] The frequent references to Jerusalem and Zion in these psalms may account for their collective identification.[2] The verbal root of "ascents" is "go up" (עלה), and since Jerusalem sits on a hill, no matter where one comes from one always "goes up" to Jerusalem. In 1 Kings 12:28, for instance, Jeroboam says to the Israelites, "You have gone up (עלה) to Jerusalem long enough." Isaiah 2:3 and Micah 4:2 envision a time when "Many peoples shall come and say, 'Come, let us go up (עלה) to the mountain of the LORD.'"

It is possible that the "ascents" referred to in Psalms 120–134 are the steps of the Temple, which Ezekiel calls "ascents (מעלות)." In Ezekiel 40:6 the prophet sees a man going into the gate of the Temple, "going

---

1. Psalm 121's superscription is slightly different, reading "A Song for the Going Up (שיר למעלות)." Psalms 122, 124, 131, and 133 add "of David (לדוד)," and Ps 127 adds "of Solomon (לשלמה)."
2. See Pss 122:1, 6; 125:1, 2; 126:1; 128:5; 129:5; 132:13; 133:3; 134:3.

up (עלה) its steps (מעלות)." Additionally, the *Mishnah* states: "fifteen steps led up within [the Court of the Women] to the Court of the Israelites, corresponding to the fifteen songs of the steps in the Psalms, and upon them the Levites used to sing"[3] and "The Levites on harps, and on lyres, and with cymbals, and with trumpets and with other instruments of music without number upon the fifteen steps leading down from the Court of the Israelites to the Women's Court, corresponding to 'The Fifteen Songs of Ascent' in the Psalms; upon them the Levites used to stand with musical instruments and sing hymns."[4]

The superscription "Song of Ascents" may reflect the very structure of the collection's psalms. Within each psalm, and often as an *inclusio* around the verses of the psalm, the Songs of Ascents contain verbal "step" connections that move the reciter through the cola and strophes of the psalm.[5] The "step connections," which were most likely fashioned as mnemonic devices, are as follows:

Psalm 120	vv. 2 and 3	"deceitful"
	vv. 5 and 6	"live, dwelling place" (ישב)
	vv. 6 and 7	"peace"
	vv. 2 and 6	"soul" (נפש)
Psalm 121	vv. 1 and 2	"my help"
	vv. 3 and 4	"slumber"
	vv. 4 and 5	"keep" (שמר)
	vv. 7 and 8	"keep" (שמר)
	v. 8 and Ps 122:1	"go" (בוא)

3. Herbert Danby, *The Mishnah* (Oxford: Oxford University Press, 1933), *m. Mid.* 2:5.

4. Ibid., *m. Sukkah* 5:4.

5. This idea was first proposed in the early nineteenth century by Wilhelm Gesenius, *Thesaurus Philologicus Criticus Linguae Hebraeae et Chaldaeae Veteris Testamenti*, 2d ed., vol. 2 (Leipzig: Fr. Chr. Wil. Vogelius, 1839), 1031–32. See the brief discussions in Loren D. Crow, *The Songs of Ascents (Psalms 120–134): Their Place in Israelite History and Religion*, SBLDS 148, ed. Michael V. Fox (Atlanta: Scholars Press, 1996), 15–18; Richard J. Clifford, *Psalms 73–150*, 216–17; and Robert Davidson, *The Vitality of Worship: A Commentary on the Book of Psalms* (Grand Rapids: Eerdmans, 1998), 404–5.

Psalm 122	vv. 2 and 3	"Jerusalem"
	vv. 4 and 5	"there" (שָׁם)
	v. 5	"thrones"
	vv. 6, 7, and 8	"peace"
	vv. 8 and 9	"for the sake of" (לְמַעַן)
	vv. 1 and 9	"house of the LORD"
Psalm 123	vv. 1 and 2	"eyes"
	vv. 2 and 3	"mercy" (חָנַן)
	vv. 3 and 4	"more than" (רַב) and "contempt" (בּוּז)
Psalm 124	vv. 1 and 2	"if it had not been the LORD"
	vv. 3, 4, and 5	"then" (אֲזַי)
	vv. 4 and 5	"flood and raging water" (מַיִם), "soul" (נֶפֶשׁ), "gone over" (עָבַר)
	vv. 4, 5, and 7	"soul" (נֶפֶשׁ)
	v. 7	"escape" (מָלַט)
Psalm 125	vv. 1 and 2	"the LORD"
	v. 2	"surround" (סָבִיב)
	v. 3	"the righteous" (צַדִּיק)
Psalm 126	vv. 1 and 4	"restore" (שׁוּב)
	vv. 2 and 3	"the LORD has done great things"
	vv. 2, 5, and 6	"shouts of joy" (רִנָּה)
	vv. 5 and 6	"sow" (זָרַע)
Psalm 127	v. 1	"if" (אִם), "in vain" (שָׁוְא), "guard, watch" (שָׁמַר)
	vv. 1 and 2	"in vain" (שָׁוְא)
	vv. 3 and 4	"sons"
	vv. 4 and 5	"warrior, man" (גֶּבֶר, גִּבּוֹר)

Psalm 128	vv. 1 and 2	"happy" (אשרי)
	vv. 1 and 4	"fear"
	vv. 2 and 5	"go well, prosperity" (טוב)
	vv. 3 and 6	"children"
	vv. 5 and 6	"Jerusalem"
Psalm 129	vv. 1 and 2	"often they have attacked me from my youth"
	v. 8	"bless"
Psalm 130	vv. 1 and 2	"voice"
	v. 5	"wait" (קוה)
	vv. 5 and 6	"my soul"
	v. 6	"those who watch for the morning"
	vv. 2 and 6	"the Lord" (אדוני)
	vv. 5 and 7	"hope" (יחל)
	vv. 3 and 8	"iniquity" (עון)
	vv. 7 and 8	"redeem" (פדה)
Psalm 131	v. 1	"not" (לא)
	v. 2	"like a weaned child" (כגמל), "with" (על)
	v. 2	"soul"
Psalm 132	vv. 5 and 7	"dwelling place" (משכן)
	vv. 8 and 14	"resting place" (מנוחה)
	vv. 9 and 16	"priests"
	vv. 9, 16, and 18	"clothe" (לבש)
	vv. 10 and 11	"turn" (שוב)
	vv. 10, 11 and 17	"David"
	vv. 11 and 12:	"throne"
	v. 12:	"sons"

Psalm 133	vv. 1 and 2	"good"
	v. 2	"beard"
	vv. 2 and 3	"run down"
Psalm 134	vv. 1, 2, and 3	"bless" and "the LORD"

In addition all of the Songs of Ascents, except Psalm 132, are uniformly brief in comparison to the rest of the psalms in the Psalter, ranging from three to nine verses. According to Erich Zenger, even including Psalm 132, the average length of the Songs of Ascents is 6.7 verses, indicating further that they were meant to be recited from memory, perhaps even "sung to catchy melodies."[6]

Whatever their origins, these "pilgrim" songs became part of a number of festal celebrations in Jerusalem. The Songs of Ascents are the psalms traditionally recited or sung at the Feast of Tabernacles (Booths or *Sukkoth*) in autumn. The Feast of Tabernacles commemorates God's care for the Israelites during the Wilderness Wanderings, reinforcing the "pilgrimage" theme of the Songs of Ascents. The six psalms preceding the Songs of Ascents are also used at festal celebrations. Psalms 113–118, the Egyptian Hallel, are recited during the spring Passover celebration and Psalm 119 is read at the Feast of Pentecost, which occurs on the fiftieth day after Passover. The concentration of festival psalms in the middle of Book Five suggests the intentional shaping of a collection of festal psalms in this portion of the Psalter.[7]

An interesting aspect of the Songs of Ascents is the wide variety of psalm types included in this relatively small collection: individual and community laments (Pss 120, 123, 126, 130), individual and community hymns (Pss 121, 122, 124, 125, 129, 131, 134, 135, 136), wisdom psalms (Pss 127, 128, 133), and a royal psalm (Ps 132). The variety of *Gattungen* [genres] represented in the Songs of Ascents has troubled many commentators, who question whether such an eclectic mix could ever have been a collection actually used in the life of ancient Israel. But Michael Goulder, in *The Psalms of the Return*, reminds us:

---

6. Frank Lothar Hossfeld and Erich Zenger, *Psalms 3*, Hermeneia, ed. Klaus Baltzer, trans. Linda M. Maloney (Minneapolis: Fortress, 2011), 295.

7. For a detailed discussion of the many proposed origins of the Songs of Ascents see Hossfeld and Zenger, *Psalms 3*, 287–95.

> Why should we think that a collection of psalms is not a unity because
> it contains pieces from different *Gattungen*? Have such critics never at-
> tended a church service that began with a confession, included lessons
> of instruction, hymns of praise and prayers, and ended perhaps with
> the General Thanksgiving?[8]

Two other aspects of the Songs of Ascents are of interest to interpreters. First, while metaphorical language abounds in the Psalter, the Songs
make extensive use of similes, usually introduced with the preposition
ki (כ): "as (כ) the eyes of a maid to the hand of her mistress" in Ps 123:2;
"like (כ) a bird from the snare" in Ps 124:7; "like (כ) the grass on the
housetops" in Ps 129:6; "like (כ) a weaned child" in Ps 131:2; "like (כ) the
precious oil on the head" in Ps 133:2. Second, while the Psalter contains
many references to everyday life, the Songs of Ascents abound with
them: "relatives and friends" in Psalm 122:8; "sowing and reaping" in
Psalms 126:5-6 and 129:6-7; "building a house" and "children" in Psalm
127:1, 3-4; "a weaned child with its mother" in Psalm 131:2; "kindred
living in unity" in Psalm 133:2.[9]

Psalm 120

Psalm 120 is the first of the group of fifteen Songs of Ascents (Pss
120–134). Its words are those of an individual who compares her current
life situation with dwelling in the hostile lands of Meshech and Kedar (v.
5). The psalm singer longs for peace but is surrounded by "lying lips" and
a "deceitful tongue" (v. 2) that she characterizes as "sharp arrows" and
"glowing coals" (v. 4). If we read the Songs of Ascents as psalms sung by
pilgrims as they made their way to Jerusalem to celebrate a number of
annual religious festivals including Passover, the feast of Weeks, and the
feast of Tabernacles, or as psalms celebrating the Israelites' return from
exile in Babylon, then Psalm 120 is a fitting introductory word. James
L. Mays writes that the psalm puts the world from which the pilgrims
come "in sharpest contrast to the peace they desire and seek in coming
to Zion."[10] But I would like to propose another reading and interpretation of the psalm.

---

8. Michael Goulder, *The Psalms of the Return (Book V, Psalms 107–150)*, JSOTSup
258 (Sheffield: Sheffield Academic Press, 1998), 24.

9. Hossfeld and Zenger, *Psalms 3*, 295–96.

10. James L. Mays, *Psalms*, IBC (Louisville: Westminster John Knox, 1994), 388.

Psalm 120:1-7

A Song of Ascents

¹In my distress I cry to the LORD,
that he may answer me:
²"Deliver me, O LORD,
from lying lips,
from a deceitful tongue."
³What shall be given to you?
And what more shall be done to
you,
you deceitful tongue?
⁴A warrior's sharp arrows,
with glowing coals of the broom
tree!
⁵Woe is me, that I am an alien in
Meshech,
that I must live among the tents of
Kedar.
⁶Too long have I had my dwelling
among those who hate peace.
⁷I am for peace;
but when I speak,
they are for war.

The NRSV translates verse 1 as "In my distress I cry to the LORD that he may answer me," suggesting that the psalmist is imploring YHWH to hear her words of distress and answer her. The MT, however, actually reads, "In my distress, to YHWH I cried out; he answered me," indicating that the psalmist is voicing words of trust in God rather than words of petition. God has heard the psalm singer's complaints of oppression in the past and has answered, giving the psalmist confidence that God will again hear and answer.[11] Thus the description of the present situation in which the psalm singer finds herself begins in verse 2. There she asks God for deliverance from "lying lips" and "a deceitful tongue." The word translated "me" in the phrase "deliver me" is נֶפֶשׁ, usually translated "soul" in the NRSV.[12] The word's root meaning is "throat," the body part through which air is breathed, speech is enacted, and sustenance is gained. Might we see here the psalm singer asking God to deliver her נֶפֶשׁ, her source of speech and breath, from those whose speech and even breath are deceitful and lying?

In verse 3 the psalmist speaks directly to "the deceitful tongue." The MT reads, "What will he [YHWH] give to you and what will he add [יֹסִף] to you?"—i.e., "What more will he give you?" The verbal pattern of this

11. For a good summary of the various options for understanding the verbs in v. 1, see Loren D. Crow, *The Songs of Ascents (Psalms 120–134): Their Place in Israelite History and Religion*, SBLDS 148 (Atlanta: Scholars Press, 1996), 32; Frank-Lothar Hossfeld and Erich Zenger, *Psalms 3*, trans. Linda M. Maloney, Hermeneia (Minneapolis: Fortress, 2011), 303–5.

12. Examples from the Psalter include Pss 23:3; 33:19; 42:3; 62:5; and 119:81.

question is modeled on oath formulas in other places in the Hebrew Bible in which parties to an oath swear allegiance at the risk of incurring the wrath of God. The usual formula was "May the LORD do to X and more also [יֹסִף]] if . . ." in which a main verbal action is intensified by יסף (add, do further or longer). In 1 Samuel 3:17, after Samuel receives a vision in the house of YHWH, he is afraid to tell Eli. But Eli calls Samuel to him and demands to know what God has said, using oath-taking words: "Do not hide it from me. May God do so to you and more also [יֹסִף], if you hide anything from me of all that he told you."[13]

In verse 4 the psalm singer proposes an answer to the oath question she posed in verse 3 with imprecatory words.[14] The deceitful tongue should have sharp arrows and glowing coals hurled against it. The word translated "deceitful" in the NRSV is from the Hebrew verbal root רמה, which means "throw, shoot, propel arrows,"[15] thus paralleling what the psalmist is receiving at the hands of her oppressor with what she calls on YHWH to do to her oppressor on her behalf. Additionally, the word translated "sharpened" is שׁנונים, closely related to "tooth" (שׁן), reflecting the bodily organ that is the cause of the psalm singer's hurt.

The word "woe" (אויה), an expression of anguished fear in the Hebrew Bible, introduces verse 5.[16] In verses 5-6 the psalmist laments having to live and have her dwelling in Meshech and Kedar. The word translated in verse 5 as "must live" and in verse 6 as "had my dwelling" is from the Hebrew root שׁכן, which means literally "settle down," "rest," and "remain." Meshech is listed in Genesis 10:2 as one of the descendants of Japheth; in Ezekiel 27:13 it is mentioned as a trading partner with Tyre, and in Ezekiel 38:2 and 39:1 as part of the kingdom of Magog. According to Josephus, Meshech was located north of Israel, in Cappadocia.[17] Ezekiel 32:26 describes the people of Meshech as "uncircumcised" ones who "spread terror in the land of the living." Kedar is, according to Genesis 25:13, the second son of Ishmael, and in other places in the biblical text his descendants (the Kedarites) are Bedouin in the Arabian desert to the southeast of Israel. Isaiah 21:16-17 describes the Kedarites as warriors with bows whose glory is about to come to an end.

13. Other examples are Ruth 1:16-17; 1 Sam 14:44; 2 Sam 3:9; 1 Kgs 2:23.

14. For a full discussion of imprecatory words in the Psalter, see the commentary for Ps 109.

15. Hossfeld and Zenger, *Psalms 3*, 302.

16. See 1 Sam 4:7; Isa 6:5; Jer 6:4; Lam 5:16.

17. Flavius Josephus, *Ant*.1.6.1.

The psalm singer may be referring to specific locations or using the designations as metaphors for places to the farthest north and farthest south of Israel, suggesting a sense of being totally surrounded by hostility. Erhard Gerstenberger maintains: "It is futile to speculate about the historicity and geographical location of such hostile tribes. Arguing from the very nature of psalm texts that were used by many people in succeeding generations, one must admit that any possible reference to a concrete situation must have acquired symbolic value in order to stay meaningful to the users of the text."[18] Erich Zenger adds: "These are data about a perspective on the world whose horizontal dimensions evoke the life-threatening 'borders' of the world of the time and are therefore a metaphor for chaos, which surrounds and menaces the world."[19]

The word translated "peace" in verses 6 and 7 is שלום. The deeper meaning of the word has to do with wholeness, wellness, and settledness. James L. Mays writes that in שלום "the hopefulness and wholesomeness of life when living is knit into the fabric of relatedness to God and others and world. It is the at-one-ness that makes for goodness."[20]

Lying lips, deceitful tongues, and those who hate "peace" are the subject of this first Song of Ascents. The psalm singer cries out to God to deliver and to make things right. The organs of speech are cited many times in the Psalter as weapons of oppression and hurtfulness.[21] "Lip" (שׂפה) occurs some twenty-eight times in the Psalter, and "tongue" (לשׁון), some thirty-five times. In addition, "lip" occurs at least thirty-eight times and "tongue" nineteen times in the book of Proverbs.

Words are a powerful commodity. The creator God has given humanity the gift of speech, and it can be used for good or for oppression and hurtfulness. The old adage "Sticks and stones may break my bones, but words will never hurt me" is a lie. Israelite pilgrims perhaps sang the words of Psalm 120 as they journeyed from their villages to Jerusalem to celebrate festal occasions or as they made their way home from exile in Babylon. But the psalm's words resonate also in many life situations in the twenty-first century. Domestic abuse may not be and often is not physical, but rather emotional and verbal. Constant belittling, accusing, and angry rants are as damaging as physical harm. Women, men, children, and

18. Erhard S. Gerstenberger, *Psalms, Part 2, and Lamentations*, FOTL 15 (Grand Rapids: Eerdmans, 2001), 319.

19. Hossfeld and Zenger, *Psalms 3*, 310.

20. Mays, *Psalms*, 388.

21. See Pss 5:9; 12:4; 50:19; 78:36; 109:2; 140:3.

people in the workplace also suffer quietly in such circumstances. The singer of Psalm 120 longs to be away from lips that speak falsehood and from deceitful tongues and to find the well-being that comes with living in the presence of God. She remembers past situations of oppression in which God has answered her (v. 1). Confident that God will be faithful again, the psalmist uses strong words of imprecation against those oppressing her (vv. 3-4). When lying lips and deceitful tongues overwhelm us, may we recall the words of the psalm singer and cry out in confident expectation that God will indeed respond. Richard Clifford suggests also that "though 'deceitful tongue' may refer to a specific calumny, it may also refer more generally to a society where mutual respect and truthfulness have disappeared (as in Pss 10:7; 12:1-4; 31:18)."[22]

Psalm 121

In Psalm 121, the second Song of Ascents, two voices come together to provide words of assurance that YHWH will provide protection and care. Some scholars suggest that the words of the psalm be heard as the departing dialogue between a pilgrim leaving home to travel to Jerusalem and members of her village providing words of blessing. Others maintain that the most likely setting is a dialogue between pilgrims as they approach the holy city, while still others understand it as the internal dialogue of an individual pilgrim at some point along the journey to Jerusalem.[23]

Perhaps more important to an interpretation of Psalm 121 is an understanding of verse 1. Many translations, including the NRSV, render the verse in a way that conveys a sense of potential peril from some mountainous barrier at which the psalmist is looking, perhaps the rugged hill country of central Palestine if the psalm's *Sitz im Leben* is seen as the beginning of a pilgrimage to Jerusalem. The phrase "lift the eyes," however, usually expresses the idea of looking expectantly, as we find in Psalm 123:1.[24] Moreover, "mountains" ordinarily do not signify anything foreboding in the biblical text but rather places of refuge,[25] high places of various ancient Near Eastern deities, and, in the case of Jerusalem,

---

22. Richard J. Clifford, *Psalms 73–150*, AOTC (Nashville: Abingdon, 2003), 219.

23. Another example of a psalmist's internal dialogue can be found in Pss 42 and 43. See Hossfeld and Zenger, *Psalms 3*, 317–18.

24. John Goldingay, *Psalms*, vol. 3: *Psalms 90–150*, BCOT (Grand Rapids: Baker Academic, 2008), 456. Hossfeld and Zenger, *Psalms 3*, 322. See also Gen 13:14 and 22:13.

25. See Gen 19:30 and 1 Kgs 19:8.

Psalm 121:1-8

A Song of Ascents*

¹I lift up my eyes to the hills—
   from where will my help come?
²My help comes from the LORD,
   who made heaven and earth.
³He will not let your foot be moved;
   he who keeps you will not
      slumber.
⁴He who keeps Israel
   will neither slumber nor sleep.
⁵The LORD is your keeper;
   the LORD is your shade at your
      right hand.

⁶The sun shall not strike you by day,
   nor the moon by night.
⁷The LORD will keep you from all evil;
   he will keep your life.
⁸The LORD will keep
   your going out and your coming in
   from this time on and forevermore.

* Ps 121 is the only Song of Ascents
in which the preposition ל is added to
מעלות, properly translated as "A Song
for the Ascents," although not reflected
in the NRSV translation.

the mountain of YHWH, as we see in Psalm 125:2 and Isaiah 2:2//Micah 4:1. Thus the second half of verse 1, "from where [מאין] will my help [עזר] come?" may be read as a rhetorical question: "From which mountain does my help come?"—a question to which the psalm singer already knows the answer, which she voices in verse 2.[26]

In that verse the psalm singer identifies YHWH as the one "who made [עשׂה] heaven and earth," employing a participial form of the verb that indicates YHWH's ongoing creative work in the world.[27] In verses 3-8 the verbal root "keep" (שמר) appears six times, always in reference to YHWH; its basic meaning is "protect, guard, watch over, take care of," and, as with "who made" in verse 2, its form in verses 3-5 is participial, conveying YHWH's present ongoing "keeping" of the psalmist. Then, in verses 7 and 8, שמר occurs in the imperfect verbal form, providing the assurance of YHWH's future care for the psalm singer.

Verses 4-6 provide concrete metaphorical images of what YHWH will do to "keep" the psalmist. YHWH neither slumbers nor sleeps (v. 4); YHWH provides shade (v. 5); YHWH provides protection from the sun by day and the moon by night (v. 6). Interestingly, in other places in the book of

26. For a full treatment of the word עזר, see the commentary for Psalm 115.

27. See the commentary on the enthronement psalms (Pss 93–100) and, in particular, Ps 96. The phrase "maker of heaven and earth" appears three times in the Songs of Ascents (Pss 121:2; 124:8; 134:3) and additionally in book 5 in Ps 146:6; it was incorporated into the Apostles' Creed with the words: "I believe in God, the Father almighty, Creator of heaven and earth."

Psalms the psalm singers call on Yʜᴡʜ to awaken (Pss 7:6; 35:23; 44:23; 59:4-5). The "sleeping deity" is a literary motif found in numerous texts in the ancient Near East. The words of Psalm 121 stand in sharp contrast to the texts accusing God of sleeping and thus not paying attention to the cries of the psalm singers.[28]

In verse 5 the psalm singer is assured that Yʜᴡʜ is her shade (צֵל). The word occurs ten times in the Psalter, often as part of the phrase "the shadow [צֵל] of your wings [כְּנָפִים]" (Pss 17:8; 36:7; 57:1; 63:7), and suggests the protection provided by a mother bird to her young chicks (cp. Isa 51:16 and Matt 23:37). In verse 6 the shade of Yʜᴡʜ will keep the sun by day and the moon by night from striking the psalmist. Erich Zenger writes: "Yʜᴡʜ is the royal protective umbrella that shades during the day from the annoying and even life-threatening heat of the sun and at night from the mysterious and dangerous powers of the moon."[29]

Verses 7 and 8 summarize all the ways in which Yʜᴡʜ will "keep" the very life (נֶפֶשׁ) of the psalm singer.[30] The phrase "your going out [יָצָא] and your coming in [בּוֹא]" is a merism, indicating that Yʜᴡʜ will guard the psalmist's every movement. Thus, at whatever point in her journey, the pilgrim psalm singer finds assurance of Yʜᴡʜ's constant, caring presence.

Psalm 121: We Lift Our Eyes to the Hills

In an article in the 2014 issue of *HTS Theological Studies*, Thinandavha D. Mashau of the University of South Africa uses verses 1 and 2 of Psalm 121 as a platform for reflecting on life in the city of Pretoria, known also as Tshwane.[31] The city was founded in 1855 during the massive Voortrekker migration (The Great Trek) from the Cape area. One of the three capital cities in South Africa, it is the seat of the administrative branch of government. As in all cities in South Africa, there is a vast gulf between the white and black populations in Pretoria, and

---

28. See Karl N. Jacobson, "Perhaps YHWH Is Sleeping: 'Awake' and 'Contend' in the Book of Psalms," in *The Shape and Shaping of the Book of Psalms: The Current State of Scholarship*, ed. Nancy L. deClaissé-Walford (Atlanta: SBL Press, 2014), 129–45.

29. Hossfeld and Zenger, *Psalms 3*, 329.

30. For a discussion of the meaning of נֶפֶשׁ, see the commentary for Ps 120:2.

31. Thinandavha D. Mashau, "Reimagining Mission in the Public Square: Engaging Hills and Valleys in the African City of Tshwane," *HTS Teologiese Studies/Theological Studies* 70 (2014): 1–11. Available at http://dx.doi.org/10.4102/hts.v70i3.2774.

South Africa in general has an overall poverty rate well above 50 percent. The population of Pretoria has grown tremendously over the years, and the inner city has become what Mashau calls a "contested place"—between local authorities, private developers, slum landlords, resident groups, landless groups, drug pushers and users, the homeless, foreigners, and street vendors. Twenty years into democracy, the scars of colonialism and apartheid have yet to heal. While much progress has been made, long strides are still needed to turn the tide against poverty, unemployment, and inequality.

Mashau, dialoguing with an "encounterological responsive reading of Psalm 121" composed by J. N. J. Kritzinger, paints a vivid picture of the stark contrast between the marginalized inhabitants of Tshwane, living in its metaphoric "valleys"— the inner city, suburbs, super-suburbs, townships, and informal settlements—and those in power who dwell on its "high hills" such as the Union Building (the seat of government), built at the highest point in Pretoria, and the Voortrekker Monument, a massive memorial to the Voortrekkers, also built on a prominent hill in Pretoria.

Kritzinger's responsive reading, used during a worship service at the Melodi ya Tshwane congregation in Pretoria, is as follows:

L: We lift up our eyes to the hills,
   to the high places in and
   around Pretoria;
   Where does our help come from?
   Does our help come from Meintijieskop,
   from the Union Buildings,
   centre of political power?

C: Our help comes from the LORD,
   who made heaven and earth

L: Does our help come from Thaba Tshwane,
   from the National Defence Force, centre of military power?

C: Our help comes from the LORD,
   who made heaven and earth

L: Does our help come from Monumentkoppie, from the Voortrekker Monument,
   reminder of the power of the past?

C: Our help comes from the LORD,
   who made heaven and earth

L: Does our help come from the high building
   of the Reserve Bank, centre of economic power?

C: Our help comes from the LORD,
   who made heaven and earth

L: Does our help come from the high buildings of Unisa or the University of Pretoria, centres of intellectual power?

C: Our help comes from the LORD,
   who made heaven and earth

L: We lift up our eyes to the hills,
   To the high places in and around Pretoria;
   Where does our help come from?

C: Our help comes from the LORD,
   who made heaven and earth;
   who is the same yesterday, today, and forever;
   who remains faithful to his

promises,
who never forsakes the work
of his hands. Amen.[32]

Mashau writes: "The future of Christian mission in the public square, like the City of Tshwane, is in critical engagement with its hills and valleys with an eye to bringing God's shalom and justice to the marginalized city dwellers." He calls on the church to fulfill its missional calling not by "sending out" missionaries but by engaging its own community missionally. "Imagine a church," Mashau says, "that does not take seriously its calling to engage urban principalities and powers that harm or destroy people's lives; such a church will never make any serious inroads in terms of impacting and transforming the community that it serves."

The racial, economic, educational, and overall societal gap in South Africa is enormous. If the church's sincere response to the vast needs in the "valleys" of cities like Tshwane is "Our help comes from the LORD," then what is the role of the church? Mashau reminds the church of its missional calling. Churches must be the eyes, ears, heart, hands, and feet of Jesus in ministering to the felt needs of those who live in their midst, not in some distant land— walking with them, listening to them, seeing them as human companions on life's journey. And then the church must be an agent of transformation, intentionally engaging social ills and political powers. The church, Mashau maintains, can and should do in and with the community things such as "providing shelter for the homeless, transferring skills to empower those on the margins to access jobs, collaborating with government and private institutions to fight poverty, joblessness and inequality, and advocacy." In doing so the church can carry out the vision of God in Isaiah 40:3-5:

> In the wilderness prepare the
>   way of the LORD,
>   make straight in the desert a
>   highway for our God.
> Every valley shall be lifted up,
>   and every mountain and hill
>   be made low;
> the uneven ground shall become
>   level,
>   and the rough places a plain.
> Then the glory of the LORD shall
>   be revealed,
>   and all people shall see it
>   together,
>   for the mouth of the LORD has
>   spoken.

Mission in the hills and valleys of Tshwane means working with God, who is the great "leveler" in society.

Nancy L. deClaissé-Walford

---

32. J. N. J. Kritzinger, "Where Does Our Help Come From? Psalm 121 in Tshwane," *Missionalia* 36 (2008): 337–38.

Psalm 122

Psalm 122, third of the fifteen Songs of Ascents, is classified as a Song of Zion (along with Pss 46, 48, 76, 84, 87, and 125). In it an individual singer, who appears to be part of a larger group of pilgrims rejoices at the prospect of going on pilgrimage to Jerusalem (v. 1) and setting foot inside the city gates (v. 2), celebrates all that the city stands for—security, gathering, and justice (vv. 3-5)—and wishes peace (שלום) for Jerusalem (vv. 6-9).

The psalm singer states in verse 1 that she is glad (שמח) to be called with other pilgrims to go to "the house of the LORD." The phrase "the house of the LORD" occurs in verses 1 and 9, forming an *inclusio* that directs the hearer's attention to the main emphasis of the psalm. The words "let us go" (הלך) in verse 1 and "go up" (עלה) in verse 4 echo a standard call formula in the Hebrew Bible in which the verbs "go" (הלך) and "go up" (עלה) occur repeatedly. In 1 Samuel 11:14, Samuel speaks to the people, saying, "Come, let us go [הלך] to Gilgal"; Jeremiah 31:6 says, "Arise, let us go up [עלה] to Zion"; Isaiah 2:3 and Micah 4:2 envision a time when many people will say, "Come [הלך], let us go up [עלה] to the mountain of the LORD." The call "let us go" is realized in verse 2 of Psalm 122, where we read that the pilgrims have arrived in Jerusalem; their feet are standing within its gates.

In verses 3-5 the psalm singer celebrates three characteristics of Jerusalem. First, in verse 3, it is a city "bound firmly together" (חבר). Interestingly, elsewhere in the Hebrew Bible חבר is never used in connection with buildings but rather applies to human agreements. The description conjures up visions of Jerusalem as a safe place, a place to which people could go in times of trouble and oppression and find security. In the ancient Near East city walls provided protection and sanctuary for inhabitants and surrounding peasant families in times of danger from enemies.

Second, verse 4 describes Jerusalem as the place to which the tribes go in order to fulfill the decree that they "give thanks to the name of the LORD," depicting it as the gathering place for the people of Israel. Third, "the thrones for judgment [משפט]" and "the thrones of the house of David" in verse 5 refer to the role of the monarchy in ancient Israel as dispenser of justice to the people. In 2 Samuel 8:15 we read: "So David reigned over all Israel; and David administered justice [משפט] and equity to all his people."[33] The prophet Micah condemns the rulers of Judah

---

33. See also 2 Sam 15:2-6 and Deut 17:8-13.

Psalm 122:1-9

A Song of Ascents. Of David.
¹I was glad when they said to me,
 "Let us go to the house of the
  Lord!"
²Our feet are standing
 within your gates, O Jerusalem.
³Jerusalem—built as a city
 that is bound firmly together.
⁴To it the tribes go up,
 the tribes of the Lord,
as was decreed for Israel,
 to give thanks to the name of the
  Lord.

⁵For there the thrones for judgment
  were set up,
 the thrones of the house of David.
⁶Pray for the peace of Jerusalem:
 "May they prosper who love you.
⁷Peace be within your walls,
 and security within your towers."
⁸For the sake of my relatives and
  friends
 I will say, "Peace be within you."
⁹For the sake of the house of the
  Lord our God,
 I will seek your good.

and Israel for abhorring justice and perverting equity (Mic 3:9-12). James Mays points out that pilgrimage season was probably a time when "conflicts and disputes unsettled in the country courts were brought to the royal officials and their successors. . . . The peace of the community depended on the establishment of justice. Pilgrimage is a journey in search of justice."[34]

Verses 6-9 of Psalm 122 are masterfully composed. The psalm singer speaks directly to Jerusalem. Each verse ends with the second-person feminine singular pronoun suffix *kᵉ* (ך, referring to the city), giving the four what Erhard Gerstenberger calls a "homophonous" quality.[35] The theme of this section of the psalm is the "peace" (שלום) of Jerusalem. Of the ten Hebrew words that make up verses 6 and 7, six contain the letters *shin* (ש) and *lamed* (ל): "pray" (שאל), "peace" (twice) (שלום), "Jerusalem" (ירושלם), "may they prosper" (שלה), and "security" (שלוה), thus acoustically and visually emphasizing the theme of שלום. In verses 8 and 9 the psalm singer addresses Jerusalem directly. She begins with "for the sake of" (למען) and then enumerates the reasons for wishing for the peace of Jerusalem—the psalm singer's "relatives and friends" and "the house of the Lord our God." Verse 9's "the house of the Lord our God" echoes the words of verse 1, forming an *inclusio* around the words of the psalm, and in verse 5, the middle of the psalm, "the house of David" provides

34. Mays, *Psalms*, 393.
35. Gerstenberger, *Psalms, Part 2, and Lamentations*, 328.

an additional focus. "The house of the LORD" symbolized the presence of God among the people of Israel; "the house of David" symbolized justice and equity among them. The peace of Jerusalem guaranteed the well-being (שלום) of the people of God. Leslie Allen writes: "Jerusalem was the focus of national unity, a unity which was grounded in worship and issued in the harmonious ordering of life."[36] J. Clinton McCann reminds us, though, that Jerusalem "is not just a place, but a symbol of God's presence in space and time."[37] On the other hand, Erich Zenger cautions against overly spiritualizing this symbol of God's presence "in such a way that the link to the concrete Jerusalem as the center of Judaism is lost."[38]

Psalm 122's repeated hopes for the peace of Jerusalem seem to answer the singer of Psalm 120's lament over the lack of peace in her current situation. The city of Jerusalem has, for millennia, been the center of contention and conflict, with various groups claiming proprietary rights. For the hundreds of thousands of pilgrims who make their way each year to Jerusalem the words of Psalm 122 ring as true today as they did when the psalm singer first uttered its words. In verse 9 the psalmist states that she will "seek" (בקש) the "good" (טוב) for Jerusalem. She will not "pray" or "hope for" but actively seek it out. One scholar describes the meaning of the Hebrew word in this way:

> This activity has in view the finding of an object which really exists or which is thought to exist, which is not close at hand to the subject at the time of seeking, but is desired most earnestly and initiates the seeking. . . . "Seeking" in the OT and elsewhere must be understood as a conscious act with a specific goal in mind, and sometimes it must be accompanied by a great deal of effort, shrewdness, and imagination.[39]

What the psalmist "seeks" is the "good" of Jerusalem, echoing the creation words of Genesis 1, where at the end of each day God declared that creation was "good" (טוב). To return not only Jerusalem but all of creation to the "good" that God intended will require a "conscious act" on the part of all and will take "effort, shrewdness, and imagination."

36. Leslie C. Allen, *Psalms 100–150*, WBC 21 (Nashville: Thomas Nelson, 2002), 159.
37. J. Clinton McCann, Jr., "The Book of Psalms," *NIB*, vol. 4 (Nashville: Abingdon, 1996), 1185.
38. Hossfeld and Zenger, *Psalms 3*, 343.
39. Siegfried Wagner, "בקש (*biqqēš*)," *TDOT*, 2:229–30.

Psalm 123

Psalm 123 is the fourth of the fifteen Songs of Ascents in book 5. Reading the Songs of Ascents as a chronological whole, we may understand Psalm 120, the first of these songs, as the lament of an individual who is far from Jerusalem and is besieged by lies, deceit, and those who hate peace. Psalm 121 is a hymn of thanksgiving sung by a psalm singer as she approaches Jerusalem with the hills of the city in view, and in Psalm 122 the pilgrim psalm singer celebrates as she arrives in Jerusalem and enters the city gates.

Psalm 123 begins with the voice of an individual singer who says, "To you I lift up my eyes," echoing the imploring words of Psalm 121:1. Whereas the singer of Psalm 121 looks to the hills in anticipation of traveling to Jerusalem, the singer of Psalm 123 is safely inside the city gates and can turn her eyes away from the world described in Psalm 120 toward God and address God directly: "O you who are enthroned in the heavens!" References to the heavens as the dwelling place of God are common in the Psalter.[40]

In verse 2 the larger community of pilgrims adds its voice to that of the individual psalmist. The pilgrims compare their confidence in God to the trust servants place in their masters and mistresses. Just as servants look to their masters and mistresses and stretch out their hands to them in supplication, so the pilgrims stretch out their hands in a plea for mercy. The word translated "mercy" is from the Hebrew root חנן. It is one of the five self-descriptive words spoken by God to Moses in Exodus 34:6. The word's basic meaning is "to show favor," and its most common use in the Hebrew Bible is in reference to "favor shown in personal relationships; it can refer to ordinary acceptance or kindness, or else favor of a special nature, such as pity, mercy, or generosity. In the latter case the usual limits established by law or custom are transcended." Further, חנן is described as "active acceptance and active favor."[41]

The metaphor employed in verse 2 presents what Erich Zenger calls a "dialectical tension."[42] It pictures God in both male and female imagery as the source of mercy or favor (חנן), but the relationship between God and worshiper is that of master over slave. Particularly troubling from a feminist interpretational standpoint are the words "mistress"

---

40. See Pss 2:4; 11:4; 115:3, 16.
41. Heinz-Josef Fabry, "חנן (ḥānan)," *TDOT*, 5:24.
42. Hossfeld and Zenger, *Psalms 3*, 350.

Psalm 123:1-4

A Song of Ascents. Of David.

¹To you I lift up my eyes,
　O you who are enthroned in the
　　heavens!
²As the eyes of servants
　look to the hand of their master,
as the eyes of a maid
　to the hand of her mistress,
so our eyes look to the LORD our God,

until he has mercy upon us.
³Have mercy upon us, O LORD, have
　mercy upon us,
for we have had more than
　enough of contempt.
⁴Our soul has had more than its fill
　of the scorn of those who are at
　　ease,
of the contempt of the proud.

and "maid." "Mistress" is the Hebrew word גברה, while "maid" is שפחה. Such a relationship is vividly portrayed in the story of Sarai and Hagar in Genesis 16. There Hagar is called a שפחה six times (vv. 1, 2, 3, 5, 6, and 8), and Sarai is called Hagar's גברה three times (vv. 4, 8, and 9). While William H. Bellinger and Walter Brueggemann observe, correctly, that this way of characterizing a relationship should not in any way suggest that servitude of one human to another is good or right, in a context in which such relationships were common the simile makes sense. But even here, they maintain, the notion of the "master" is transformed. The psalmist who calls on the Lord as master knows no dread or fear, only mercy.[43] This master is one exclusively sought out for salvation: "our eyes look to the LORD our God, until he has mercy on us" (v. 2). Richard Clifford characterizes Psalm 123 as a "primer on prayer" in which the psalmist "lifts his or her eyes to heaven, symbolically forswearing every other means of support" and "embraces the status of servant and waits, eyes fixed on the hand of the Lord."[44]

The expression of trust in God's mercy (חנן) becomes a twice-repeated petition in verse 3, followed by the reason for the petition in verses 3 and 4. The psalm singers "have had more than enough" of "contempt" and their soul "has had more than its fill" of "scorn" from those who are at ease and proud. The words translated "more than enough" and "more than its fill" in verses 3 and 4 are both from שבע, which means "eat one's fill, be sated, have enough."

43. Walter Brueggemann and William H. Bellinger Jr., *Psalms*, NCBC (Cambridge: Cambridge University Press, 2014), 531.
44. Clifford, *Psalms 73–150*, 229.

The word translated "soul" in verse 4 is the Hebrew נפש, whose basic meaning is "throat," denoting the organ of the body that provides breath and sustenance to the body and that is "the organ of life itself."[45] Thus the collective throat of the psalm singers is filled to its limit (שבע) with the contempt and scorn of those who are at ease. Psalm 123 ends with those words of lament, inviting the reader to move on to Psalm 124 to find resolution to Psalm 123's cry for mercy (חנן).

Psalm 124

Psalm 124, the fifth of the Songs of Ascents, answers the cry for mercy voiced by the singers of Psalm 123, who feel overwhelmed by the "contempt" and "scorn" of "those who are at ease" (123:3-4). Thus Psalm 124 may be heard as words of trust and praise in answer to the singers of Psalm 123.[46]

The voice of an individual psalmist speaks the opening phrase of the psalm, "If it had not been the LORD who was on our side," and invites Israel to join in with the words "Let Israel now say." From that point forward we hear the voice of the community of psalm singers. Verses 1 and 2 begin with "if not" (לולי), while verses 3-5 begin with "then" (אזי), forming an "if . . . then" structure. לולי is used in biblical Hebrew only to express an unreal condition,[47] indicating that the psalm singers are confident that God is on their side. Verses 3-5 state what might have been if that had not been so. Loren Crow maintains that the statement in verses 1-5 "is not an 'if . . . then' statement in the tradition of the Greek logicians but rather a narrative about what might have occurred without YHWH's aid."[48]

---

45. Hossfeld and Zenger, *Psalms 3*, 316.

46. For another example of a lament psalm whose final words of trust and praise may be located in the following psalm, see Nancy L. deClaissé-Walford, "An Intertextual Reading of Psalms 22, 23, and 24," in *The Book of Psalms: Composition and Reception*, ed. Peter W. Flint and Patrick D. Miller, VTSup 99 (Leiden: Brill, 2005), 139–52; and Nancy L. deClaissé-Walford, *Introduction to the Psalms: A Song from Ancient Israel* (St. Louis: Chalice Press, 2004), 35–40.

47. Ludwig Koehler and Walter Baumgartner, *The Hebrew and Aramaic Lexicon of the Old Testament* 1, trans. and ed. M. E. J. Richardson (Leiden: Brill, 2001), 524; and Bruce K. Waltke and Michael P. O'Connor, *An Introduction to Biblical Hebrew Syntax* (Winona Lake, IN: Eisenbrauns, 1990), 637–38.

48. Crow, *The Songs of Ascents (Psalms 120–134)*, 52–53.

Psalm 124:1-8

A Song of Ascents. Of David.

[1]If it had not been the LORD who was
  on our side
—let Israel now say—
[2]if it had not been the LORD who was
  on our side,
  when our enemies attacked us,
[3]then they would have swallowed us
  up alive,
  when their anger was kindled
  against us;
[4]then the flood would have swept us
  away,
the torrent would have gone over
  us;
[5]then over us would have gone
  the raging waters.
[6]Blessed be the LORD,
  who has not given us
  as prey to their teeth.
[7]We have escaped like a bird
  from the snare of the fowlers;
the snare is broken,
  and we have escaped.
[8]Our help is in the name of the LORD,
  who made heaven and earth.

In verse 2 the attacker is rendered in the NRSV as "enemies," but it is actually the Hebrew collective noun אדם, recalling the creation story in Genesis 2 in which humanity (אסד) is formed by God from the ground (אדמה). Verses 1 and 2 contrast the power of God with the powerlessness of the human community (אדם) that rises up against the people of Israel.

Beginning with verse 4 the psalm singers use vivid images of water—the flood, the torrent, the raging waters—to describe the calamities that might have befallen them if the Lord had not been with them. Images of watery chaos occur often in the Psalter[49] as well as in other ancient Near Eastern literature, such as the Mesopotamian creation myth Enuma Elish.[50] The word translated "us" at the end of verse 4 and in verse 5 is the same Hebrew word, נפש, that is translated as "soul" in Psalm 123:4. In Psalm 123 the psalm singers' "very being" or "throat" is filled with the contempt and scorn of those taunting them; in Psalm 124 the "very beings" or "throats" of the psalmists are saved from the torrent and the raging waters.

49. See Pss 69:1-2; 74:13-14; 93:3-4; 107:23-27.

50. For a thorough treatment of water imagery in the book of Psalms, see William P. Brown, *Seeing the Psalms: A Theology of Metaphor* (Louisville: Westminster John Knox, 2002), 105–34. For Enuma Elish, see Bill T. Arnold and Bryan E. Beyer, eds., *Readings from the Ancient Near East: Primary Sources for Old Testament Study* (Grand Rapids: Baker Academic, 2002), 31–50.

In verses 6 and 7 the psalmists praise God for their past deliverance with a metaphorical image of fowlers attempting to snare a bird for food. A bird caught in a snare is another common metaphor for danger in both the Hebrew Bible and the ancient Near East.[51] In the famous Taylor Prism inscription the seventh-century Assyrian king Sennacherib boasted of his near-defeat of King Hezekiah: "He himself I shut up like a caged bird within Jerusalem, his royal city."[52]

Psalm 124's final verse is a declaration of trust by the psalm singers in which they declare that their "help" (עֵזֶר) is in the name of the LORD.[53] The phrase "who made the heavens and the earth"—a merism, indicating all-encompassing totality—occurs three times in the Songs of Ascents (Pss 121:2; 124:8; 134:3) and also in Psalm 146:6.

Thus the singers of Psalm 124 affirm that God indeed is on the side of the faithful ones of Israel. The "enemy" (אָדָם) who rises up over the faithful (v. 2) is, in the end, mere humanity. Psalm 124 has a poetic and repetitive quality that suggests it was meant to be recited liturgically in a worship setting. The opening words of the first two verses, "if not," followed by the opening words of the next three verses, "then," act as strong repetitive devices. Vivid images, repeated in successive verses— floods, torrents, raging waters, and fowlers' snare—add to the psalm what Richard Clifford characterizes as "swiftness and drama."[54] As God can calm the raging waters and provide escape for small birds from the fowlers' snare, so God is a help (עֵזֶר) to the pilgrims who have arrived in Jerusalem, showing them mercy (חָנַן, Ps 123:3) and providing peace (שָׁלוֹם, Ps 122:6-8).

The translation of the Hebrew word אָדָם in verse 2 as "enemies" seems, to this commentator, to allow for a certain degree of abstraction of the ones who are threatening to "swallow up alive" the psalm singers. An "enemy" can become a nameless, faceless entity—an "other." The Hebrew word used here connotes no such idea. The Common English Bible translation renders the word "those people," conveying a sense of full knowledge of the names and faces of those threatening to "swallow up."

When we confront many of the larger issues facing the world in which we live—income disparity that affects equal access to secure housing and

---

51. See Pss 91:3; 141:9; Prov 6:5; Qoh 9:12.
52. Arnold and Beyer, *Readings from the Ancient Near East*, 146–47.
53. For a discussion of the word "help" (עֵזֶר) in the Hebrew Bible, see the commentary for Ps 115:9-11.
54. Clifford, *Psalms 73–150*, 229.

nourishing food, child trafficking and prostitution, inequalities of money and power—the "enemy" is often abstracted, becoming a nameless, faceless "other." The "enemy" in each case, though, is "those people," people more interested in their own profit, well-being, and lifestyle than in the good of "all people." The singers of Psalm 124 have named "those people" as אדם; they are humanity, all who contribute to the vast divide separating those of privilege and those struggling to contribute and survive. Nevertheless, the psalm singers accept and celebrate God's help in escaping the raging waters and snares that threaten them. Unless we, like them, can find it within ourselves to name "those people" and perhaps recognize ourselves in "those people," we will not be able to fully enlist and accept the "help" of God in finding a solution for these troubling issues in our world today.

Psalm 125

Psalm 125 is the sixth in the collection of Songs of Ascents. In Psalm 122 the psalmist has arrived in Jerusalem, and in Psalms 123 and 124 she celebrates the mercy and deliverance of God. The focus of Psalm 125 is Jerusalem—Mount Zion—and, like Psalms 46, 48, 76, 84, 87, and 122, is known as a Song of Zion. It continues the celebration of arriving at and being in Jerusalem begun in Psalm 122.

The psalm opens in verse 1 with the psalm singer likening those who trust in the Lord to Mount Zion, which "cannot be moved." "Moved" (מוט) occurs twenty-five times in the Psalter. In Psalm 46, for instance, the psalm singers state confidently that Jerusalem will not "be moved" (v. 5, מוט), though the mountains should "shake" (v. 3, מוט) and kingdoms "totter" (v. 6, מוט). The enthronement psalms (Pss 93–100) celebrate God's sovereignty over the world and its inhabitants. The world shall never be moved (Pss 93:1 and 96:10, מוט), and the psalm singer's foot will not slip (Ps 94:18, מוט).

Verse 2 of Psalm 125 declares that just as the mountains surround Jerusalem, so God surrounds God's people "from this time on and forevermore." While Jerusalem itself sits on a hill, it is actually overshadowed by higher mountains to the east. The pilgrim celebrating a festival in Jerusalem looks out at the surrounding mountains and likens them to the way God protectively surrounds God's people. Erich Zenger thus maintains, concerning the significance of verses 1 and 2, "What is crucial is not that the people trust in unshakeable Zion, but that they trust in YHWH, the God of Zion."[55]

---

55. Hossfeld and Zenger, *Psalms 3*, 361.

Psalm 125:1-5

A Song of Ascents.

¹Those who trust in the LORD are like Mount Zion,
which cannot be moved, but abides forever.
²As the mountains surround Jerusalem,
so the LORD surrounds his people, from this time on and forevermore.
³For the scepter of wickedness shall not rest
on the land allotted to the righteous,
so that the righteous might not stretch out
their hands to do wrong.
⁴Do good, O LORD, to those who are good,
and to those who are upright in their hearts.
⁵But those who turn aside to their own crooked ways
the LORD will lead away with evildoers.
Peace be upon Israel!

Verse 3 begins with the particle "for" (כי) and contrasts the "scepter of wickedness" with the "land allotted to the righteous." The word translated as "scepter" is שבט, often rendered "tribe," while "land allotted" is גורל, often translated "inheritance." Both words appear repeatedly in the account of the settlement and allotting of the land of promise in the book of Joshua, with "scepter/tribe" (שבט) occurring some thirty times in the book and "land allotted/inheritance" (גורל) twenty-two times. The psalmist states confidently that "the scepter of wickedness" (רשע) will not rest on "the land allotted to the righteous" (צדיק), "so that" the righteous will not "stretch out their hands to do wrong." The contrast between the "wicked" and the "righteous" is the theme of Psalm 1 and is one of the structuring elements of the book of Psalms.[56]

Verses 4 and 5 offer another contrast between the wicked and the righteous: those who are "upright in their hearts" and those who "turn aside to their own crooked ways." "Heart" here is לב, which means much more than the beating organ in one's chest; rather, it connotes the "vital center" of a person.[57] In verse 3 the psalmists mention the "wicked" first and the "righteous" second, while in verses 4 and 5 the "upright" are mentioned first, creating an envelope structure: wicked is to righteous as upright is to crooked. Or perhaps the structure leads the reader or hearer from the wicked to the righteous and then back out

---

56. See Pss 7:9; 11:5; 32:10-11; 37:16; 58:10; 75:10; 92:7, 12; 94:12-14; 112:6-10; 129:4; 140:8-13.

57. Heinz-Josef Fabry, "לב (*leb*)," *TDOT*, 7:412–34.

again in a final condemnation of the crooked ones. The reversal places the righteous ones in the middle of the literary structure of verses 3-5, a focal point for the message of the psalm.

Psalm 125 ends with the brief petition, "Peace [שלום] be upon Israel." The same petition occurs in Psalm 128:6, and the word "peace" appears in five other places in the Songs of Ascents (120:6, 7; 122:6, 7, 8). The pilgrims gathered in Jerusalem for festival celebrations come from the surrounding countryside; the stronghold of the city, Zion, was a temporary shelter. The righteous, those who trust in YHWH, could carry the assurance of the stability of Zion with them back to wherever home was.

Verse 3's words concerning "the land allotted [גורל, inheritance] to the righteous" evoke the promises of land made to the Israelite ancestors and the division of the land in the book of Joshua, and its words call our modern world to reflect on "the land allotted." Recall that גורל occurs twenty-two times in the book of Joshua, along with fifty occurrences of the synonymous Hebrew word נחלה, also translated "allotted/inheritance." According to the storyline of the book of Psalms (see the introduction, pp. l–lv), book 5 is set in the postexilic period of ancient Israel's history. The people were under the rule of the Persians, so the "land allotted," "the inheritance," was no longer their land. It was possessed by the Persian Empire and the people were vassals, small cogs in a great empirical machine. How did the returnees from Babylon understand their relationship to the land of promise?

Perhaps there was and had always been another way to understand and appropriate the inheritance God promised. In Psalm 119, the massive wisdom acrostic celebrating the law (תורה, Torah), the concept of "inheritance" shifts from physical dirt to the law (תורה) of the Lord. Verse 111 reads, "Your decrees" (עדות, one of the seven Hebrew words used as synonyms for law [תורה] in Psalm 119) "are my heritage [נחלה] forever; they are the joy of my heart." What does Torah have to do with the land, with "place"? At Sinai God made a covenant with the people of Israel, with strict instructions concerning how to live as God's people in the land of promise, particularly how to care for the land and those who live on it. Ellen Davis writes: "The descendants of Israel were given, not a land, but the *use* of a land, along with precise instructions for its good care."[58]

Today we live in a highly mobile world, sometimes by choice but often because of the difficulties and oppressions that confront us. Those who

---

58. Ellen F. Davis, *Scripture, Culture, and Agriculture: An Agrarian Reading of the Bible* (Cambridge: Cambridge University Press, 2009), x. Italics supplied.

stay in the same place feel a sense of "inheritance" while those who are forced to move experience a sense of "disinheritance." Conflict over who belongs and who does not is inevitable since, as Walter Brueggemann reminds us, "Land is never simply physical dirt but is always physical dirt freighted with social meanings derived from historical experience." It is never "contextless space";[59] it is what this commentator calls "storied place." When people move to a new place, whether voluntarily or involuntarily, they encounter other peoples' "storied places," and the intrusion of other "stories" can be disturbing and disruptive for both. But in the end the earth, the land, our inheritance belong to God. Wendell Berry, an American novelist, poet, environmental activist, cultural critic, and farmer, offers apt concluding words:

> We have been given the earth to live, not on, but with and from, and only on the condition that we care properly for it. We did not make it, and we know little about it. In fact, we don't, and will never, know enough about it to make our survival sure or our lives carefree. Our relation to our land will always remain, to a significant extent, mysterious.[60]

Don't Take Away My Land

When I read the words of verse 3, "For the scepter of wickedness shall not rest on the land allotted to the righteous," my thoughts immediately travel to a one-hundred-acre farm in southern Indiana in the American Midwest. My great-grandfather bought the farm in the mid-1800s; my grandfather, then my father and aunt, and now I and my sister have inherited it. It is my "land allotted," and my family is committed to farming it and keeping it in the family. It is my firm grounding, the place to which I return time after time, and the place to which my husband and I plan to retire a few years from now. But for centuries before my great-grandfather acquired the land it was occupied by the Native American tribe called the Shawnee. In an 1804 treaty the United States government "purchased" the land from the Shawnee and resettled them farther west in the United States. Thus, long before I came to this farmland it was someone else's firm grounding. Land—the land, my land, our land. It is a nostalgic, evocative, heart-stirring concept and one that occurs repeatedly in the text of the Hebrew Bible.

---

59. Walter Brueggemann, *The Land: Place as Gift, Promise, and Challenge in Biblical Faith*, 2nd ed., OBT (Minneapolis: Fortress, 2002), 2, 55.

60. Wendell Berry, "Foreword," in Davis, *Scripture, Culture, and Agriculture*, ix.

In an article in the South African newspaper *Mail and Guardian* I found these words: "The biggest humiliation you can visit upon an African is to take away his land. You can't separate us from the land. We are one with it."[61] I suspect the Native American Shawnees who were displaced from southern Indiana could have expressed the same sentiment. How, then, do I understand my relationship and responsibility to my hundred-acre farm? I turn to the biblical text.

Ellen Davis, in *Scripture, Culture, and Agriculture: An Agrarian Reading of the Bible*, maintains that those who composed the Holiness Code in the Torah (Lev 17–27) "perceived that the land cares how it is used or misused."[62] Norman Habel, a biblical interpreter and advocate for social justice, writes that the social model implied in the Holiness Code is "an agrarian theocracy" and goes on to say: "As a jealous landowner, YHWH desires responsible tenants who will maintain an attitude of reverence and concern for the very soil and soul of the land."[63] An agrarian theocracy acknowledges humanity's fleeting relationship with the land; we are temporary residents and caretakers of a timeless earth.

Psalms 90 and 91 remind us that the earth, birthed and nurtured by God ages ago (see Pss 90:2 and 91:1), belongs to God and God alone. The enthronement psalms (Pss 93–100) affirm that our creator God is ever-present in the workings of the world and that the land belongs to God. And Psalm 125 emphasizes the importance of the "land allotted" (v. 3). God entrusts the care of the land, the earth, to transient humanity, but that trust comes with tremendous responsibility. As industrialization, modernization, and consumerism evolve and grow in our world, so does the struggle to maintain an "agrarian theocracy."

A telling modern-day example of the struggle is the story of the residents of the Umgungundlovi community of Xolobeni in the Eastern Cape of South Africa. For twenty years they have been fighting to stop the South Africa Department of Mineral Resources from issuing a permit to Transworld Energy and Minerals for titanium dune mining on lands on which, according to an article in the South African newspaper *Saturday Star*, "several hundred people and their

---

61. Lucas Ledwaba, "Healing Resurrects Blighted Land above Mamelodi," *Mail and Guardian* (29 March–5 April 2018), 18.

62. Davis, *Scripture, Culture, and Agriculture*, 110. See, e.g., Lev 19:9-10; 23:9-14; 25:1-7.

63. Norman Habel, *The Land Is Mine: Six Biblical Land Ideologies*, OBT (Minneapolis: Fortress, 1995), 110.

ancestors have lived according to their customs and traditions for centuries."[64] The article contains the content of numerous postcards sent by members of the Xolobeni community to the Department of Mineral Resources. Mabhude "Camago" Danca wrote: "The natural streams provide us with water and we use the land to grow our crops. The mine will use up all of the water and take away the wealth of the land." Themba Yalo wrote: "This land is healthy and we have worked with it for many generations, it is part of us." And Fakazile Joyce Ndovela wrote: "I have cattle, sheep and goats. I grow crops and plough my fields. I don't have a husband. I survive off the land. The water feeds everything, the crops, the animals and my family. I don't want to change the way I live."[65] On April 23, 2018, the matter was brought before the Pretoria High Court; on December 3, 2018, the High Court ruled in favor of the Xolobeni.[66]

Who "owns," who has "rights to" the land? Ellen Davis reminds us that "the land cares how it is used or misused."[67] And recall the words of Norman Habel above about YHWH being a jealous landowner who desires responsible tenants.[68] May we, may I, be ever mindful of the "jealous landowner" and our / my role as responsible tenants.

Nancy L. deClaissé-Walford

Psalm 126

Psalm 126 is the seventh in the collection of fifteen Songs of Ascents. It is a community lament in which the gathered community calls on God to come to its aid. The psalm singers begin in verse 1 by remembering a time in their past when God restored their lives and did great things among them; they then petition God in verse 4 to once again restore their lives so that they can rejoice. James L. Mays characterizes and summarizes Psalm 126 as "joy remembered and joy anticipated."[69]

64. Sheree Bega, "Murder, Intimidation—Finally Rural People Have Day in Court," *Saturday Star* (April 28, 2018), 5.

65. Ibid.

66. See https://www.business-humanrights.org/en/so-africa-court-orders -consultation-with-xolobeni-community-prior-to-granting-mining-permission-to -australian-company. The court ruled that the minister of mineral resources would have to obtain full and formal consent from the Xolobeni community prior to grant- ing mining rights.

67. Davis, *Scripture, Culture, and Agriculture*, 110.

68. Habel, *The Land Is Mine*, 114.

69. Mays, *Psalms*, 399.

Psalm 126:1-6

A Song of Ascents.

¹When the LORD restored the fortunes of Zion,
  we were like those who dream.
²Then our mouth was filled with laughter,
  and our tongue with shouts of joy;
then it was said among the nations,
  "The LORD has done great things for them."

³The LORD has done great things for us,
  and we rejoiced.
⁴Restore our fortunes, O LORD,
  like the watercourses in the Negeb.
⁵May those who sow in tears
  reap with shouts of joy.
⁶Those who go out weeping,
  bearing the seed for sowing,
shall come home with shouts of joy,
  carrying their sheaves.

A major interpretational issue in Psalm 126 revolves around the phrases in verses 1 and 4 that the NRSV, the NIV, and the ESV translate as "restored the fortunes of Zion" and "Restore our fortunes."[70] The phrase in verse 1 is שוב . . . . את־שיבת ציון. The word שיבת, the direct object of the verb שוב, is a *hapax legomenon* that Leslie Allen suggests is formed from the verbal root שוב, making it a cognate accusative, and thus he offers a translation of "turn with a turning toward."[71] The *qere* of the phrase in verse 4 is שוב . . . . את־שביתנו, and thus, along with a few Hebrew manuscripts and the Septuagint, many translators harmonize verse 1's שיבת to verse 4's שבית. Leslie C. Allen suggests, though, that the psalmist(s) crafted verses 1 and 4 as parallel statements using similar Hebrew words. He writes: "The stylistic variation of form between שיבת and שבות may have been intended as a pointer to a new beginning at v. 4 and as a means of differentiating the changes of fortune as separate events."[72]

The psalm singers describe themselves in verse 1 as "like ones dreaming." These words do not mean that the people could not believe what was happening and thought they were dreaming. In the ancient Near East dreams were often understood as the medium through which the gods revealed what would happen in the future (e.g., Joseph in Gen 37;

---

70. The CEB renders vv. 1 and 4 with the phrase "change for the better," the KJV as "turn again the captivity," and the NASB as "brought back the captive ones" (v. 1) and "restore our captivity" (v. 4).

71. The phrase שוב שבית, the verb with its cognate accusative, is used extensively in the Hebrew Bible, particularly in prophetic material, to describe the people's change in life circumstances when God's wrath is turned away and God's favor returns. See Deut 30:3; Hos 6:11; Ezek 39:25; Jer 29:14; 30:3; Joel 3:1; Amos 9:14; Zeph 2:7; 3:20.

72. Allen, *Psalms 101–150*, 231.

Pharaoh in Gen 41; Nebuchadnezzar in Dan 2). Erich Zenger writes: "The event [the turning back] was reality, but it was as unexpected and God-sent as a dream whose full achievement, though in progress, was still in the future."[73]

Verse 2 describes the people's reaction to God's restorative actions in verse 1: their mouth is filled with laughter, their tongue with shouts of joy (רִנָּה). "Shouts of joy" (רִנָּה) is repeated three times in Psalm 126, in verses 2, 5, and 6, suggesting that it is the unifying theme of the psalm. The result of restoration in the past was shouts of joy, just as the result of restoration in the future will be shouts of joy. In addition, the nations saw what God had done on behalf of the people and declared among themselves, "The LORD has done great things for them" (v. 2). This declaration is in sharp contrast with the taunting from the nations in other psalms in the Psalter. In Psalm 42:3 the people ask continually, "where is your God?" In Psalm 3:2 the psalmist laments that many are saying, "there is no deliverance for him in God!" In Psalm 126:3 the psalm singers repeat the words spoken by the nations in verse 2 by saying, "The LORD has done great things for us," and they conclude their words of trust in God in verse 3 with "we rejoiced."

In verse 4 water is used as a metaphoric image to introduce another theme of the psalm. The water channels, seasonal wadis that fill with nourishing water in the rainy season in the desert lands of the Negev, were something the people counted on to enliven a parched landscape year after year and provide sustaining crops. In verses 5 and 6, though, the nourishing waters give way to the tears and weeping of those sowing the arid fields in hopes of a good crop that will feed their households and allow for joyful weeping and shouts of joy (רִנָּה). Erhard Gerstenberger suggests that the metaphors of "sowing and reaping" evince wisdom influence as the psalmists employ day-to-day images of human toil to describe God's restorative work.[74] The two terms "sowing and reaping" constitute a "merism," understood as representative of the whole season's process: the planting, the watchful care, the weeding, and finally the harvest.

Sowing and reaping also suggest the fertility traditions of the ancient Near East. Sowing the seed in the ground is akin to the burial of the dead; thus the sowers weep as they bury the seed in the ground, as in many ancient Near Eastern fertility rituals. When the seedlings emerge from the ground and mature and the "sheaves" are harvested, shouts of

---

73. Hossfeld and Zenger, *Psalms 3*, 376.
74. Gerstenberger, *Psalms, Part 2, and Lamentations*, 341.

joy ensue. J. Clinton McCann reminds us that, while we may read these verses against the background of ancient fertility rituals, "it is just as important to observe that sowing is always an act of anticipation and hope,"[75] echoing James Mays's words: Psalm 126 is "joy remembered and joy anticipated."[76] The repetition of the word "shout for joy" (רנן) in verses 2, 5, and 6 connects the rejoicing of the people at their restoration by God with the rejoicing of the reapers at the harvest. The metaphor is brought full circle: the people are confident that they will rejoice in this new event of restoration just as they did in the past.

The memory of restoration in the past was, according to most biblical commentators who adhere to the storyline of the Psalter, about the return to Jerusalem after the Babylonian exile. The singers of Psalm 126, who have arrived in Jerusalem to celebrate a sacred festival, find themselves in a situation of despair and seek God's help. In doing so they recall the restoration to Zion, something the people in exile hoped for but never dreamed would happen. Psalm 126 presents what LeAnn Snow Flesher calls "life's ebbs and flows." She maintains that our ancestors in the faith understood the ebbs and flows described in the book of Psalms and that the psalms provide the "liturgical tools" to make sense of and deal with them, in the form of laments and words of praise. She continues:

> Yet this balance has not been the emphasis of the contemporary Christian church, which has increasingly bought into a doctrine of prosperity that teaches individuals of faith to expect only good in their life, and condemns their lack of faith when bad things happen to them. Such a doctrine does not give credence to the idea that life is filled with positives and negatives, and that evidence of faith and faithfulness is exhibited in how people and communities respond to both sets of circumstances.[77]

Psalm 127

Eighth in the group of the fifteen Songs of Ascents, Psalm 127 is classified as a wisdom psalm, the first of three wisdom psalms in the Songs of Ascents and one of six in book 5: Psalms 112, 119, 127, 128, 133, and 145. A wisdom psalm may be defined as one that "provides instruction in right living and right faith in the tradition of the other wisdom

---

75. McCann, "The Book of Psalms," 1195.
76. Mays, *Psalms*, 399.
77. LeAnn Snow Flesher, "Psalm 126: Between Text and Sermon," *Int* 60 (2006): 434–36.

Psalm 127:1-5

A Song of Ascents. Of Solomon.

[1]Unless the LORD builds the house,
    those who build it labor in vain.
Unless the LORD guards the city,
    the guard keeps watch in vain.
[2]It is in vain that you rise up early
    and go late to rest,
eating the bread of anxious toil;
    for he gives sleep to his
        beloved.

[3]Sons are indeed a heritage from the
    LORD,
    the fruit of the womb a reward.
[4]Like arrows in the hand of a warrior
    are the sons of one's youth.
[5]Happy is the man who has
    his quiver full of them.
He shall not be put to shame
    when he speaks with his enemies
        in the gate.

writings in the Hebrew Bible—Proverbs, Ecclesiastes, and Job."[78] Additionally, Psalm 127 is one of only two psalms in the Psalter ascribed to Solomon, the other being Psalm 72. Its theme is found in the first verse of the psalm—"house"—a rich and multivalent word in biblical Hebrew, perhaps reflecting Solomon's role in building the first Jerusalem temple.

Psalm 127 is most likely composed of two distinct proverbial sayings (vv. 1-2 and vv. 3-5), joined together by a common theme of building a "house." Verse 5's initial word "happy" (אַשְׁרֵי) marks it as a wisdom composition.[79] "House" (בִּיִת) has a wide range of meanings in the Hebrew Bible. It can refer to family dwellings (Gen 19:2; Judg 11:31; 2 Kgs 4:2), to whole households (Gen 46:27; Ruth 1:8; Josh 7:18), to the whole people of Israel (Exod 40:38; 1 Kgs 20:31; Ezek 36:22), to ruling dynasties (2 Sam 3:1; 7:11; 1 Kgs 16:3), and to the temple in Jerusalem (2 Kgs 22:3; Ezra 6:15; Jer 7:2).

Verses 1 and 2 form the first of the two proverbial sayings. Verse 1 is highly structured, with two parallel units in which the first line of each begins with "if the LORD does not" (אִם . . . לֹא) and the second with "in vain" (שָׁוְא). "House" (בִּיִת) in verse 1 most likely refers to the Jerusalem temple, just as "city" (עִיר) most probably refers to the city of Jerusalem since the Songs of Ascents are pilgrimage songs sung by worshipers who have arrived in the city to celebrate various festivals. The polyvalent nature of "house" (בִּיִת) in the Hebrew Bible, however, allows for a wide-ranging understanding of the words of verse 1.

78. deClaissé-Walford, *Introduction to the Psalms*, 25.
79. For a discussion of the word אַשְׁרֵי, see the commentary for Ps 112.

Verse 2 begins with "in vain" (שׁוא), the same word used in verse 1 to describe the activities of "those who build" and "the guard," this time in reference to spending long days in "anxious toil." The final line of the verse begins with כן, translated in the NRSV as "for," but with a meaning more akin to "in comparison with the above"[80]—stating that YHWH provides for the beloved. Richard Clifford describes verse 2 as "a beautifully constructed tricolon with a hard-hitting and unexpected final colon."[81] The words of verse 2 do not indicate that one should shun hard work, but they remind the reader or hearer that God can and will provide. Further, in the context of Psalm 127 the words of verse 2 are a caution against neglecting home and family as one works to provide for them.

In the MT the word "indeed" (הנה) occurs at the beginning of verse 3 rather than as rendered in the NRSV translation. It signals the beginning of a new strophe of the psalm, introducing the second proverbial saying. The admonitions in verses 1 and 2 thus move to assurance and declaration in verses 3-5.[82] The word translated in verse 3 as "sons" is בנים, whose acoustic similarity to the words "build" (בנה) and "house" (בית) in verse 1, coupled with the polyvalent meaning of the word "house," strongly connects the two portions of the psalm. The word "heritage" (נחלה) is used no fewer than fifty times in the book of Joshua (as well as extensively in the Pentateuch) in reference to the inheritance of the promised land by the Israelites.[83]

"Reward" (שׂכר) in Psalm 127:3 echoes Genesis 15, the story of the covenant between God and Abram. God says to Abram: "Do not be afraid, Abram, I am your shield; your reward [שׂכר] shall be very great" (15:2). Abram objects because he is childless, but God says to him: "Look toward heaven and count the stars, if you are able to count them . . . so shall your descendants be" (15:5). "Building a house" in early Israel and the ancient Near East—whether a family, a house, a temple, or a dynasty—required the proper building material. That material for families and dynasties was sons, although the strategic daughter might prove

---

80. See Waltke and O'Connor, *An Introduction to Biblical Hebrew Syntax*, 39.3.4e. For another suggestion on the translation of כן, see John A. Emerton, "The Meaning of *šēnā'* in Psalm CXXVII," *VT* 24 (1974): 15–31.

81. Clifford, *Psalms 73–150*, 240.

82. Patrick D. Miller, "Psalm 127—The House That YHWH Builds," *JSOT* 22 (1982): 119–32, at 127.

83. For a discussion of other words used in Joshua that have to do with "inheritance," see the commentary for Ps 125:3.

useful.[84] Indeed, the word "sons" (בנים) is actually a collective, inclusive of all offspring of an individual.

The psalmist employs warrior imagery in verses 4-5 to describe the gift of sons—arrows, quivers, and mighty ones. The word translated "warrior" in verse 4 is the adjective גבור, meaning "strong, vigorous, hero, champion," often used to describe military or heroic figures. In verse 5 an alternate form of גבור (גבר) is translated as "man." In David's lament over the death of Saul and Jonathan in 2 Samuel 1 he describes the shield of Saul as "the shield of the mighty" (גבר); 2 Samuel 23:8 names David's "mighty men" (גבר); and in 2 Kings 24:16 the king of Babylon took captive all of the גבר of Jerusalem, seven thousand.

The "gate" (שער) of a city in the ancient Near East was the gathering place for the elders and judges who settled disputes, rendered judgments, and made important decisions regarding the community. In Amos 5:12 the prophet condemns those "who afflict the righteous, who take a bribe, and push aside the needy in the gate." Boaz goes to the city gate in order to settle the matter of his marriage to Ruth (Ruth 4:1-6). In Deuteronomy 21:18-19 we read that if parents have a rebellious son they should "bring him out to the elders of his town at the gate of that place," and the husband of the "strong woman" in Proverbs "is known in the city gates" (31:23).

The word translated "enemies" (איב) occurs some seventy-five times in the Psalter and can refer to either personal foes or enemies of the larger community. As in most psalms, the "enemies" in Psalm 127 are not specified but are unnamed foes. But verse 5 states with confidence that with the support of children the mighty one (גבר) will not be ashamed (בוש) when he speaks in the gates of the city.[85]

Psalm 127 reminds its readers/hearers that without God it is useless to build a house, watch over a city, rise early, work late, and worry endlessly. The psalm also celebrates the gift of children. Few who read the psalm fail to hear echoes of the prophet Nathan's words to David in 2 Samuel 7:11-13:

> The LORD declares to you that the LORD will make you a house [בית]. When your days are fulfilled and you lie down with your ancestors, I will raise up your offspring after you, who shall come forth from your body, and I will establish his kingdom. He shall build a house [בית] for my name, and I will establish the throne of his kingdom.

---

84. See, for instance, Rebekah, Genesis 24; Leah and Rachel, Genesis 29; Michal, 1 Samuel 18.

85. Horst Seebass, "בוש (bôsh)," *TDOT*, 2:50–60, at 51.

What we build and keep watch over, what we rise early for and stay up late tending matters only if God is involved. Children are indeed a "building project" of life. But as we see more couples struggling with infertility, more persons choosing a single lifestyle, more broken families, and more nonconventional relationships, we are called to expand the term "children" to include far more than our biological offspring. My "child" might be my niece or nephew who can no longer live with a biological parent; a project to provide adequate food and shelter to homeless women and children; weekly visits with folks in assisted living facilities; tutoring young students who struggle to learn; fostering a child who needs a stable home life; mentoring the teen who lives down the street and seems to have lost his way. These children, these "building projects," are the sources of one's happiness in life (v. 5) for which God gives restful sleep (v. 2).

Psalm 128

Ninth of the Songs of Ascents, Psalm 128 is classified, like the preceding Psalm 127, as a wisdom psalm, continuing the theme of home and family. It combines wisdom words in verses 1-4, called by Samuel Terrien "sapiential salutations," with benedictory words in verses 5-6, described by him as a "priestly blessing."[86] In reference to its sapiential elements John Goldingay maintains that Psalm 128 is "for the most part, a poem that could have appeared in Proverbs,"[87] while in reference to its priestly elements Walter Brueggemann and William H. Bellinger suggest that the psalm reflects a cultic background.[88]

Verses 1-4 contain much of the vocabulary we encounter in Psalm 127: "happy" (אשרי), "house" (בית), "children" (בנים, translated "sons" in Ps 127), "thus" (הנה, translated "indeed" in Ps 127), and "man" (גבור, translated as "warrior" in Ps 127). The opening verse of Psalm 128, which begins with "happy" (אשרי), parallels the message of the opening of the Psalter in Psalm 1:1, but whereas Psalm 1 is addressed to an individual ("man," איש), Psalm 128 addresses "everyone" (כל).[89] The statements in verses 1 and 4 concerning the one who "fears [ירא] the LORD" form an

---

86. Samuel Terrien, *The Psalms: Strophic Structure and Theological Commentary*, ECC (Grand Rapids: Eerdmans, 2003), 832.

87. Goldingay, *Psalms 90–150*, 507.

88. Brueggemann and Bellinger, *Psalms*, 545.

89. For a full discussion of אשרי, see the commentary for Ps 112.

Psalm 128:1-6

A Song of Ascents.

¹Happy is everyone who fears the
    LORD,
  who walks in his ways.
²You shall eat the fruit of the labor of
    your hands;
  you shall be happy, and it shall go
    well with you.
³Your wife will be like a fruitful vine
  within your house;

your children will be like olive shoots
  around your table.
⁴Thus shall the man be blessed
  who fears the LORD.
⁵The LORD bless you from Zion.
  May you see the prosperity of
    Jerusalem
  all the days of your life.
⁶May you see your children's children.
  Peace be upon Israel!

inclusio around the first four verses of Psalm 128. In twenty-first-century culture the idea of fear is usually connected with the basic human instincts to run, defend, or retaliate. ירא in the Hebrew Bible is a synonym for "love" (אבה, Deut 10:12), "cling to" (דבק, Deut 10:20), and "serve" (עבד, Deut 6:13; Josh 24:14). At its root the word denotes obedience to the divine will. Erich Zenger defines ירא as "a foundational trust in YHWH as the good, life-promoting creator God."[90]

In contrast to Psalm 127:2, which suggests that anxious human toil is "in vain" (שוא), Psalm 128:2 says "the fruit of the labor of your hands you shall eat." Erich Zenger points out that while the message of Psalm 127 is that a satisfying life is a gift from God, regardless of human labor and effort, Psalm 128 reminds the reader or hearer that humanity can and must contribute to attaining that "satisfying life."[91]

Verse 3 celebrates a "happy" (אשרי) Near Eastern family environment, depicting one's wife (אשה) as a fruitful vine and children (בנים) like olive shoots. The word translated "within" (your house) in the NRSV is in Hebrew ירכה, connoting the inner chambers or recesses of the house; that, coupled with the reference to "your table," suggests the intimacy of family relationships.

Verses 5 and 6 may be understood as priestly or cultic sayings, compared by many commentators with the priestly blessing of Numbers 6:24. They begin with words of hope: "The LORD bless you from Zion," followed by the repeated imperative "May you see." These verses use the

90. Hossfeld and Zenger, *Psalms 3*, 400.
91. Ibid., 405.

literary device of advancing repetition (anadiplosis) to emphasize the extent to which the psalm singer will be blessed all her days, including seeing her children's children.[92] Psalm 128 thus moves the reader or hearer a step further in the wisdom admonitions found in Psalm 127, offering words of blessing and bringing the psalm singer home to Jerusalem, the place of "prosperity" (טוב) and "peace" (שלום) and a long and satisfying life.

As observed in the commentary on Psalm 127, a spouse and children are not the only means to blessing by God. Each of our heartfelt endeavors in life can be likened to spouses and children, those in whom we invest our lives at the cost of all else. Psalm 128 promises that such endeavors, if they are undertaken with a firm "reverence for the LORD" (Ps 128:1, 4), will be blessed. In due season they also contribute to the well-being of Jerusalem—that is, the whole body of believers.

Psalm 129

Psalm 129 is the tenth of the Songs of Ascents. It continues the agricultural theme of Psalms 126–128, but its tone is quite different. The psalm's opening words are a call to the people of Israel to speak as one about an ongoing oppressive situation in which they find themselves. The repetition of "often they have attacked [צרר] me from my youth" in verses 1 and 2 emphasizes the relentlessness of the situation. The word translated "attacked [צרר]" carries a basic meaning of "cramp, bind, wrap up, shut up, confine." It occurs some twenty-five times in the Psalter and in its noun form is translated variously in the NRSV as "foe," "adversary," or "enemy."[93] Yet even though the psalm singers feel attacked, they state with confidence in verse 2, "yet they have not prevailed against me."

Verse 3 employs agricultural imagery to convey the severity of Israel's oppression. Israel's back is likened to a field being plowed, with the plowshares driving long furrows in the soil. In Isaiah 51:23 God says to the people, "you have made your back like the ground and like the street for them [your tormentors] to walk on," and the prophet Micah declares: "Zion shall be plowed as a field" (Mic 3:12; Jer 26:18). The psalm singers compare their oppression to the relentless movement of a plow through the ground, churning up buried soil, bringing it to the surface, and then returning it, broken apart, to the depths from which it came. Here is a

92. See similar blessings in Gen 50:23 (Joseph) and Job 42:16 (Job). Hossfeld and Zenger, *Psalms 3*, 403.

93. See, for example, Pss 7:7; 10:5; 23:5; 31:12; 59:17; 74:23; 102:3; 107:6.

Psalm 129:1-8

A Song of Ascents.

1"Often have they attacked me from
my youth"
—let Israel now say—
2"often have they attacked me from
my youth,
yet they have not prevailed
against me.
3The plowers plowed on my back;
they made their furrows long."
4The LORD is righteous;
he has cut the cords of the wicked.
5May all who hate Zion
be put to shame and turned
backward.
6Let them be like the grass on the
housetops
that withers before it grows up,
7with which reapers do not fill their
hands
or binders of sheaves their arms,
8while those who pass by do not say,
"The blessing of the LORD be upon
you!
We bless you in the name of the
LORD!"

powerful image of oppressors continually opening old wounds, pouring
salt in them, and then returning them to the depths of the oppressed one's
very being. Elaine James suggests that the image of the plowed "back"
may also be understood as referring to sexual violence, particularly in
the context of warfare.[94]

Verse 4 is the turning point in the psalm. The singers express in simple
yet powerful words the hope that the oppressor will not ultimately
prevail: "The LORD is righteous [צדיק]." Being "righteous" (צדיק) has a
very simple meaning in Hebrew: "doing the right thing."[95] The Lord
is righteous and will do the right thing by "cutting the cords of the
wicked." The word "cord" (עבת) continues the agricultural imagery of
verse 3, suggesting the ropes used by farmers to tether and guide the
plow animals through the fields. It may also suggest the instruments of
punishment used by the Egyptians and others on the backs of subject
people (see Ps 2:3).

Verses 5-8 outline the fate of the attackers. "Hate" (שׂנא) is a powerful
word in Hebrew, conveying emotion as well as act. It is used over 170
times in the Hebrew Bible, with both humankind and God as subjects.
God's hate is directed most often toward behaviors and actions rather
than specific persons. Examples include Deuteronomy 12:31 (Canaanite

94. Elaine James, " 'The Plowers Plowed': The Violated Body in Psalm 129," *BibInt*
25 (2017): 172–89.
95. For a full discussion of "righteous" (צדיק), see the commentary for Ps 111:3-4.

cultic practices); Deuteronomy 16:22 (the erection of sacred pillars); Isaiah 1:14 (the insincere festivals of the Israelites); and Isaiah 61:8 (unholy offerings). While "hate" in the Hebrew Bible is an emotionally charged word, its consequence usually implies a distancing of oneself from another person or thing, both emotionally and physically, rather than wishing the other harm. In verse 5 the psalm singer wishes for "all who hate Zion" to be ashamed and turned backward, echoing the concept of distancing tied to the word's meaning.

The agricultural metaphor begun in verse 3 continues in verses 6-8 as the psalmist wishes that those "who hate Zion" may be like the grass that grows on top of a sod-covered roof, grass that lacks the necessary root system to produce a crop that the reaper or the binder of sheaves can profitably use. The words of verse 8 seem best understood when they are tied to the agricultural metaphor of verses 6-7. In Ruth 2:4 Boaz greets the reapers in his field with the words, "The LORD be with you," and they reply, "The LORD bless you." In Psalm 129:8 the psalm singer expresses a wish that those "who hate Zion" will not gain the blessing of the harvest.[96]

A wise German relative once said to me, "Was auch immer du säst, das wirst du ernten": "Whatever you sow, you will reap." Oppression is a pervasive presence in our world today—child and spousal abuse, discrimination against "the other," economic injustices that range from lack of food in developing countries to food deserts in developed ones, political corruption, the fallout of warfare that includes sexual exploitation, and so forth. The words of the singers of Psalm 129, "Often" and "from my youth" (vv. 1, 2), remind us that oppression is an age-old human phenomenon and that we cannot rest until all such oppression is addressed at its root cause and quashed—until the oppressors are "ashamed and turned backward" (Ps 129:5) and are never allowed to plow those fields again.

Psalm 130

In the eleventh of the Songs of Ascents an individual psalm singer calls on God for deliverance from what seems to be some threatening situation in life. Verse 1's "out of the depths" echoes words used elsewhere in the Hebrew Bible in reference to the sea, specifically the Mediterranean, a place of watery storm and potential death.[97] The psalmist likens the

---

96. Clifford, *Psalms 73–150*, 246; Hans-Joachim Kraus, *Psalms 60–150: A Commentary*, trans. Hilton C. Oswald, CC (Minneapolis: Fortress, 1993), 462; Mays, *Psalms*, 404–5.

97. See Isa 51:10; Ezek 27:34; Ps 69:2, 14; Jonah 2:2-6.

Psalm 130:1-8

A Song of Ascents.

¹Out of the depths I cry to you, O Lᴏʀᴅ.
²Lord, hear my voice!
Let your ears be attentive
to the voice of my supplications!
³If you, O Lᴏʀᴅ, should mark
iniquities,
Lord, who could stand?
⁴But there is forgiveness with you,
so that you may be revered.
⁵I wait for the Lᴏʀᴅ, my soul waits,
and in his word I hope;

⁶my soul waits for the Lord
more than those who watch for
the morning,
more than those who watch for
the morning.
⁷O Israel, hope in the Lᴏʀᴅ!
For with the Lᴏʀᴅ there is
steadfast love,
and with him is great power to
redeem.
⁸It is he who will redeem Israel
from all its iniquities.

TRANSLATION MATTERS

In Psalm 130 the psalmist employs two words used commonly in the Hebrew Bible to address God and translated in the NRSV respectively as Lᴏʀᴅ and Lord. The word translated "Lᴏʀᴅ" in verses 1, 3, 5, and 7 is יהוה, the personal name of God given to Moses in Exodus 3, Yʜᴡʜ. The name is derived from God's words to Moses when Moses asked for God's name in verse 13, after God commands that he return to his people and lead them out of the oppression of Egyptian slavery. Moses says: "If I come to the Israelites and say to them, 'The God of your ancestors has sent me to you,' and they ask me, 'What is his name?' what shall I say to them?" The Lord answered אהיה אשר אהיה, which can be translated as "I am who I am," "I am who I will be," "I am the one being" (according to the LXX). From this self-declaration of the Lord we derive the personal name of God, altered from first-person "I am" to third-person "he is" as Yʜᴡʜ: "He is how he is," "he is who he will be," "he is the one being."

The word translated as "my Lord" in verses 2, 3, and 6 of Psalm 130 is אדני (*'adonai*). It is the word אדון (lord) with a first-person pronoun suffix attached to it. Two forms of אדון (lord) appear in the Hebrew Bible, one used to address God and the other to address humans of a higher standing than oneself. The form used in Psalm 130 is used to address God; thus we find in Psalm 130 two synonymous addresses to the God of Israel, Lᴏʀᴅ (יהוה) and Lord (אדני).

current situation to that of one lost at sea and asks God to "hear" and "be attentive." "Hear" (שמע) occurs frequently in an initial position in pleas, both to God and from God,[98] while "be attentive" (קשב) is almost always used in conjunction with "ears," providing a vivid image of a God who pauses and turns an ear to the cries of humanity. The word translated in verse 2 as "supplications" adds further support to this image of God. It is derived from the Hebrew root חנן, translated in numerous places in the Psalter as "gracious" or "mercy/merciful,"[99] and is one of the self-declarative attributes God spoke to Moses in Exodus 34:6. The word means literally "to look kindly upon," in many cases where breaches of trust have taken place, as we see in the Golden Calf incident (Exod 32). The attribute is used almost exclusively in descriptions of God in the Hebrew Bible and in concert with other descriptive terms, suggesting the multifaceted character of God.[100] In Psalm 130 the psalm singer calls on God to be attentive (קשב) to the singer's "supplication" (חנן) by appealing to a basic characteristic of God. The Latin name for Psalm 130 is *De profundis* ("out of the depths"); it is used in many countries for invitations to funerals.[101] The mourners cry *de profundis*, and their only request is that God hear and be attentive.

In verses 3 and 4 the psalm singer expresses confidence that God will indeed "hear" and "be attentive" because God does not "mark iniquities" and offers "forgiveness." "Iniquity" (עון) occurs over two hundred times in the Hebrew Bible and is the primary word used to describe human sin and guilt in the prophetic writings.[102] The basic meaning of the word is "to bend, curve, turn aside, or twist," thus providing a vivid image of "iniquity" as an act or mistake that is not upright or just but is instead bent or twisted.

God provides forgiveness, according to verse 4, and so God is to "be revered." Here again we find the Hebrew root word ירא, most often translated in the NRSV as "fear." As noted above, today we usually associate the idea of fear with the basic human instincts to run, defend, or retaliate, but ירא encompasses a larger meaning of "awe, reverent respect, honor," as we see in the NRSV translation of this verse.

---

98. See Deut 6:4; Pss 4:1; 64:1; 102:1; Mic 3:9.

99. See Pss 30:8; 59:6; 102:8; 109:12; 111:4; 112:4; 123:3.

100. Heinz-Josef Fabry, "חנן (*ḥānan*)," *TDOT*, 5:22–36, at 23, 30.

101. Terrien, *The Psalms*, 839.

102. The word occurs twenty-four times in Isaiah, twenty-three times in Jeremiah, thirty-eight times in Ezekiel, and eleven times in Hosea.

As in verses 1 and 2, verses 5 and 6 use two designations for God: Lord (יהוה) and Lord (אדני), although here the words are spoken *about* God, whereas in verses 1 and 2 they are addressed *to* God. The repetition of the words "wait" and "watch" highlights verses 5 and 6 as the focus of Psalm 130. J. Clinton McCann states that the repetition "draws out the poetic line; thus it reproduces literally the effect of waiting."[103] "Wait," from the Hebrew root קוה, conveys a sense of tense expectation, like pulling on two ends of a rope and waiting for it to snap. The psalm singer waits, with more intense expectation "than those who watch [שמר] for the morning." Sentinels often stood guard on city walls, as did soldiers in camps during times of war, watching in the darkness for danger and waiting expectantly for the safety of daylight, when the possibility of attack from enemies was lessened.

In verses 7 and 8 the psalm singer turns her attention to "Israel"—in the context of the Songs of Ascents perhaps to companion travelers who have arrived in Jerusalem to worship together. The singer has renewed confidence in God and calls on those traveling alongside her to "hope" (יחל), best understood as "wait expectantly." "Hope" (יחל) is far less intense than "wait" (קוה) but seems to clearly tie the psalm singer's declaration in verse 5 to the admonition to "Israel" in verse 7. "Wait and hope," and God will redeem Israel from all of its "iniquities" (עון) because, according to verse 3, "If you, O Lord, should mark iniquities [עון], Lord, who could stand?" The psalm singer bases her trust in God's redemptive power on another of God's self-declarative attributes spoken to Moses in Exodus 34:6: God's "steadfast love" (חסד). "Steadfast love" is rendered in various translations as "faithful love," "lovingkindness," "unfailing love," and "mercy." The Hebrew word has to do with the covenant commitment between God and Israel and thus may also be translated as "covenant love."[104]

Psalm 130 is one of the seven penitential psalms sung during the season of Lent in the medieval church.[105] By order of Pope Innocent III (1198–1216) the psalms were to be prayed while kneeling each day of the Lenten season, or at least every Friday, reminding the singer of both humanity's "iniquity" (עון) and God's "steadfast love" (חסד). One of Martin Luther's best-known hymns is his metrical version of Psalm 130,

103. McCann, "The Book of Psalms," 1205.

104. For a detailed treatment of "steadfast love [חסד]," see "Translation Matters" in the commentary for Ps 118.

105. The others are Pss 6, 32, 38, 51, 102, 130, and 143.

and he called it "a proper master and doctor of Scripture." John Wesley wrote, after hearing Psalm 130 sung at St. Paul's Cathedral in London, that his heart was "strangely warmed," much as happened to the two disciples on the Emmaus Road in Luke 24 who felt their "hearts burning within" them as they talked with Jesus about "the law of Moses, the prophets, and the psalms."[106]

Psalm 130 calls us again to imagine pilgrim travelers to Jerusalem: one village or family group meeting another, exchanging greetings, traveling to, and finally arriving in Jerusalem. The pilgrims sing as they travel along and when they arrive in the city. Psalm 130 in its canonical setting is a song sung by a pilgrim after she has arrived in the city. In its words we hear a heartfelt cry and a resounding sense of assurance that God forgives iniquities and redeems. Each time we enter our own "Jerusalems," our "sanctuaries," we bring with us the incidents in our lives that have caused us, intentionally or unintentionally, to commit iniquity (עָוֹן), that is, to bend, curve, turn aside, or twist what is right. And we are not alone; we live in a world of twisting, curving, and bending what is right and just in order to accommodate selfish needs. One has only to log on to various news feeds, pick up a newspaper, or watch the evening news to witness such. This psalm invites the faithful who embrace God's "steadfast love" (חֶסֶד) to help turn the tide of our world's and our own selfish iniquity (עָוֹן)—our self-seeking turning and twisting.

"Wait" and "Hope" Even in the Depths

Psalm 130 opens with a cry of despair in verses 1-2: "Out of the depths I cry to you, O LORD. . . . Let your ears be attentive." The psalmist gradually moves, though, from feelings of despair to hope and peace as she remembers and reflects on God and takes her eyes off herself and places them on God, acknowledging that God alone is able to save.

The occasion of one of my birthdays caused me to reflect on what a beautiful experience it is to grow up, but it also brought frustration and sadness as I recalled the desires of my heart that have not materialized at my age. Family members, friends, and fellow church members continually ask:

---

106. See further McCann, "The Book of Psalms," 1206.

"When are you getting married? When will you buy a car? When are you finishing your studies? When are you buying a house? Why are you not preaching yet?" They mean well, but somehow it seems to them that I am incomplete without these things. Do I *need* a husband, a car, a house, and all these things to be deemed successful in society? And yet the more I hear the questions, the more these things become my own desires! As I try to reconcile God's timing to the expectations of others that are now my own expectations, I find the words of Psalm 130 reassuring!

Out of the depths I cry to you, O Lord. Lord, hear my voice! Let your ears be attentive to the voice of my supplications! Sometimes, in the midst of the noise from others and my own doubts and fears, I feel very alone. I feel as though I am indeed in the depths: a desolate land or an abyss, a place of isolated hopelessness and lonely anguish where food and water are scarce. "The depths" bring to mind the townships and slums of Third World countries, places all too familiar to a person like myself. And yet the psalm singer, one who dwells in "the depths," in a dark, unreachable place where poverty is rife and opportunity rare, feels empowered to cry out to God to hear her voice. The words of Psalm 130 resonate deeply with someone like me whose voice is often marginalized. "Hear me, because no one has ever taken the time to hear me. I am but a small voice among many in this desolate land; hear me!"

If you, O Lord, should mark iniquities, Lord, who could stand? If God were to hold any person truly accountable for their acts and thoughts none would be able to stand, for, as Romans 3:23 tells us, "all have sinned and fall short of the glory of God." Verse 4 of Psalm 130 reminds us, though, of God's great forgiveness, embodied in the life of Jesus, that frees us from condemnation.

I wait for the Lord, my soul waits, and in his word I hope. When it seems that things in my life are not coming to me as and when I expect or hope, the psalm singer reminds me to "wait" and "hope." The words of the psalm suggest that the psalm singer at some crucial point in her life makes the decision to wait on the Lord and continue to hope. I too must "wait" and "hope." Being overly anxious and not trusting in God's good timing might lead me into temptation. I might end up compromising: settling for a job that pays more money but steers me away from my life's purpose, all for a car and a house; settling for a life partner who does not bring out the best in me, all for the sake of getting married at the expected time. No, I must "wait" and "hope."

My soul waits for the Lord more than those who watch for the morning, more than those who watch for the morning. These words are my supplication! I will wait on the Lord! Even when I do not feel like it I will choose to wait like the psalm singer, with an attitude of eagerness and hopeful expectation (more than those who watch for the morning). Waiting is a humbling act that prepares our hearts to receive the good from God. And we do not wait in vain. The promises of God are not like the promises of our governments that so often fail to materialize; God's promises are, in the words of 2 Corinthians 1:20, "Yes" and "Amen."

O Israel, hope in the LORD. . . with him is steadfast love . . . and with him is great power. As God's people we are instructed to hope in the Lord for that very reason: because of God's steadfast love and great power. Unlike the love of people that so often fails because it discriminates against gender and status, God's love transcends petty categorization and moves in realms of grace and forgiveness. Finally, God has great power to redeem us from the most dejected conditions as we struggle to have our voices heard in a society that seems to be happy to leave us "in the depths." Psalm 130 reminds us that God's power is great and more than sufficient to lift us out of the "depths" of the seemingly repressive society in which we live and that God will indeed "hear our voice" and "redeem" us.

Siphokazi Dlwati

"Out of Depths I Cry to You"

At the end of apartheid in 1994, South Africa declared eleven official languages for the country: Afrikaans, English, IsiNdebele, IsiXhosa, IsiZulu, Sepedi, Sesotho, Setswana, Siswati, Tshivenda, and Xitsonga. I am an Afrikaans-speaking South African. The language was derived from several European languages and many of its words resemble Dutch, Flemish, and German. Afrikaans became part of South African history after the country became the Union of South Africa in 1910. At that time Dutch and English were the two official languages. On the eighth of May 1925 the "Official Languages of the Union Act Number 8 of 1925" was passed and Dutch was replaced by Afrikaans. Afrikaans is a beautiful language that has many unique ways of saying and explaining things. When it comes to the concept of listening, two sayings in Afrikaans come to mind: *Die ene ore wees* ("being all ears," meaning to listen very intently) and *Met 'n halwe oor luister* ("listen with half an ear," meaning not to listen). These two sayings have become quite relevant in the current culture of South Africa. As a result of the sad history of apartheid (which itself is an Afrikaans word), the Afrikaans language is viewed by many South Africans as the language of the oppressor.

How may this Afrikaans-speaker communicate his desire for forgiveness and reconciliation to those who feel oppressed when he desires that they "be all ears" (*Die ene ore wees*) but they only seem to listen with "half an ear" (*Met 'n halwe oor luister*)? And how do those who have been oppressed for so long come to be able to listen with "all ears" when they themselves have only been listened to for decades with "half an ear"?

When I read Psalm 130's words, "Out of the depths I cry to you, O LORD. Lord, hear my voice!" I picture death and the underworld as being at the ends of the sea, in the bottom of a well or a cistern—somewhere far away from YHWH. YHWH is in heaven, so to be in the depths or the underworld is be outside of YHWH's realm, and yet the psalmist continues to cry out and asks God's ear to be attentive—asking for God to be *Die ene ore wees* (listen intently) and not *Met 'n halwe oor luister* (not listen). YHWH, lean your ear down from heaven and "be all ears" to the cries of this supplicant. This psalm singer seeks forgiveness and needs you to hear.

Verses 3-4 of Psalm 130 affirm that God alone "marks" sinfulness and forgives; verses 5-6 are words of waiting and hoping for the presence of God in the psalmist's troubling situation; verses 7-8 provide affirmation that YHWH does indeed redeem from all sinfulness. The depths spoken of in verse 1 of Psalm 130 are for Afrikaans the history of apartheid in South Africa: the depths of suppression of indigenous languages and cultures; the depths of oppression based on skin color; the depths of servitude of the African population by the European colonists.

The Afrikaans language has become repulsive to those who lived through and are heirs of apartheid in South Africa, but it is my language, my way of expressing my need for forgiveness and reconciliation. How might my language be heard again as a language of reconciliation rather than as a language of division and oppression? In his article "Mandela and Afrikaans: From Language of the Oppressor to Language of Reconciliation," Michael le Cordeur explains how Nelson Mandela also concluded that the Afrikaans language must be made part of the process of reconciliation. Mandela famously said: "If you talk to a man in a language he understands, you talk to his mind. But if you talk to him in his own language, you talk to his heart."[98] I am an Afrikaans-speaking South African and I

---

107. Michael Le Cordeur, "Mandela and Afrikaans: From Language of the Oppressor to Language of Reconciliation," *International Review of Social Sciences and Humanities* 10 (2015): 32–45.

love my language. I am afraid that if my language is not heard, it will die.

"Out of the depths I cry . . . hear my voice!" Whatever language we speak, we speak from the heart. Perhaps the story in Acts 2 can provide some measure of hope for the divided world in which South Africa finds itself. At the Pentecostal gathering in Jerusalem after the ascension of Jesus the diverse crowd came together, and "the crowd gathered and was bewildered, because each one heard them speaking in the native language of each" (Acts 2:6). My native tongue says *Ek getuig dat ek lief die Here* ("I confess that I love the Lord"). The words have more meaning in one's own language.

Lodewyk Sutton

Psalm 131

Erhard Gerstenberger calls this brief psalm "a jewel of simplicity";[108] H.-J. Kraus characterizes it as the most tender and intimate of the pilgrimage songs;[109] Hermann Gunkel notes, "A few simple sentences, but of such depth and authenticity that they dare more than a great, artistic poem."[110] It is one of three of the Songs of Ascents ascribed to David (Pss 122, 124, and 131), thus giving the psalm something of a "royal" starting point for interpretation, but its metaphoric imagery allows the reader or hearer to move past the psalm's "royal" overtones and find a rich feminine picture of God.

The psalm singer begins the psalm with an invocation, "O Lord," calling on Yhwh to hear her prayer. She continues with a threefold negative declaration: "my heart [לב] is not lifted up; my eyes are not raised too high; I do not occupy myself [הלך] with things too great." The word "heart" (לב) in Hebrew refers to the seat of human intellect and will and parallels the English concept of "mind," while the word translated "occupy myself" is the verb הלך, which means "to walk, move about." The psalm singer maintains that she does not think better of herself than of others and she does not walk about with eyes raised high, dwelling on things too great and marvelous for her. The reference to "heart" (לב, mind) reflects the inner demeanor of the psalm singer, while "eyes" and

---

108. Gerstenberger, *Psalms, Part 2, and Lamentations*, 359.

109. Kraus, *Psalms 60–150*, 470.

110. Hermann Gunkel, *Die Psalmen übersetzt und erklärt* HKAT 2/2 4th ed. (Göttingen: Vandenhoeck & Ruprecht, 1929), 563.

Psalm 131:1-3

A Song of Ascents. Of David.

1O LORD, my heart is not lifted up,
my eyes are not raised too high;
I do not occupy myself with things
too great and too marvelous for me.
2But I have calmed and quieted my
soul,

like a weaned child with its
mother;
my soul is like the weaned child
that is with me.
3O Israel, hope in the LORD
from this time on and
forevermore.

"occupied" (הלך, walk about) reflect the outer demeanor and actions of the psalmist.

Instead, the psalmist's soul (נפש) is calmed and quieted. The word translated "calm" (שוה) means "to be even, smooth." Verse 2 likens the evenness and quietness of the psalm singer to a weaned child with its mother.[111] The basic meaning of the word for weaned (גמל) is "treat kindly, deal fully or adequately with someone, complete or perfect" and came by analogy to mean "wean." In Genesis 21:8 we read of Isaac: "The child grew and was weaned [גמל]; and Abraham made a great feast on the day." Hannah tells her husband Elkanah in 1 Samuel 1:22 that she will take Samuel to Shiloh "as soon as the child is weaned [גמל]," and in Isaiah 28:9 the prophet cries out: "Who will he teach knowledge? . . . those who are weaned [גמל] from milk, those taken from the breast?" Thus in a number of places in the biblical text גמל refers to the completion of a child's weaning from her mother's breast; she no longer cries out in hunger for the breast but still seeks out the mother for her warm embrace and nurturing care.

גמל, however, is also used in the Hebrew Bible to express the idea of dealing with someone in a full or adequate manner. David sings in 2 Samuel 22:21: "The LORD rewarded [גמל] me according to my righteousness." In Psalm 13:6 the psalm singer says, "I will sing to the LORD because he has dealt bountifully [גמל] with me," and the singer of Psalm 116 says in verse 3, "Return, O my soul, to your rest, for the LORD has dealt bountifully [גמל] with you." Thus verse 2 of Psalm 131 might also depict a still-nursing child who is well fed and fully satisfied (גמל), resting

---

111. A child in the ancient Near East was usually weaned sometime in its third or fourth year of life.

peacefully in the mother's embrace.[112] However one understands the metaphor, it is a powerful image of one who finds calm and quiet in the embrace of a feminine God, as twice repeated in verse 2. Erich Zenger summarizes well the two understandings of גמל in Psalm 131:

> If one sees the specific aspect of the mother-child relationship that here serves as a comparison for the relationship between God and the human being not so much as the difference between nursling and weanling, but more generally in the act of nursing a child, then the psalm evokes the child's *twofold experience* of receiving from its mother everything necessary for and promoting life *and thereby* learning the personal care and closeness of the mother as literally a "space to live in."[113]

The final verse of Psalm 131, with the admonition to "hope [יחל]" in the LORD," echoes the words of Psalm 130:5, 7, suggesting that the two psalms be read together. The words also unite the individual psalm singer in verses 1 and 2 of Psalm 131 with the whole community of pilgrim worshipers in verse 3 of the psalm, as we find in other Songs of Ascents.[114]

The strong feminine imagery in Psalm 131 has led a number of scholars to suggest that it may have been composed by a woman.[115] It certainly gives voice to the quiet repose of a mother and her satisfied, resting child. Assigning authorship to any psalm is problematic, however, and the metaphor of God as parent and Israel as child is found elsewhere in the Hebrew Bible. In Hosea 11:3-4 God says of Israel, "yet it was I who taught Ephraim to walk, I took them up in my arms. . . . I was to them like those who lift infants to their cheeks." In Deuteronomy 1:31, Moses says to the people: "in the wilderness . . . you saw how the LORD your God carried you, just as one carries a child, all the way that you traveled until you reached this place."[116] Regardless of the gender of the voice in Psalm 131, its words reflect a basic trust in God by pilgrims coming to Jerusalem for festivals and celebrations and singing the words of the Songs of Ascents.

---

112. See Goldingay, *Psalms 90–150*, 537.

113. Hossfeld and Zenger, *Psalms 3*, 452.

114. See Pss 122, 123, 130.

115. See, for instance, Gottfried Quell, "Struktur und Sinn des Psalms 131," in *Das Ferne und nahe Wort. Festschrift Leonhard Rost*, ed. Fritz Maass, BZAW 105 (Berlin: Töpelmann, 1967), 181–85; Allen, *Psalms 101–150*, 198; McCann, "The Book of Psalms," 1208; Bernard W. Anderson with Stephen Bishop, *Out of the Depths: The Psalms Speak for Us Today*, 3rd ed. (Louisville: Westminster John Knox, 2000), 179; Hossfeld and Zenger, *Psalms 3*, 446. But see also Gerstenberger, *Psalms, Part 2, and Lamentations*, 362; Crow, *The Songs of Ascents (Psalms 120–134)*, 97–98.

116. See also Isa 46:3-4 and Jer 31:20.

The message of Psalm 131 is simple. Pride, haughtiness, and seeking after great and wondrous things will not provide the calm and quiet that simple reliance on God brings. In the New Testament, Jesus told the disciples that anyone who did not become like a child would never enter the kingdom of heaven (Matt 18:13-15; Mark 10:13-16). Psalm 131 teaches us in vivid metaphoric imagery what it means to be a child in the presence of a feminine God.

Psalm 132

Psalm 132 is the thirteenth of the fifteen Songs of Ascents. Its length, subject matter, and location within the Songs of Ascents seem to suggest a special function for it in this grouping of psalms. First, with eighteen verses this psalm is considerably longer than any of the other Songs of Ascents, which range in length from three verses (Ps 134) to nine (Ps 122). Second, Psalm 132 reiterates the promises given to David by God in 2 Samuel 7 and the choice of Zion/Jerusalem as God's dwelling place. Third, according to the "storyline" of book 5's Songs of Ascents its placement near the end of the collection suggests that it was recited by pilgrims who had traveled to Jerusalem and now, perhaps nearing the end of their pilgrimage time, stand within the city, pondering God's past promises to David and further considering their own lives and futures.

Psalm 132 has two sections: a prayer in verses 1-10 and a response to that prayer in verses 11-18.[117] The "prayer" portion of the psalm begins in verses 1-5 with a recollection of a vow by David to God. The psalm singer calls on God to remember for the sake of David all that David experienced in his life and all David promised to do to create a dwelling place for God. The words of verses 1-5 echo the sentiments of David in 2 Samuel 7 when he announces to the prophet Nathan that he plans to build a house for the ark of God (2 Sam 7:2). While no other biblical text states that David vowed that he would not "enter my house or get into my bed . . . until I find a place for the LORD," the author of the New Testament book of Acts characterizes David as "a man after God's own heart" (Acts 13:22).

The word "dwelling place [מִשְׁכָּן]" in verses 5, 7, and 13 derives from a verbal root that means "settle down, inhabit, reside." It is the same word

---

117. See esp. Allen, *Psalms 101–150*, 204–9; McCann, "The Book of Psalms," 1211–12. For an intriguing alternate structure for the psalm, see James Limburg, *Psalms*, WBiC (Louisville: Westminster John Knox, 2000), in which he suggests the following: vv. 1-10, a chosen place; vv. 11-12, a chosen person; vv. 13-18, a chosen place and a chosen person.

Psalm 132:1-18

A Song of Ascents

¹O Lord, remember in David's favor
all the hardships he endured;
²how he swore to the Lord
and vowed to the Mighty One of
Jacob,
³"I will not enter my house
or get into my bed;
⁴I will not give sleep to my eyes
or slumber to my eyelids,
⁵until I find a place for the Lord,
a dwelling place for the Mighty
One of Jacob."

⁶We heard of it in Ephrathah;
we found it in the fields of Jaar.
⁷"Let us go to his dwelling place;
let us worship at his footstool."
⁸Rise up, O Lord, and go to your
resting place,
you and the ark of your might.
⁹Let your priests be clothed with
righteousness,
and let your faithful shout for joy.
¹⁰For your servant David's sake
do not turn away the face of your
anointed one.

used to describe God's presence in the tabernacle during the wilderness wanderings (Exod 40:35) and in the temple in Jerusalem (1 Kgs 8:12). "Dwelling place [מֹשְׁכָּן]" is a unifying theme for the psalm, along with the word used in parallel with it, "resting place [מְנוּחָה]" (vv. 8 and 14), from the verbal root נוח. "Dwelling place" and "resting place" bring to mind for the singers of Psalm 132 the promise and ultimate fulfillment of God's enduring presence in their midst.

The "prayer" continues in verses 6 and 7 with the story of the ark of the covenant as found in 1 Samuel 4–6; it acted as the footstool of Yhwh in the tabernacle and in the temple. The direct objects of the two verbs in verse 6 are feminine singular (though translated "it"), indicating perhaps that what the singers have heard of and found is a "place" (מָקוֹם, v. 5a) for Yhwh to dwell.[118] Erich Zenger posits that the referent could be the ark (אָרוֹן), which appears in verse 8, since while the word is usually masculine in Hebrew, in 1 Samuel 4:17 and 2 Chronicles 8:11 it is feminine.[119] The word "resting place [מְנוּחָה]" in verse 8 is also feminine, perhaps paralleling the reference to "place [מָקוֹם]" in verse 5.

---

118. David J. A. Clines, ed., *The Concise Dictionary of Classical Hebrew* (Sheffield: Sheffield Phoenix, 2009), 240, indicates that מָקוֹם can be both masculine and feminine. Goldingay, *Psalms 90–150*, 549–50, argues that the "it" can refer to both "place" (masculine singular) and "dwelling place" (feminine plural), since the feminine singular is "the regular way of referring to an indeterminate 'it.'"

119. Hossfeld and Zenger, *Psalms 3*, 456.

Psalm 132:1-18 (cont.)

[11]The L<small>ORD</small> swore to David a sure
   oath
   from which he will not turn back:
"One of the sons of your body
   I will set on your throne.
[12]If your sons keep my covenant
   and my decrees that I shall teach
      them,
their sons also, forevermore,
   shall sit on your throne."
[13]For the L<small>ORD</small> has chosen Zion;
   he has desired it for his habitation:
[14]"This is my resting place forever;
here I will reside, for I have
   desired it.
[15]I will abundantly bless its provisions;
   I will satisfy its poor with bread.
[16]Its priests I will clothe with salvation,
   and its faithful will shout for joy.
[17]There I will cause a horn to sprout
   up for David;
   I have prepared a lamp for my
   anointed one.
[18]His enemies I will clothe with
   disgrace,
   but on him, his crown will gleam."

Thus readers or hearers could understand that the psalm singers "heard of" a place/resting place in Ephrathah and "found" the ark in the fields of Jaar (v. 6). The place names bring to mind the story of the capture of the ark of the covenant by the Philistines in 1 Samuel 4–6 and the bringing of the ark to Jerusalem by David in 2 Samuel 6. Psalm 132:6's reference to Ephrathah most likely indicates the area surrounding Bethlehem, the home of David, while Jaar seems to refer to Kiriath-jearim, where the ark was housed from the time of its return from the Philistines (1 Sam 7:2) until David brought it to Jerusalem (2 Sam 6).[120] The prayer portion of Psalm 132 culminates in verses 9-10 with words on behalf of the priests, of the faithful, and of David, echoed in verses 16-17. The words "priests" and "faithful" in verse 9 are a merism that encompasses the whole of Israel, asking for righteousness for the priests so that the faithful may "shout for joy [רנן]."[121]

Verses 11-18 offer a response to the prayer of verses 1-10, beginning in verses 11-12 with a reiteration of God's promises to David in 2 Samuel 7. Verses 13-15 take up verses 6-8's theme of finding a dwelling place for the

120. In 1 Sam 5 the Philistines capture the ark of the covenant, which the Israelites had taken into battle. The Philistines place the ark in the temple of Dagon, one of the Philistine gods. After the presence of the ark causes the destruction of the statue of Dagon (1 Sam 5:1-5) and brings illness upon the inhabitants of the cities of the Philistines (1 Sam 5:6-12), they send the ark back to the Israelites and, according to 1 Sam 7:2, "the ark was lodged at Kiriath-jearim."

121. For a discussion of רנן, see the commentary for Ps 95.

ark. Verses 13 and 14 state that Yнwн has chosen Zion for his "habitation" (משׁכֶן) and a "resting place" (מְנוּחָה) in which God will "reside." Zion is thus the "resting place" (מְנוּחָה) of both the ark (v. 8) and Yнwн (vv. 8 and 14). Verse 15's promises of "provisions" for Zion and care for its "poor" call to mind the words of Psalms 107:33-42 and 145:14-20, which state that God can provide the faithful with all their needs: a habitable land, productive fields and vineyards, children, food for the hungry, care for the needy, and an ear to the cries of those who are oppressed. The end of Psalm 132, in verses 16-18, echoes verses 9 and 10, using the merism "priests" and "faithful" to once again include all of Israel in the promise of salvation and shouts of joy (רנן).

Psalm 132 calls to our remembrance two important elements of identity for the ancient Israelites: a dwelling place for God and the kingship of David—temple and court. The prayer of verses 1-10 and the response of assurance in verses 11-18 give hope to the postexilic pilgrims to Jerusalem that God is indeed dwelling among them. Temple and court may be foreign concepts to Christians today, but J. Clinton McCann suggests that we see in the words of Psalm 132 a reminder that God's presence among us is real and concrete, occupying both time and space.[122] Elizabeth F. Huwiler, commenting on the "we" voice of the psalm, writes: "The 'we,' the voice of the worshiping community, functions both to bring the David story from the historical past into the liturgical present and to transport the congregants from the current worship setting into that same historical past."[123]

McCann's and Huwiler's contention that Psalm 132 brings the past to the present and the present to the past reminds us that God's presence among us occupies both time and space. Each of us is heir to a particular past and present, a particular time and space in which we experience the ebb and flow of God's absence and presence. In the times when God seems absent the memory of God's presence in the past, in one time and space, can give us the strength to move through the absence to presence once again in this time and this space. But what about those who are emotionally and physically abused, those who live in constant despair and fear, the hungry, the homeless? For those who live in the "privileged" world, perhaps the words of Psalm 132 can be a reminder that "all Israel" is included in the promises of the psalm: all are entitled to "shout for joy" (רנן, vv. 9 and 16) and to have "provisions" and "bread" (v. 15). The

122. McCann, "The Book of Psalms," 1213.
123. Elizabeth F. Huwiler, "Patterns and Problems in Psalm 132," in *The Listening Heart: Essays in Wisdom and the Psalms in Honor of Roland E. Murphy, O.Carm.*, ed. Kenneth G. Hogland, et al., JSOTSup 58 (Sheffield: JSOT Press, 1987), 199–215, at 207.

words of Psalm 132 can be a clarion cry to envision a "dwelling place" or multiple "dwelling places" for YHWH realized among all people.

Psalm 133

Psalm 133 is fourteenth of the fifteen Songs of Ascents. It is one of three wisdom psalms in the grouping—Psalms 127, 128, and 133[124]—and in its three short verses the singer of the psalm summarizes the goodness and pleasantness of kindred living together in unity, using two metaphoric images: oil and dew. Scholars maintain that the core of Psalm 133 is a traditional proverbial or wisdom saying in Israel:

> Behold, how good and how pleasant it is when kindred dwell together in unity. It is like good oil on the head, running down upon the beard. It is like the dew of Hermon.[125]

The two simple metaphoric images of oil and dew, further designated in verses 2 and 3 as oil on the head of the high priest Aaron and dew on Mount Hermon, which provided needed water to Jerusalem, transformed the proverbial saying into a psalmic celebration of Jerusalem.

In its proverbial setting the wisdom words of verse 1—"how good [טוב] and how pleasant [נעים]"—recall the exclamation of blessing uttered by a traveler or visitor upon entering the home of another in ancient Israel. "Good" echoes God's assessment of creation in Genesis 1. Verses 4, 10, 12, 18, and 21 of Genesis 1 say that "God saw that it was good [טוב]." In verse 31 God declares creation not just "good" but "very good." In the Genesis 2 creation story, however, God declares "It is *not* good that the man [אדם] should be alone" (2:18). From the beginning of creation God saw the need for humanity to dwell together, and the words of Psalm 133 emphasize the importance of humans living in community.[126] The word "pleasant" in verse 1 derives from the root נעם, and its meanings include "pleasant, lovely, sweet, good, attractive, friendly, joyous." It occurs frequently in the biblical text in parallel constructions with טוב.[127]

---

124. The other wisdom psalms in the Psalter are Pss 1, 32, 37, 49, 73, 79, 112, 119, and 145.

125. See, for example, Allen, *Psalms 101–150*, 215; McCann, "The Book of Psalms," 1214; Crow, *The Songs of Ascents*, 109; Mays, *Psalms*, 413; and Hossfeld and Zenger, *Psalms 3*, 472. Psalm 133 has been popularized in the Shabbat hymn "*Hinneh Mah Tov.*"

126. For a full discussion of the Genesis 2 story, see Nancy L. deClaissé-Walford, "Genesis 2: It Is Not Good for the Human to Be Alone," *RevExp* 103 (2006): 343–58.

127. See Gen 49:15; Ps 147:1; Job 36:11; Prov 24:25.

Psalm 133:1-3

A Song of Ascents.

¹How very good and pleasant it is when kindred live together in unity!
²It is like the precious oil on the head,
running down upon the beard,
on the beard of Aaron,
running down over the collar of his robes.
³It is like the dew of Hermon,
which falls on the mountains of Zion.
For there the LORD ordained his blessing,
life forevermore.

Oil from the olive was an important commodity in the dry environment of the Near East. Olive oil was mixed with sweet-smelling spices and used for care of the hair and skin. Verse 2 likens the goodness and pleasantness of dwelling together metaphorically to "precious [טוב] oil." A basic act of hospitality when visitors entered the homes of others was to wash their feet and pour soothing and refreshing oil on their heads; the oil poured on men's heads ran down into the beard. The oil in Psalm 133 is poured on the head of Aaron, and the oil runs down into his beard and onto the collar of his garments. In Leviticus 8:10-12, Moses anoints his brother Aaron as high priest of ancient Israel with "anointing oil [שמן המשחה]." Thus the oil used to anoint the head of the visitor to one's home is likened to the oil used to anoint the head of Aaron the high priest, infusing the act with a sense of sacredness and elevating the visitor to the status of an esteemed guest in the home.

In verse 3 the goodness and pleasantness of dwelling together is likened to the dew on Mount Hermon. Located some 125 miles north of Jerusalem, the mountain was known for its abundant dew that provided an important agricultural resource to Palestine, which saw little rainfall between the months of April and October. Without the nightly accumulation of dew the land would be parched and dry for many months of the year. In the metaphorical language of Psalm 133 the dew from Hermon falls on the "mountains of Zion," providing blessing.

The metaphoric images of oil and dew in Psalm 133 are strong symbols of the blessing available to those who dwell together in unity. Psalm 133 reminded the pilgrims who gathered in Jerusalem that they were family, kindred living together in unity, and that they could partake of the "precious oil" and the "dew of Hermon" celebrated by the psalm singers. In its position in the book of Psalms, then, Psalm 133 is a proclamation of delight sung by pilgrims who have arrived for festal celebrations in Jerusalem.

The singers of Psalm 133 would most likely have remembered the proverbial wisdom saying on which the psalm was based—kindred who dwell together in unity being likened to good oil and dew, representing the joy and goodness of dwelling together as brothers and sisters—but the words of the whole psalm reminded the people that their family relationship was established not by blood but by their mutual sharing in the community of God. The celebrations of festivals in Jerusalem transformed pilgrims coming from different places and family groups into a united family that for a holy time ate and dwelt together. Psalm 133 was a song of greeting, of anticipation, and of celebration of that holy time.

In the Christian tradition Psalm 133 is used as a text for the observance of the Eucharist, calling the whole people of God to a family table where all are welcome. Augustine of Hippo boldly claimed that Psalm 133 inspired the foundation of monasteries because its words paint a picture of the ideal of brothers, fellow pilgrims in the faith, dwelling together in unity. In the twenty-first century the table remains a powerful image of kinship and unity, as do the ideals of basic sustenance: the oil and the dew. Yet we often exclude from our tables—knowingly or unwittingly—those who do not seem to conform to what we envision as "kindred in unity" (אחים גם יחד). This psalm invites us to ensure that no one be excluded from our tables and that all experience the "precious oil" and the "dew of Hermon."

Sitting at the Table

With whom we sit at table matters because being at table with others builds the bonds that hold communities together. It is the place where relationships develop and communities form in organic ways. Around the table, families talk about the calendar and listen to what happened in one another's days. Roommates work out issues over dinner, talk about what is going on in their lives, and often learn from one another's cooking habits. Church members sharing meals together solve problems, plan church events, and learn about each other's joys and problems outside of church. At shared tables friends pick up where they left off, lovers reconnect, and strangers discover chemistry that leaves them wanting more.

The table is also a place where we learn to draw boundaries regarding what is acceptable behavior and what is not. The selection of those we welcome at the table and those we do not welcome signals who belongs in our community and who does not belong. It is often where we learn who is important and powerful in our community and who is considered inconsequential. A quick stroll through any middle-school cafeteria will demonstrate this principle in action.

In reality this boundary-setting behavior is active on most of the occasions when we sit together at table. It does not matter whether we are at a church dinner or a fancy company party; the articulated and unarticulated rules regarding who is supposed to sit where are understood. The product of this kind of rule-setting is often the exclusion from our tables of people who do not meet certain expectations.

Psalm 133 paints a beautiful picture of what it means for us all to dwell in kindred community with one another as God's people. In the Christian tradition this unity is expressed most fully when we celebrate communion together at God's table. This is a table where every human being is welcome to sit, to fully participate in the community, and to receive all the nourishment God's table has to offer.

Because all are welcome, God's table is full of diversity, inclusion, and often unlikely dinner partners. God's table welcomes all: the CEO and the homeless LGBTQ teen, the philanthropist and the money launderer, the nun and the sex worker, the mothers of the Black Lives Matter movement and the white supremacist. All are welcome at God's table. The refugee, the military captain, the socialist, the capitalist, the

chaplain who has lost faith, and the victim of assault who can't let go of faith are welcome and invited to bring a friend.

Even on our best days the ideal of Psalm 133 is difficult to imagine. Diverse community has never been easy. As humans we have always found it simpler to sit with those who are most like us than to try to figure out how to sit with people who are different from us. For this reason we too often find ways to avoid engaging in this kind of challenging community. Some of us avoid diverse community because we are afraid of conflict. Some of us are afraid that if we make our ideas known in diverse spaces we will face ridicule or even retribution. Some of us do not push for more diversity in our communities because we know that our world often rewards those who maintain the boundaries of our monolithic communities over those who strive to destroy divisive boundaries. Often we are afraid that if we begin to participate in diverse communities we will be disconnected from other communities in which we participate. Sometimes the ideological, theological, and political divides are so deep in diverse communities that we simply do not have the creative vision to imagine how we will ever be able to sit at God's table together. The reality of an open and inclusive table means that some are present who have hurt others at the table and some are present at the table who devalue the lives of others who are there. Diverse community is hard.

And yet . . . God has called us to manifest the kindred unity of the community of God in the world by making room for everyone at the table. We must reflect on the reasons we avoid participating in the fullness of the diverse community of God. When we do we will learn ways to care for ourselves so we can be fully present. Then, when we find ourselves sitting at God's table with people we never imagined would be there we will discover that, while the labels we allowed to divide us remain, they are no longer the measure by which anyone's welcome at the table is determined. At God's table there are no more boundary-setting rules. At God's table everyone will have a place and everyone will be welcome.

Nikki C. Hardeman

Psalm 134

Psalm 134, the last of the Songs of Ascents, may be read or heard as departing words of blessing for the pilgrims who have come to Jerusalem as they ready themselves to return to their homes in the surrounding countryside. A worship leader calls on the people to offer a final word of blessing to YHWH, whose dwelling place is in Jerusalem.

The word translated "bless" (ברך) occurs over four hundred times in the Hebrew Bible, and its basic meaning is "bend the knee, kneel," a sign of acquiescence to another. Humans bless other humans (Gen 27:30; Deut 33:1; 2 Sam 6:20); humans bless God (Gen 24:48; Josh 22:33; Ps 66:8); God blesses various God-given entities (animals in Gen 1:22; the seventh day in Gen 2:3; bread and water in Gen 23:25); and God blesses humankind (Gen 12:2; Exod 20:24; Ps 115:12).

"Servants [עבד] of the LORD" is a common designation for the whole of the community of ancient Israel. They, along with the ones who "stand in the house of the LORD in the nighttime," are called on to lift their hands and bless YHWH. Isaiah 30:29 and Psalm 3:5 suggest that night vigils were held in the temple in Jerusalem for the purpose of prolonged festive celebration or seeking God's deliverance from life-threatening situations.[128]

In verse 3 the leader invokes God's blessing on the pilgrims, reminding them that God is in Zion (Ps 132:13) and is the "maker of heaven

---

128. See Karel van der Toorn, "Ordeal Procedures in the Psalms and the Passover Meal," *VT* 38 (1988): 427–45, for a full discussion.

Psalm 134:1-3

A Song of Ascents.

¹Come, bless the Lord, all you
  servants of the Lord,
who stand by night in the house of
  the Lord!

²Lift up your hands to the holy place,
  and bless the Lord.
³May the Lord, maker of heaven and
  earth,
bless you from Zion.

and earth," the sustainer God who guides the people from the dwelling place in their midst.[129]

The words of Psalm 134 call on the people to bless Yhwh and then for Yhwh to bless them in a reciprocal relationship. The psalm singers' pilgrimage to Jerusalem is at its end; they have carried out acts of worship, have spoken, and have heard words from God, and thus they ready themselves to return to their lives away from Jerusalem. Psalm 134 is the final doxology or, perhaps better, invocation, calling the people to bless God and God to bless the people.

Worship in the sanctuary of God is a wonderfully moving experience, a time of withdrawal and renewal, but we cannot remain in the sanctuary; we must return to the world. Each worship service in the Christian tradition closes with words of benediction: concluding words that prepare the congregation to leave the sanctuary and return to the world. One memorable benediction is that of John Rowan Claypool IV:

> Depart now
> in the fellowship of God the Father,
> and as you go, remember:
> In the *Goodness* of God
> you were born into this world;
> By the *Grace* of God
> you have been kept
> all the day long,
> even until this hour;
> And by the *Love* of God,
> fully revealed in the face of Jesus,
> you . . . are being . . . *Redeemed*.
> Amen.[130]

---

129. See also Pss 121:2 and 124:8.

130. John R. Claypool IV was pastor of Crescent Hill Baptist Church, Louisville, KY, 1960–1971. For this and other benedictions at Crescent Hill, see http://www.chbc -lky.org/oldsite/benedict.htm.

Psalms 135–137

On Whose Shoulders Are We Standing?

Psalms 135–137, untitled psalms, are located in book 5 after an extensive collection of psalms used at various festival functions in the life of Israel: Psalms 113–118 at Passover; Psalm 119 at Pentecost; Psalms 120–134 at Tabernacles and various other festivals. Just before these psalms are a call to worship, Psalm 111, and a call to response, Psalm 112. Framing all of them are Psalms 108–110 and 138–145, attributed, in their superscriptions, to David, the great sovereign of ancient Israel. He was a prominent figure in books 1 and 2 of the Psalter but is virtually absent in books 3 and 4;[1] he then reappears in book 5, with fourteen of its forty-four psalms attributed to him. The question of the function of Psalms 135–137, and especially 137, in the overall "storyline" of the Psalter has drawn some attention from scholars.

Psalm 137 is an apt concluding word to the Songs of Ascents (Pss 120–134) due primarily to its shared focus with the Songs of Ascents on

---

1. While thirty-nine of the forty-one psalms in book 1 and eighteen of the thirty-one psalms in book 2 are attributed to David, only one psalm in book 3 and two psalms in book 4 are associated with him.

Jerusalem and Zion.[2] J. Clinton McCann writes: "The combination of first-person plural and singular voices, the focus on Jerusalem, and even the length of the psalm make it similar to the Songs of Ascents."[3] He posits: "Given the similarities between Psalms 134 and 135, as well as Psalms 135 and 136, it is likely that Psalms 135–137 form a sort of appendix to the Songs of Ascents."[4] John Goldingay adds: "Like many of the Songs of the Ascents, Ps. 137 represents a unique take on the nature of one of the standard psalm forms; it is a distinct kind of community prayer psalm."[5] In addition, some commentators also read Psalms 135 and 136, along with Psalm 137, as concluding words not just to the Songs of Ascents but to Psalms 111–112 and 113–118. Klaus Seybold maintains that the acrostic Psalm 111 is "theology" and its "twin" acrostic, Psalm 112, is "anthropology," outlining God's good provisions for humanity and humanity's response to those provisions.[6] He proposes that "anthropology" follows in Psalms 113–134 with humanity's words to God in various festival celebrations in the life of Israel, while Psalms 135 and 136 frame the collection with a concluding "theology." Judith Gärtner states that Psalms 135 and 136 "turn out to be key hermeneutical texts in the Psalter, since through them the commitment to Yʜᴡʜ as the one God in creation and history is placed in a significant pivotal point for the formation of the Psalter."[7]

Psalm 135

Psalm 135 evinces a number of ties to the psalms that precede it as well as to Psalm 136.[8] The psalm begins and ends (vv. 1-3 and 21) with

---

2. See Ps 137:1, 3, 5, 6, 7. References to Jerusalem and Zion occur ten times in the Songs of Ascents: Pss 122:2, 3, 6; 125:1, 2; 126;1; 128:5 (2x); 129:5; 132:13.

3. J. Clinton McCann Jr., "The Book of Psalms," *NIB*, vol. 4 (Nashville: Abingdon, 1996), 1227. Psalm 137 is nine verses long and, according to Erich Zenger, the average length of the psalms in the Songs of Ascents, including the lengthy Psalm 132, is 6.7 verses (Frank-Lothar Hossfeld and Erich Zenger, *Psalms 3*, trans. Linda M. Maloney, Hermeneia [Minneapolis: Fortress, 2011], 295).

4. McCann, "The Book of Psalms," 1227.

5. John Goldingay, *Psalms*, vol. 3: *Psalms 90–150*, BCOT (Grand Rapids: Baker Academic, 2008), 601.

6. Klaus Seybold, *Die Psalmen*, HAT (Tübingen: Mohr, 1996), 400.

7. Judith Gärtner, "The Historical Psalms: A Study of Psalms 78; 105; 106; 135; and 136 as Key Hermeneutical Texts in the Psalter," *Hebrew Bible and Ancient Israel* 4: *The Historical Psalms* (Tübingen: Mohr Siebeck, 2015): 373–99, at 398.

8. For a full discussion of Ps 135's ties to Ps 136, see the commentary for Ps 136.

Psalm 135:1-21

¹Praise the LORD!
  . Praise the name of the LORD;
  give praise, O servants of the LORD,
²you that stand in the house of the
    LORD,
  in the courts of the house of our
    God.
³Praise the LORD, for the LORD is good;
  sing to his name, for he is gracious.
⁴For the LORD has chosen Jacob for
    himself,
  Israel as his own possession.
⁵For I know that the LORD is great;

our Lord is above all gods.
⁶Whatever the LORD pleases he does,
  in heaven and on earth,
  in the seas and all deeps.
⁷He it is who makes the clouds rise at
    the end of the earth;
  he makes lightnings for the rain
  and brings out the wind from his
    storehouses.
⁸He it was who struck down the
    firstborn of Egypt,
  both human beings and animals;
⁹he sent signs and wonders

a summons to "praise the LORD" (הללויה), which occurs nine times in Psalms 111–117, opening and/or closing each of them. The verbal root הלל has a range of meanings that include "shout, jubilation, rejoice" and the substantive "song of joy" and is most likely onomatopoetic, a word formed "by imitation of a sound made by or associated with its referent." Thus "hallelujah!" may be imitative of the shouted joy of a worshiper standing in Jerusalem in the presence of God. Verse 1 of Psalm 135 specifies those summoned as "the servants [עבד] of the LORD," as do the opening words of Psalms 113 and 134.[9]

After summoning the worshipers to praise, verses 1-4 of Psalm 135 outline the reasons for doing so. The worshipers are called in verse 1 to praise the "name [שם]" of YHWH; in verse 3 they are admonished to "sing to" the "name"; in verse 13 the psalm singer states, "Your name, O LORD, endures forever." References to the name of YHWH occur no fewer than fifteen times in Psalms 111–118 and the Songs of Ascents (Pss 120–134).[10] Verse 2's words, "you that stand in the house of the LORD, in the courts of the house of our God," echo Psalms 111:1; 116:19; 117:26; 122:1-2; 132:5;

9. Psalm 134 does not summon "the servants of the LORD" to praise the Lord; rather, it summons them to "bless [ברך] the LORD." The final verse of Ps 135 declares, "Blessed be [ברוך] the LORD."

10. See Pss 111:9; 113:2; 115:1; 116:13; 118:10; 122:4; 124:8; 129:8. For a discussion of the significance of "name" in the Hebrew Bible, see the commentary for Ps 113.

Psalm 135:1-21 (cont.)

into your midst, O Egypt,
against Pharaoh and all his
servants.
¹⁰He struck down many nations
and killed mighty kings—
¹¹Sihon, king of the Amorites,
and Og, king of Bashan,
and all the kingdoms of Canaan—
¹²and gave their land as a heritage,
a heritage to his people Israel.

¹³Your name, O LORD, endures forever,
your renown, O LORD, throughout
all ages.
¹⁴For the LORD will vindicate his
people,
and have compassion on his
servants.
¹⁵The idols of the nations are silver
and gold,
the work of human hands.

134:1. Further, verse 3 of Psalm 135 employs the poetic parallel "good [טוב]" and "gracious/pleasant [נעים]" just as Psalm 133:1 does.[11]

Verse 4's notice that God has chosen Jacob/Israel for a possession (סגלה) acts as a prelude for the historical recital by the psalm singer in verses 8-14.[12] Verses 5-7 affirm YHWH's position as greater than "all gods [כל אלהים]," and continue with creation language describing God's sovereignty over heaven and earth, the sea and the deeps, the clouds and lightning, and the wind and the rain.[13] The words "Whatever the LORD pleases [חפץ] he does" in verse 6 recall the words of Psalm 115:3 and prepare the reader or hearer for the words about God's power over the "idols of the nations" in verses 15-18 of Psalm 135, recalling in turn the words of Psalm 115:4-8. Verse 7's repeated "he makes [עשה]" is anticipated by Psalms 115:15; 121:2; 124:8; and 134:3's repeated celebration of God as "the maker [עשה] of heaven and earth."

Verses 8-14 resume the narrative begun in verse 4, affirming God's choosing of Jacob and Israel for a possession by recounting the provisions of God during the exodus from Egypt, the wilderness wandering, and the settlement in the land. God "struck down [נכה] the firstborn of

11. The NRSV renders נעים as "pleasant" in Ps 133:1 and as "gracious" in Ps 135:3.

12. In Exod 19:5 God says to the people, "if you obey my voice and keep my covenant, you shall be my treasured possession [סגלה] out of all the peoples." See also Deut 7:6; 14:2; 26:18.

13. Verse 5's words bring to mind the words of Jethro to Moses in Exod 18:11, "Now I know that great is the LORD, more than all the gods [כל האלהים]."

¹⁶They have mouths, but they do not
speak;
they have eyes, but they do not
see;
¹⁷they have ears, but they do not hear,
and there is no breath in their
mouths.
¹⁸Those who make them
and all who trust them

shall become like them.
¹⁹O house of Israel, bless the LORD!
O house of Aaron, bless the LORD!
²⁰O house of Levi, bless the LORD!
You that fear the LORD, bless the
LORD!
²¹Blessed be the LORD from Zion,
he who resides in Jerusalem.
Praise the LORD!

Egypt" (v. 8; see Exod 12:29); "sent signs and wonders [אתות ומפתים]" (v. 9; see Exod 7–12); "struck down" Sihon, king of the Amorites, and Og, king of Bashan (v. 11; see Num 21); and gave their land as a "heritage" (נחלה) to "his people Israel" (v. 12).[14] The psalm singer then, in verse 13, celebrates YHWH as a god whose "name" (שם) and "renown" (זכר) endure "throughout all ages."

Verses 15-18 are a near parallel to Psalm 115:4-8, depicting the powerlessness of the idol-gods of the nations. Such are the works of human hands, made of silver and gold (v. 15; Ps 115:4); they have mouths but do not speak, eyes but do not see (v. 16; Ps 115:5), ears but do not hear (v. 17; Ps 115:6); they have no breath in them (v. 17; Ps 115:7); and those who make them will become like them (v. 18; Ps 115:8).

Verses 19 and 20 of Psalm 135 then admonish the "house of Israel," the "house of Aaron," the "house of Levi," and "you that fear the LORD" to "bless [ברך] the LORD." Again the words are a near parallel to Psalm 115:9-11, but with two differences. The singer of Psalm 115 calls on three groups of people (Israel, the house of Aaron, and those who fear the Lord) to "trust [בטח] in the LORD." In Psalm 135, however, the psalm singer calls on four groups to "bless the LORD," adding the house of Levi to the groups mentioned in Psalm 115. The additional group named in Psalm 135 may suggest a concern by the singer of the psalm to make a distinction between the house of Aaron and the house of Levi.

---

14. Other references to Sihon and Og are found in Deut 1:4; 2:26–3:11; 29:6; 31:4; Judg 11:19-22.

Excursus: The House of Aaron and the House of Levi

According to the books of Ezekiel and Chronicles and the Priestly account in the book of Numbers the temple personnel were all members of the tribe of Levi, but they were stratified into the Aaronid priests and the Levites, with the Levites subordinate to the priests. In Numbers 3:6 we read:

> Bring the tribe of Levi near and set them before Aaron the priest, that they may serve him. And they shall perform the duties for him and for the whole congregation before the tent of meeting, to do the service of the tabernacle. You shall thus give the Levites to Aaron and to his sons; they are wholly given to him from among the children of Israel.

It seems that originally all members of the tribe of Levi were set aside for special service to the Lord, but those who could show descent directly from Aaron—and from Zadok, according to Ezekiel—occupied higher positions within the cult than the other Levites (see Ezek 44:10-16 and Neh 7:63-65). Nehemiah reestablished the Levites in the Jerusalem temple during his term as provincial governor (see Neh 13:10-13), but the Levites performed the more "menial" chores while the Aaronid priests were the ruling elite of the temple.

Verse 21's reference to Zion and Jerusalem echoes the tenfold mention of them in the Songs of Ascents[15] and affirms that Yhwh "resides" (שׁכֵן) in Jerusalem. The psalm closes by repeating its opening "hallelujah" (הַלְלוּ יָהּ). The Septuagint, however, omits this closing "hallelujah" and places it instead at the beginning of Psalm 136, perhaps to tie it to Psalm 135 and Psalms 111–118.[16]

Psalm 135, a hymn of praise to God sung by a gathered community of worshipers, echoes other words in the Old Testament: Exodus 18:11 and Psalm 115:3-11, as discussed above, as well as Deuteronomy 7:6 in verse 4; Jeremiah 10:13 in verse 7; and Deuteronomy 32:36 in verse 14. Leslie Allen writes:

> In Ps 135 older materials are unashamedly recycled to create a new composition of praise. The harmony of concerted worship, for which

---

15. Pss 122:2, 3, 6; 125:1, 2; 126:1; 128:5 (2x); 129:5; 132:13.

16. For a discussion of the placement of the "hallelujah" openings and closings for these psalms, see the commentary for Ps 115.

it pleads in vv. 19-20, itself finds artistic illustration in the blending of older voices to form a contemporary medley.[17]

John Goldingay maintains that "if ever the term 'mosaic' applied to a psalm, then it is to Ps. 135."[18] Why a mosaic, a gathering together of other traditional texts to speak to the reader or hearer of Psalm 135? According to the storyline of the book of Psalms (see the introduction, pp. l–lv), book 5 relates the story of the postexilic community's quest for identity and survival as a part of a number of vast world empires: the Persians, the Greeks, and then the Romans. The people were once again living in their own land; the temple was rebuilt and worship had resumed; they were free but not free. According to James Sanders, in an article titled "Adaptable for Life: The Nature and Function of Canon," in such situations sometimes "only the old, tried, and true has any real authority. A new story will not do; only a story with old, recognizable elements has the power for life required."[19]

In times of transition, in those times when we wonder what our next step in faith should be, it is often helpful to look back over our past. What words have sustained us in the past? On whose shoulders are we standing? What are the very foundations of our faith? The singers of Psalm 135 employed familiar words and ideas to express their faith in God, for indeed sometimes "only the old, tried, and true" has any real meaning.

Additionally, in the global world in which we live in the twenty-first century the words of Psalm 135 can act as a caution to faith communities to be wary of self-entrenchment, of coming to believe that "their idea of God" is above all other ideas of God. Walter Brueggemann and William H. Bellinger remind us of the dangers of claiming that "our God" is exclusive, what they term "religious patriotism."[20] Samuel Terrien adds:

> The Christian church became an arrogant sect when it took itself to be the New Israel, uniquely chosen and exclusive of other nations or religions. This hymn to the Creator of all humankind [Ps 135] is marred,

17. Leslie C. Allen, *Psalms 101–150*, WBC 21 (Nashville: Thomas Nelson, 2002), 227–28.

18. John Goldingay, *Psalms 90–150*, 577.

19. James A. Sanders, "Adaptable for Life: The Nature and Function of Canon," in *From Sacred Story to Sacred Text* (Philadelphia: Fortress, 1987), 18.

20. Walter Brueggemann and William H. Bellinger Jr., *Psalms*, NCBC (Cambridge: Cambridge University Press, 2014), 567.

like other psalms of Zion, when it yields to the temptation of theological imperialism.[21]

The "old, tried, and true" words of Psalm 135 are a clarion call to remember our roots, roots that give us grounding and vision for the future. But roots, allowed to spread and grow in fertile soil, produce new sprouts and give new life to new generations.

Psalm 136

Each verse of Psalm 136 follows a fixed format: a call to give thanks (הודו) followed by a refrain that states the reason for thanks: "for his [God's] steadfast love [חסד] endures forever."[22] The same refrain occurs in a number of liturgical passages in the Hebrew Bible and in other psalms in the Psalter.[23] The somewhat parallel liturgical refrain formats of Psalm 118:1-4 and the whole of Psalm 136 are an additional argument for the ties between Psalms 135–137 and the psalms that precede them. In Psalm 118 the refrain occurs just after the *athnah* in each verse, as it does in Psalm 136.

The layout of Psalm 136 in the Masoretic Text emphasizes its highly structured format, with the refrain in each verse separated spatially from its call to praise:

v. 1 : כי לעולם חסדו   הודו ליהוה כי־טוב

v. 2 : כי לעולם חסדו   הודו לאלהי האלהים

Verse 1's call to "give thanks [הודו] to the LORD, for he is good [טוב]" echoes the same call in verses 1 and 29 of Psalm 118, further linking the two psalms. Links to Psalm 135 are numerous as well. The phrase "the LORD is good" appears in Psalm 135:3, and verses 2 and 3's declaration that YHWH is the "God of gods" (אלהי האלהים) and "Lord of lords" (אדני האדנים) recalls Psalm 135:5. Verses 4-9 of Psalm 136 recount the creative doings (עשׂה) of God, as does Psalm 135:6-7: the heavens and the earth, the waters, the great lights, and the sun and moon and stars. The singer of Psalm 136 employs participial forms in verses 4-7, conveying to

---

21. Samuel Terrien, *The Psalms: Strophic Structure and Theological Commentary*, ECC (Grand Rapids: Eerdmans, 2003), 859.

22. For a discussion of חסד, see the commentary for Ps 118.

23. See 1 Chr 16:34; 2 Chr 5:13; 7:3; 20:21; Ezra 3:11; Pss 100:5; 106:1; 107:1; 118:1-4, 29.

Psalm 136:1-26

¹O give thanks to the LORD, for he is good,
for his steadfast love endures forever.
²O give thanks to the God of gods,
for his steadfast love endures forever.
³O give thanks to the Lord of lords,
for his steadfast love endures forever;
⁴who alone does great wonders,

for his steadfast love endures forever;
⁵who by understanding made the heavens,
for his steadfast love endures forever;
⁶who spread out the earth on the waters,
for his steadfast love endures forever;
⁷who made the great lights,

the reader or hearer God's ongoing creative work in the world: "doing, making" (עשׂה) in verses 4, 5, and 7 and "spreading out" (רקע) in verse 6. While in Psalm 135 the verb עשׂה occurs in the perfect aspect in verses 6 and 7's celebration of God's creative work, verse 7's "makes rise" (מעלה) and "brings out" (מוצא) are participles, affirming, as does Psalm 136, the ongoing nature of God's creative work.[24]

Verse 4 of Psalm 136 describes God as the one "who alone does great wonders" (נפלאות). The Psalter uses the word often in reference to the Israelites' deliverance from Egypt and God's provision for them in the wilderness wandering.[25] Its occurrence in verse 4, prefacing the psalm's creation language, suggests that God's creative work is as much a "great wonder" as is God's work in Israel's history. It thus provides a tie from verses 4-9 to verses 10-22 of the psalm, where, in language nearly identical to that found in Psalm 135:8-12, the psalm singer recounts the acts of God on behalf of the Israelites during the exodus, wilderness wandering, and settlement in the land. While Psalm 135 does not employ participles in its historical recounting, Psalm 136 does, further confirming the close connection between God's creative and sustaining work in the world.

"Struck/struck down" (נכה) in verses 10 and 17, "brought out" (יצא) in verse 11, "split" (גזר) in verse 13, and "led" (הלך) in verse 17 are participles. Both Psalms 135 and 136, though, compare God "striking down" (נכה) the firstborn in Egypt with the "striking down" of "mighty" (עצום,

24. See Gärtner, "The Historical Psalms," 395.
25. See Pss 78:4; 86:10; 105:2, 5; 106:2.

Psalm 136:1-26 (cont.)

for his steadfast love endures
forever;
⁸the sun to rule over the day,
for his steadfast love endures
forever;
⁹the moon and stars to rule over the
night,
for his steadfast love endures
forever;
¹⁰who struck Egypt through their
firstborn,
for his steadfast love endures
forever;
¹¹and brought Israel out from among
them,
for his steadfast love endures
forever;

¹²with a strong hand and an
outstretched arm,
for his steadfast love endures
forever;
¹³who divided the Red Sea in two,
for his steadfast love endures
forever;
¹⁴and made Israel pass through the
midst of it,
for his steadfast love endures
forever;
¹⁵but overthrew Pharaoh and his
army in the Red Sea,
for his steadfast love endures
forever;
¹⁶who led his people through the
wilderness,

Ps 135:10) and "great" (גדול, Ps 136:17) kings, and both psalms name Sihon and Og as two of those "struck down."[26] In verses 23-25, paralleling Psalm 135:13-14, the psalm singer recalls God's remembrance and rescue in the past (vv. 23-24) and affirms, once again employing a participial form, God's ongoing provision for the people in the present with verse 25's affirmation that God "gives [נתן] food to all flesh [בשר]."

The affirmation in verse 25 may at first glance seem out of place in a celebration of God as "God of gods" and "Lord of lords" (vv. 2-3) and as creator and deliverer (vv. 10-22), but food is a theme that, while not common in the Psalter, is especially prominent in the Songs of Ascents. Psalm 126:5-6 celebrates reaping the harvest food; in Psalm 127:2 the reader or hearer is cautioned against "eating the bread of anxious toil"; Psalm 128:2 promises that the one who "fears the LORD" will eat "the fruit of the labor of your hands"; Psalm 129:7 states that the wicked will not reap a crop sufficient to fill their hands; and in Psalm 132:15 God promises abundant food for the poor. James Limburg further reflects on Psalm 136's closing description of God, writing: "Psalm 136 puts the gift of daily food on the same plane as the great acts of creation,

---

26. Other references to Sihon and Og are found in Deut 1:4; 2:26–3:11; 29:6; 31:4; Judg 11:19-22.

for his steadfast love endures
forever;
¹⁷who struck down great kings,
for his steadfast love endures
forever;
¹⁸and killed famous kings,
for his steadfast love endures
forever;
¹⁹Sihon, king of the Amorites,
for his steadfast love endures
forever;
²⁰and Og, king of Bashan,
for his steadfast love endures
forever;
²¹and gave their land as a heritage,
for his steadfast love endures
forever;

²²a heritage to his servant Israel,
for his steadfast love endures
forever.
²³It is he who remembered us in our
low estate,
for his steadfast love endures
forever;
²⁴and rescued us from our foes,
for his steadfast love endures
forever;
²⁵who gives food to all flesh,
for his steadfast love endures
forever.
²⁶O give thanks to the God of
heaven,
for his steadfast love endures
forever.

exodus, and conquest."[27] A major role for women in the ancient Near East was to provide the food that daily sustained their families. Carol Meyers categorizes women of the household as "bread-producers," an undertaking that involved converting the grain to flour, preparing the dough, and baking the bread. Additionally, women were most likely responsible for drink production in the form of brewing beer, and for drying foods such as fruits, legumes, and herbs for future use.[28] The promise by God of abundant food for all flesh may be seen as another feminine image of YHWH. Psalm 136 has been designated "The Great Hallel," and the Babylonian Talmud offers this explanation: "And why is it called 'Great Hallel' (הלל הגדול)? Rabbi Johanan says: 'Because the Holy One, blessed be he, is enthroned on high in the universe and yet gives food to all creatures.' "[29]

Psalm 136 ends as it begins, forming an *inclusio* around the psalm but with something of a twist. While verse 1 calls on worshipers to "give thanks [הודו] to the LORD for he is good [טוב]," verse 26 calls them to "give

27. James Limburg, *Psalms*, WBiC (Louisville: Westminster John Knox, 2000), 464.
28. Carol Meyers, *Rediscovering Eve: Ancient Israelite Women in Context* (Oxford: Oxford University Press, 2013), 128–32.
29. b. Pesaḥ, 118a.

thanks [הודו] to the God of heaven [אל השמים]." John Goldingay suggests that the designation "God of heavens" expands the concept of a God who is "good" to Israel to the God of creation who is "good" to all.[30] In an interesting insight Erhard Gerstenberger points out that the creation/historical recitation of Psalm 136 encompasses twenty-two verses (vv. 4-25), the number of letters in the Hebrew alphabet.[31] If Gerstenberger's insight is accepted we may perhaps understand Psalm 136 as imaginatively imitating Psalms 111 and 112, the alphabetic acrostics that introduce the festival psalms in the middle of book 5 (Pss 113–134), thus forming, along with Psalm 135, an *inclusio* around the grouping of psalms.

Those who shaped the Psalter into its final form may have purposely placed Psalms 135 and 136 after Psalms 111–118 and the Songs of Ascents. James L. Mays describes the two psalms as "partners in praise to resume the 'praise of the LORD' and 'O give thanks to the LORD' psalms in Psalms 111–118, after the interval of prayer for the law of the LORD (Psalm 119) and the pilgrim voices of the songs of ascents."[32] J. Clinton McCann suggests that the two psalms "form an appendix to the Songs of Ascents" and maintains that "it is as if the editors of the Psalter intended for Psalms 135–136 to articulate the praise invited by Ps 134:1-2."[33] John Goldingay further opines that Psalms 135 and 136 provide the "reasons or content" for the worship that Psalm 134 calls for but in which no "reasons or content" are given.[34] And Erich Zenger asserts that the two psalms "introduce the historical-theological perspective that was lacking in the Pilgrim Psalter. . . . In a sense, they offer the reasons for the pilgrimage to Jerusalem, a reminder of how the pilgrimages became possible."[35]

Psalm 136 summons the faithful to a repetitious communal response to the actions of God on their behalf—"for his steadfast love [חסד] endures forever." Leslie Allen writes of "the regular heartbeat of the congregational refrain" in the psalm.[36] A similar liturgical structure can be observed in a form of Psalm 145 included in the Dead Sea Scroll 11QPsa. Each verse of the psalm is followed by the refrain "Blessed is God and blessed is his name for all time," giving the psalm the following form:

---

30. Goldingay, *Psalms 90–150*, 596.

31. Erhard S. Gerstenberger, *Psalms, Part 2, and Lamentations*, FOTL 15 (Grand Rapids: Eerdmans, 2001), 385.

32. James L. Mays, *Psalms*, IBC (Louisville: Westminster John Knox, 1994), 415.

33. McCann, "The Book of Psalms," 1219.

34. Goldingay, *Psalms 90–150*, 577.

35. Hossfeld and Zenger, *Psalms 3*, 500, 509.

36. Allen, *Psalms 101–150*, 234.

I will extol you my god the King; and I will bless your name for all time and beyond.

Blessed is God and blessed is his name forever.

Every day I will bless you, and I will praise your name for all time and beyond.

Blessed is God and blessed is his name forever.

Great is the LORD and highly to be praised, and his greatness is unsearchable.

Blessed is God and blessed is his name forever. (vv. 1-3)

Psalm 136 is a powerful liturgical composition (as is Psalm 145 in 11QPs[a]). In *Abiding Astonishment*, a study of Psalms 78, 105, 106, and 136, Walter Brueggemann reminds us of the power of liturgy. Liturgical recitals are "world building": "They create, evoke, suggest, and propose a network of symbols, metaphors, images, memories and hopes so that 'the world,' in each successive generation, is perceived, experienced, and practiced in a specific way."[37]

As the singers of Psalm 136 enunciated the words of the psalm they brought the past powerfully into the present with repeated use of participial verbal forms. God who created is creating. God who delivered is delivering. God who sustained is sustaining. Christian liturgical acts serve the same purpose. With each recitation of the Lord's Prayer, the Apostles' Creed, the Peace of Christ, we bring the past redemptive acts of God powerfully into the present.

But those redemptive acts on God's part fall on "deaf ears" for those who do not see the actions of God in their lives. Where is the god who "brought Israel out" (v. 11), "overthrew" (v. 15), "led" (v. 16), "struck down" (v. 17), and "gave . . . a heritage" (vv. 21-22), the god who "remembered" and "rescued" and "gives food" (vv. 23-25)?

As this author writes these words thousands of people fleeing from oppression, gang violence, corrupt governments, and abject poverty are making their way on a migrant march from Central America through Mexico to the southern borders of the United States. Imagine the words of Psalm 136 on their lips as they walk, day after day: "O give thanks to the God of gods, for his steadfast love endures forever; . . . who led the people through the wilderness, for his steadfast love endures forever; . . . and gave their land as a heritage . . . and rescued us from our foes . . . who gives food to all flesh, for his steadfast love endures forever."

---

37. Walter Brueggemann, *Abiding Astonishment: Psalms, Modernity, and the Making of History*, LCBI (Louisville: Westminster John Knox, 1991), 21, 26.

Signs of God's Love and Majesty

It is hard sometimes to imagine how big God's love for us is. Many times I wonder why God loves me when I am a sinful human being. But then I recall the words of 2 Corinthians12:8-9, that God's grace is sufficient for us and God's power is made perfect in our human weakness. God loves me because of grace even though I am a sinner. Grace is one of the many means through which God shows love to humanity. In the words of Psalm 136 we are told that God shows love to humanity through creation, through power, through leadership, and through mercy. The psalm opens in verses 1-3 with a reminder to humanity that we owe gratitude to God because of God's goodness and majesty.

Verses 4-9 celebrate God's majesty and love for us through creation. Verse 4 introduces this section of the psalm with the declaration that God does "great wonders." I come from Malawi, where many people rely on agricultural produce, a source of both food and income, in order to sustain themselves. Verse 5 tells us that God made the heavens. The heavens are the source of rain that waters the crops that sustain my people. Verse 6 tells us that God made the earth, where the crops are grown and human beings and animals live and thrive. In verse 8 we are reminded that God also made the sun, thought by others in the ancient Near East to be a

god in its own right, but given by God to the earth and humanity to allow plants to grow and life to flourish. God also gave the moon and stars to the earth (v. 9) as a source of light to help guide humanity through the night. The light helps us to not fear the terror of night (Ps 91:5) as we are able to see what is ahead of us and around us.

Verses 10-15 remind us that God had power over the events in the lives of our ancestors in the faith who were oppressed and enslaved in Egypt. I wonder sometimes why God delivered the Israelites but allows other people to suffer through oppression, discrimination, marginalization, stigmatization, and much more. At the same time, the end of apartheid in South Africa and the breakthroughs in the fight against the HIV pandemic, particularly in terms of acceptance of and medication for those who are living with HIV, are two examples of God's power over events in the lives of humanity.

Verses 16-22 assure us that God leads us through the most difficult times. The journey from Egypt to the land of promise was not easy for the Israelites, but God led them all the way. It is only up to us to believe in God and to trust that God will lead us to become the person each of us was created to be. God's love and majesty will lead us to the great things prepared for us.

The last part of Psalm 136, verses 23-26, reminds us that

God's mercy ("steadfast love" in the NRSV) is the driving force behind what God does on behalf of humanity and, indeed, on behalf of creation. God remembers, protects, and provides for creation even when creation falls short of deserving mercy time and again. Psalm 136 reminds humanity, and indeed all of creation, that God's creation (vv. 4-9), power (vv. 10-15), leadership (vv. 16-22), and mercy (vv. 23-25) bear witness to God's unlimited care for the created world and for humanity.

William Chisa

Psalm 137

Richard Clifford writes that "Psalm 137 has the distinction of having one of the most beloved opening lines and the most horrifying closing line of any psalm."[38] This psalm is classified as a community lament, but additionally its content places it within a group of psalms in the Psalter called "imprecatory."[39] In imprecatory psalms the singers invoke the wrath of God upon a foe. In nearly every psalm in the Psalter that laments oppression by a foe or adversary, the foe is not named. In Psalm 137, though, the foe is clearly identified as Babylon, indicating that the psalm most likely dates to during or just after the Babylonian exile (596–538 BCE).[40]

Verses 1-3 establish the setting of the psalm, what Erich Zenger calls "a vivid topography of the exilic situation."[41] The psalm singers are sitting and weeping "beside the rivers of Babylon." Verses 1 and 2 begin with the same Hebrew word, עַל, a preposition with a range of meanings that carry the basic idea of being "over, upon, on, at." The psalm singers are "upon/at [עַל] the rivers of Babylon" (v. 1) and they hang their harps "upon [עַל] the willow trees [of Babylon]" (v. 2). The repetition of "there [שָׁם]" in verses 1 and 3 emphasizes the location of the psalm's setting. James L. Mays describes the double use of the word as "pointing a verbal finger."[42]

38. Richard J. Clifford, *Psalms 73–150*, AOTC (Nashville: Abingdon, 2003), 275. Brueggemann and Bellinger, *Psalms*, 573, state further that the psalm is "familiar to contemporary readers both because of its stunning beginning and its troubling ending."

39. The imprecatory psalms are Pss 12, 58, 83, 94, 109, 137, and 139. A number of other psalms contain imprecatory language. For a full discussion of imprecatory psalms, see the commentary for Ps 109.

40. See the comments by Erich Zenger in Hossfeld and Zenger, *Psalms 3*, 513–14.

41. Ibid., 514.

42. Mays, *Psalms*, 422.

Psalm 137:1-9

¹By the rivers of Babylon—
   there we sat down and there we
      wept
   when we remembered Zion.
²On the willows there
   we hung up our harps.
³For there our captors
   asked us for songs,
and our tormentors asked for mirth,
     saying,
   "Sing us one of the songs of Zion!"
⁴How could we sing the LORD's song
   in a foreign land?
⁵If I forget you, O Jerusalem,
   let my right hand wither!
⁶Let my tongue cling to the roof of my
     mouth,

   if I do not remember you,
   if I do not set Jerusalem
     above my highest joy.
⁷Remember, O LORD, against the
     Edomites
   the day of Jerusalem's fall,
how they said, "Tear it down! Tear it
     down!
   Down to its foundations!"
⁸O daughter Babylon, you
     devastator!
   Happy shall they be who pay you
     back
   what you have done to us!
⁹Happy shall they be who take your
     little ones
   and dash them against the rock!

Moreover, the repetition of the first-person-plural suffix נו nine times in verses 1-3 evokes what Leslie Allen describes as a "ring of pathos."[43]

The word translated "captor" in verse 3 is an active participle derived from the Hebrew root שבה, which means "make prisoners of war, lead into captivity."[44] The word for "tormentors" here is also an active participle from the Hebrew root תלל. It is an unusual root in biblical Hebrew, occurring in the participial form only in Psalm 137 and in other verbal forms in eight places in the Hebrew Bible; it is translated variously as "deal falsely" (Exod 8:25), "mock" (Judg 16:10), and "deceive" (Job 13:9; Jer 9:4). The Septuagint translates "tormentors" in verse 3 as οἱ αἰχμαλωτεύσαντες ἡμᾶς ("the ones leading us away"), while the Aramaic Targum renders it "our plunderers."

The psalm singers lament that their "captors" and "tormentors" ask them for "songs" and "mirth," specified more exactly in the last colon of verse 3 as "one of the songs of Zion [שיר ציון]." שיר is the word used in the superscription of each of the Songs of Ascents (Pss 120–134). The words of the captors and tormentors in verse 3 may be likened to the words of taunters in other psalms who say to the psalmist, "Where is your God?" (Pss 42:3, 10; 79:10).

43. Allen, *Psalms 101–150*, 241.
44. Benedikt Otzen, "שבה (šāḇâ)," in *TDOT*, 14:286–94, at 286–87.

Verse 4 is the thematic centerpiece of Psalm 137. There the psalm sing-ers cry out, "How [אֵיךְ] could we sing?" אֵיךְ is commonly used to intro-duce words of mourning in the Hebrew Bible (see Lam 1:1; 2:1; 4:1; Hos 11:8; 2 Sam 1:25). Interestingly, the psalm singers transform the words of their captors' demand—"sing us one of the songs of Zion"—into "how could we sing the LORD's song?" Zion was the dwelling place of the God of the Israelites; any song of Zion was thus a song of YHWH, and sing-ing a song of Zion was not possible in a "foreign land [אַדְמַת נֵכָר]." Erich Zenger said, however, that the words of the psalm do not mean that one could not sing YHWH songs outside the Land. Rather, the use of the term אַדְמַת נֵכָר indicates "foreign soil," the "soil" of foreign gods, in this case Marduk, the primary god of the Babylonians. He writes:

> A YHWH song, sung by the conquered and deported YHWH-musicians for the entertainment of the adherents of Marduk, in the midst of Baby-lon, was simply impossible—especially if the deportees wanted to hold fast to *their* faith in YHWH and remain true to their memory of Zion.[45]

Verses 5 and 6, characterized as an "oath," are the only portion of Psalm 137 sung by an individual voice. The mingling of individual and commu-nity voices is not unusual in lament psalms.[46] An individual, speaking on behalf of the community of singers, voices three oaths, all formulated with the particle אִם, which introduces the *protasis* of a real conditional oath—one that is capable of being fulfilled.[47] The three אִם clauses in verses 5 and 6—"If [אִם] I forget you, O Jerusalem," "if [אִם] I do not remember you," and "if [אִם] I do not set Jerusalem above my highest joy"—along with the twofold reference to "Jerusalem," form an *inclusio* around the *apodoses* of the *protases* of verses 5 and 6: "may my right hand forget" and "may my tongue cleave to the roof of my mouth." If the psalmist forgets (שׁכח) Jerusalem, then the psalmist's right hand will forget (שׁכח), and if the psalmist forgets, she will be unable to speak. The terms "right hand" and "tongue" may be thought of as a merism, referring to all human action, thus condemning completely the one who forgets Jerusalem. Other scholars maintain that the reference is to the "right hand" that strums the harp and the "tongue" that sings, meaning that the psalmist vows never to sing again if she forgets Zion.[48]

---

45. Hossfeld and Zenger, *Psalms 3*, 516.

46. The same phenomenon may be observed in book 5, in Pss 108 and 123.

47. Bruce K. Waltke and Michael P. O'Connor, *An Introduction to Biblical Hebrew Syntax* (Winona Lake, IN: Eisenbrauns, 1990), 636.

48. See Goldingay, *Psalms 90–150*, 605; Brueggemann and Bellinger, *Psalms*, 574; Hossfeld and Zenger, *Psalms 3*, 517; McCann, "The Book of Psalms," 1228. For a dis-cussion of the word "remember" (זכר), see the commentary for Ps 119:49-56.

In verses 7-9 the community of psalm singers reunites with the individual psalmist and voices the imprecatory words of Psalm 137. They begin with a plea to YHWH to "remember" (זכר), echoing their pledge to "not forget" (שׁכח) and to "remember" (זכר) in verses 5 and 6. In verse 7 the singers call on God to remember the children (בנים) of Edom. According to the book of Genesis the Edomites are descended from Esau, the twin brother of Jacob, son of Isaac and grandson of Abraham (Gen 25:30), and the book of Obadiah states that the Edomites took part in the sacking of the temple and destruction of Jerusalem by the Babylonians in 587.

Verses 8 and 9 are the culmination of the imprecatory words of the psalm. Verse 8 calls "daughter [בת] Babylon" the "devastator" (שׁדד) to account. The biblical text regularly uses the term "daughter" (בת) in reference to Jerusalem and to cities that surround a primary or capital city.[49] The word "happy" (אשרי) introduces two phrases in verses 8 and 9. The word occurs twenty-six times in the Psalter, most often as the introductory word of a wisdom psalm.[50] Only in Psalm 137, though, does it introduce imprecatory words.

The imprecatory words of Psalm 137 cannot be tamed; they are harsh and venomous. Perhaps a close study of the words in their Hebrew context can help us to understand their full import. The word translated "pay you back" in verse 8 is ישׁלם, derived from the Hebrew root שׁלם, which means "peace, wholeness, or well-being," and in its verbal idea "complete, repay." It is most probably employed as a play on words with Jerusalem (ירושׁלם). Thus those who "pay back" Babylon for what was done to them are restoring the "wholeness" or "well-being" of Jerusalem. That payback, though, involves the dashing of "little ones" (עולל) against rocks. The Hebrew word means "children and nursing infants," so there is no equivocation about the sentiment. Perhaps the reader or hearer may understand the words in the context of the condemnatory cry against "daughter Babylon," the "mother" of such children. Or perhaps, as Erich Zenger suggests, these words may evoke "the royal house in Babylon, whose continuation is to be thwarted through the death of the children of 'daughter Babylon.' That the aim of making 'daughter Babylon' 'childless' is to put an end to its 'royal rule' is a central perspective also."[51]

---

49. See, for instance, Isa 1:8; 23:10; Mic 1:13; 4:10; Pss 9:14; 45:12.
50. See, for instance, Pss 1:1; 2:12; 112:1; 119:1; 127:5; 128:1, 2; 144:15; 146:5.
51. Hossfeld and Zenger, *Psalms 3*, 520.

However we choose to interpret the words of verse 9, there is no way to soften or alter their sentiment. And we should not try to do so. Psalm 137 is a heartfelt lament sung to God, asking for God's justice in the face of absolute despair and hopelessness. It is a song of revenge sung on behalf of the victims of Babylon's destruction. Psalm 137, along with the other imprecatory psalms in the Psalter, reminds us of the basic human desire for revenge when we or those we love have been wronged. God does not ask us to suppress those emotions but rather to speak about them in plain and heartfelt terms. In the speaking out we give voice to the pain, the feelings of helplessness, and the burning anger. In speaking out to God we give the pain, the helplessness, and the burning anger to God, trusting that God's justice will be done. Not to remember and not to speak is to suppress and acquiesce. J. Clinton McCann interprets the words of Psalm 137 in the context of the Holocaust (the *shoah*). He writes:

> To remember is painful; grief is always painful. To remember is unsettling; anger always unsettles. But to remember is also to resist the same thing's happening again. To remember is to choose to live and be faithful to God's purpose of life for all people.[52]

Charles Spurgeon wrote this about Psalm 137:

> Let those find fault with it who have never seen their temple burned, their city ruined, their wives ravished, and their children slain; they might not, perhaps, be so velvet-mouthed if they had suffered after this fashion.[53]

And Erich Zenger says this about the psalm:

> Psalm 137 is not the song of people who have the power to effect a violent change in their situation of suffering, nor is it the battle cry of terrorists. . . . It is an attempt, in the face of the most profound humiliation and helplessness, to suppress the primitive human lust for violence in one's own heart, by surrendering *everything* to God—a God whose word of judgment is presumed to be so universally just that even those who pray the psalm submit themselves to it.[54]

---

52. McCann, "The Book of Psalms," 1229.

53. Charles H. Spurgeon, *The Treasury of David: Spurgeon's Classic Work on the Psalms* (Grand Rapids: Kregel, 2004), 627.

54. Erich Zenger, *A God Vengeance? Understanding the Psalms of Divine Wrath*, trans. Linda M. Maloney (Louisville: Westminster John Knox, 1996), 48.

"If I Forget You, O Jerusalem"

Psalm 137 is, for me, an expression of a cry for help and a longing for liberation from the bondages of patriarchy that have left me enslaved physically, psychologically, and spiritually. Verses 1-2 say, "By the rivers of Babylon—there we sat down and there we wept when we remembered Zion. On the willows there we hung up our harps. For there our captors asked us for songs, and our tormentors asked for mirth." These words remind me of how we women in South Africa weep as we are being abused physically, emotionally, and spiritually every day. It is even more difficult for young women like myself who live in rural societies, where the traditional patriarchal culture and its beliefs and customs are still strongly embraced. Women are expected to submit joyfully and obediently to what is so often an oppressive and harmful cultural system as "the natural way of things." I remember reading these verses of Psalm 137 at a time when I was labeled as rebellious in my church because I asked a lot of questions and rejected some church practices I felt were unjust.

The unjust and oppressive world in which I was living was my own Babylon, while Jerusalem was the image to me of how the church ought to be. To me church should be an inclusive place that allows all its members, regardless of their gender, to be active and to exercise their spiritual gifts. Church should be a place where sins committed by women are seen in the same way as and not as more shameful than sins committed by men. In the end, church should be a place where everyone feels a sense of belonging and safety.

In verses 4 and 5 of the psalm the singers ask, "How could we sing the LORD's song in a foreign land? If I forget you, O Jerusalem, let my right hand wither! Let my tongue cling to the roof of my mouth . . . if I do not set Jerusalem above my highest joy." When I read this I think to myself: "How do society and the church expect us women to sing when we are being oppressed and continually told by the patriarchal society that it is the natural way of things?" I cannot believe that the rules and norms of patriarchal society are "the natural way of things." I cannot forget Jerusalem—the way church ought to be! When I voiced these concerns in my church I became an outcast, and, as painful as that was, I was never ready to conform and lose myself.

To me, seeking justice and equality is not being disobedient to God. Jerusalem remains my greatest joy. Jerusalem is a church where everyone is treated equally. If I fail to hold on to this idea of equality, justice, and having a sense of belonging in the church, then indeed let my tongue stick to the roof of my mouth and leave me unable to speak. I am willing to be labeled a rebellious outcast to uphold these ideals.

Verses 7-9 of Psalm 137 cry out: "Remember, O Lord, against the Edomites the day of Jerusalem's fall, how they said, 'Tear it down! Tear it down! Down to its foundations!' O daughter Babylon, you devastator! Happy shall they be who pay you back what you have done to us! Happy shall they be who take your little ones and dash them against the rock!" I still have faith that patriarchy will be destroyed in South Africa just as apartheid was, though we still have a long way to go in the quest for racial equality.

Patriarchy has done so much damage in our society, destroying women but also destroying men. Men may appear to be strong, but they are fragile human beings like the rest of us. South Africa has the highest rate of femicide in the world, caused by the physical, psychological, and spiritual dominance of men over women in our society. Imagine those men who genuinely love and respect their mothers, sisters, wives, and daughters and yet condone and practice this dominance and abuse in order to be accepted into the patriarchal society. The toll on women is tragically obvious in the number of women murdered by men, but there must be a tremendous toll on these men as well.

It is painfully clear that the patriarchal system in South Africa has a negative impact on both women and men, and thus the system with its roots in religion, culture, and traditions needs to be "smashed against the rock." We must create new social systems that will be inclusive for all and oppressive for none, systems that do not discriminate based on gender, race, or background. Most important, we must build churches in which everyone feels welcome and knows their voices and their questions will be heard and respected. Then, and only then, can we truly celebrate being in the midst of Jerusalem.

Yenziwe Shabalala

Psalms 138–145

All Flesh Will Bless God's Holy Name

Psalms 138–145, all ascribed to David, form a closing chorus of words of David in book 5. Together with Psalms 108–110 they create an *inclusio* around the acrostic Psalms 111–112 and the festival Psalms 113–134. Additionally, Psalms 138 and 145 share no fewer than thirteen terms and verbal roots, forming an envelope structure around this last Davidic collection: "give thanks/praise" (ידה, 138:1, 2, 4; 145:10); "name" (שם, 138:2; 145:1, 2, 21); "steadfast love" (חסד, 138:2, 8; 145:8, 10, 13, 17); "faithfulness/faithful/sincerely" (אמת, 138:2; 145:13, 18); "exalted/great/abounding" (גדל, 138:2, 5; 145:3, 6, 8); "cry out/call on" (קרא, 138:3; 145:18); "hear" (שמע, 138:4; 145:19); "glory/glorious" (כבוד, 138:5; 145:5, 11, 12); "extol/be high" (רום, 138:6; 145:1); "hand" (יד, 138:7, 8; 145:16); "forever" (לעולם, 138:8; 145:1, 21); "deliver/save" (ישע, 138:7; 145:19); "work/make/do/deed" (עשה, 138:8; 145:4, 9, 10, 13, 17).

Michael Goulder divides the whole of book 5 into three major sections, Psalms 107–119, Psalms 120–134, and Psalms 135–150. He sees the Songs of Ascents (Pss 120–134) as the centerpiece of the book, with the surrounding psalms related to one another in the following ways:

105–106	Historical Psalms	135–136
107	Return from Exile	137
108–110	David Psalms	138–145
111, 112	Alphabetic Psalms	145
113–118	Hallel Psalms	146–150
119	Praise of the Law	1
Songs of Ascents (Pss 120–134)		

Goulder justifies the inclusion of Psalm 1 in the suggested arrangement thus: "We might therefore bear in mind the possibility that the Jews of the fourth century BCE viewed the Psalter as a cycle, in the same way that the Torah is traditionally read as a cycle."[1]

Within the last Davidic collection, Psalms 138–143 are psalms of an individual (classified as either individual hymns of thanksgiving or individual laments); Psalm 144 is a royal psalm; Psalm 145 is a wisdom acrostic. J. Clinton McCann maintains that "the core of this collection consists of psalms of lament, culminating in Psalm 144," which is classified as a royal psalm but is "a royal lament."[2] McCann continues:

> Thus, near the end of both Books IV and V, there are royal laments [Psalms 101 and 144] . . . that effectively call to mind the ongoing theological crisis of exile. Significantly, Psalm 145 responds to Psalm 144 by affirming God's steadfast love. . . . Actually, Psalm 145 proves to be transitional. Not only does it conclude the Davidic collection, forming with Psalm 138 an envelope of praise around a core of laments, but it also anticipates Psalms 146–150.[3]

We turn now to an examination of each of the psalms in the final Davidic collection in the Psalter.

Psalm 138

Psalm 138 is traditionally classified as an individual hymn of thanksgiving, in which an individual singer praises God for goodness to or on

1. Michael D. Goulder, *The Psalms of the Return (Book V, Psalms 107–150)*, JSOTSup 258 (Sheffield: Sheffield Academic, 1998), 16.
2. J. Clinton McCann Jr., "The Book of Psalms," *NIB*, vol. 4 (Nashville: Abingdon, 1996), 664.
3. Ibid.

Psalm 138:1-8

Of David.

¹I give you thanks, O LORD, with my
　　whole heart;
　　before the gods I sing your praise;
²I bow down toward your holy temple
　　and give thanks to your name for
　　　　your steadfast love and
　　　　your faithfulness;
　　for you have exalted your name
　　　　and your word
　　above everything.
³On the day I called, you answered
　　me,
　　you increased my strength of soul.
⁴All the kings of the earth shall praise
　　you, O LORD,
　　for they have heard the words of
　　　　your mouth.

⁵They shall sing of the ways of the
　　LORD,
　　for great is the glory of the LORD.
⁶For though the LORD is high, he
　　regards the lowly;
　　but the haughty he perceives from
　　　　far away.
⁷Though I walk in the midst of trouble,
　　you preserve me against the
　　　　wrath of my enemies;
　　you stretch out your hand,
　　and your right hand delivers me.
⁸The LORD will fulfill his purpose for
　　me;
　　your steadfast love, O LORD,
　　endures forever.
　　Do not forsake the work of your
　　　　hands.

behalf of that person, usually for deliverance from some trying situation.[4] Hermann Gunkel describes the occasion on which such words to God may have been offered: "A person is saved out of great distress, and now with a grateful heart he brings a thank offering to [YHWH]; it was customary that at a certain point in the sacred ceremony he would offer a song in which he expresses his thanks."[5]

In verses 1-3 second-person pronouns occur eleven times, as the psalmist addresses God directly in an exuberant burst of praise. The psalmist says in verse 1 that she sings her praise "before the gods" (אלהים).[6] Psalms 135 and 136 also talk of "the gods." In Psalm 135:5 the singer declares, "the LORD is great; our Lord is above all gods," and in Psalm 136:2-3 we read: "give thanks to the God of gods . . . give thanks to the Lord

4. For a discussion of the elements of an individual hymn of thanksgiving, see Nancy L. deClaissé-Walford, *Introduction to the Psalms: A Song from Ancient Israel* (St. Louis: Chalice Press, 2004), 21–23.

5. Hermann Gunkel, *The Psalms: A Form-Critical Introduction*, trans. Thomas M. Horner (Philadelphia: Fortress, 1967), 17.

6. The LXX translates אלהים in v. 1 as "angels" (ἀγγέλων).

of lords." In Psalm 138, however, the psalm singer is not only claiming Yhwh's sovereignty over any claimants to the appellation "god" but she is doing so "before [in the presence of] the gods." John Goldingay suggests: "Perhaps there is a confrontational edge to the 'before' (cf. 23:5), which would fit the references to the gods in 135:5; 136:2-3."[7] Erich Zenger maintains, however, that "the place indication here lacks any hint of a polemic relationship of the gods to the one and only God Yhwh"; rather, it reflects the reality of the Diaspora situation: "on foreign soil, in the presence of other gods."[8]

In verse 2 of the psalm the singer continues her words of thanks, this time to the "name" (שם) of God because of God's "steadfast love" (חסד) and "faithfulness" (אמת).[9] "Steadfast love" (חסד) is used often in parallel constructions with "faithfulness" (אמת). These are two of the self-descriptive words given by God to Moses on Mount Sinai (Exod 34:6-8).[10] In Psalm 85:10 the psalm singer announces:

> Steadfast love and faithfulness will meet;
> righteousness and peace will kiss each other.

The verbal root of אמת is אמן, meaning "be firm, be reliable, be permanent," and is the root from which the word "amen" is derived.

The psalm singer states her reason for giving thanks, singing, and bowing down (vv. 1, 2) with verse 2's words: "for you have exalted your name and your word above everything." The word translated in verse 2 as "word" is not the usual term for "word" in the Hebrew Bible (דבר). Rather, the psalmist refers to God's אמרה, a word derived from the verbal root אמר that means "say." A more accurate translation for אמרה in Psalm 138 might be "saying," which emphasizes the activity of voicing a word rather than the product of the activity. Additionally, אמרה is one of the seven synonyms for "Torah" (תורה) used in Psalm 119, suggesting perhaps that the "word" (אמרה) to which the psalm singer refers in verse 2 is the Torah.

---

7. John Goldingay, *Psalms*, vol. 3: *Psalms 90–150*, BCOT (Grand Rapids: Baker Academic, 2008), 617.

8. Frank-Lothar Hossfeld and Erich Zenger, *Psalms 3*, trans. Linda M. Maloney, Hermeneia (Minneapolis: Fortress, 2011), 528, incorporating the words of Beat Weber, *Werkbuch Psalmen* 2 (Stuttgart: Kohlhammer, 2003), 339.

9. For a discussion of "name" (שם), see the commentary for Ps 113; for a discussion of "steadfast love" (חסד), see the commentaries for Pss 103 and 118.

10. Examples of the parallel use of "steadfast love" (חסד) and "faithfulness" (אמה) in the Psalter include Pss 25:10; 26:3; 40:10, 11; 57:4, 10; 69:14; 86:15; 108:5; 115:1.

In verse 3 the psalmist outlines what God has done on her behalf, thus prompting the words of thanks. The opening phrase of the verse, in English "on the day" (ביום), seems to suggest a particular point in time in which the psalmist cried out. In Hebrew, however, the phrase has a broader temporal frame of reference, best understood as "whenever." Thus the psalm singer thanks God for answering whenever she cries out. The two verbs "cry out" (קרא) and "answer" (ענה) are employed in a cause-and-effect construction numerous times in the Psalter.[11] The psalm singer states that by answering her cry God has "increased" her strength of "soul" (נפש). The singer of Psalm 138 celebrates that her נפש, the essence of who she is, was "increased in strength" by God's attentiveness to her cry for help.[12] The word translated "increased," רהב, actually means "storm against," "be bold," and "be boisterous." John Goldingay translates this portion of verse 3 as "you made me defiant in spirit with strength," and writes: "When one has seen Yhwh act, it changes one's stance in the world."[13]

In verse 4 the venue of thanks and singing to YHWH shifts from the realm of the gods (v. 1) to the realm of earthly kings. There the emboldened נפש of the psalmist confidently declares in the presence of God that "all the kings of the earth shall praise you" because "they have heard the words [אמרה] of your mouth." "Words" in verse 4 is derived from the same Hebrew root as we find in verse 2. God's word (אמרה) is exalted and the kings of the earth have heard it—perhaps from the psalmist, from the "throat [נפש]" of the emboldened psalm singer.

In verse 5 the psalm singer's mode of reference to God shifts. While in verses 1-4 the psalmist speaks directly to YHWH, using second-person pronouns, in verses 5-6 she consistently refers to God in the third person. After declaring to YHWH that the kings of the earth have heard God's words, the psalmist asserts in verses 5 and 6 with confident assurance that the kings will join in singing about YHWH, mingling their voices with those of people whom God regards despite the exigencies of their lives. Walter Brueggemann and William H. Bellinger insightfully point out that the singing (שיר) of the kings of the earth in Psalm 138:5 contrasts with the lament of the singers of Psalm 137 that they cannot "sing [שיר] the LORD's song" in a foreign land (v. 3). They write: "Psalm 138 is a simple summary of Israel's faith, but it is still powerful, because it

11. See Pss 17:6; 27:7; 81:7; 86:7; 91:15; 99:6; 102:3; 120:1.
12. For a discussion of "soul (נפש)," see Translation Matters for Psalm 103.
13. Goldingay, *Psalms 90–150*, 618.

reflects faith in a world with chaos knocking at the door, likely in the aftermath of exile."[14]

In the last two verses of Psalm 138 the psalm singer shifts the focus once again from the earthly realm of kings to the "trouble" (צרה) brought on by her "enemies" (איב). She speaks of hands (יד) three times—"your hand" and "your right hand" in verse 7 and "the works of your hands" in verse 8. In verse 7 she remembers God's "hand" and "right hand" that preserved and delivered her. In verse 8 the psalmist implores God not to forsake the work of her hands. She has experienced God's upholding hands over and over in the past, enough to embolden her to proclaim the words (אמרה) of God to the kings of the earth, and now she petitions God to continue to uphold and protect her.

The opening psalm of the final Davidic collection in the Psalter celebrates God's answering the cry for help from the psalm singer and emboldening her to declare God's word (אמרה) to "all the kings of the earth." In the aftermath of the Babylonian exile the Israelites questioned their very identity and future as the people of God. With the full knowledge of the "steadfast love" (חסד) and "faithfulness" (אמת) of Yhwh, though, the postexilic Israelite community could find a way to "sing" (שיר) God's praise in the aftermath of an exile in which they could not "sing" (שיר) the songs their captors requested (Ps 137:4).

Psalm 139

Psalm 139 is the second in a collection of eight psalms of David at the end of book 5. Like Psalm 138, it is classified as an individual hymn of thanksgiving, praising God for goodness to or on behalf of the psalm singer, usually for deliverance from some trying situation.[15] Frank-Lothar Hossfeld, following the lead of Hermann Gunkel, maintains that the designation "'hymn' was adequate to the basic mood of the psalm, in which the one praying sinks with astonishment and reflection into the mysteries of Yhwh."[16] Erhard Gerstenberger states, however:

> The discussion about [Ps 139's] genre classification has been going on for a long time with no end in sight. Elements and inklings of various categories of psalms can be detected in the different subunits. The exegete

14. Walter Brueggemann and William H. Bellinger Jr., *Psalms*, NCBC (Cambridge: Cambridge University Press, 2014), 579.

15. deClaissé-Walford, *Introduction to the Psalms*, 21–23.

16. Hossfeld and Zenger, *Psalms 3*, 537.

Psalm 139:1-24

To the leader. Of David. A Psalm.

¹O LORD, you have searched me and
known me.
²You know when I sit down and when
I rise up;
you discern my thoughts from far
away.
³You search out my path and my
lying down,
and are acquainted with all my
ways.
⁴Even before a word is on my tongue,
O LORD, you know it completely.
⁵You hem me in, behind and before,
and lay your hand upon me.

⁶Such knowledge is too wonderful
for me;
it is so high that I cannot attain it.
⁷Where can I go from your spirit?
Or where can I flee from your
presence?
⁸If I ascend to heaven, you are there;
if I make my bed in Sheol, you are
there.
⁹If I take the wings of the morning
and settle at the farthest limits of
the sea,
¹⁰even there your hand shall lead me,
and your right hand shall hold me
fast.

who insists that one single aspect must be determinative for the whole psalm may choose among complaint, thanksgiving, hymn, and wisdom discourse. All these avenues have been tried, to the effect that the picture of our psalm is very colorful in OT research.[17]

Four verses of the psalm, 19-22, stand in stark contrast with the rest. They are often omitted in reading and studying the psalm,[18] but scholars suggest that they may provide the hermeneutical key to understanding the circumstances under which it was composed John Goldingay writes that the "particular meaning in its [Ps 139's] context emerges only at the end."[19] In verses 19-22 the psalm singer calls on God to "kill the wicked" (v. 19) and wishes that "the bloodthirsty" and those who "speak maliciously" against God would depart the psalmist's presence (vv. 19-20). The psalmist further expresses "hatred" for those who hate YHWH (vv. 21-22), suggesting that she is someone who has been hurt by others, who feels or has felt the pressing in of the wicked, the bloodthirsty, the speakers of

17. Erhard S. Gerstenberger, *Psalms, Part 2, and Lamentations*, FOTL 15 (Grand Rapids: Eerdmans, 2001), 405.

18. In the Revised Common Lectionary, Ps 139:1-6 and 13-18 are included in Years B and C, and Ps 139:1-12 and 23-24 are included in Year A.

19. Goldingay, *Psalms 90–150*, 625. See also Sigmund Mowinckel, *The Psalms in Israel's Worship*, vol. 2 (Oxford: Blackwell, 1967), 75.

Psalm 139:1-24 (cont.)

¹¹If I say, "Surely the darkness shall cover me,
and the light around me become night,"
¹²even the darkness is not dark to you;
the night is as bright as the day,
for darkness is as light to you.
¹³For it was you who formed my inward parts;
you knit me together in my mother's womb.
¹⁴I praise you, for I am fearfully and wonderfully made.

Wonderful are your works;
that I know very well.
¹⁵My frame was not hidden from you,
when I was being made in secret,
intricately woven in the depths of the earth.
¹⁶Your eyes beheld my unformed substance.
In your book were written
all the days that were formed for me,
when none of them as yet existed.
¹⁷How weighty to me are your thoughts, O God!
How vast is the sum of them!

maliciousness against God, and those who hate God. In this context of conflict and hostility the psalm singer speaks in trust and thankfulness for God's presence.

In verses 1-6 the psalmist speaks directly to God, using the divine name YHWH twice and pronouns referring to God ten times. In addition, the psalmist refers to herself eleven times. The concentration of personal pronouns in the first six verses of Psalm 139 marks it as a reflection of the profound relationship of the "I" and "you" in ancient Israel.[20] James L. Mays comments: "Of course it could be said that the concern of all psalms is the relation between God and those who use them as praise and prayer. But here that relation is the single unrelieved concern."[21]

In the opening verse the psalmist states that God has "searched" (חקר) her and "known" (ידע) her. The two words, חקר and ידע, form an *inclusio* around Psalm 139; in verse 1 the singer says that God has "searched" her and "known" her, and in verse 23 she asks that God continue to do so. The verb חקר carries a meaning of "explore, examine, search out, or test" and is used in two ways in the Hebrew Bible, shedding some light, perhaps, on its meaning as used in Psalm 139. First, God "searches/

---

20. James L. Mays, *Psalms*, IBC (Louisville: Westminster John Knox, 1994), 427; see also Walter Brueggemann, "The Psalms as Prayer," in *The Psalms and the Life of Faith*, ed. Patrick D. Miller (Minneapolis: Fortress, 1995), 34–39.

21. Mays, *Psalms*, 426.

¹⁸I try to count them—they are more than the sand;
I come to the end—I am still with you.
¹⁹O that you would kill the wicked, O God,
and that the bloodthirsty would depart from me—
²⁰those who speak of you maliciously,
and lift themselves up against you for evil!

²¹Do I not hate those who hate you, O LORD?
And do I not loathe those who rise up against you?
²²I hate them with perfect hatred;
I count them my enemies.
²³Search me, O God, and know my heart;
test me and know my thoughts.
²⁴See if there is any wicked way in me,
and lead me in the way everlasting.

examines" persons, as we see in Psalm 139 but also in Psalm 44:21; Job 13:9; Jeremiah 17:10. Second, God's ways cannot be "sought out," as we see in Job 5:9; 9:10; 36:26; and Isaiah 40:28. God, whose ways are "unsearchable," "searches out" the ways of humanity, and in that "searching out" in Psalm 139 God comes to "know" the psalm singer. "Knowing" is a major theme of the psalm. The word occurs seven times (vv. 1, 2, 4, 6, 14, 23 [2x]), four of them in verses 1-6. Its verbal root is יד״ע, and it encompasses a wide range of meanings from simple recognition to intimate sexual relationship. God knows all there is to know about the psalmist, inside and out: every detail of her daily routine and every unspoken thought.

Verse 2 continues the psalmist's musings over God's "knowing" (ידע) her, using the merism "sit down" and "rise up" to encompass all her daily activities.²² Verse 2b summarizes those activities, calling them the singer's "thoughts" (רע). רע has a multiplicity of meanings in Hebrew, including "companion, friend, noise, thought." In the concluding phrase of verse 2 the psalm singer's use of רע indicates how, where, and with whom she spends her time. The word will appear again in verse 17, there in reference to God's רע.

Verse 3 uses a set of poetic parallels to convey God's knowledge of the psalmist: "search out" and "are acquainted" and "my lying down" and "my ways." The word translated "search out" in verse 3 of the NRSV is not the same Hebrew word as in verse 1. It is זרה, which means "scatter" or "stretch out," and in the context of Psalm 139 may indicate, according

---

22. For other uses of this merism, see Deut 6:7; 11:19; Ps 127:2.

to John Goldingay, "the picture of God extending the span of a hand over something, to get the dimensions of it."[23] The poetic parallel line in verse 3b confirms such an understanding, since the word translated "acquainted with" comes from a rare verbal root in biblical Hebrew, סכן, that means "become familiar with." Thus the psalm singer portrays Yhwh as one who has spread a divine hand over the doings of the psalmist and is familiar with her movements and motivations.

The theme continues in verses 4-6. Yhwh, who is familiar with the psalm singer's movements and motivations, knows (ידע) her word (מלה) even before she utters it and thus "hems" (צור) her in "behind and before" (v. 5). Thus she declares in verse 6, "Such knowledge [ידע] is too wonderful for me." צור, translated in the NRSV as "hem in," has a basic meaning of "bind, tie up" and, by analogy, "besiege, confine." While the word can convey a sense of protection, J. Clinton McCann comments that it may convey some measure of ambivalence in the psalmist's mind about the nature of God. He writes: "Ambivalence would be understandable. . . . To be fully known is to be completely vulnerable."[24] John Goldingay adds, " 'Bind' (*ṣārar*) is a neatly ambiguous verb; one can bind things to protect them or to restrict them."[25] McCann goes on to say, though, that "the psalmist certainly celebrates as good news the marvelous and mysterious reality that his or her life is accessible to God in every way and at every moment."[26]

In verses 7-12 the psalm singer muses over the idea that God is all-encompassing and all-present. No matter where the psalmist tries to flee from God—the heavens (v. 8), Sheol (v. 8), the sea (v. 9), the darkness (vv. 11-12)—God is there. The heavens/the heights and Sheol/the depths are another merism used in Psalm 139, indicating the boundaries and all that lies between them. The heavens were the dwelling places of the gods in the ancient Near East, not accessible to humanity, while Sheol was the shadowy realm to which all the dead went.[27] Brueggemann and Bellinger remind us: "The poetic images do not stand as flat, literal propositions of doctrine but as poetic figures to affirm divine presence in the farthest heights and depths."[28]

---

23. Goldingay, *Psalms 90–150*, 629.
24. McCann, "The Book of Psalms," 1236.
25. Goldingay, *Psalms 90–150*, 630.
26. McCann, "The Book of Psalms," 1236.
27. For a discussion of Sheol, see the commentary for Ps 116.
28. Brueggemann and Bellinger, *Psalms*, 583.

"The sea" in verse 9 is most likely a reference to the vast Mediterranean Sea that lies to the west of Palestine. Even if the psalmist sought out the wings of the dawn (in the east) and settled in a remote region of the sea (in the west), God could find her. Verses 11 and 12 round out another merism in verse 9-12, "the dawn, the day, the light" (אוֹר) and "the darkness [חֹשֶׁךְ] and the night." Darkness, as the antithesis of light, was a realm of uncertainty and fear in the ancient Near East (see Job 12:22 and Pss 35:6; 88:6, 12; 107:10, 14). At the beginning of the creation story in Genesis 1 the earth is described as "formless and void," with "darkness [חֹשֶׁךְ] upon the face of the deep" (Gen 1:2). The creative words of God harnessed the darkness, separating it from the light (אוֹר) (Gen 1:4), and in that new light God created the world. The singer of Psalm 139 muses in verse 7, "Where can I go from your spirit? Or where can I flee from your presence?" Is the psalm singer expressing once again some ambivalence about God's intimate knowledge of her movements and whereabouts?

The words of verses 13-18 begin to resolve somewhat the struggle of the psalm singer to comprehend God's intense interest in her. In these verses the focus shifts from "space" (as we see in vv. 7-12) to "time."[29] In verse 13 the psalmist acknowledges that God "formed" (קנה) her inward parts and "knit" (סכך) her together in her mother's womb. The basic meaning of קנה is "acquire, possess," and apart from its use in Psalm 139 it occurs only three times in the Hebrew Bible in the sense of begetting a child.[30] In Genesis 4:1, according to the NRSV, Eve says: "I have produced [קנה] a man [Cain] with the help of the LORD." In Deuteronomy 32:6 Moses says to the people: "Is not he [God] your father, who created [קנה] you, who made you and established you?" And in Proverbs 8:22 Woman Wisdom affirms: "The LORD created [קנה] me at the beginning of his work." In Psalm 139 we may be permitted to see the psalm singer voicing a connection between her own "forming" and the first child of humanity (Gen 4:1), the children of Israel (Deut 32:6), and Woman Wisdom (Prov 8:22).[31]

29. Goldingay, *Psalms 90–150*, 626.

30. Frank-Lothar Hossfeld, in Hossfeld and Zenger, *Psalms 3*, 541, points out that קנה, "in older usage, meant 'acquire by purchase' (cf. Pss 74:2; 78:54), and only in the postexilic period came to have the creation-theological significance of 'create.'"

31. For a discussion of Woman Wisdom, see the introduction, pages • • •, and Pss 92, 101, 104, and 107.

The word translated "fearfully" in verse 14 is derived from the verbal root ירא, often translated as "fear" but better understood as "reverence and awe."[32] The word translated "wonderfully" in verse 14 comes from the verbal root פלא, which means "be different, striking, remarkable— outside the power of human comprehension." It is used repeatedly in the Psalter to describe the acts of God on behalf of psalm singers (Pss 9:2; 40:5; 71:17; 96:3), particularly God's actions in the history of the ancient Israelites (Pss 78:4, 11; 105:2, 5; 106:7, 22). Psalm 106:22 employs both of the words (נוראות and נפלאים) used in Psalm 139:14:

> wondrous works [נפלאות] in the land of Ham,
>   and awesome deeds [נוראות] by the Red Sea.[33]

Verse 15's reference to being shaped in "the depths of the earth" echoes the creation story in Genesis 2, where we read, "then the LORD God formed the human from the dust of the ground" (עפר מן־האדמה, Gen 2:7).

The word translated "unformed substance" in verse 16a is גלם, a *hapax legomenon*; it occurs nowhere else in the text of the Hebrew Bible. In Babylonian Aramaic the word designates a formless mass or an incomplete vessel, while the Syriac word *galma* means "uncultivated soil."[34] The remainder of the verse is as difficult to interpret as its beginning. Other references to a scroll (book) of God occur in Exodus 32:32-33 and Psalms 56:8 and 69:28. We read in none of those passages, however, about the numbering of the days of an individual life; the reference is to a scroll in which God has written names (Exod 32 and Ps 69) and kept account of humanity's troubles (Ps 59). Whatever the exact meaning of this verse, it suggests that the psalmist acknowledges that God holds all of her life in God's hands.

Verses 17 and 18 form something of a doxological close to the first sixteen verses of Psalm 139. The psalmist marvels at the thoughts (רע) of God, using the same word as in verse 2b, in which she says to God, "you discern my thoughts [רע] from far away." God's thoughts are weighty, mighty, and more numerous than the sand.

As stated above, verses 19-24 may provide the setting in life for the composition of Psalm 139. Verse 19 begins with words of imprecation by the psalmist against the wicked and the bloodthirsty. She continues in verses 21-22 first with a rhetorical question and then with an adamant statement concerning those who hate (שׂנא) YHWH. She states that she "hates" (שׂנא) them, "loathes" (קוט) them, and counts them as her "ene-

---

32. For a discussion of ירא, see the commentary for Ps 111.
33. See also Exod 34:10 and Ps 145:5, 6.
34. *HALOT*, 1:194.

mies" (אֹיֵב). The psalm singer does not say she is being oppressed by the wicked and bloodthirsty, but Goldingay suggests that perhaps "they are trying to [pressure] the psalmist into joining them," but she "will have nothing to do with them and totally repudiates what they stand for."[35]

Psalm 139 closes with the same words as its opening: "Search [חֲקֹר] me and know [יָדַע] me." While the words in verse 1 are in the perfect aspect, "O LORD, you have searched me and known me . . . you discern my thoughts," in verse 23 they are in the imperative aspect, "Search me, O God, and know my heart."

Each of us was formed and framed by God. God's eyes beheld our unformed substances. Each of us was reverently, wondrously, remarkably, differently made—in ways that are beyond human explanation. In any time, in any place where the faithful face wickedness, bloodshed, and deceit, the words of Psalm 139 can provide comforting assurance of God's sovereign creation of and care for each individual.[36]

"Where Can I Flee from Your Presence?"

Carolyn Pressler, in an article titled "Certainty, Ambiguity, and Trust: Knowledge of God in Psalm 139," writes that while Psalm 139 is "lauded as a hymn praising God's all-encompassing knowledge, presence, and power, it has also been interpreted as the cry of one for whom God is an ambiguous and even oppressive presence."[37] In the psalm's first eighteen verses God knows, knows, knows (vv. 1-4); God searches (vv. 1, 4); God discerns (v. 2); God hems in behind and before (v. 5). God's hand is upon the psalmist (vv. 5, 10). God knows every word the psalm singer is going to say, even before it is on her tongue (v. 4). No matter where the psalmist flees, God will find her, even if she tries to hide in the darkest places (vv. 7-12). In fact, God was there at her conception and watched her carefully throughout her gestation (vv. 13-16). Pressler writes: "Whether near (v. 5) or far off (v. 2), the psalmist is never outside of the sphere of divine consciousness."[38]

---

35. Goldingay, *Psalms 90–150*, 637.

36. References to the creation by God of an individual are rare in the Hebrew Bible. See Jer 1:6 and Pss 22:9; 71:6 for the only other examples.

37. Carolyn Pressler, "Certainty, Ambiguity, and Trust: Knowledge of God in Psalm 139," in *A God So Near: Essays on Old Testament Theology in Honor of Patrick D. Miller*, ed. Brent A. Strawn and Nancy R. Bowen (Winona Lake, IN: Eisenbrauns, 2003), 91–99, at 91.

38. Ibid., 93.

All of this seems to be too much for the psalm singer, who says, "Such knowledge is too wonderful for me" (v. 6), and, "How weighty to me are your thoughts, O God! How vast is the sum of them" (v. 17). For most readers Psalm 139 is a comforting word of assurance that God is ever present and intimately involved in the lives of humanity, and that is the way commentators have almost uniformly interpreted the psalm.

For women and girls relentlessly controlled by husbands, boyfriends, fathers, and others, though, many of the words and sentiments of Psalm 139 could be difficult to hear. Rather than finding comforting assurance in verse 5's "You hem me in, behind and before, and lay your hand on me," an abused woman might wonder, "Is God another 'male figure' in my life who 'hems me in,' restricting and controlling me, never letting me out of his sight?"

In an article titled "The Sexual Politics of Gender-Based Violence in South Africa: Linking Public and Private Worlds," Carolyn S. Stauffer writes of the subordinated position of black women in South African society because of a number of factors. First, traditional South African culture, like many traditional cultures, was and in many cases continues to be highly patriarchal, a culture in which women are commodities purchased for a "bride price" (*lobola*), and who can be bought, sold, or exchanged at the will of male relatives.[39] According to L. Juliana M. Claassens and Amanda Gouws such patriarchal societies create "relationships of power that very often exclude women from decision-making positions and control over their own lives and bodies."[40]

Second, while apartheid-era legislation restricted the rights and movements of all indigenous African people it particularly reinforced patriarchal control of women. Following customary South African law, apartheid legislation deemed women minors under the guardianship of their husbands; women were not allowed to own property, open a bank account, or travel without their husband's consent.[41] Claassens and Gouws point out that while in the postapartheid era the South African government passed a plethora of laws to ensure equal rights and protection for

39. Carolyn S. Stauffer, "The Sexual Politics of Gender-Based Violence in South Africa: Linking Public and Private Worlds," *Journal for the Sociological Integration of Religion and Society* 5 (2015): 1–16, at 10.

40. L. Juliana M. Claassens and Amanda Gouws, "From Esther to Kwezi: Sexual Violence in South Africa after Twenty Years of Democracy," *International Journal of Public Theology* 8 (2014): 471–87, at 473.

41. Stauffer, "Sexual Politics," 10.

women, twenty years later a great many women in South Africa still experience patriarchal domination.

Third, in the apartheid era white males dominated the public domain, white women dominated the private domain, and black women, as domestic laborers, were able to integrate themselves into the "private domain," thus establishing for themselves a place in the societal order. For black males, though, according to Stauffer, "no provision was made for them to receive legitimation by an externally validated masculinity script."[42] In the postapartheid era, while black men are an ever-growing segment of the public domain, young black males make up the highest percentage of the unemployed population, at a staggering 52 percent in 2013 for those between the ages of fifteen and twenty-four. For these men a "validated masculinity script" still does not exist, and thus, left adrift in the social order, searching for a "script," a "narrative of identity," such men may turn to domestic domination to find their "script," their "identity."[43]

Finally, religious teaching has reinforced and continues to reinforce the idea of male dominance. The church's primary image of God as "male" and the husband/wife relationship as one of domination and subordination as seen in so much of Scripture has numerous unintended consequences.

Carolyn Pressler writes that the singer of Psalm 139 resolves the feelings of ambiguity about God's continual presence and moves to a level of trust in verse 18 ("I am still with you") that opens to entreaty and petition in verses 19-24 ("O that you would kill the wicked, O God").[44] I wonder if women who live in an oppressive male-dominated society and who read Psalm 139, questioning whether God is just another controlling male figure in their lives, are able to move so quickly to the resolution the singer of the psalm reached. The pervasive male images of and language about God in faith communities can only be a barrier for those who experience relentless oppression and control from the men in their lives. Images of and language about God that move beyond traditional patriarchal ideals may allow such women, in the words of J. Clinton McCann Jr. to "celebrate as good news the marvelous and mysterious reality that . . . [their lives are] accessible to God in every way and at every moment."[45]

Nancy L. deClaissé-Walford

---

42. Ibid., 7.
43. Ibid., 6.
44. Pressler, "Certainty," 98.
45. McCann, "The Book of Psalms," 1236.

Psalm 140

Psalm 140 picks up, in many ways, where Psalm 139 leaves off. In the closing verses of Psalm 139 the psalm singer declares complete hatred for those who hate God (vv. 21-22) and calls on God to kill the wicked (v. 19). In Psalm 140 the psalmist cries out to God about wicked and violent people who plan evil things in their minds and calls on God to punish them with burning coals, pits, and landlessness. The psalm contains all the elements of a lament psalm: invocation (vv. 1, 4, 6, 7, 8), complaint (vv. 1-5), petition (vv. 8-11), expression of trust (vv. 6-7, 12), and expression of praise (v. 13), and it begins a series of four individual laments (Pss 140–143).

TRANSLATION MATTERS

סלה occurs seventy-one times in thirty-nine psalms in the Psalter. All but two of its occurrences are in books 1, 2, and 3. In books 4 and 5 סלה occurs only in Psalms 119 and 140. It is left untranslated in most English versions and is a musical or liturgical notation, placed at key junctures in the psalms to indicate some sort of pause in the recitation or singing. The verbal root of the word is most likely סלל, which means "a lifting up of the eyes or the voice." An Aramaic root, *sl'*, means "pray, bow down." The Septuagint translates סלה as διάψαλμα, meaning "pause in singing." The Targums define סלה as "forever" or "everlasting," perhaps a directive to insert a benediction, refrain, or prayer. Michael Goulder builds on this idea and suggests that סלה means something like "recitative" and marks a pause in the psalm at which a prayer or story from ancient Israel is recited. He writes that at Psalm 44:8 the סלה signals a pause for the reading of Joshua 24, and at Psalm 85:3's סלה excerpts from Exodus 32–34 are read.[46] The common thread running through the various speculations about the function of סלה is that it indicates some sort of pause in the recitation or singing of the psalm, either for some bodily movement—raised hands, raised eyes, bowing down—or for a musical interlude, congregational song, or recitation of words.

On a humorous note, David Alan Hubbard is said to have maintained that "*selah*" is what David said when he broke a string on his musical instrument, which, according to John Goldingay, is the most "illuminating theory because there is no logic about when you break a string, and there is no logic about the occurrence of *selâ*."[47]

Psalm 140 is a highly structured composition. Richard Clifford's outline centers on the placement of the psalm's three סלהs. He observes that

---

46. Michael D. Goulder, *The Psalms of the Sons of Korah*, JSOTSup 20 (Sheffield: Sheffield Academic, 1982), 103–6.

47. Goldingay, *Psalms 90–150*, 643.

Psalm 140:1-13

To the leader. A Psalm of David.
¹Deliver me, O Lᴏʀᴅ, from evildoers;
  protect me from those who are
    violent,
²who plan evil things in their minds
  and stir up wars continually.
³They make their tongue sharp as a
    snake's,
  and under their lips is the venom
      of vipers.   *Selah*
⁴Guard me, O Lᴏʀᴅ, from the hands
      of the wicked;
  protect me from the violent
    who have planned my downfall.

⁵The arrogant have hidden a trap for
    me,
  and with cords they have spread
    a net,
  along the road they have set
      snares for me.   *Selah*
⁶I say to the Lᴏʀᴅ, "You are my God;
  give ear, O Lᴏʀᴅ, to the voice of
    my supplications."
⁷O Lᴏʀᴅ, my Lord, my strong deliverer,
  you have covered my head in the
    day of battle.
⁸Do not grant, O Lᴏʀᴅ, the desires of
    the wicked;

verses 1-3 contain twenty-three Hebrew words, ending with סלה; verses 4-5 contain twenty-three words, ending with סלה; verses 6-8 contain twenty-four words, ending with סלה; verses 9-11 contain twenty-three words; and verses 12-13 provide a closing statement of trust.[48] In addition, verses 1 and 4a end with the same words, מאיש חמסים תנצרני, although they are translated differently in the two verses in the NRSV,[49] while verses 3 and 5b both begin with אשר. J. Clinton McCann, building on the work of Leslie Allen, sees Psalm 140 as a chiastic composition whose center, verses 6-7, proclaims the sovereignty of God:

vv. 1-2:   persons of violent ways

  v. 3:   lips

  vv. 4-5:   wicked, plot

    vv. 6-7:   the sovereignty of God

  v. 8:   wicked, plot

  vv. 9-10:   lips

v. 11:   persons of violent ways

  vv. 12-13:   the acts of the sovereign God

48. Richard J. Clifford, *Psalms 73–150*, AOTC (Nashville: Abingdon, 2003), 284.
49. The end of v. 1 reads, "protect me from those who are violent," and the end of v. 4a reads, "protect me from the violent."

Psalm 140:1-13 (cont.)

do not further their evil plot.   *Selah*
⁹Those who surround me lift up their
heads;
let the mischief of their lips
overwhelm them!
¹⁰Let burning coals fall on them!
Let them be flung into pits, no
more to rise!
¹¹Do not let the slanderer be
established in the land;

let evil speedily hunt down the
violent!
¹²I know that the LORD maintains the
cause of the needy,
and executes justice for the
poor.
¹³Surely the righteous shall give
thanks to your name;
the upright shall live in your
presence.

McCann also notes that the words "evil" (רע), "violent" (חמס), "lip" (שׂפה), and "wicked" (רשע) in verses 1-4 are repeated in reverse order in verses 8-11.[50]

Psalm 140 opens rather abruptly in verses 1-4 with words of complaint about those who devise "evil" and "violence" and whose tongues and lips are sharp and filled with venom, perhaps confirming its placement as a continuation of Psalm 139. The word translated "deliver" in verse 1 is not the usual word for "deliver" in the Hebrew Bible (ישע) but rather is from the verbal root חלץ, which means "to draw out, pull out, extricate." The psalm singer, whom God knows intimately (Ps 139), asks God to take her away (perhaps snatch her away) from the evil and violence being plotted against her. The word "tongue" (לשׁון) occurs some thirty-five times in the Psalter and nineteen times in the book of Proverbs, while "lip" (שׂפה) occurs twenty-eight times in Psalms and thirty-eight times in Proverbs, conveying the power of words in human relationships. In the book of Psalms references to the speech organs are almost always negative, connoting the harm of hateful words and plotting against others.[51]

In verses 4 and 5 the focus shifts from the thoughts and words of the psalm singer's oppressors (the "wicked") to the devices they are planning to deploy in order to bring about her downfall: traps and nets and snares. The opening words of verse 4, "guard me," are not as urgent as those we find in verse 1. The psalmist asks God to guard or keep her

---

50. McCann, "The Book of Psalms," 1239–41. Leslie C. Allen, *Psalms 101–150*, WBC 21 (Nashville: Thomas Nelson, 2002), 267.
51. See the commentary for Ps 120, vv. 2 and 3.

safe (שמר) rather than extricating her from the actions of the wicked. The words translated "planned my downfall" (חשבו לדחות פעמי) mean literally "planned how to trip my footsteps," thereby causing the psalmist to fall into the traps and nets and snares laid for her. But with God's guarding and watchful care she can maneuver the pitfalls.

In verses 6 and 7 the psalm singer speaks again to God, mixing praise with petition. God is her God, God is her Lord and strong "deliverer"; this time she uses the more usual Hebrew word ישע rather than חלץ as in verse 1.[52] McCann writes: "While it would appear from vv. 1-5 that the violent are in control, the psalmist affirms . . . that God is sovereign."[53] The phrase "you have covered [סכך] my head [ראש] in the day of battle" in verse 7 refers to verse 2's complaint that the evildoers "stir up wars continually." Brueggemann and Bellinger conclude that the words of verse 7 are "an image of protection in the face of violent opponents."[54]

The petition of verses 8-11 echoes the complaint of verses 1-5. The psalmist cries out to God to inflict on people of violent ways punishments equal to their evil acts against her. For those who "plan evil things" (v. 2), the psalmist asks that God not grant their desires (v. 8). For those who sharpen their tongues and have venom under their lips (v. 3), a literal reading of verse 9 is "the head [ראש] of those who surround me, may the mischief of their lips [שפה] cover [כסה], paralleling סכך in v. 7] them." For those who conceal a trap, spread out a fowler's net, and place snares at the side of the road (vv. 5-6), the psalmist asks God to rain down burning coals of fire upon them, cause them to fall into a pit, and render them homeless (vv. 10-11). As with the closing verses of Psalm 139 (vv. 19-22), the modern reader may find such words of retribution difficult to voice. But as McCann reminds us in his commentary on Psalm 109:

> Evil, injustice, and oppression must be confronted, opposed, hated because God hates them. From this perspective the psalmist's desire for vengeance amounts to a desire for justice and righteousness in self and society. . . . The anger is expressed, but it is expressed in prayer and thereby submitted to God. . . . Thus this vehement, violent sounding prayer is, in fact, an act of non-violence.[55]

---

52. The words of Ps 140:6-7 echo those of Ps 31:14-15.
53. McCann, "The Book of Psalms," 1240.
54. Brueggemann and Bellinger, *Psalms*, 586.
55. McCann, "The Book of Psalms," 1127.

In the closing verses of Psalm 140 the psalmist sings words of trust and praise to God. In verse 12 she expresses confidence that God will defend and provide justice for the needy and the poor, a common theme in the Psalter. The word translated "needy" is עָנִי and occurs some forty times in the book of Psalms; "poor," אֶבְיוֹן, occurs more than twenty times. The two words are used interchangeably and often in poetic parallelism.[56] The singer of Psalm 140 laments her own oppressive life situation but finds protection from the "LORD, my Lord, my strong deliverer" (v. 7). Thus she turns outward in verse 12, away from her inward struggles, to express confidence that YHWH executes justice (מִשְׁפָּט) for those who are least able to defend themselves against oppression.[57] The psalm singer closes with words of certainty that the righteous (צַדִּיק) will give thanks to the name of God and that the upright (יָשָׁר) will live in God's presence. Despite the seeming despair that surrounds her the psalm singer can praise God as one who cares for and protects the righteous and the upright despite their life circumstances.

A Prayer against Xenophobic Attacks

I am a Malawian who has been studying in South Africa since 2013. I first learned about xenophobia, the fear of or prejudice against people from other countries, in 2008 when there were xenophobic attacks in South Africa that were reported in a number of media outlets in Malawi. I was young at the time and therefore did not take the issue too seriously. The second attacks—as far as I know—happened in 2015. I was in South Africa by then, doing my third year of studies. I was no longer far away in Malawi where I could only hear stories; I was in the thick of it. I should point out that I did not experience the xenophobic attacks directly, but this was one of the most terrifying points in my life. When I walked to and from the university campus in Pietermaritzburg I constantly prayed to God to protect me and to rescue fellow foreigners who were suffering from the attacks. I use psalms sometimes as prayers for different things depending on what I am going through at the moment. In this situation of xenophobia Psalm

---

56. See Psalms 9; 10; 37:14; 70:5; 47:21; 109:16.

57. Along with the "needy" and the "poor" the writers of the Hebrew biblical text are also concerned with the "widow," the "orphan," and the "stranger." See the commentary for Ps 94.

140 came to be a useful prayer for me.

Verses 1-3 of the psalm are a call to God to rescue persons from those who attack them. During xenophobic attacks people assault others based not on how they look but on where they come from. The oppressors set up checkpoints in areas such as bus stops and roadways where they stop people and ask them to speak in a local language in order to pick out foreigners. If the people are unable to speak the local language they are threatened with deportation and some are scorned and even harmed. Psalm 140's words of entreaty for deliverance from those "who plan evil" and "make their tongue sharp as a snake's" offer a source of comfort for those caught up in such threatening situations. God encourages us to cry out when we are in troubling situations (Ps 50:15), and the words of Psalm 140:1-3 help us to give voice to our trouble.

Verses 4-8 help us find the words we can use to pray for protection against the plans of those who seek to attack us. During the xenophobic attacks in 2015, I received text messages from friends, South African and foreign alike, telling me for my safety where not to go and which roads not to take. My friends, as the hands of God, guarded me (v. 4) from the traps, the nets, and the snares (v. 5) laid by those who planned to bring harm to me and others. This reminds me of Isaiah 54:17, which tells us that no weapon designed to harm us shall prosper and that we can condemn every tongue that rises against us in judgment.

The words of verses 9-11, a prayer that harm may come to those who attack the psalmist, might be interpreted in the twenty-first century as wrong, but in the face of overwhelming hatred and prejudice it is an amazing gift to have the ability to pour out our hearts and say whatever we wish to God in prayer. It helps us get closer to God and instils within us more confidence in our ability to be honest with God. God invites us to ask for what we need, giving foreigners like me the ability to confidently ask for protection in the face of xenophobic attacks.

Not all South Africans are involved in these attacks. Such people are only a small contingent, and there is actually a strong backlash against such assaults. Verses 12 and 13 confirm that God is just and takes up the cause of those who are vulnerable and that those who suffer from xenophobic attacks or the fear of them can call on God and God will "execute justice" (v. 12). The world does not belong to any particular group of human beings; it belongs to God who created it. In this sense no one has the right to harm others in the land God made for everyone to live in. We are all passing through this earth; we are citizens of heaven (Phil 3:20), and so we need to embrace one another as one people of God.

William Chisa

Psalm 141

The many verbal links between Psalms 140 and 141 (no fewer than eleven) indicate their connectedness; thus while we may read Psalm 140 as a continuation of Psalm 139, we may also read Psalm 141 as a continuation of Psalm 140. The words "give ear" (אזן) and "voice" (קול) occur in 141:1 and 140:6; "watch, protect" (נצר) in 141:3 and 140:1; "guard, keep" (שמר) in 141:3, 9 and 140:4; "lip" (שפה) in 141:3 and 140:3, 9; "wicked" (רשע) in 141:4, 10 and 140:4, 8; "evil" (רע) in 141:4, 5 and 140:1, 2, 11; "righteous" (צדיק) in 141:5 and 140:13; "LORD (GOD), my Lord" (יהוה אדני) in 141:8 and 140:7; and "trap" (פח) and "snare" (מוקש) in 141:9 and 140:5.

In Psalm 140 the psalmist cries out to God for deliverance from "evildoers" and "those who are violent." In Psalm 141 she asks God for help so that the psalmist's own heart will not be turned toward "evil" and "wicked deeds" (Ps 141:4). In Psalm 140 the psalmist cries out to God to be delivered from those who "Make their tongue sharp as a snake's," with the poison of a viper "under their lips" (140:3), while in Psalm 141 the psalmist implores God to "set a guard over" the psalmist's own mouth, to "keep watch over the door of my lips" (141:3). Leslie Allen suggests that the singer of Psalm 141 has been associating with evil people and engaging in their deeds and speech and is coming before God asking for protection and guidance.[58] Others, such as Hans-Joachim Kraus and J. Clinton McCann, maintain that the psalmist is being tempted to join in the deeds and speech of evil people but has not yet done so.[59]

The twofold repetition of "I call" (קרא) together with the imperative "give ear" (אזן) in verse 1 suggest a sense of urgency on the part of the psalm singer as she comes into the presence of YHWH. Commentators differ in their translations and interpretations of verse 2. Is the psalmist bringing her prayer with uplifted hands to YHWH in place of incense and sacrifice? The NRSV translation suggests such an understanding. Or is she bringing the incense and offering to YHWH with prayer and uplifted hands? No marker is given in the Hebrew text to indicate the relationship between prayer and incense or between lifting up the hands and evening sacrifice. Kraus writes that Psalm 141 pictures "the spiritualization of the older practice of sacrifice. . . . The prayer song, which in earlier times

---

58. Allen, *Psalms 101–150*, 344.

59. Hans-Joachim Kraus, *Psalms 60–150: A Commentary*, CC (Minneapolis: Fortress, 1993), 527; McCann, "The Book of Psalms," 1243.

Psalm 141:1-10

A Psalm of David

¹I call upon you, O Lᴏʀᴅ; come
  quickly to me;
  give ear to my voice when I call
    to you.
²Let my prayer be counted as
  incense before you,
  and the lifting up of my hands as
    an evening sacrifice.
³Set a guard over my mouth, O Lᴏʀᴅ;
  keep watch over the door of my
    lips.
⁴Do not turn my heart to any evil,

to busy myself with wicked deeds
in company with those who work
  iniquity;
  do not let me eat of their
    delicacies.
⁵Let the righteous strike me;
  let the faithful correct me.
Never let the oil of the wicked anoint
  my head,
  for my prayer is continually
    against their wicked deeds.
⁶When they are given over to those
  who shall condemn them,

may have accompanied the presentation of the sacrifice, now takes the place of the offering."[60]

Other commentators point out that in the Hebrew Bible prayer and sacrifice/offering go hand in hand, citing Ezra 9:5, which says, "At the evening sacrifice I got up from my fasting, with garments and my mantle torn, and fell on my knees, spread out my hands to the Lᴏʀᴅ my God, and said . . ."[61] James L. Mays writes that Psalm 141 does not imply a spiritualization of sacrifice and that "word and sacrament are not at odds here."[62] John Goldingay adds: "Prayers accompanied offerings, so that as usual worship of Yhwh is multifaceted; it involves words, music, gestures, and offerings. Prayers would not be substitutes for offerings unless offerings were impossible for some reason."[63]

The psalmist petitions God in verse 3 to place a guard (שמר) over her mouth and to keep watch (נצר) over the door (דל) of her lips. "Guard" and "keep watch" are the same words used in Psalm 140:4 in the singer's petition to Yʜᴡʜ to protect her from the violent and wicked, but in Psalm 141 she asks that God protect her from any tendency on her own part to engage in sharp or venomous speech (Ps 140:3). דל is a *hapax legomenon* (it does not occur elsewhere in the text of the Hebrew Bible), the usual form

60. Kraus, *Psalms 60–150*, 527.
61. For other references to the evening sacrifice, see 2 Kgs 16:15 and Dan 9:21.
62. Mays, *Psalms*, 431.
63. Goldingay, *Psalms 90–150*, 655.

Psalm 141:1-10 (cont.)

then they shall learn that my words were pleasant.	in you I seek refuge; do not leave me defenseless.
⁷Like a rock that one breaks apart and shatters on the land, so shall their bones be strewn at the mouth of Sheol.	⁹Keep me from the trap that they have laid for me, and from the snares of evildoers.
⁸But my eyes are turned toward you, O God, my Lord;	¹⁰Let the wicked fall into their own nets, while I alone escape.

in biblical Hebrew being דלה. Frank-Lothar Hossfeld suggests that the form דל is used purposely in verse 3 because it is a homonym of "poor, weak" (דל), emphasizing the psalmist's feelings of vulnerability in the face of those who plan evil things in their minds (Ps 140:2).[64]

The singer continues her petition in verse 4, asking God to keep her from turning her heart (לב, the seat of thought) to evil and joining in the company of "those who work iniquity." In fact, she adds, "do not let me eat of their delicacies." The book of Proverbs contains many warnings about whom a person chooses for companionship and with whom one shares a table. Proverbs 24:1-2 advises: "Do not envy the wicked, nor desire to be with them; for their minds devise violence and their lips talk of mischief."[65] Walter Brueggemann and William H. Bellinger observe: "The pervasive power of the enemies could become attractive. The prayer is that YHWH will keep the petitioner from indulging in evil behavior among the wicked."[66]

Verses 5-7 are fraught with textual difficulties that render translation and interpretation difficult. In verse 5 the psalmist seeks correction from the righteous (צדיק) and the faithful (חסד) and, according to the NRSV, prays that the oil of the wicked may not anoint her head. Other translations such as the KJV, ESV, NASB, and NIV characterize the oil as the kind reproof of the righteous.[67] Whether we understand the oil to be that of

---

64. Hossfeld and Zenger, *Psalms 3*, 559.

65. See also Prov 3:31; 16:29; 22:24-25; 23:6-8, 17.

66. Brueggemann and Bellinger, *Psalms*, 590.

67. See also Hossfeld and Zenger, *Psalms 3*, 555. The difficulty in translation centers on the understanding and interpretation of the MT שמן ראש אל־יני ראשי. The LXX translates שמן ראש (the oil of the head) as ἔλαιον δὲ ἁμαρτωλοῦ (the oil of the sinful).

the wicked or the oil of kind reproof, the psalm singer states at the end of verse 5 that her prayer is continually against these others' wicked deeds.

Verse 6 continues with textual difficulties, the textual comments in *BHS* stating that verse 6 is "corrupt." While the NRSV renders the first portion of the verse "When they are given over to those who shall condemn them," the MT has "Their judges [שפטים] will be thrown down at the hands of the cliff." The identity of "their judges" in verse 6 is not clear, but perhaps the reference is to the leaders among verse 4's "those who work iniquity." John Goldingay suggests that the use of the verbal root שפט in verse 6 provides "an ironic link with the preceding psalm" where verse 12 states that YHWH will "execute justice" (שפט) for the poor. When the wicked find themselves without judges, then perhaps they will realize that the psalmist's words are "pleasant" (נעם).[68] Verse 7 is also marked in *BHS* as "corrupt." The interpretation of the verse hinges on the translation of the suffix on the word "bones [עצם]." The MT has "our bones [עצמינו]," while the NRSV follows a number of Septuagint manuscripts and the Syriac translation and renders the word "their bones." If the translation is "their bones" it continues the narrative of verse 6, stating the ultimate fate of either the "judges of the wicked" or the "wicked" themselves. If the translation is "our bones," then it begins the petition of the closing verses (vv. 8-10) of Psalm 141. Brueggemann and Bellinger observe:

> The most common rendering takes v. 6 as an announcement of judgment on the wicked and an exoneration of the petitioner. . . . In this interpretation, the verses express the hope that retribution will come on the wicked and that the petitioner will be spared. That reading of the verses seems plausible, but the text is difficult, so any interpretation must be tentative.[69]

Verse 8 begins the final petition of Psalm 141. The psalm singer states that her eyes are turned toward YHWH and implores YHWH not to leave her "defenseless." The Hebrew literally says, "do not lay bare my very being [נפשי]," leading into the final words of the psalm, which recall those of Psalm 140:5. The psalm singer pleads with God not to "lay her bare" to the "trap" (פח), the "snares" (מקשות), and the "nets" (מכמר) of the wicked but to allow her to escape while they fall into their own nets, echoing and perhaps bringing to full circle the words of Psalm 140:5. The singer

---

68. See the commentary for Ps 133:1.

69. Brueggemann and Bellinger, *Psalms*, 590.

of Psalm 141 recognizes how seductive wrong paths in life can be and cries out to God to preserve her from them.

An interesting phenomenon in Psalms 140 and 141 is the abundant use of "body language": heart (לֵב, 140:2; 141:4), tongue (לָשׁוֹן, 140:3), lips (שָׂפָה, 140:3, 9; 141:3), hands (יָד, 140:4; 141:2), ear (אֹזֶן, 140:6; 141:1), voice (קוֹל, 140:6; 141:1), head (רֹאשׁ, 140:7, 9; 141:5), mouth (פֶּה, 141:3), bones (עֶצֶם, 141:7), eyes (עַיִן, 141:8), inmost being (נֶפֶשׁ, 141:8). The psalm singers are not depicted as disembodied worshipers and suppliants; rather, they bring the whole of themselves before God. The singers of Psalms 140 and 141 refer to elements of the human body no fewer than nineteen times in the psalms' twenty-three verses. In an article titled "Body Images in the Psalms" Susanne Gillmayr-Bucher observes that there are more than one thousand explicit references to the body and its parts in 143 of the 150 psalms in the Hebrew Psalter.[70] She writes, "The persons in the Psalms do not so much *have* a body, they rather *are* a body." She goes on to say, "The way the body and its parts are used shapes substantially the development of the line of thought and the discourse of the psalms."[71] The singers of Psalms 140 and 141 refer to the body parts of the oppressors as well as to her/their own and, further, describe what those parts of the body *do*. The "mind" (לֵב) of the oppressors "plans evil [רַע] things" in Psalm 140:2, while the singer of Psalm 141 petitions God not to turn her "heart [לֵב] to any evil [רָע]" (v. 4). The tongues of the oppressors in Psalm 140:3 are "sharp as a snake's" and under their lips is "the venom of vipers." The singer of Psalm 141, in contrast, asks God to guard her mouth and keep watch over the door of her lips (v. 3). In Psalm 140 the hands of the oppressors hide traps, spread a net, and set snares (vv. 4-5), while the psalm singer lifts her hands in prayer in Psalm 141:2. The oppressors "lift up their heads" in Psalm 140:9, but the singer of Psalm 141 praises God for "covering her head" in verse 7 and asks that the oil of the wicked not anoint her head in verse 5. By giving attention to the body parts mentioned by the psalm singers and what those body parts *do*, the reader or hearer observes a movement in the discourse of the two psalms—a contrast between the wicked and evildoers and the faithful (albeit struggling) psalmist. Coming before God with our whole created being rather than a disembodied "self" or "soul" allows for a more genuine and "human" relationship with the God who created us as we are.

70. Susanne Gillmayr-Bucher, "Body Images in the Psalms," *JSOT* 28 (2004): 301–26, at 301.

71. Ibid., 303.

"It Is So Difficult to Be a Woman in South Africa"

I read Psalm 141 in the light of a conversation I had with my friend. She was recently appointed to a top management position, and in South Africa not many women fill such positions. Her colleagues are overwhelmingly male and in most of the meetings she attends she is the only woman present. One day she sent me a panicked message expressing her fear, as she felt unsafe in the presence of these men; in her concluding sentence she exclaimed, "It is so difficult to be a woman in this country right now!" Her fear is not without reason or cause. Daily, women in South Africa are being abused, violated, and even murdered, not just by criminals but by the people who, arguably, are supposed to care for them (i.e., boyfriends, husbands, fathers, and so forth). How do women protect themselves from abuse, violation, and even murder by people they love and whom they think love them? The reality of never knowing who to trust has devastating effects on many women in South Africa.

The words of Psalm 141 provide me with some hope, though, that God is able to preserve us South African women from evil. In verse 1 the psalm singer comes to God in great need with a heartfelt plea to "give ear to my voice." Often the voices of the marginalized in society are not heard by human ears, but God gives an ear to the voices of the voiceless. We who often do not have a voice know that we can call on God when our earthly support systems fail us—our friends, our family, the government—those who are supposed to be caring for us. We have an unwavering assurance that we can call to God when all other avenues have been exhausted, because God is inexhaustible. And so the psalm singer comes before God in prayer and incense and evening sacrifice in verse 2. The words of this verse remind me of the story of Hannah in 1 Samuel; she is desolate and desperate, but she comes to God in prayer, trusting in God's goodness and deliverance from her present situation of oppression.

The words of verse 3 are a firm reminder that the power of life and death is in the tongue (Prov 18:21). We must choose our words wisely and with careful consideration, even in situations of discrimination and oppression. It is easy to "run our mouths dry," but we, along with the psalmist, must ask that God watch over our mouths to discern the right times to speak and the times to be quiet.

A common reaction to discrimination and abuse is to attempt to carry out the same "evil" against the oppressors as they are inflicting on the oppressed. In the current social and economic circumstances in South Africa it is tempting to turn to underhanded devices and oppression of others as the means for living. It is easy for the heart to be overcome by feelings of revenge and resentment, but Psalm 141 calls us back and reminds us that we should not turn our "heart to any evil . . . busy [ourselves] with wicked deeds in company with those who work iniquity." In fact, we ought not even share a table with them, enticed by their delicacies.

Verse 5 offers the way in which those who are oppressed and abused can survive. Oftentimes we are overcome by great distress, but a true sign of humility and growth is the ability to accept learning from others who have been through more than we have and can provide words of wisdom about how to stay out of the company of the wicked and persevere in resisting them.

Verses 6 and 7 are words of hope and vision for the abused and oppressed. Good will eventually win over evil and the wicked will learn that the words of the psalm singer— here the marginalized, abused women of South Africa—are "pleasant." Thus the singer of Psalm 141 turns confident eyes to God in the assurance that God is her refuge and will keep her from the traps and snares laid for her by those who seek to marginalize and abuse her. In fact, they will fall into their own nets: the system of abuse they have perpetuated. God is not just a person but a place, a place where gender-based discrimination and violence has no home. There all can live in equality and freedom.

Siphokazi Dlwati

Psalm 142

Psalm 142, like Psalms 140, 141, and 143, is an individual lament, but unlike the other three it is identified in its superscription as a "Maskil" (מַשְׂכִּיל) rather than a "Psalm" (מִזְמוֹר). Thirteen psalms in the Hebrew Psalter (Pss 32, 42, 44, 45, 52–55, 74, 78, 88, 89, and 142) are designated מַשְׂכִּיל. The root of the word is שׂכל, and in the form in which we find it in the Psalter it means "have insight, teach." Scholars believe that the מַשְׂכִּיל is meant to be an artistic or teaching song. John Goldingay suggests that Psalm 142 could be "offering a pattern for prayer or praise," but he adds that "contemplative poem" and "skillful poem" are further possibilities.[72]

Psalm 142 is also one of thirteen psalms in the Psalter whose super-scriptions place them in specific events in the life of David, but it is the only instance of such in books 4 and 5.[73] The biblical text narrates two

---

72. Goldingay, *Psalms 90–150*, 664.
73. The others are Pss 3, 7, 18, 34, 51, 52, 54, 56, 57, 59, 60, and 63.

Psalm 142:1-7

A Maskil of David.
When he was in the cave. A Prayer.

[1]With my voice I cry to the LORD;
  with my voice I make supplication
    to the LORD.
[2]I pour out my complaint before him;
  I tell my trouble before him.
[3]When my spirit is faint,
  you know my way.
In the path where I walk
  they have hidden a trap for me.
[4]Look on my right hand and see—
  there is no one who takes notice
    of me;

no refuge remains to me;
  no one cares for me.
[5]I cry to you, O LORD;
  I say, "You are my refuge,
    my portion in the land of the living."
[6]Give heed to my cry,
  for I am brought very low.
Save me from my persecutors,
  for they are too strong for me.
[7]Bring me out of prison,
  so that I may give thanks to your
    name.
The righteous will surround me,
  for you will deal bountifully with me.

instances in the life of David in which he flees to a cave in fear for his life. In 1 Samuel 20–22 David escapes from Saul to the cave of Adullam, and in 1 Samuel 23–24 he flees to a cave in Engedi when he learns that Saul is plotting to kill him.[74] Verbal links to both of these stories occur in verses 6 and 7 of Psalm 142.

Many scholars ignore the superscriptions of the psalms when offering commentary on them, arguing that the superscriptions were later scribal additions and that placing the psalms in specific historical settings anchors them too securely in the past rather than allowing them to speak relevantly in the modern context.[75] Others pay close attention to the superscriptions, pointing out that they provide an initial context in which to read and interpret the psalms. James Sanders sums it up best:

> Does not such editorial work indicate the intense interest of redactors in date lines and historical contexts? They seem to be saying fairly clearly, if the reader wants to understand the full import for his or her (later) situation of what Scripture is saying, he or she had best consider the original historical context in which this passage scored its point.[76]

74. The superscription of Ps 142 is very similar to that of Ps 57.
75. See, for instance, Brevard Childs, *Introduction to the Old Testament as Scripture* (Philadelphia: Fortress, 1979), 520–22.
76. James A. Sanders, "Canonical Context and Canonical Criticism," *HBT* 2 (1980): 173–97; reprinted in *From Sacred Story to Sacred Text: Canon as Paradigm* (Philadelphia: Augsburg Fortress, 1987; repr. Eugene, OR: Wipf and Stock, 1999), 153–74, at 170.

The superscriptions call readers to go back and review the incidents in the life of David to which they refer. They provide initial concrete "story-worlds" for the psalms that may allow readers or hearers to "walk into" and "live in" the psalms for themselves. Walter Brueggemann and William H. Bellinger write: "The superscription is not so much about the origin of the psalm as it is about a life setting in which readers can envision the praying of the psalm."[77]

Verses 1 and 2 of Psalm 142 echo in some ways the first two verses of Psalm 141, but two significant differences may be observed. First, whereas the singer of Psalm 141 speaks directly *to* YHWH, in Psalm 142 she speaks *about* YHWH. Second, while both psalms state that the psalmist is calling on God and admonishing God to act in some way, different Hebrew verbal forms are used. In Psalm 141:1 the word translated "call" is קְרָא, whose basic meaning is something like "attract someone's attention by the sound of one's voice," thereby suggesting a range of meanings, including "call, summon, invite, read, and pray."[78] The verbal root translated "cry" in Psalm 142:1 is זעק, which conveys the idea of an emotional crying out in acute distress and seeking deliverance from a perilous situation. The verbal root occurs only five times in the Psalter; two of those occurrences are in Psalm 142 (vv. 1 and 5). The other occurrences are in Psalm 22:5 ("To you they [our ancestors] cried, and were saved") and in Psalm 107:13 and 19 ("Then they cried to the Lord in their trouble, and he saved them from their distress"). זעק in Psalm 142:1 is paralleled in verse 2 by "pour out" (שפך), which carries the idea not of a slow pouring out but of a dense, continuous movement, an inundation.[79]

Beginning with verse 3 the psalm singer shifts from speaking *about* God to speaking directly *to* God. The word translated "spirit" is רוח, referring to the psalmist's very breath of being, further underscored with the emphatic use of the second-person pronoun (אתה) and the verb "know." The psalmist continues in the remainder of verses 3 and 4 to enumerate the circumstances that have prompted her "cry" and "pouring out" to God. Her oppressors have hidden a trap (פח; see Pss 140:5; 141:9) in the path she walks, and no one takes notice or provides a refuge for her. The word translated "refuge" is מנוס, the same word used by David in 2 Samuel 22:3 ("my stronghold and my refuge [מנוס], my savior; you save

77. Brueggemann and Bellinger, *Psalms*, 592–93.

78. Frank-Lothar Hossfeld and E.-M. Kindl, "קְרָא (*qārāʾ*)," *TDOT*, 13:109–16, at 109–10.

79. Rüdiger Liwak, "שפך (*šāpak*)," *TDOT*, 15:431–42, at 432.

me from violence") and perhaps better translated "escape" or "flight" from the trap that is hidden.[80]

In verse 5 the psalmist again cries (זעק) to God, but this time with words of confidence. "You are my refuge [מחסה], my portion [חלק] in the land of the living." The word translated "refuge" in verse 5 is the more common term for refuge in the Psalter, occurring twelve times and consistently indicating a physical place of safety. "My portion [חלק] in the land of the living" echoes the dividing of the land of promise in the wilderness wandering and settlement narratives, in which the word occurs some thirty times. Each tribe except that of Levi was allotted a portion (חלק) of the land. John Goldingay adds that in ancient Israel a family's possession of its "portion" was directly linked to the family's vulnerability.[81] Brueggemann and Bellinger maintain that "implicit" in the psalm singer's statement is that she "will remain in the land of the living and not go down to the realm of death, Sheol."[82]

In verse 6 the psalm singer, who is "brought very low," petitions YHWH to give heed to her "cry," but the Hebrew word used here is not זעק, the word she employs in verses 1 and 5, but rather רנה, derived from the verbal root רנן. רנה can indeed mean "cry or entreaty," as we find, for example, in Psalms 17:1; 61:2; and 106:44, but more often in the Psalter it is "joy, singing, and glad songs," as we see in Psalms 30:6; 105:43; and 118:15. Moreover, the verbal root רנן is almost always used in a positive sense in the Hebrew Bible, never with a sense of oppression.[83] Thus in the context of Psalm 142 we might understand that the psalm singer's רנה in verse 6, while a cry for help, may anticipate the declaration in verse 7 that she will be able to "give thanks" (ידה) if YHWH will save her and bring her out of her prison. The word translated here as "prison" (מסגר) is most likely another metaphor the singer of Psalm 142 employs to describe the situation of oppression and entrapment she feels.[84] It may also have provided the inspiration for the superscription of the psalm.

The psalm closes with words of confident trust that if YHWH will bring her "out of prison" (deliver her from those persecuting her), then the

80. The word occurs only one other time in the Psalter, in 57:17, and is translated in the NRSV as "refuge." For other uses see Job 11:20; Jer 25:35; Amos 2:14.

81. Goldingay, *Psalms 90–150*, 667.

82. Brueggemann and Bellinger, *Psalms*, 593.

83. See, for example, its repeated use in the enthronement psalms: Pss 95:1; 96:12; 98:4, 8.

84. מסגר occurs elsewhere in the Hebrew Bible only in Isa 24:22 and 42:7.

righteous will surround her as God deals bountifully (גמל) with her, providing yet another tie to the historical event in the life of David suggested in Psalm 142's superscription. In 2 Samuel 22:21 David sings: "The Lord rewarded [גמל] me according to my righteousness."

Psalm 142 voices the lament of a person whose "spirit is faint," who is confronted by "traps" wherever she goes, with no one "taking notice." She has no "refuge" except in God, no place she feels safe, and she compares her life situation to being in "prison." In 2017, according to the United States Census Bureau, 39.7 million people in the United States, 12.3 percent of the population, lived below the poverty level.[85] While in households headed by a woman with no husband present the percentage was 25.7, that percentage jumped to an astounding 40.8 percent if children under eighteen were part of the household and 48.4 percent if there were children under the age of six.[86] Many more women than men are living on the brink of poverty. Low wages, lack of affordable housing and slum landlords, lack of affordable childcare, no sick leave time from work, no employer-provided healthcare, and no time or opportunity for education and job training all contribute to the endless cycle of poverty that can make a woman feel as though there are imprisoning traps laid for her wherever she goes. Even for those who manage to "get by" from paycheck to paycheck, a sick child, a car in need of repair, or any other unexpected expense can be overwhelming.

The singer of Psalm 142 cries out to God, saying, "you know my way." I can imagine her saying further, "I do my best. I go to work every day so that I can feed and clothe and provide shelter for my children." And yet, according to verse 3, "In the path where I walk, they have laid a trap for me . . . and no one takes notice." "When my child is sick and I have to take unpaid time off work to care for her; when the kitchen floods and the landlord does nothing; when I work hard and others get promoted over me; when my paycheck and the aid I receive don't buy enough groceries to get us through the week . . . no one notices, no one seems to care. I feel as though I am in some kind of life prison with no way of escaping."

---

85. Kayla Fontenot, Jessica Semega, and Melissa Kollar, "Income & Poverty in the United States: 2017," *United States Census Bureau Current Population Report* (Washington, DC: US Department of Commerce, 2017), 12–13, tables 3 and 4.

86. In households headed by a male with no wife present the percentage was 12.4 percent. In such households with children under eighteen it was 19.1 percent, and with children under six it was 22.6 percent.

The psalm singer thus appeals to God. She has been faithful; God knows her ways. If God will save her from this endless cycle of despair she will offer thanks in full confidence that God "will deal bountifully" with her. The word translated "bountifully" in verse 7 is גמל, which means in its most basic sense "be kind, treat kindly, be helpful, deal fully or adequately with."[87] An interesting occurrence of גמל is in Psalm 131. There the psalm singer likens her sense of quiet and contentment in the presence of YHWH to that of a child in the arms of her mother. Verse 2 reads, "my soul [נפש] is like the weaned [גמל] child that is with[in] me." Here גמל is translated "weaned," a meaning derived from the word's basic idea of dealing fully or adequately with something.[88] גמל, however, is also used in the Hebrew Bible to express the idea of dealing with someone in a full or adequate manner, and thus the image in Psalm 131 could also be that of a still-nursing child who is well-fed and fully satisfied (גמל), resting peacefully in the mother's embrace.[89] Both meanings provide an apt expression of the confidence shown by the singer of Psalm 142. God will "deal bountifully" with her, weaning her from the traps that have kept her bound in her prison of endless poverty or near-poverty or providing for her until she is like a sated child who finally is fully fed (able to provide for herself and those in her care) and who can now rest peacefully on life-giving breasts.

Psalm 143

Psalm 143, along with Psalms 140, 141, and 142, is an individual lament, a group of four laments of David framed by Psalms 138 and 139 (individual hymns of thanksgiving) and Psalms 144 and 145 (a royal psalm and a wisdom psalm).[90] Psalm 143 has a number of thematic and verbal links with Psalms 140–142, indicating their integrity as a group. A unique characteristic of Psalm 143 is the psalmist's reference to self in relation to God as "your servant" in verses 2 and 12. The reference may be in anticipation of the royal psalm that follows; besides, as Frank-Lothar Hossfeld suggests, "It describes, or includes, belonging, a special relationship to YHWH as well as the humility of the human being before

---

87. Klaus Seybold, "גמל (*gāmal*)," *TDOT*, 3:23–33, at 23–25.

88. See Gen 21:8; 1 Sam 1:22; Isa 28:9.

89. See Goldingay, *Psalms 90–150*, 537.

90. Ps 143 is the last lament psalm in the Psalter, with a series of hymns (Pss 144–150) following.

Psalm 143:1-12

A Psalm of David

¹Hear my prayer, O LORD;
   give ear to my supplications in
      your faithfulness;
   answer me in your righteousness.
²Do not enter into judgment with your
      servant,
   for no one living is righteous
      before you.
³For the enemy has pursued me,
   crushing my life to the ground,

making me sit in darkness like
      those long dead.
⁴Therefore my spirit faints within me;
   my heart within me is appalled.
⁵I remember the days of old,
   I think about all your deeds,
   I meditate on the works of your
      hands.
⁶I stretch out my hands to you;
   my soul thirsts for you like a
      parched land.   *Selah*

God."[91] In addition, the Septuagint and Vulgate add to the superscription ("a psalm of David") the words "when his son [Absalom] pursued him" (see Ps 3). As with the superscription to Psalm 142, which places it in a particularly turbulent time in the life of David, so Psalm 143's added superscription gives the reader a historical context for reading the psalm.

Psalm 143 begins with a threefold plea to God to "hear," "give ear," and "answer." The word translated "supplications" in verse 1 is from the Hebrew root חנן, "to show favor," and the phrase "give ear to my supplications" echoes Psalm 140:6, the opening psalm of this cluster of laments of David, as well as the first verse of Psalm 142.

In verse 2 the psalm singer admonishes God not to enter into judgment against her, calling herself God's "servant" and adding that no one living is righteous before God. The sentiment expressed in verse 2 occurs most frequently in the books of Job and Ecclesiastes, suggesting perhaps a sapiential tradition behind Psalm 143.[92]

The complaint portion of the psalm begins in verse 3, using words and phrases common to individual laments. The enemy (אויב), who appears here and twice in the petition of the psalm (vv. 9 and 12), pursues and crushes, leaving the psalmist sitting in darkness, akin to the "prison" of Psalm 142:7. Thus, in verse 4, the spirit (רוח) of the psalmist faints, just as does the spirit (רוח) of the singer of Psalm 142 (v. 3), and her heart (לב) is appalled (שמם). שמם occurs in the *hithpolel* (the form we find in v. 4) only

---

91. Hossfeld and Zenger, *Psalms 3*, 573.

92. For "enter into judgment," see Job 9:32; 14:3; 22:4; Qoh 11:9; 12:14; for the idea that no human is righteous before God see Job 9:2; 15:14; 25:4.

[7]Answer me quickly, O LORD;
  my spirit fails.
Do not hide your face from me,
  or I shall be like those who go
    down to the Pit.
[8]Let me hear of your steadfast love in
    the morning,
  for in you I put my trust.
Teach me the way I should go,
  for to you I lift up my soul.
[9]Save me, O LORD, from my enemies;
  I have fled to you for refuge.

[10]Teach me to do your will,
  for you are my God.
Let your good spirit lead me
  on a level path.
[11]For your name's sake, O LORD,
  preserve my life.
In your righteousness bring me
  out of trouble.
[12]In your steadfast love cut off my
    enemies,
  and destroy all my adversaries,
  for I am your servant.

five times in the Hebrew Bible. It indicates something of a crippling state, a sense of numbness, disbelief, or dismay.[93]

In the midst of the darkness, fainting, and desolation the psalm singer remembers, in verse 5, the days of old. "Remember" (זכר) is a powerful and pervasive word in the Hebrew Bible. It occurs nearly two hundred times and generally conveys the idea of "the presence and acceptance of something in the mind."[94] The psalmist remembers and then "thinks about" (הגה) and "meditates on" (שׂיח) the works of God's hands. שׂיח, translated in verse 5 as "meditate on," is from the same Hebrew word translated "complaint" in Psalm 142:2. There the psalmist is agitated by oppression and complains to God; in Psalm 143 she remembers the works of God in the world and meditates on them, spreading out her hands as her "soul" (נפשׁ, very being) thirsts for God (v. 6). The outspread hands in Psalm 143 bring to mind the uplifted hands of the singer of Psalm 141:2. Hossfeld maintains, however, that "thought, reflection, and memory are not intended positively; they are an effect of the distressed situation, indicating the tension between the past actions of God and the absence of God's action in the present. The prayer gesture in v. 6a is also anything but a confession of trust; it is a sign of the petitioner's cry for help."[95] John Goldingay adds, "Recollecting how things once were is a

---

93. The other occurrences of the verb in the *hithpolel* are Isa 59:16 and 63:5; Qoh 7:16; Dan 8:27. Ivo Meyer, "שׁמם (*šāmam*)," *TDOT*, 15:238–48, at 238–39, 242.

94. Hermann Eising, "זכר (*zākăr*)," *TDOT*, 4:64–82, at 65.

95. Hossfeld and Zenger, *Psalms 3*, 571.

common feature of a prayer psalm, adding to the force of the lament by contrasting past and present."[96]

Hossfeld's assessment of the mindset and intention of the psalm singer is seemingly confirmed by the next verses of the psalm. Beginning with verse 7 the psalmist embarks on what Leslie Allen calls "an urgent, breath-less series of appeals"[97] that lasts for six verses, continuing the three-fold petition of verses 1 and 2 and, in verses 9 and 12, pointing out the "enemy" (אויב) mentioned in verse 3. She cries out to YHWH: "answer me quickly," "do not hide your face," "let me hear," "teach me," "save me," "teach me," "let your good spirit lead me," "preserve my life," "bring me out of trouble," "cut off my enemies," and "destroy my adversaries."

The "Pit" (בור) in verse 7 is a word commonly used in parallel with "Sheol."[98] The petition from the psalm singer to God in verse 8 to "hear of your steadfast love in the morning" may refer to the singer's lament that she sits "in darkness" (v. 3) and is in "prison" (Ps 142:7), and she "lifts up" (נשא) her "soul" (נפש) just as the singer of Psalm 141:2 "lifts up" (נשא) her hands. The phrase "your good spirit" (רוחך טובה) appears only in verse 10 of Psalm 143 and in Nehemiah 9:20 in the Hebrew Bible, where the people have gathered to confess God's care for them throughout their history. In recounting the time of the wilderness wanderings Ezra says, "you gave your good spirit [רוחך טובה] to instruct them." In verse 10 of Psalm 143 the psalmist asks that God's good spirit lead her on a level path. In verse 11 the singer pleads with YHWH to preserve her life and in verse 12 to cut off her enemies and destroy her adversaries. She closes with the words "I am your servant," echoing verse 2.

Psalm 143 is one of the seven penitential psalms of the Psalter (Pss 6, 32, 38, 51, 102, 130, and 143), used in the Lenten liturgy of the medieval church, reminding reciters of the great divide between God and humanity and giving voice to humanity's entreaties to God to "hasten, answer, and deliver." Thus Psalm 143 may be interpreted as the prayer of someone who comes to God, naming herself as God's servant and recognizing her own unrighteousness (v. 2) and pleading with God to "teach" (vv. 8, 10) her God's will and way.

An additional understanding of Psalm 143 may be found by examin-ing closely the words of verse 11 and reading this psalm in the context

---

96. Goldingay, *Psalms 90–150*, 674.

97. Allen, *Psalms 101–150*, 356.

98. See Pss 30:3 and 88:3-4. For a discussion of Sheol, see Translation Matters for Ps 116.

of the five psalms of David that precede it. In Psalm 138 the singer declares God's regard for the lowly in the midst of trouble (vv. 6 and 7); in Psalm 139 the psalmist praises a nurturing God who has known her even before she was born (vv. 15-16); in Psalms 140–142 she laments the "traps" (Pss 140:5; 141:6; 142:3), the "snares" (Pss 140:5; 141:6), and the "cords" (Ps 140:5) that evildoers, the arrogant, the wicked, persecutors, and enemies have put in her path.

In verse 11 the psalm singer expresses what may be the motivation for her urgent petitions to YHWH: "for your name's sake" (לְמַעַן־שִׁמְךָ).[99] The "name" of YHWH is a powerful force in the Hebrew Bible. In Exodus 3, Moses asks for God's name so that he can return to Egypt and lead the Israelites to freedom. In the story of Rahab in the book of Joshua, Rahab says to the spies she has hidden: "The LORD your God is indeed God in heaven above and on earth below" (Josh 2:11). In 1 Samuel 12:22, Samuel says to the people: "For the LORD will not cast away his people, for his great name's sake." The phrase occurs in the Psalter as part of a plea to YHWH to deliver and/or forgive, or in recounting the rationale for YHWH's deliverance. In Psalm 31:3-4 the psalmist says to God: "for your name's sake lead me and guide me, take me out of the net that is hidden for me." The singer of Psalm 25 cries out in verse 11, "for your name's sake, O LORD, pardon my guilt, for it is great." In Psalm 106:8 we read: "Yet he saved them for his name's sake, so that he might make known his mighty power."

Brueggemann and Bellinger therefore maintain that the singer of Psalm 143 "in a show of considerable chutzpah, stands in the prayer tradition of Israel and seeks to leverage YHWH by appealing to YHWH's own self-regard."[100] J. Clinton McCann writes that the psalm singer's appeal to two of God's inherent characteristics, "faithfulness" (אמונה) and "righteousness" (צדקה), in verse 1 sets the tone for the psalm, and the words of verse 11 confirm that the issue presented in Psalm 143 is "fundamentally one of God's character."[101] We are invited to read in the words of Psalm 143 the bold demands of a woman who has had enough of "traps" and "nets" and "snares" and "prison" and "darkness" and who now boldly challenges YHWH to "preserve her life" by appealing to YHWH's own reputation in the world.

99. For a full discussion of "name" (שם), see the commentary for Ps 113.

100. Brueggemann and Bellinger, *Psalms*, 597–98.

101. McCann, "The Book of Psalms," 1251.

Psalm 144

With Psalm 144 the tone of the final Davidic collection shifts from lament (Pss 140–143) to words of confidence in God, who is a rock, a fortress, and a stronghold for the psalm singer (v. 2). It is classified as a royal psalm, the third in book 5,[102] but it is an interesting composition containing echoes of a number of other psalms in the Psalter, including Psalm 8:4 in 144:3, Psalm 39:5-6 in 144:4, Psalm 33:2 and 3 in 144:9, and Psalm 33:12 in 144:12. The most extensive connections in Psalm 144, though, are to Psalm 18, one of four royal psalms in book 1. Psalm 144:1 uses the same language as Psalm 18:34; 144:2 echoes 18:2, 46, and 47; 144:5 parallels 18:9; 144:6 employs the same imagery as 18:14; 144:7 and 11 use language identical to 18:16, 44, 45; and verse 10 of Psalm 144 recalls the superscription of Psalm 18. Walter Brueggemann and William H. Bellinger describe Psalm 144 as a "rereading" of Psalm 18.[103] Given that Psalm 18 is a duplicate of the song sung by David in 2 Samuel 22, we may say also that Psalm 144 (by association) is firmly anchored in the life story of David, the great king of ancient Israel.[104] James L. Mays writes:

> The composer of Psalm 144 must have found in [Psalm 18] a promise for the psalmist's own time. So the psalmist composed a psalm of praise and prayer to the God who [according to 144:10] "gives salvation to kings and rescues his servant David" as a context for petitions for deliverance from the aliens of the psalmist's time. By re-praying Psalm 18 in a new version, the writer appealed to the LORD to do for the people what the LORD had done for the LORD's servant David.[105]

Erhard Gerstenberger cautions, though, that likeness does not necessarily equate to borrowing:

> The process of composing psalms has to be thought of much more in terms of a broad transmission of sacred texts that to a large extent consisted of traditional vocabulary, stock phrases, and form elements. . . . Conscious use of particular, already existing psalms by late composers would be very difficult to ascertain.[106]

---

102. The other two are Pss 110 and 132. Royal psalms are so classified because their subject matter is the person of the king. Nine psalms in the Psalter are identified as royal: Pss 2, 18, 20, 21, 45, 72, 101, 110, and 132.

103. Brueggemann and Bellinger, *Psalms*, 599.

104. The LXX expands the superscription of Ps 144, adding to the MT's "of David" "against Goliath."

105. Mays, *Psalms*, 436.

106. Gerstenberger, *Psalms, Part 2, and Lamentations*, 427.

Psalm 144:1-15

Of David.

¹Blessed be the LORD, my rock,
  who trains my hands for war, and
    my fingers for battle;
²my rock and my fortress,
  my stronghold and my deliverer,
my shield, in whom I take refuge,
  who subdues the peoples under
    me.
³O LORD, what are human beings that
    you regard them,
  or mortals that you think of them?
⁴They are like a breath;
  their days are like a passing
    shadow.

⁵Bow your heavens, O LORD, and
  come down;
  touch the mountains so that they
    smoke.
⁶Make the lightning flash and scatter
    them;
  send out your arrows and rout
    them.
⁷Stretch out your hand from on high;
  set me free and rescue me from
    the mighty waters,
  from the hand of aliens,
⁸whose mouths speak lies,
  and whose right hands are false.
⁹I will sing a new song to you, O God;

In verses 1 and 2 of Psalm 144 the psalm singer praises God with a piling up of descriptive phrases and the pronouns "my," "I," and "me" (ten times in vv. 1-2). While the singer of Psalm 18 opens with the words "I love you, O LORD," the singer of Psalm 144 opens with "Blessed be the LORD" and goes on to laud God as "my rock, who trains [למד] my hands for war, and my fingers for battle." למד echoes Psalm 143's petition to YHWH to "teach [למד] me to do your will" (v. 10). The word "hand" (יד) figures prominently in Psalm 144, in verses 1, 7, 8, and 11, with a strong distinction made between the divine and the human hand.

The NRSV emends the beginning of verse 2 from "my חסד" to "my rock" in order to harmonize the verse with Psalm 18:2 and 2 Samuel 22:2-3. There is no textual support for emendation, however, and numerous differences between the three texts make emendation unwarranted. The use of חסד in fact connects Psalm 144 with the collection of psalms of David of which it is a part (Pss 138–145). In Psalm 138:2 the psalmist gives "thanks to your name for your steadfast love [חסד]," and the word occurs as well in Psalms 141:5; 143:8, 12; and 145:8.

In a rather abrupt change in thought in verse 3 the psalm singer ponders God's regard for humanity, employing the parallel terms "human beings" (אדם) and "mortals" (בן־אנוש), bringing to mind the words of Psalm 8:5. The two verses, Psalms 144:3 and 8:5, exhibit a number of differences that are masked somewhat in English translations. The term translated "human beings" in 8:5 is בן־אדם and the word translated

Psalm 144:1-15 (cont.)

upon a ten-stringed harp I will play
to you,
¹⁰the one who gives victory to kings,
who rescues his servant David.
¹¹Rescue me from the cruel sword,
and deliver me from the hand of
aliens,
whose mouths speak lies,
and whose right hands are false.
¹²May our sons in their youth
be like plants full grown,
our daughters like corner pillars,
cut for the building of a palace.
¹³May our barns be filled,

with produce of every kind;
may our sheep increase by
thousands,
by tens of thousands in our fields,
¹⁴and may our cattle be heavy
with young.
May there be no breach in the walls,
no exile,
and no cry of distress in our
streets.
¹⁵Happy are the people to whom such
blessings fall;
happy are the people whose God
is the LORD.

"mortals" is אנוש, while in 144:3 "human being" is אדם and "mortal" is בן־אנוש. In 8:5 the psalmist wonders that God is "mindful of" (זכר) and "cares for" (פקד) humanity, while in 144:3 the verbs used of God are "regard" (ידע) and "think of" (חשב).

Verse 4 of Psalm 144 likens humanity to a breath (הבל) and a shadow (צל), recalling the words of Psalms 39:5-6 and 11; 62:9; 78:33; and 109:23. הבל is the word used by the author of Qoheleth nearly forty times to describe life.[107] The term is introduced in Qoheleth 1:2 and is translated in the NRSV as "vanity of vanities" (הבל הבלים), better translated as "breath of breaths." Erhard Gerstenberger maintains that verses 3 and 4 of Psalm 144 "lean toward sapiential thinking."[108]

In another change in mood, but perhaps as a result of her pondering over the ephemeral state of humanity, the psalm singer in verses 5-8 petitions God for protection, echoing verses 9, 14-16, and 44-45 of Psalm 18. Using language associated with theophanies in the Hebrew Bible, the psalmist calls on God to come down from the heavens and cause the mountains to smoke and lightning to flash.[109] "The mighty waters" (מים רבים) is used in poetic parallelism in verse 7 with "the hand of aliens" (יד בני נכר). The phrase translated "aliens" is rendered in various

107. See Lisa M. Wolfe, *Qoheleth*, WCS 24 (Collegeville, MN: Liturgical Press, 2019).
108. Gerstenberger, *Psalms, Part 2, and Lamentations*, 428.
109. See Exod 19:16 and 1 Kgs 19:11-12.

English translations as "strangers" (CEB), "foreigners" (ESV and NIV), "strange children" (KJV), and "aliens" (NASB and NRSV). The LXX translates it υἱῶν ἀλλοτρίων, "children of others." The phrase is common in the Hebrew Bible, occurring in Genesis 17:12; Exodus 12:43; Leviticus 22:25; Isaiah 56:3, 6; 60:10; 61:5; 62:8; Ezekiel 44:7, 9; Nehemiah 9:2; and Psalm 18:44, 45; in each case it refers to those outside the community of ancient Israel. The psalmist maintains in verse 8 that the "aliens" speak "lies" (שׁוא) and that their "right hands" (ימין) are "false" (שׁקר) and asks God to stretch out God's hand (plural in Hebrew, ידים) to "free" (פצה) and rescue her from them. Passages in the Hebrew Bible that describe God's hand delivering God's people employ the singular form of "hand," while passages that describe God's creative work in the world use the plural form.[110] Frank-Lothar Hossfeld writes: "Evidently the intent is to represent the theophanic YHWH also as the creator God."[111]

In verse 9 the psalm singer states that she will sing a "new song" to God upon a "ten-stringed harp." "A new song" (שׁיר חדשׁ) occurs elsewhere in the Psalter in the enthronement Psalms 96 and 98 and in Psalm 148, one of the final Hallel psalms. Verse 10 references David, the great warrior and song singer of ancient Israel, recalling the superscription of Psalm 18.

The phrase "David his servant" ties Psalm 144 to the end of Psalm 143 in which the psalm singer calls herself "your servant." Likewise, the term translated "rescue" in verse 10, describing what God has done for David, is the same word, פצה, that the psalmist uses in her petition to God in verse 7 to "set me free." The singer of Psalm 144 calls on God to set her free just as God set David free. Verse 11 is virtually identical to verses 7 and 8, employing פצה once again and forming perhaps something of an *inclusio* around verses 9-10, focusing them as the key to understanding Psalm 144.

The tone of the psalm changes once more with verse 12. The first-person-singular voice gives way to the first-person-plural voice, as perhaps the individual singer joins her voice with those of others in the community, asking for God's good provision for them—or we might understand the individual psalm singer as speaking on behalf of her community.

The items mentioned in verses 12-14—sons, daughters, grain, sheep, and cattle—were important assets to ancient Near Eastern families. The list is strikingly similar to the one in Deuteronomy 28:4, part of the blessings for obedience promised to the children of Israel as they prepare

110. Note the singular form in Ps 138:7; Exod 15:6 and 7; Deut 5:15 and 6:21; and the plural form in Pss 8:7; 138:8; 143:5.

111. Hossfeld and Zenger, *Psalms 3*, 585.

to enter the land. Verse 14 has been translated and interpreted in two very different ways. The NRSV adds "in the walls" to the MT and uses "exile" to translate the Hebrew word יוֹצֵאת, from the root יצא (go out).[112] The KJV, ESV, and NASB, on the other hand, do not refer to walls and translate יוֹצֵאת as "going out," "loss," and "failure in bearing." Thus two understandings of the final portion of verse 14 are possible: that there may be enough food produced in the city to support it and make it less vulnerable to outside attack (the NRSV) or that there may be enough food produced—with no miscarriages among the cattle—to ensure that there is sustenance for all, no cries of hunger and despair in the streets (ESV and NASB). Psalm 144 ends with two אַשְׁרֵי statements in verse 15, the first summarizing the good that comes to people who receive the blessings outlined in the previous verses, the second an affirmation of the good that comes to people who acknowledge Yhwh as their God.

Psalm 144 is a masterful example of appropriating traditional phrases, images, and ideas to ever-new situations in life. Whether the psalmist borrowed from book 1 of the Psalter in general, from Psalms 8, 18, and 32 in particular, or from a stock of traditions shared by a faith community, the resulting song is a witness to the power of what James Sanders calls "the old, tried, and true." He writes:

> In crisis situations, only the old, tried, and true has any real authority. Nothing thought up at the last minute, no matter how clever, can effect the necessary steps of recapitulation and transcendence needed by the threatened community, if it is to survive with identity. A new story will not do; only a story with old, recognizable elements has the power for life required.[113]

John Goldingay writes that Psalm 144 "takes up the declarations in Ps. 18 and elsewhere but refracts them through the lens of present situation and need."[114] Book 5 of the Psalter tells the story of ancient Israel as it returned from exile in Babylon and attempted to find a way to be God's people in a radically changed world.[115] Old words, words that rang true in the past, are attributed to David and paint a picture of new hope for a struggling community.

112. See also the CEB and NIV.
113. Sanders, "Adaptable for Life: The Nature and Function of Canon," in *From Sacred Story to Sacred Text*, 21.
114. Goldingay, *Psalms 90–150*, 691.
115. See the introduction, pp. liv–lv.

Set Us Free from Those Whose Mouths Speak Lies

An article in the May 13, 2019, issue of *Time Magazine* titled "South Africa's Dividing Line"[116] states that twenty-five years after the end of apartheid in South Africa the World Bank has declared that country the world's most unequal society, largely divided along racial lines. The top 10 percent of the population owned some 70 percent of the country's assets while the bottom 60 percent controlled 7 percent, and most of the bottom 60 percent live on less than five dollars a day.

According to the article, the source of the inequality "is multifaceted. Unemployment, poor education programs and a collapsing public health system all play a role. But the largest dividing line is land."[117] That divide manifests itself in the number of "informal settlements"[118] that have grown up around the major cities in South Africa. Their number in 1994, before the end of apartheid, was three hundred; in 2019, twenty-five years after the end of apartheid, the number is 2,700. Imizamo Yethu, near Cape Town, is an example. It is described in the *Time* article as a "ramshackle settlement . . . made up of small brick houses, corrugated-aluminum shacks and lean-tos constructed from old shipping pallets."[119] Six thousand families live there in an area about the size of an American shopping mall. In Cape Town 60 percent of the population, mostly black, live in townships and informal settlements like Imizamo Yethu, far from the business areas of the city. Travel from the townships and informal settlements to places of employment is expensive and erratic; trains from the townships to the city cost a third of a typical worker's daily wages, and minibuses that serve the informal settlements are crowded and sometimes dangerous.

Separating the informal settlements and townships from Cape Town's center are vast tracts of unused public land, some of which used to be bustling villages on the edge of the city. One example is District Six, a 150-acre stretch of land that until 1966 was home to sixty thousand people of various backgrounds. In 1966 the apartheid regime declared the

---

116. Aryn Baker, "South Africa's Dividing Line," *Time Magazine* (May 13, 2019): 42–47.

117. Ibid., 45.

118. This author will use the term "informal settlements" to refer to both black townships and the "makeshift settlements" that sit on the outskirts of South Africa's major cities.

119. Baker, "South Africa's Dividing Line," 43.

area "whites only," and by 1982 most of the buildings had been demolished and the residents relocated to a township eighteen miles away.

The irony is that District Six was never developed as a white neighborhood, and now the land is used as a parking lot for commuters to downtown Cape Town. After 1994 residents of District Six were allowed to return, but the process for establishing ownership and gaining permission to return is caught up in government red tape. Thus far only 139 homes have been rebuilt in the district. Construction began on a three-hundred-unit apartment complex in 2013, but according to the article it has barely progressed. By now many of those who were relocated in 1982 are too elderly to be able to return to District Six. The issues that plague Cape Town are not unique to that South African city.

Black South Africans have been driven off their lands since the colonial era, but in 1948 the South African government instituted a policy of separation of races. The country's black citizens were "legally" stripped of their land and forcibly relocated to designated developments. In the postapartheid era reclaiming lost land is a major issue for South African blacks, but in 2019, twenty-five years after the end of apartheid, little progress has been made. The questions of land ownership and land rights seem to be tied up in the very government that promised repatriation.

As I read the words of verses 7-8 and 11 of Psalm 144, "set me free . . . from [those] whose mouths speak lies and whose right hands are false," I cannot but think about the people in South Africa who hoped that with the end of apartheid they might have a new beginning and a new chance at lives for themselves, their children, and their children's children. But those hopes have been dashed by what can only be described as lies and false dealings. The hope for sons to flourish like growing plants and daughters to be able to be strong, with plenty of food and no cries of distress in the streets (vv. 12-14), seems like a distant dream. But may God "bow the heavens, touch the mountains, and stretch out God's hand" and bring those hopes to reality.

Nancy L. deClaissé-Walford

Psalm 145

Psalm 145 is the last of the group of eight psalms (Pss 138–145) at the end of book 5 of the Psalter that are ascribed, in their superscriptions, to

Praise. Of David.

א ¹I will extol you, my God and King,
and bless your name forever
and ever.

ב ²Every day I will bless you,
and praise your name forever
and ever.

ג ³Great is the LORD, and greatly to be
praised;
his greatness is unsearchable.

ד ⁴One generation shall laud your
works to another,
and shall declare your mighty acts.

ה ⁵On the glorious splendor of your
majesty,

and on your wondrous works, I
will meditate.

ו ⁶The might of your awesome deeds
shall be proclaimed,
and I will declare your greatness.

ז ⁷They shall celebrate the fame of
your abundant goodness,
and shall sing aloud of your
righteousness.

ח ⁸The LORD is gracious and merciful,
slow to anger and abounding in
steadfast love.

ט ⁹The LORD is good to all,
and his compassion is over all
that he has made.

David. It is an acrostic in which in each verse of the psalm begins with a successive letter of the Hebrew alphabet.[120]

The Babylonian Talmud tractate Berakot 4b states that Psalm 145, like the *Shema* (Deut 6:4-5: "Hear, O Israel, the LORD is our God; the LORD alone. You shall love the LORD your God with all your heart, and with all your soul, and with all your might"), is to be recited three times a day and everyone who does so "may be sure that he [or she] is a child of the world to come."[121] Psalm 145 appears in the Jewish Prayer Book more than any other psalm in the Psalter, and the Psalm scroll 11QPsᵃ from Qumran contains a version of this psalm in which the refrain "Blessed is the LORD and blessed is his name forever and ever" is included after each verse, pointing to some sort of liturgical use. All indications are that the words of this psalm were and are a vital part of the faith of the Jewish people.

120. The נ line, which should be between vv. 13 and 14, is missing in the MT. It is included in 11QPsᵃ, the LXX, and in the Syriac tradition. It reads "YHWH is faithful in all his words and loyal in all he does." The NRSV includes the missing line as part of verse 13. See pp. 109–10 on the nature and function of acrostic poems.

121. S. D. Goitein designated Psalm 145 as the *"shema"* of the book of Psalms in his *Biblical Studies* (Tel Aviv: Yavneh, 1957), 228.

Psalm 145:1-21 (cont.)

׳ ¹⁰All your works shall give thanks to you, O Lᴏʀᴅ,
and all your faithful shall bless you.

כ ¹¹They shall speak of the glory of your kingdom,
and tell of your power,

ל ¹²to make known to all people your mighty deeds,
and the glorious splendor of your kingdom.

מ ¹³Your kingdom is an everlasting kingdom,

and your dominion endures throughout all generations.
The Lᴏʀᴅ is faithful in all his words,
and gracious in all his deeds.

ס ¹⁴The Lᴏʀᴅ upholds all who are falling,
and raises up all who are bowed down.

ע ¹⁵The eyes of all look to you,
and you give them their food in due season.

פ ¹⁶You open your hand,

Psalm 145's superscription, unique to the Hebrew Psalter, is "Praise [תהלה]. Of David." The psalm begins with the psalmist's individual words of praise and blessing addressed directly to "my God the king."[122] While the idea of God as king is expressed many times in the Psalter,[123] only here and in Psalm 98:6 does the psalmist refer to God as *the* king. The singer's direct address to God continues in verse 2, where she declares that she will "bless" (ברך) and "praise" (הלל) Yʜwʜ's "name" (שם) for all time.[124] Verses 1 and 2 and verse 21 frame Psalm 145 with the repeated words "bless," "praise," "name," and "forever and ever." Verse 3 gives the reason why Yʜwʜ is worthy of praise: Yʜwʜ's "unsearchable greatness" (גדולתו אין חקר). God's "unsearchable greatness" contrasts with the psalm singer's acknowledgment in Psalm 139:1 "O Lᴏʀᴅ, you have searched [חקר] me and known me."

In verse 4 the psalm singer proclaims, "One generation shall laud your works to another," and in verse 6 announces that she too will declare God's greatness. Leslie Allen writes: "The poet willingly owns himself to be a link in this living chain of worship of the great king."[125] Verses 4-7 employ seven verbs to express the way in which the generations and the

---

122. The NRSV translates v. 1 as "my God and king," but the Hebrew text contains the definite article before "king," requiring a translation of "the king."

123. See especially the collection of enthronement psalms in book 4, Pss 93, 95–99.

124. For a discussion of the significance of "name" in the Hebrew Bible, see the commentary for Ps 113.

125. Allen, *Psalms 100–150*, 372.

satisfying the desire of every
living thing.

צ ¹⁷The Lᴏʀᴅ is just in all his ways,
and kind in all his doings.

ק ¹⁸The Lᴏʀᴅ is near to all who call
on him,
to all who call on him in truth.

ר ¹⁹He fulfills the desire of all who
fear him;

he also hears their cry, and
saves them.

ש ²⁰The Lᴏʀᴅ watches over all who
love him,
but all the wicked he will destroy.

ת ²¹My mouth will speak the praise of
the Lᴏʀᴅ,
and all flesh will bless his holy
name forever and ever.

psalm singer will praise God's greatness. The generations will "laud" (שבח) and "declare" (נגד, make known) in verse 4. In verse 5 the psalm singer says, "I will meditate," from the verbal root שׂיח, which can mean "muse, speak, talk," even "sing."[126] The generations and the psalmist will "proclaim" (אמר, say) and "declare" (ספר, recount) in verse 6; in verse 7 the generations will "celebrate" and "sing aloud." The word translated "celebrate" is from the root נבע, which means "bubble up, pour out," and "sing aloud" is from רנן, meaning "give a ringing cry."[127] The psalm singer and the generations will not simply make known God's greatness; they will proclaim it eagerly and joyously tell it.

In verses 4-6 the psalm singer uses four different words to describe the acts of God on behalf of humanity. The first, in verse 4, is "works," from the root עשׂה, which means simply "do, make, manufacture, prepare." The second word, also in verse 4, translated "mighty works," is derived from the root גבר and means "achieve, be strong, increase." In verse 5 the psalmist meditates on God's "wondrous works" (נפלאות), which is derived from the verbal root פלא meaning "be unusual, wonderful, miraculous." "Wondrous works" (נפלאות) is often used in the Hebrew Bible to describe God's actions on behalf of the Israelites during the exodus from Egypt and the wilderness wandering. In Exodus 3:20 God says to Moses, "I will stretch out my hand and strike Egypt with all my wonders [נפלאות] that I will perform in it," and in Exodus 34:10, "Behold I make a covenant. Before all your people I will perform marvels [נפלאות], such as have not been performed in all the earth or in any nation." In Psalm

126. Note its occurrence in Pss 142:3 and 143:5.
127. See the repeated use of רנן in the enthronement psalms (93–100).

86:10 the psalm singer says of God, "You are great and do wondrous things [נִפְלָאוֹת]," and the singer of Psalm 136:4 affirms that God alone "does great wonders [נִפְלָאוֹת]."

In verse 6 of Psalm 145 the psalmist describes the acts of God on behalf of humanity as "awesome deeds" (נוֹרְאוֹת), from the root ירא, "be awesome, terrible, terrifying." Brueggemann and Bellinger state that the psalm is "a good example of a poetic structure of intensification as descriptions pile up."[128] We observe this in the "piling up" of the words used to describe God's workings in the world and the numerous verbs used to convey the means by which the generations and the psalm singers will make God's greatness known in verses 4-7.

Verse 8 echoes God's self-descriptive words given to Moses on Mount Sinai in Exodus 34.[129] Verse 9 acts as something of a summary statement of the preceding verses. Yhwh is "good" (טוֹב) and compassionate (רַחֲמִים) "over all that he has made." The word translated "compassion" in verse 9 and the one translated "merciful" in verse 8 are both derived from the word רחם, which literally means "womb," depicting here an image of the womb-love of a feminine God for her created world.[130] Verse 10 continues the psalm singer's direct address to Yhwh, stating that both the creation and the faithful ones (חֲסִידִים) will thank and bless God, but it acts as something of a summary of the verses that precede it and an introduction to the verses that follow. Frank-Lothar Hossfeld maintains that the verse functions as "a kind of intermediate introduction, like a superscription."[131]

The centerpiece, both physically and thematically, of the acrostic Psalm 145 is verses 11-13. Verse 11 begins with the Hebrew letter *kaf* (כ), verse 12 with *lamed* (ל), and verse 13 with *mem* (מ). The initial letters of these lines, reversed, spell the Hebrew word for king, *melek* (מלך), and within verses 11-13 the word "kingdom" (מלכות) occurs four times. In the Hebrew text the word appears at the beginning of verse 11, the end of verse 12, and twice at the beginning of verse 13, forming a triangular structure with its apex at the end of verse 12 and its base at the beginnings of verses 11 and 13.

---

128. Brueggemann and Bellinger, *Psalms*, 604.

129. The ordering of the descriptors of Yhwh in Ps 145 differ from those in Exod 34 because of the acrostic structure of the psalm. Verse 8 is the ח line of the acrostic and thus חנון appears first, while in Exod 34 it is רחום that comes first.

130. See the commentary for Ps 116:5.

131. Hossfeld and Zenger, *Psalms 3*, 599.

11 מלכות . . . .

12 . . . . מלכות מלכות

13 מלכות. . . . .

These verses emphasize the theme of Psalm 145, the reign of God over the "faithful" (חסידים) and all of God's "works" (מעשׂים).[132]

Verses 14-20, like verses 3-9, are descriptions of God. But whereas the words of verses 3-9 declare attributes of God, the words of verses 14-20 describe actions of God on behalf of creation. In a series of active participles the psalm singer outlines God's generous care: God "upholds" and "raises up" (v. 14), "gives" food (v. 15), "opens his hand" and "satisfies" (v. 16), "is near" (v. 18), "fulfills desires" and "hears cries" (v. 19), and "watches over" (v. 20).[133] Here we observe concrete actions by the sovereign Yhwh for those who diligently seek God. Verse 20 contrasts the fate of those who love God with the fate of the wicked, recalling the words of Psalm 1. While these words may seem in contradiction to verse 9's statement that God has "compassion over all that he has made," J. Clinton McCann reminds us:

> The happiness or prosperity of the righteous (see Ps 1:1, 3) is not so much a reward as it is their experience of being connected to the true source of life—God. Similarly, the destruction of the wicked is not so much a punishment as it is the result of their own choice to cut themselves off from the source of life.[134]

The final words of Psalm 145 begin with the individual voice of the psalm singer and expand to encompass the voice of all flesh in the praise of God as sovereign. "Praise" (תהלה), "bless" (ברך), "name" (שׁם), and "forever and ever" (לעולם ועד) occur in verse 21 just as they do in verses 1 and 2, providing a framing or *inclusio* for the psalm. Psalms 146–150, the concluding doxology of the Psalter, will continue to voice the praise of God that is initiated in Psalm 145.

Might we read Psalm 145 as the summary statement of the theme of the Hebrew Psalter, that Yhwh *is sovereign over all the generations of the*

132. The enthronement psalms (Pss 47, 93–100) also celebrate the sovereignty of God, using much the same language as that found in Ps 145. For a discussion of the use of the term "reign" rather than "kingship," see the discussion for Ps 93.

133. For similar language about God, see Pss 107:33-42 and 72:1-14.

134. McCann, "The Book of Psalms," 1260–61.

Israelites and over all flesh? And might we hear David, the former earthly king of ancient Israel, leading the Israelites and all flesh in a joyous celebration of that confession? All indications are that the answer to the question is a resounding yes. In the words of Psalm 145, a new world has been powerfully and decisively spoken into being.

The message for those who pray the psalms today is simple and yet complex. In the midst of the turmoil and uncertainty in the twenty-first-century world, praising God as sovereign and making God's sovereignty known to all flesh may be a way to find peace in the midst of the turmoil. But what does that mean? We can speak the words, but how do we put them into action? God is indeed sovereign, but for that sovereignty to be truly realized we must be the hands and feet of God in God's world—what some scholars call "a communitization" of kingship. In the ancient Near East the role of the sovereign was to provide a safe place of habitation for humanity. That safety included dwelling places, farm land, drinking water, abundant harvests, increase of animals, and fertility within the family (see Pss 72 and 107). In our twenty-first-century world many people do not have the basic elements of safe habitation, whether as a result of poverty, societal violence, political corruption, disease, prejudice, or outright neglect. The psalm invites us, in addition to calling on God for help, to be the eyes and ears and hands and feet of God and "uphold all who are falling," "raise up all who are bowed down," "open our hands and give food," and "hear the cry" of those who are less able to care for themselves and respond. That is to say: we must, in God's name, provide for all that the sovereignty of God over the world promises.

Psalms 146–150

Let All That Have Breath . . .
Women and Men Alike

The praise of God as sovereign in Psalm 145 begins with the words of the individual psalm singer in verse 1, expands to the generations of the faithful in verse 4, and encompasses all of God's "works" (מעשׂים) in verse 10. The psalm's closing verse summarizes the movement, from "my mouth" to "all flesh." Psalms 146–150, the final Hallel of the Psalter, each begin and end with "Praise the LORD" (הללו־יה) and together form the closing doxology of book 5 and the Psalter as a whole. The group follows the movement observed in Psalm 145, from an individual hymn (Ps 146) to a community hymn (Ps 147) to a creation psalm (Ps 148) to exuberant praise (Pss 149–150).

Psalm 146

Psalm 146, the opening psalm of the final Hallel, is classified as an individual hymn of thanksgiving in which the psalm singer praises God (vv. 1-2), offers words of admonition not to trust in earthly rulers (vv. 3-4), celebrates YHWH as creator and sustainer (vv. 5-8b), contrasts the fate of the righteous and the wicked (vv. 8c-9), and celebrates YHWH's sovereignty for all time (v. 10). Erich Zenger maintains, "Psalm 146 takes

Psalm 146:1-10

[1]Praise the LORD!
Praise the LORD, O my soul!
[2]I will praise the LORD as long as I live;
I will sing praises to my God all
my life long.
[3]Do not put your trust in princes,
in mortals, in whom there is no
help.
[4]When their breath departs, they
return to the earth;
on that very day their plans perish.
[5]Happy are those whose help is the
God of Jacob,
whose hope is in the LORD their
God,
[6]who made heaven and earth,
the sea, and all that is in them;
who keeps faith forever;
[7]who executes justice for the
oppressed;
who gives food to the hungry.
The LORD sets the prisoners free;
[8]the LORD opens the eyes of the
blind.
The LORD lifts up those who are
bowed down;
the LORD loves the righteous.
[9]The LORD watches over the strangers;
he upholds the orphan and the
widow,
but the way of the wicked he
brings to ruin.
[10]The LORD will reign forever,
your God, O Zion, for all
generations.
Praise the Lord!

up the principal theme of the preceding Psalm 145, praise of YHWH's universal royal rule, and places it within the dramatic horizon of world politics."[1]

In verse 1 the psalmist admonishes her "soul" (נפש, "inmost being") to praise (הלל) YHWH and continues in verse 2 with a statement that she will praise (הלל) and sing praises (זמר) to God for the duration of her life.[2] In verses 3 and 4 the singer warns those listening to her song of praise not to trust in "princes" (נדיבים), since they are "mortals" (בן־אדם) who return to the "earth" (אדמה) when their breath leaves them.[3] These words recall Genesis 2, in which the first human (אדם) is formed by God from the earth (אדמה), and they remind us of the transitory nature of human existence. In addition, they tie Psalm 146, the beginning of the end of the Psalter, to Psalms 1 and 2, the beginning of the Psalter. The words of verse 3 echo the sentiments of Psalm 2 while the end of verse 4 states

---

1. Frank-Lothar Hossfeld and Erich Zenger, *Psalms 3*, trans. Linda M. Maloney, Hermeneia (Minneapolis: Fortress, 2011), 616.
2. For a discussion of נפש, "soul," see Translation Matters for Ps 103.
3. For a similar warning see Ps 118:8-9.

that the plans of "princes," who are mere "mortals" will "perish" (אבד),
as will the wicked in Psalm 1 and the kings and rulers in Psalm 2.

Continuing the connection to the beginning of the Psalter, verse 5
opens with the wisdom word "happy" (אשרי), the same word with which
Psalm 1 opens and Psalm 2 closes. While the NRSV employs plural forms
("those" and "their") in verse 5, the MT has singular forms, denoting
one's individual relationship with "the God of Jacob" as her "help" (עזר)
and her "hope" in YHWH. That person is "happy"—in comparison, perhaps, to the one who puts her trust in "mortal princes."[4]

In verses 6-8b the singer of Psalm 146 describes the actions and attributes of God in what Erhard Gerstenberger calls "a Yahweh hymn,"[5]
using language similar to Psalm 145:14-20. As in Psalm 145 so here in
Psalm 146, in a continuous series of participles, the psalm singer first celebrates God as creator and then outlines God's generous care for creation.
God cares and provides for the "oppressed," the "hungry," "prisoners,"
"the blind," and "those who are bowed down." The passive participle
translated "those who are bowed down" (כפופים) occurs in the Psalter
only here and in Psalm 145:14.

Continuing with participles that indicate God's ongoing care, in verses
8c-9a the psalm singer states that YHWH loves the righteous and watches
over the strangers. Abruptly the participles cease and the singer uses
imperfect verbs in the remainder of verse 9. The psalmist affirms that
God will uphold the orphan and the widow, but the way of the wicked
(רשעים) God will bring to ruin. The contrast between the fate of the righteous and the fate of the wicked recalls once again the words of Psalm
1. Walter Brueggemann and William H. Bellinger summarize well the
sentiment of verses 7-9:

> The recurring subject is the socially vulnerable and powerless who
> stand in need of an advocate. . . . This is indeed "God's preferential
> option" for the vulnerable and needy, the ones who are outsiders and
> who are kept outsiders in familiar economic arrangements in order to
> maintain a certain arrangement of social power and social possibilities.[6]

---

4. For a discussion of אשרי ("happy"), see the commentary for Ps 112.

5. Erhard S. Gerstenberger, *Psalms, Part 2, and Lamentations*, FOTL 15 (Grand Rapids:
Eerdmans, 2001), 438.

6. Walter Brueggemann and William H. Bellinger Jr., *Psalms*, NCBC (Cambridge:
Cambridge University Press, 2014), 607.

Verse 10 reiterates the words of Psalm 145:1, 11-13 and book 4's en-thronement psalms (Pss 93–100). "The LORD will reign forever, your God, O Zion, for all generations." Thus the beginning of the end of the Psalter states unequivocally the conclusion toward which the story of the Psalter has been moving.[7]

James L. Mays calls Psalm 146 a "sung lesson," one in which those who recite it along with those who hear it teach and are taught that God is the eternal sovereign over the world.[8] The words of Psalm 146 have as much to say to those of us who live in the twenty-first-century world as they did to the ancient Israelites. Earthly rulers will return to their earthen states, but the creator God continues to care and provide for the oppressed, the hungry, the prisoners, the blind, those who are bowed down, the strangers, and the orphans and widows. How does God ac-complish such care? Those who believe that God is sovereign must be the hands and feet, the voice, and the eyes and ears of God in this world and act with mind and will and soul (inmost being) to carry out God's care and provision for those whom Brueggemann and Bellinger call the "socially vulnerable and powerless."[9]

Psalm 147

Psalm 147 is the second of the five Hallel psalms that form the doxo-logical end of the book of Psalms. Classified as a community hymn, it celebrates God's sovereign reign over the community of faith and all of creation.

The psalm opens with two phrases introduced by the particle כִּי, trans-lated in the first phrase as "how" and in the second as "for." The psalm singer states that it is "good" (טוֹב) to "sing praises" (זַמֵּר) to God, echoing her words in Psalm 146:2, perhaps as an invitation for the community of faith to join her praise. Erich Zenger maintains, though, that "strictly speaking, v. 1 is not an explicit exhortation to praise God but an emphatic appreciation of divine praise that as such is an implicit invitation."[10] The reason for singing praises to God is that God is "gracious." The word translated "gracious" by the NRSV is נָעִים, an adjective that means "pleas-

---

7. See the introduction, pp. l–lv, for the story of the shape and shaping of the Psalter.

8. James L. Mays, *Psalms*, IBC (Louisville: Westminster John Knox, 1994), 440.

9. Brueggemann and Bellinger, *Psalms*, 607.

10. Hossfeld and Zenger, *Psalms 3*, 623.

Psalm 147:1-20

¹Praise the LORD!
How good it is to sing praises to our
God;
for he is gracious, and a song of
praise is fitting.
²The LORD builds up Jerusalem;
he gathers the outcasts of Israel.
³He heals the brokenhearted,
and binds up their wounds.
⁴He determines the number of the
stars;
he gives to all of them their
names.

⁵Great is our Lord, and abundant in
power;
his understanding is beyond
measure.
⁶The LORD lifts up the downtrodden;
he casts the wicked to the ground.
⁷Sing to the LORD with thanksgiving;
make melody to our God on the
lyre.
⁸He covers the heavens with clouds,
prepares rain for the earth,
makes grass grow on the hills.
⁹He gives to the animals their food,

ant" or "delightful,"[11] and the NRSV is the only major English translation that uses the word as a descriptor for YHWH, "for he is gracious." In other translations, such as the KJV, CEB, ESV, NASB, and NIV, נעים is translated as "pleasant" and is used as a descriptor of the praise offered to YHWH.[12] However we understand the use of נעים, the psalm singer states in the last half of verse 1 that "a song of praise [תהלה] is fitting," recalling the superscription of Psalm 145, "Praise. Of David [תהלה לדוד]."

In verses 2-6, in a series of participles like those found in Psalms 145 and 146, the psalmist describes God's actions in the history of the community of faith (vv. 2-3, 6) and in all creation (v. 4). YHWH "builds," "gathers," "heals," "binds up," "determines," "names," "lifts up," and "casts down." YHWH builds up the sacred city of Jerusalem and gathers the people (the outcasts) together. In the story of the Psalter, book 5 celebrates the return to Jerusalem from exile in Babylon and the rebuilding of the city and the temple.[13]

Verse 7 issues a twofold invitation to participate in singing Psalm 147: "Sing [ענה] to the LORD with thanksgiving" and "make melody [זמר, see Pss 146:2 and 147:1] to our God." The verbal root ענה is most often trans-

11. See Ps 133:1: "How very good [טוב] and pleasant [נעים] it is when kindred live together in unity."
12. In the NIV, for example, v. 1 reads, "Praise the LORD. How good it is to sing praises to our God, how pleasant and fitting to praise him!"
13. See the introduction to the commentary, pp. liv–lv.

and to the young ravens when
they cry.
¹⁰His delight is not in the strength of
the horse,
nor his pleasure in the speed of a
runner;
¹¹but the Lord takes pleasure in those
who fear him,
in those who hope in his steadfast
love.
¹²Praise the Lord, O Jerusalem!
Praise your God, O Zion!
¹³For he strengthens the bars of your
gates;
he blesses your children within
you.
¹⁴He grants peace within your borders;
he fills you with the finest of wheat.

¹⁵He sends out his command to the
earth;
his word runs swiftly.
¹⁶He gives snow like wool;
he scatters frost like ashes.
¹⁷He hurls down hail like crumbs—
who can stand before his cold?
¹⁸He sends out his word, and melts
them;
he makes his wind blow, and the
waters flow.
¹⁹He declares his word to Jacob,
his statutes and ordinances to
Israel.
²⁰He has not dealt thus with any other
nation;
they do not know his ordinances.
Praise the Lord!

lated "answer," but it is used in the sense of "sing" in Psalm 119:172 and in the introduction to the so-called Song of Miriam in Exodus 15:21: "And Miriam sang [ענה] to them: 'Sing [שׁיר] to the Lord, for he has triumphed gloriously; horse and rider he has thrown into the sea.'"

After verse 7's call to "sing," verses 8-11 resume the participial descriptions of God's ongoing work in the world begun in verses 2-6. In verses 8 and 9 God the creator "covers," "prepares," "makes grow," and "gives food." In something of a summary statement in verses 10-11 the psalm singer states that God does not "delight" (חפץ) in "the strength of the horse" and does not take "pleasure" (רצה) in "the speed of a runner." Rather, God takes "pleasure" (רצה) in those who "fear" (ירא) and "hope" (יחל) in God's "steadfast love" (חסד).[14]

Verse 12 issues the third call to participate in singing Psalm 147, "Praise [שׁבח] the Lord, O Jerusalem! Praise [הלל] your God, O Zion," echoing the words of Psalm 146:10. The pronoun "your" in verse 12 is feminine, as are the three instances of the pronoun in verse 13; the psalm singer is calling on the city of Jerusalem, the dwelling place of the presence of Yhwh to join her

14. For a treatment of ירא, "fear," see the commentary for Ps 111.

in song.[15] The particle כִּי at the beginning of verse 13 renders the structure of this section of the psalm (vv. 13-20) parallel to the first section (vv. 1-12). Two reasons to participate in praising God follow: "he strengthens the bars of your gates" and "he blesses your children within you." Martin Luther wrote regarding the word "bars" (בְּרִיחַ) in this verse: "We must understand [them] not only as the iron bar which a smith can make, but, by synecdoche, everything else that helps to protect us, such as good government, good city ordinances, good order, . . . and pious, faithful, and wise rulers."[16]

Participles dominate once again beginning with verse 14, in concluding words about God's actions in the life of the community of faith (vv. 14, 19-20) and creation (vv. 15-18). The language used in verses 15-18 is reminiscent of that found in Job 38, God's speech to Job "out of the whirlwind." Verses 15 and 18 speak of God "sending out" (שׁלח) his "word" (דבר) to the earth. Psalm 119 uses דבר twenty-two times as one of the seven synonyms for Torah. In verses 15-18 YHWH's "word" is linked with YHWH's creative work, recalling the words of Genesis 1 and linking them to the Torah. In verse 19 the "word" (דבר) that YHWH "sent out" (שׁלח) to the earth is now declared to Jacob, echoing the words of Psalm 146:5. The words "statutes" (חק) and "ordinances" (משׁפט) are two other of the seven synonyms for Torah used in Psalm 119. Erich Zenger writes: "The judging and saving power of the creator God and world king YHWH to create order has achieved its recognizable and transmittable form in the Torah given to Jacob/Israel."[17]

Psalm 146, the words of an individual psalm singer, gives way in Psalm 147 to the words of the community of the faithful, indicated by Psalm 147's references to Jerusalem, Zion, Jacob, and Israel (vv. 2, 12, 19). In both Psalms 146 and 147 the psalm singers celebrate God as sovereign over all creation as well as over the community of the faithful. James L. Mays sums it up well:

> The history of the community of faith is a small part of reality, but the power that moves its course is the same that governs the stars. On the other hand, the processes of the world are vast, impersonal, and uncaring, but the sovereignty at work in the world is the saving, caring God whom Israel has come to know in its history.[18]

15. For similar language see Isa 54:13.

16. Martin Luther, *Selected Psalms*, in *Luther's Works*, vols. 12–14 (St. Louis: Concordia, 1955–58), 3:113–23.

17. Hossfeld and Zenger, *Psalms 3*, 626.

18. Mays, *Psalms*, 442.

Psalm 148

Psalm 148 is the third of the five doxological psalms that close the Hebrew Psalter, each beginning and ending with "hallelujah" (הללו־יה). The word הלל occurs twelve times in Psalm 148, perhaps in anticipation of Psalm 150's final unbridled words of praise to God. Psalm 148 is classified as a creation psalm;[19] it continues the movement of the final doxological hymns of the Psalter from individual praise (Ps 146) through the praise of the community of faith (Pss 147 and 149) to the praise of all creation (Pss 148 and 150).

Verses 1-6 call on all the inhabitants and components of the heavenly realm to praise God: angels (מלאכים), host (צבא), sun and moon, stars, the highest heavens, and the waters above the heavens. The word translated in verse 2 as "angels" is derived from the verbal root לאך, which means "send." The word מלאך is used in the Hebrew Bible to refer both to humans, where it is translated "messengers" (Gen 32:6; 1 Sam 23:27; Ezek 23:40), and to heavenly beings, where it is translated as "angels" (Gen 19:1; Judg 13:3; 1 Kgs 13:18). "Host" comes from the verbal root צבא, meaning "go forth to war." The word occurs extensively in the Hebrew Bible in general and in the Psalter in particular in reference to human armies (Pss 44:9; 60:10; 68:12; 108:11) and to "the LORD of hosts" (Pss 24:10; 46:10; 69:6; 80:4). "Angels" and "host" in the heavens perhaps reflect the ancient Near Eastern idea of a heavenly world that parallels earthly societal structures.

The sun, moon, and stars were considered by other peoples in the ancient Near East to be individual gods. The words of the psalmist in Psalm 148 reflect the creation theology of Genesis 1: the God of the Israelites created the sun, the moon, and the stars (in Gen 1:16 "the two great lights . . . and the stars"). The great lights and the stars are not gods to be worshiped but objects that worship God.[20]

The phrase "the highest heavens" (שמי השמים) in verse 4 also occurs in Deuteronomy 10:14 and 1 Kings 8:27. It reflects the ancient Near Eastern concept of the world in which the heavens were separated into the heavens above the "dome" or "firmament" (רקיע, see Gen 1:6-8) and the heavens below the dome. The heavens below the dome were the realm of earthly existence (the atmosphere); the heavens above the dome were

---

19. The other creation psalms in the Psalter are Pss 8, 19, 65, and 104.
20. Recall the story in Josh 10, where Joshua commands the sun and moon to stand still and witness what God has done on behalf of the Israelites.

Psalm 148:1-14

¹Praise the LORD!
Praise the LORD from the heavens;
  praise him in the heights!
²Praise him, all his angels;
  praise him, all his host!
³Praise him, sun and moon;
  praise him, all you shining stars!
⁴Praise him, you highest heavens,
  and you waters above the
  heavens!
⁵Let them praise the name of the LORD,

  for he commanded and they were
  created.
⁶He established them forever and
  ever;
  he fixed their bounds, which
  cannot be passed.
⁷Praise the LORD from the earth,
  you sea monsters and all deeps,
⁸fire and hail, snow and frost,
  stormy wind fulfilling his command!
⁹Mountains and all hills,

the realm of the gods. In Psalm 148 the heavens above the dome (the realm of the gods) are called on to praise the God of Israel. Psalm 148:4's "the waters above the heavens" also refers to the division that took place with creation of the "dome" (רקיע), dividing the waters above from the waters below. The waters below the dome were the source of springs, rivers, and seas, while the waters above the dome, which lay between the heavens below and the heavens above, were the source of rainfall.

In verse 5 the singer of Psalm 148 issues a summary call, now in the jussive voice rather than the imperative, for all that God has created to praise YHWH, and then provides the reasons why they should give praise, introduced by the particle כי (see Ps 147:1, 13). All should praise God because (כי) at God's command all was created (ברא), continuing the connections with Genesis 1 (see Gen 1:1, 21, 27). The first half of verse 6 affirms the everlasting nature of God and God's creation, echoing the sentiments of Psalms 145:11-13, 21 and 146:10. While the NRSV renders the last half of the verse "he fixed their bounds, which cannot be passed," the word for "bounds" is חק, translated in Psalm 147:19 as "statutes," and is one of the seven synonyms for Torah employed in Psalm 119. A better translation of this portion of the verse, one that ties it to the creation/ Torah language of Psalm 147, is "he gave [נתן] a statute [חק] that cannot be transgressed [עבר]."²¹

In verses 7-12 the focus of the psalm singer's call to praise moves from the heavenly realm to the whole of the earthly realm. Using language

---

21. Such an understanding also ties Ps 147 to the creation and Torah words of Ps 19.

Psalm 148:1-14 (cont.)

fruit trees and all cedars!
¹⁰Wild animals and all cattle,
   creeping things and flying birds!
¹¹Kings of the earth and all peoples,
   princes and all rulers of the earth!
¹²Young men and women alike,
   old and young together!
¹³Let them praise the name of the
   LORD,

for his name alone is exalted;
   his glory is above earth and
      heaven.
¹⁴He has raised up a horn for his
   people,
   praise for all his faithful,
   for the people of Israel who are
      close to him.
Praise the LORD!

reminiscent of both Job 38 (see Ps 147) and Genesis 1, the singer calls on sea monsters, hail, snow, frost, stormy wind, mountains, hills, fruit trees, cedars, wild animals, cattle, creeping things, and flying birds, along with kings, peoples, princes, young men and young women, and the old and the young to join in the praise. Interestingly, humanity is called last to praise God, preceded by the rest of creation, perhaps in parallel to the creation story in Genesis 1.[22]

Verse 13 calls all creation to praise "the name of the LORD" and once again provides the reason why, introduced by the particle כִּי (see v. 5 and Ps 147:1, 13).[23] The phrase "earth and heaven," reversing the usual order "the heavens and the earth," in the verse occurs elsewhere in the Hebrew Bible only in Genesis 2:4, the beginning of the so-called second creation account, confirming Psalm 148's ties to the creation account in Genesis 1 and 2. In verse 14 the focus returns to Israel (see Pss 146:5 and 147:12-14, 19-20) and anticipates Psalm 149 in which the children of Israel are called on to "rejoice in their King" (149:2). The "horn" (קֶרֶן) is a common metaphor in the Hebrew Bible for strength, dignity, and superiority.[24]

Psalm 148 is an invitation to all of creation and its inhabitants—the earth and the heavens—to join in the praise of God. All are included; none are excluded from the call. Richard Clifford observes: "Though moderns tend to think of worship as the response of rational creatures to their God, this psalm rather regards worship as virtually inherent in the

22. See Brueggemann and Bellinger, *Psalms*, 613.
23. For a discussion of "name" (שֵׁם) in the Hebrew Bible, see the commentary for Ps 113.
24. See Num 23:22; Deut 33:17; 1 Sam 2:10; Pss 92:10; 112:9; 132:17.

world's structure."[25] All creation, animate and inanimate, can participate in celebration of the creator God. John Goldingay reflects:

> Praise is an inarticulate noise, a la-la-la-la sound, so being unable to articulate sentences is not a barrier to giving praise. Much of the heavens and the earth is noisy, and its noise has the ring of praise about it. Its noise draws attention to the one who made it the way it is.[26]

Psalm 19:3-4 affirms the whole creation's participation in praising God:

> There is no speech, nor are there words;
>   their voice is not heard;
> yet their voice goes out through all the earth,
>   and their words to the end of the world.

Psalm 149

Psalm 149 is the fourth of the five final Hallel psalms that form the closing doxology of the Psalter. It begins and ends with "Praise the LORD" (הללו־יה), as do the other final Hallel psalms, but it seems somewhat out of place in this collection since its final verses focus on God's vengeance on the nations in defense of God's people (vv. 7-9). James L. Mays writes that Psalm 149 "seems to be a hymn in preparation for holy war."[27] In *The Message of the Psalms*, Walter Brueggemann states simply: "I do not know what to make of this, for it is quite unexpected in the hymns."[28]

The message of the psalm's first four verses echoes that of the other final Hallel psalms. In verse 1 the psalm singer calls on the "assembly of the faithful" to "sing to the LORD a new song [שירו ליהוה שיר חדש]." The word translated "faithful" is הסידים, formed from the word חסד, which refers to the covenant faithfulness between God and the people of Israel; the faithful are those who honor the covenant. The call to sing a "new song" (שירו ליהוה שיר חדש). The call to sing a "new song" occurs also in Psalms 96 and 98 and in each instance seems to refer to some sort of new beginning or new insight into the relationship between God and the people. Samuel Terrien maintains that the phrase "new song" does not indicate a song tune that has never been heard before but rather

25. Richard J. Clifford, *Psalms 73–150*, AOTC (Nashville: Abingdon, 2003), 313.
26. Goldingay, *Psalms 90–150*, 735. See also the enthronement psalms (93–100).
27. Mays, *Psalms*, 446.
28. Walter Brueggemann, *The Message of the Psalms: A Theological Commentary* (Minneapolis: Augsburg, 1984), 166.

¹Praise the LORD!
Sing to the LORD a new song,
 his praise in the assembly of the
  faithful.
²Let Israel be glad in its Maker;
 let the children of Zion rejoice in
  their King.
³Let them praise his name with
  dancing,
 making melody to him with
  tambourine and lyre.
⁴For the LORD takes pleasure in his
  people;
 he adorns the humble with victory.
⁵Let the faithful exult in glory;

let them sing for joy on their
  couches.
⁶Let the high praises of God be in
 their throats
 and two-edged swords in their
  hands,
⁷to execute vengeance on the nations
 and punishment on the peoples,
⁸to bind their kings with fetters
 and their nobles with chains of
  iron,
⁹to execute on them the judgment
  decreed.
This is glory for all his faithful ones.
Praise the LORD!

refers to the beginning of a new era, a new epoch in history.[29] J. Clinton McCann writes that the psalm's "theological thrust is to assert God's universal sovereignty and to invite God's people to join God at God's work in the world."[30]

Verses 1-3 are filled with images of singing, celebrating, and dancing— "a new song" and "praise" in verse 1; "glad" and "rejoice" in verse 2; "praise," "dancing," "making melody" in verse 3. Singing and dancing were common parts of cultic activity in the ancient Near East. In Exodus 15, Miriam "took a tambourine in her hand" and all the women followed "with tambourines and with dancing." In 2 Samuel 6:14 we read that when the ark of the covenant was being brought into Jerusalem "David danced before the LORD with all his might." According to 1 Chronicles 25:4-6 David appointed temple musicians such as the sons and daughters of Heman, who were "under the direction of their father for the music in the house of the LORD with cymbals, harps, and lyres for the service of the house of God."

---

29. Samuel Terrien, *The Psalms: Strophic Structure and Theological Commentary*, ECC (Grand Rapids: Eerdmans, 2003), 924.
30. J. Clinton McCann Jr., "The Book of Psalms," *NIB*, vol. 4 (Nashville: Abingdon, 1996), 1276–77.

Verse 4 announces a twofold reason for offering praise to YHWH. First, the Lord takes pleasure (רצה) in the people. The word used here is the same as we find in Psalm 147:10-11, which states that YHWH does not take "pleasure" in the speed of a runner but rather in those who fear God. Second in verse 4, the Lord "adorns" (פאר) the "humble" (עני) with victory. "Adorns" comes from an Egyptian loanword meaning "headdress, head wrap" and is used to describe the head coverings of upper-class women of Jerusalem in Isaiah 3:20, priests in Exodus 39:28 and Ezekiel 44:18, and a bridegroom in Isaiah 61:10. We see here a wonderful depiction of God rewarding the humble (also translated as the "poor") with the trappings of victory over those who oppress them. Erich Zenger writes: "YHWH chooses the 'poor,' that is the despised, the oppressed, the powerless, and the degraded in order to reveal his glory in them and so to give *them . . .* honor and dignity."[31]

Verses 5-7 resume the call to praise begun in verses 1-3 and summon the faithful to "exult" and "sing for joy" (רנן) with the "high praises of God in their throats."[32] But in the middle of verse 6 comes a radical and disturbing shift in the tenor of the psalm. Along with the praise of God in their throats, the faithful are to have "two-edged swords in their hands, to execute vengeance on the nations and punishment on the peoples."

The word translated "vengeance" is from the Hebrew root נקמה and may be defined as "an invocation of judgment, calamity, or curse uttered against one's enemies, or the enemies of God." נקמה is used almost exclusively in the Hebrew Bible in reference to the vengeance of God on those who violate the basic order and balance of the created world.[33] In Psalm 149 this divine prerogative is meted out to the "faithful." Verse 9 gives the reason for the vengeance outlined in the previous verses: "to execute on them the judgment decreed." The word translated "decreed" is כתוב, which means "written" in Hebrew, probably referring to the instructions written in the Torah regarding right living in relation with others and God. The idea of vengeance is difficult for many twenty-first-century Christians to embrace. James L. Mays reminds us that the vengeance called for in Psalm 149 is not "the emotion of a hate reaction but in the sphere of legal custom. 'Vengeance' was an act to enforce or

---

31. Hossfeld and Zenger, *Psalms 3*, 650.

32. רנן occurs repeatedly in the enthronement psalms to convey creation's celebration of the sovereignty of God. See Pss 95:1; 96:12; 98:4, 8.

33. See Num 31:2-3; Jer 20:12; Ezek 25:14.

restore justice where the regular legal processes were not competent or had failed."[34] John Goldingay comments:

> To translate *něqāmâ* [נקמה] as vengeance gives a misleading impression. . . . Indeed, the function of the redress is to rebuke them (cf. the world order in 141:5). It is to put them in their place, to chastise them for their attitudes and get them to see the truth about their position in the world and before Yhwh.[35]

The words of Psalm 149 have been used to incite and justify war against those deemed to be the enemies of God. It was used to provoke the Peasant Revolt in Germany in the sixteenth century and to call the Roman Catholics to a holy war against the Protestants, beginning the Thirty Years' War in the seventeenth century. The author of the book of Hebrews writes, however, that "the word of God is living and active, sharper than any two-edged sword" (4:12). As believers today seek God's justice in the world, words can be a powerful weapon in the hands of the "faithful" against those who cause or allow others to suffer injustice.

Psalm 150

In the last psalm of the final Hallel collection in the Psalter the word "praise" (הלל) begins each verse and occurs a total of thirteen times, forming a resounding doxological close to the book of Psalms.[36] The first two verses describe the God to whom the worshipers are called to offer praise; verses 3-5 describe the method by which they are to offer praise; the final verse of the psalm includes all of creation in the praise of God.

The Israelites viewed the temple in Jerusalem as the dwelling place of God (or the name of God) on earth.[37] In verse 1 of Psalm 150 the psalm singer asserts that God is in his "sanctuary" (קדש), God's earthly dwelling among the people. She then calls on those who hear her to "praise" (הלל) God in God's mighty "firmament" (רקיע). In the act of worship the earthly, God's "holy place" (קדש), the temple or sanctuary, and the heavenly, the "firmament" (רקיע), meet and commune, transcending the boundaries between the two. Erich Zenger observes, "Our psalm is especially concerned with bringing together the earthly (v. 1b) and

---

34. Mays, *Psalms*, 302–3.
35. Goldingay, *Psalms 90–150*, 742.
36. The word "hallelujah" occurs twelve times in Ps 148.
37. See Exod 40:34-35; Deut 12:10-11; 14:22-23; 1 Kgs 8:10-13; Pss 74:2; 135:21.

Psalm 150:1-6

¹Praise the LORD!
Praise God in his sanctuary;
  praise him in his mighty
    firmament!
²Praise him for his mighty deeds;
  praise him according to his
    surpassing greatness!
³Praise him with trumpet sound;
  praise him with lute and harp!
⁴Praise him with tambourine and
  dance;
  praise him with strings and pipe!
⁵Praise him with clanging cymbals;
  praise him with loud clashing
    cymbals!
⁶Let everything that breathes praise
  the LORD!
Praise the LORD!

heavenly (v. 1c) praise of YHWH and filling the whole cosmos with it."[38] Verse 2 then offers the reasons for such praise—God's mighty deeds and surpassing greatness.

Verses 3-5 detail the way in which the worshipers are to offer their praise to YHWH. While in Psalms 146–149 the worshipers announce their intent to sing and make music to God (see Pss 146:2; 147:1, 7; 149:1, 3), Psalm 150 depicts the realization of that intent, with details of the types of instruments to be used in worship: "trumpet" (שׁופר), "lute" (נבל), "harp" (כנור), "tambourine" (תף), "strings" (מן), "pipe" (עוגב), and "cymbals" (צלצלים). Richard Clifford describes the array as "a full symphony" in which "every instrument of the orchestra joins the human voice in giving praise."[39] Verse 6's call to "everything that breathes" (כל הנשמה) to praise the Lord echoes the proclamation made by the singer of Psalm 145 in its closing verse 21 that "My mouth will speak the praise of the LORD, and all flesh will bless his holy name forever and ever," forming an envelope structure around the final doxological words of the Psalter.

38. Hossfeld and Zenger, *Psalms 3*, 658.
39. Clifford, *Psalms 73–150*, 319.

Epilogue

How, indeed, does one go about writing a feminist commentary on the book of Psalms? This writer has attempted to let this timeless text speak for itself and out of itself. As I stated in the introduction to the commentary, the words of the psalmists are genderless and timeless; they are the words of every person in every time and place and testify to the multifaceted dimensions of humanity's relationship with God and one another in all times and places.

The Psalter begins with the wisdom words of Psalm 1, calling on the faithful to delight in and meditate on the Torah, and with Psalm 2's admonition to acknowledge God's role in providing a ruler for the faithful. The book then chronicles humanity's joy and sorrow, wonder and skepticism, gratitude and anger either directed to or about the God we worship. Each word of the psalms is part and parcel of the fabric that makes up the saga of this journey through life. We find words of awe and wonder in Psalm 8:3-4:

> When I look at your heavens, the work of your fingers . . .
> what are human beings that you are mindful of them?

Words of utter despair in Psalm 22:1, 6:

> My God, my God, why have you forsaken me? . . .
> I am worm, and not human;
> scorned by others, and despised by the people.

Words of longing for God in Psalm 42:1:

> As a deer longs for flowing streams,
> so my soul longs for you, O God.

Words accusing God in Psalm 74:1:

> O God, why do you cast us off forever?
> Why does your anger smoke against the sheep of your pasture?

And words of confident trust in Psalm 97:11:

> Light dawns for the righteous,
> and joy for the upright in heart.

The multitudes of human emotions expressed in the psalms reflect the ebb and flow of human life. We move often, in our daily lives, our daily walks, from feelings of hope to ones of despair, from questioning to assurance, from awe to doubt. The book of Psalms echoes that ebb and flow. We do not find a tidy grouping of psalms of despair followed by psalms of hope followed by psalms of awe and wonder. Rather, the book of Psalms is a seemingly "messy mix" of psalm types reflecting, I maintain, the human condition—a psalm of hope gives way to one of despair, one of awe to one of doubt.

As a counter to my reading of the psalms as a white, relatively affluent female living in suburban North America, this author enlisted readers from a very different part of the world, South Africa, to contribute commentary on various psalms out of their life experiences. They offered words of anger and anguish, words of hope in the ultimate goodness of humanity, words of confidence that God does indeed hear our prayers, and words of admonition to those in power to work to effect change. The richness of their insights strengthened my own contention that the book of Psalms is indeed words of every person in every time and place in their quest to understand God and the world around them.

And to conclude, only after the whole range of expressions of the human condition has been articulated, heard, and pondered do the psalm singers offer the final *hallelujah* praises to God, culminating in Psalm 150's emotive cry to "let everything that breathes praise the LORD." For those who accept the story as their own and accept God as sovereign, the only response is unbridled praise. *Hallelujah* (הללו־יה)!

Works Cited

Allen, Leslie C. *Psalms 101–150*. WBC 21. Nashville: Thomas Nelson, 2002.

Anderson, Bernard W., with Stephen Bishop. *Out of the Depths: The Psalms Speak for Us Today*. 3rd ed. Louisville: Westminster John Knox, 2000.

Arnold, Bill T., and Bryan E. Beyer, eds. *Readings from the Ancient Near East: Primary Sources for Old Testament Study*. Grand Rapids: Baker Academic, 2002.

Bail, Ulrike. " 'O God Hear My Prayer': Psalm 55 and Violence against Women." In *Wisdom and Psalms: A Feminist Companion to the Bible*, edited by Athalya Brenner and Carole Fontaine, 242–63. 2nd ser. Sheffield: Sheffield Academic, 1998.

Baker, Aryn. "South Africa's Dividing Line." *Time Magazine*, May 13, 2019, 42–47.

Bauckham, Richard. *The Bible and Ecology*. Waco, TX: Baylor University Press, 2010.

Baumann, Gerlinde. *Die Weisheitsgestalt in Proverbien 1–9: Traditionsgeschichtliche und theologische Studien*, FAT 16. Tübingen: Mohr [Siebeck], 1996.

Beah, Ishmael. *A Long Way Gone: Memoirs of a Boy Soldier*. New York: Macmillan, 2008.

Bega, Sheree. "Murder, Intimidation—Finally Rural People Have Day in Court." *Saturday Star*, April 28, 2018, 5.

Berlin, Adele. "The Rhetoric of Psalm 145." In *Biblical and Related Studies Presented to Samuel Iwry*, edited by Ann Kort and Scott Morschauser, 17–22. Winona Lake, IN: Eisenbrauns, 1985.

Bishop, Edmund. *Liturgica Historica: Papers on the Liturgy and Religious Life of the Western Church*. Oxford: Clarendon, 1918.

Blevins, Carolyn. "Under My Wings: Jesus' Motherly Love: Matthew 23:37-39." *RevExp* 104 (2007): 365–74.

Boring, M. Eugene. "Psalm 90–Reinterpreting Tradition." *Mid-Stream* 40 (January–April 2001): 119–28.

Braude, William G. *The Midrash on Psalms*. Vol. 2. New Haven: Yale University Press, 1987.

Brenner, Athalya, and Fokkelien Van Dijk-Hemmes. *On Gendering Texts: Female and Male Voices in the Hebrew Bible*. Leiden: Brill, 1993.

Brooke, George J. "A Long-Lost Song of Miriam." *BAR* 20 (1994): 62–65.

Brown, William P. *Seeing the Psalms: A Theology of Metaphor*. Louisville: Westminster John Knox, 2002.

———. "The Lion, the Wicked, and the Wonder of It All." *Journal for Preachers* (2006): 15–21.

Brueggemann, Walter. *Abiding Astonishment: Psalms, Modernity, and the Making of History*. LCBI. Louisville: Westminster John Knox, 1991.

———. *The Land: Place as Gift, Promise, and Challenge in Biblical Faith*. 2nd ed. OBT. Minneapolis: Fortress, 2002.

———. *The Message of the Psalms: A Theological Commentary*. Minneapolis: Augsburg, 1984.

———. "The Psalms as Prayer." In *The Psalms and the Life of Faith*, edited by Patrick D. Miller, 34–39. Minneapolis: Fortress, 1995.

Brueggemann, Walter, and William H. Bellinger Jr. *Psalms*. NCBC. Cambridge: Cambridge University Press, 2014.

Burns, Rita J. *Has the Lord Indeed Spoken Only Through Moses? A Study of the Biblical Portrait of Miriam*. SBLDS 84. Atlanta: Scholars Press, 1987.

Camp, Claudia V. *Wisdom and the Feminine in the Book of Proverbs*. Sheffield: Almond Press, 1985.

Ceresko, Anthony R. "The Sage in the Psalms." In *The Sage in Israel and the Ancient Near East*, edited by John G. Gammie and Leo G. Perdue, 217–30. Winona Lake, IN: Eisenbrauns, 1990.

Childs, Brevard S. *Introduction to the Old Testament as Scripture*. Philadelphia: Fortress, 1979.

Claassens, L. Juliana M. *Mourner, Mother, Midwife*. Louisville: Westminster John Knox, 2012.

———. "Rupturing God-Language: The Metaphor of God as Midwife in Psalm 22." In *Engaging the Bible in a Gendered World*, edited by Katherine Doob Sakenfeld, et al., 166–75. Louisville: Westminster John Knox, 2006.

Claassens, L. Juliana M., and Amanda Gouws. "From Esther to Kwezi: Sexual Violence in South Africa after Twenty Years of Democracy." *International Journal of Public Theology* 8 (2014): 471–87.

Clifford, Richard J. *Psalms 73–150*. AOTC. Nashville: Abingdon, 2003.

Clines, David J. A., ed., *The Concise Dictionary of Classical Hebrew*. Sheffield: Sheffield Phoenix, 2009.

Creach, Jerome. *Yahweh as Refuge and the Editing of the Hebrew Psalter*. Sheffield: Sheffield Academic, 1996.

Crow, Loren D. *The Songs of Ascents (Psalms 120–134): Their Place in Israelite History and Religion*. SBLDS 148. Atlanta: Scholars Press, 1996.

Danby, Herbert. *The Mishnah*. Oxford: Oxford University Press, 1933.

Davidson, Robert. *The Vitality of Worship: A Commentary on the Book of Psalms*. Grand Rapids: Eerdmans, 1998.

Davis, Ellen F. *Scripture, Culture, and Agriculture: An Agrarian Reading of the Bible*. Cambridge: Cambridge University Press, 2009.

deClaissé-Walford, Nancy L. "An Intertextual Reading of Psalms 22, 23, and 24." In *The Book of Psalms: Composition and Reception*, edited by Peter W. Flint and Patrick D. Miller, 139–52. VTSup 99. Leiden: Brill, 2005.

———. *Introduction to the Psalms: A Song from Ancient Israel*. St. Louis: Chalice Press, 2004.

———. "Genesis 2: It Is Not Good for the Human to Be Alone." *RevExp* 103 (2006): 343–58.

———. "Psalm 44: O God, Why Do You Hide Your Face?" In *My Words Are Lovely*, edited by Robert L. Foster and David M. Howard, 121–31. New York: T&T Clark, 2008.

deClaissé-Walford, Nancy L., Rolf A. Jacobson, and Beth LaNeel Tanner. *The Book of Psalms*. NICOT. Grand Rapids: Eerdmans, 2014.

Duffy, Eamon. *Marking the Hours: English People and Their Prayers 1240–1750*. New Haven: Yale University Press, 2006.

Emerton, John A. "The Meaning of šēnā' in Psalm CXXVII." *VT* 24 (1974): 15–31.

Flesher, LeAnn Snow. "Psalm 126: Between Text and Sermon." *Int* 60 (2006): 434–36.

Fontenot, Kayla, Jessica Semega, and Melissa Kollar, "Income & Poverty in the United States: 2017." United States Census Bureau Current Population Report. Washington, DC: US Department of Commerce, 2017.

Freedman, David Noel. "Other than Moses . . . Who Asks (or Tells) God to Repent?" *BRev* 1 (1985): 56–59.

———. *Psalm 119: The Exaltation of Torah*. BJSUCSD 6. Winona Lake, IN: Eisenbrauns, 1999.

Frye, Northrop. *Fearful Symmetry: A Study of William Blake*. Princeton, NJ: Princeton University Press, 1969.

Gafney, Wilda C. *Daughters of Miriam: Women Prophets in Ancient Israel*. Minneapolis: Fortress, 2008.

Gammie, John G., and Leo G. Perdue, eds. *The Sage in Israel and the Ancient Near East*. Winona Lake, IN: Eisenbrauns, 1990.

Gärtner, Judith. "The Historical Psalms: A Study of Psalms 78; 105; 106; 135; and 136 as Key Hermeneutical Texts in the Psalter." *Hebrew Bible and Ancient Israel: The Historical Psalms* 4 (2015): 373–99.

Gerstenberger, Erhard S. *Psalms, Part 2, and Lamentations*. FOTL 15. Grand Rapids: Eerdmans, 2001.

Gesenius, Wilhelm. *Thesaurus Philologicus Criticus Linguae Hebraeae et Chaldaeae Veteris Testamenti*. 2nd ed. Vol. 2. Leipzig: Fr. Chr. Wil. Vogelius, 1839.

Gillmayr-Bucher, Susanne. "Body Images in the Psalms." *JSOT* 28 (2004): 301–26.

Goitein, S. D. *Biblical Studies*. Tel Aviv: Yavneh Publishing House, 1957.

Goldingay, John. *Psalms*. Vol. 3: *Psalms 90–150*. BCOT. Grand Rapids: Baker Academic, 2008.

Gottwald, Norman K. *The Hebrew Bible: A Socio-Literary Introduction*. Philadelphia: Fortress, 1985.

Goulder, Michael D. *The Psalms of the Return (Book V, Psalms 107–150)*. JSOTSup 258. Sheffield: Sheffield Academic, 1998.

———. *The Psalms of the Sons of Korah*. JSOTSup 20. Sheffield: Sheffield Academic, 1982.

Gunkel, Hermann. *An Introduction to the Psalms: The Genres of the Religious Lyric of Israel*. Completed by Joachim Bergrich. Translated by James D. Nogalski. MLBS. Macon, GA: Mercer University Press, 1998.

———. *The Psalms: A Form-Critical Introduction*. Translated by Thomas M. Horner. Philadelphia: Fortress, 1967.

Habel, Norman C. *The Land Is Mine: Six Biblical Land Ideologies*. OBT. Minneapolis: Fortress, 1995.

Häusl, Maria. "Ps 17—Bittgebet einer kinderlosen Frau?" In *"Wer darf hinaufsteigen zum Berg YHWH's": Beiträge zu Prophetie und Poesie des alten Testaments*, edited by Hubert Irsigler, 205–22. St. Ottilien: EOS Verlag, 2002.

Hayes, Elizabeth. "The Unity of the Egyptian Hallel Psalms 113–18." *BBR* 9 (1999): 145–56.

Hopkins, Denise Dombkowski. *Psalms: Books 2–3*. WCS 21. Collegeville, MN: Liturgical Press, 2016.

Huwiler, Elizabeth F. "Patterns and Problems in Psalm 132." In *The Listening Heart: Essays in Wisdom and the Psalms in Honor of Roland E. Murphy, O.Carm.*, edited by Kenneth G. Hogland, et al., 199–215. JSOTSup 58. Sheffield: JSOT Press, 1987.

Hossfeld, Frank-Lothar, and Erich Zenger. *Psalms 2*. Translated by Linda M. Maloney. Hermeneia. Minneapolis: Fortress, 2005.

———. *Psalms 3*. Translated by Linda M. Maloney. Hermeneia. Minneapolis: Fortress, 2011.

Howard, David. "A Contextual Reading of Psalms 90–94." In *The Shape and Shaping of the Psalter*, edited by J. Clinton McCann Jr., 52–70. JSOTSup 159. Sheffield: JSOT Press, 1993.

Jacobson, Karl N. "Perhaps YHWH Is Sleeping: 'Awake' and 'Contend' in the Book of Psalms." In *The Shape and Shaping of the Book of Psalms: The Current State of Scholarship*, edited by Nancy L. deClaissé-Walford, 129–45. Atlanta: SBL Press, 2014.

James, Elaine. "'The Plowers Plowed': The Violated Body in Psalm 129." *BibInt* 25 (2017): 172–89.

Janzen, J. Gerald. "Song of Moses, Song of Miriam: Who Is Seconding Whom?" *CBQ* 54 (1992): 211–20.

Kirkpatrick, A. F. *The Book of Psalms*. Cambridge: Cambridge University Press, 1910.

Knowles, Melody D. "Feminist Interpretation of the Psalms." In *The Oxford Handbook of the Psalms*, 424–36. Oxford: Oxford University Press, 2014.

Koehler, Ludwig, and Walter Baumgartner. *The Hebrew and Aramaic Lexicon of the Old Testament*. Vol. 1. Translated and Edited by M. E. J. Richardson. Leiden: Brill, 2001.

Kraus, Hans-Joachim. *Psalms 1–59: A Commentary*. Translated by Hilton C. Oswald. CC. Minneapolis: Augsburg, 1988.

———. *Psalms 60–150: A Commentary*. Translated by Hilton C. Oswald. CC. Minneapolis: Augsburg, 1993.

Kritzinger, J.N.J. "Where Does Our Help Come From? Psalm 121 in Tshwane." *Missionalia* 36 (2008): 337–38.

Lacocque, André, and Paul Ricoeur. *Thinking Biblically: Exegetical and Hermeneutical Studies*. Translated by David Pellauer. Chicago: University of Chicago Press, 1998.

Le Cordeur, Michael. "Mandela and Afrikaans: From Language of the Oppressor to Language of Reconciliation." *International Review of Social Sciences and Humanities* 10 (2015): 32–45.

Ledwaba, Lucas. "Healing Resurrects Blighted Land above Mamelodi." *Mail and Guardian*, March 29–April 5, 2018, 18.

LeMon, Joel. *Yahweh's Winged Form in the Psalms: Exploring Congruent Iconography and Texts*. Fribourg: Academic Press, 2010.

Limburg, James. *Psalms*. WBiC. Louisville: Westminster John Knox, 2000.

Luther, Martin. *First Lectures on the Psalms 2*. Luther's Works. Vol. 13. St. Louis: Concordia, 1976.

Lutzky, Harriet. "Shadday as a Goddess Epithet." *VT* 48 (1998): 15–36.

Mandela, Nelson R. *Notes to the Future: Words of Wisdom*. New York: Atria Books, 2012.

Mashau, Thinandavha D. "Reimagining Mission in the Public Square: Engaging Hills and Valleys in the African City of Tshwane." *HTS Teologiese Studies/ Theological Studies* 70 (214): 1–11.

Mays, James L. *Psalms*. IBC. Louisville: Westminster John Knox, 1994.

McCann, J. Clinton, Jr. "The Book of Psalms." In *NIB*, 639–1280. Vol. 4. Nashville: Abingdon, 1996.

Meyers, Carol. *Rediscovering Eve: Ancient Israelite Women in Context*. Oxford: Oxford University Press, 2013.

Miller, Patrick D. "Psalm 127—The House That Yhwh Builds." *JSOT* 22 (1982): 119–32.

Mowinckel, Sigmund. *The Psalms in Israel's Worship*. 2 vols. Translated by D. R. Ap-Thomas. Nashville: Abingdon, 1962.

Murphy, Roland E. *The Tree of Life: An Exploration of Biblical Wisdom Literature*. 2nd ed. Grand Rapids: Eerdmans, 1996.

Nasuti, Harry P. *Tradition History and Psalms of Asaph*. SBLDS 88. Atlanta: Scholars Press, 1988.

Nelson, Richard D. "Psalm 114." *Int* 63 (April 2009): 172–74.

O'Connor, Kathleen. *Lamentations and the Tears of the World*. Maryknoll, NY: Orbis Books, 2003.

———. *The Wisdom Literature*. Collegeville, MN: Liturgical Press, 1988.

Oppenheim, Claire E. "Nelson Mandela and the Power of Ubuntu." *Religions* 3 (2012): 369–88.

Patterson, Richard D. "Psalm 92:12-15: The Flourishing of the Righteous." *BSac* 166 (2009): 271–88.

Pressler, Carolyn. "Certainty, Ambiguity, and Trust: Knowledge of God in Psalm 139." In *A God So Near: Essays on Old Testament Theology in Honor of Patrick D. Miller*, edited by Brent A. Strawn and Nancy R. Bowen, 91–99. Winona Lake, IN: Eisenbrauns, 2003.

Pritchard, James B., ed. "The Hymn to the Aton." In *Ancient Near Eastern Texts Relating to the Old Testament*, 369–71. 3rd ed. with suppl. Princeton, NJ: Princeton University Press, 1969.

Quell, Gottfried. "Struktur und Sinn des Psalms 131." In *Das Ferne und nahe Wort. Festschrift Leonhard Rost*, edited by Fritz Maass, 181–85. BZAW 105. Berlin: Töpelmann, 1967.

Rensberger, David. "Ecological Use of the Psalms." In *The Oxford Handbook of the Psalms*, 608–20. Oxford: Oxford University Press, 2014.

Sanders, James A. "Adaptable for Life: The Nature and Function of Canon." In *From Sacred Story to Sacred Text*, 9–39. Philadelphia: Fortress, 1987.

Sanders, Scott Russell. "Letter to a Reader." In *Writing from the Center*, 169–88. Bloomington: Indiana University Press, 1995.

Schökel, Luis Alonso. *A Manual of Hebrew Poetics*. Translated by Adrian Graffy. Rome: Editrice Pontificio Istituto Biblico, 1998.

Schroer, Silvia. *Wisdom Has Built Her House: Studies on the Figure of Sophia in the Bible*. Translated by Linda M. Maloney and William McDonough. Collegeville, MN: Liturgical Press, 2000.

Seybold, Klaus. *Die Psalmen*. HAT. Tubingen: Mohr, 1996.

Shäfer, Peter. *Mirrors of His Beauty: Feminine Images of God from the Bible to the Early Kabbalah*. Princeton: Princeton University Press, 2002.

Spurgeon, Charles H. *The Treasury of David: Spurgeon's Classic Work on the Psalms*. Grand Rapids: Kregel, 2004.

Stanton, Elizabeth Cady. *The Woman's Bible*. New York: Prometheus Books, 1999.

Stauffer, Carolyn S. "The Sexual Politics of Gender-Based Violence in South Africa: Linking Public and Private Worlds." *Journal for the Sociological Integration of Religion and Society* 5 (2015): 1–16.

Tate, Marvin E. *Psalms 51–100*. WBC 20. Nashville: Thomas Nelson, 2000.

Terrien, Samuel. *The Psalms: Strophic Structure and Theological Commentary*. ECC. Grand Rapids: Eerdmans, 2003.

Trible, Phyllis. "Bringing Miriam Out of the Shadows." *BRev* 5 (1989): 14–25.

———. *God and the Rhetoric of Sexuality*. OBT. Philadelphia: Fortress, 1978.

———. "Take Back the Bible." *RevExp* 97 (2000): 425–31.

Tucker, W. Dennis, Jr. *Constructing and Deconstructing Power in Psalms 107–150*. Atlanta: SBL Press, 2014.

van der Toorn, Karel. "Ordeal Procedures in the Psalms and the Passover Meal." *VT* 38 (1988): 427–45.

Walker-Jones, Arthur. *The Green Psalter*. Louisville: Westminster John Knox, 2009.

Wallace, Robert E. *The Narrative Effect of Book Four of the Hebrew Psalter*. StBibLit 112. New York: Peter Lang, 2007.

Waltke, Bruce K., and Michael P. O'Connor. *An Introduction to Biblical Hebrew Syntax*. Winona Lake, IN: Eisenbrauns, 1990.

Weber, Beat. *Werkbuch Psalmen* 2. Stuttgart: Kohlhammer, 2003.

Westermann, Claus. *The Psalms: Structure, Content & Message*. Translated by Ralph D. Gehrke. Minneapolis: Augsburg, 1980.

Wolfe, Lisa M. *Qoheleth*. WCS 24. Collegeville, MN: Liturgical Press, 2019.

Wright, Christopher J. H. *God's People in God's Land: Family, Land, and Property in the Old Testament*. Grand Rapids: Eerdmans, 1990.

Zenger, Erich. *A God of Vengeance? Understanding the Psalms of Divine Wrath*. Translated by Linda M. Maloney. Louisville: Westminster John Knox, 1996.

———. " 'Du kannst das Angesicht der Erde erneuern' (Ps 104,30). Das Schöpferlob des 104. Psalms als Ruf zur ökologischen Umkehr." *BL* 64 (1991): 75–86.

———. "The God of Israel's Reign over the World." In *The God of Israel and the Nations: Studies in Isaiah and the Psalms*, edited by Norbert Lohfink and Erich Zenger, translated by Everett R. Kalin, 161–90. Collegeville, MN: Liturgical Press, 2000.

Index of Scripture References

Index of Subjects

Author

Nancy L. deClaissé-Walford is the Carolyn Ward Professor of Old Testament and Biblical Languages at the McAfee School of Theology at Mercer University in Atlanta, Georgia. She holds a PhD in biblical studies from Baylor University and is the author of several articles and books on the Psalms. DeClaissé-Walford is an active participant in and part of the steering committee of the Book of Psalms Section of the Society of Biblical Literature and is also the Old Testament editor for the Word Biblical Commentary series.

Volume Editor

Linda M. Maloney, PhD, ThD, is a native of Houston, Texas. She studied at St. Louis University (BA, MA, PhD), the University of South Carolina (MIBS), and Eberhard-Karls-Universität Tübingen, where she earned her ThD in New Testament in 1990 under the direction of Prof. Gerhard Lohfink. She has taught at public and private colleges, universities, and seminaries in the United States and was academic editor at Liturgical Press from 1995 to 2005. She is a priest of the Episcopal Church (USA) and lives in Vermont and California.

Series Editor

Barbara E. Reid, OP, is a Dominican Sister of Grand Rapids, Michigan. She holds a PhD in biblical studies from The Catholic University of America and is Carroll Stuhlmueller, CP, Distinguished Professor of New Testament studies at Catholic Theological Union, Chicago. Her most recent publications are *Wisdom's Feast: An Invitation to Feminist Interpretation of the Scriptures* (2016) and *Abiding Word: Sunday Reflections on Year A, B, C* (3 vols.; 2011, 2012, 2013). She served as vice president and academic dean at CTU from 2009 to 2018 and as president of the Catholic Biblical Association in 2014–2015.